Kathryn Ochwat 12 '96

BOOKS BY THOMAS MERTON

The Seven Storey Mountain

The Sign of Jonas

New Seeds of Contemplation

Conjectures of a Guilty Bystander

Zen and the Birds of Appetite

The Collected Poems of Thomas Merton

The Literary Essays of Thomas Merton

Mystics and Zen Masters

The Hidden Ground of Love (Letters I)

The Road to Joy (Letters II)

The School of Charity (Letters III)

The Courage for Truth (Letters IV)

Witness to Freedom (Letters V)

Love and Living

The Monastic Journey

The Asian Journal

Run to the Mountain (Journals I)

Entering the Silence (Journals II)

A Search for Solitude (Journals III)

Turning Toward the World

THE JOURNALS OF THOMAS MERTON / Volume 4: 1960–1963 / Patrick Hart, O.C.S.O. General Editor

Thomas Merton

Turning Toward the World

The Pivotal Years

EDITED BY VICTOR A. KRAMER

HarperSanFrancisco
An Imprint of HarperCollins*Publishers*

Grateful acknowledgment is made for permission to reprint previously
published material: From *Conjectures of a Guilty Bystander* by Thomas
Merton. Copyright © 1966 by The Abbey of Gethsemani. Used by
permission of Doubleday, a division of Bantam Doubleday Dell
Publishing Group.

HarperCollins Web Site: http://www.harpercollins.com
HarperCollins®, 📖 ®, and HarperSanFrancisco™ are trademarks
of HarperCollins Publishers, Inc.

Book design by David Bullen

FIRST EDITION

Library of Congress Cataloging-in-Publication Data
Merton, Thomas, 1915–1968.
    Turning toward the world : the pivotal years / Thomas
Merton ; edited by Victor A. Kramer. — 1st ed.
    (The journals of Thomas Merton ; v. 4)
    "1960–1963."
    Includes bibliographical references and index.
    ISBN 0–06–065480–5 (cloth)
    ISBN 0–06–065481–3 (pbk.)
    1. Merton, Thomas, 1915–1968—Diaries.   2. Trappists—United
States—Diaries.   3. Catholic Church—United States—Clergy—
Diaries.   I. Kramer, Victor A.   II. Title.   III. Series:
Merton, Thomas, 1915–1968.   Journals of Thomas Merton ; v. 4.
BX4705.M3516A3   1996
    271'.12502—dc20
    [B]   96–16561

96 97 98 99 00 RRDH 10 9 8 7 6 5 4 3 2 1

Inexorably life moves on towards crisis and mystery.

August 16, 1961

Contents

Acknowledgments

Numerous persons have assisted me in the preparation of this journal. Above all, the monks of the Abbey of Gethsemani have provided an atmosphere of quiet and continuing support during my many visits to that monastery and when I have telephoned. Brother Patrick Hart, as friend and as General Editor of *The Journals of Thomas Merton*, has tirelessly answered questions about everything from Merton's script to monastic customs. Other monks – Matthew Kelty and Chrysogonus Waddell at Gethsemani, Bernard Johnson at Our Lady of the Holy Spirit at Conyers – have generously answered my many queries.

Graduate students have assisted in deciphering, transcribing, and word processing. Sometimes they have corrected readings of Merton's tight, hurried handwriting and assisted with proofreading. Two people who have assisted in these ways and been invaluable with this project are David Remy and Paul Wise, both of whom have helped me to read Merton's hand and to turn Xerox copies into typescript.

All this help as the project moved forward from deciphering holograph, to seeking references in libraries, to proofreading has made it possible to assemble the many pieces of what sometimes seemed an almost overwhelming puzzle provided by the energetic Father Louis. Georgia State University awarded a research grant that provided some funds for research, equipment, and travel, as well as one year of support for graduate research assistance in 1993–1994. The Department of English provided one quarter of graduate research cost-share funding that year.

Interlibrary loans as well as the resources of many libraries in Atlanta have made it possible for the editing of this project to become mostly a pleasure as well as an ongoing learning exercise, which I am sure will lead to still other related projects. I am especially thankful for the support provided by the reference and interlibrary staffs of Georgia State University. I am thankful for the assistance of library personnel at the Pitts Theological Library of Emory University and the Columbia Theological Seminary

Library in Decatur, as well as for assistance from various public libraries in the Greater Atlanta area.

My fellow editor Jonathan Montaldo (Volume 2) has provided steady encouragement, especially during the concluding year of this project as deadlines were adjusted to meet publishing needs. Fr. Laurence Bourget provided an invaluable reading of the penultimate version of the manuscript. His wisdom clarified much of what Merton wrote. Other editors of the complete journal project have also provided encouragement, answers to questions, and assistance with details as the project unfolded. Both Lawrence Cunningham (Volume 3) and Robert Daggy (Volume 5) have made useful suggestions. Numerous visits to the Thomas Merton Studies Center at Bellarmine College; queries answered by Robert Daggy, the curator there; and assistance by Marquita Breit of the Bellarmine College Library have facilitated the completion of this project.

Similarly, many visits to the card catalog in the library of the Abbey of Gethsemani were necessitated as month by month this project became less of a puzzle and more of a pleasure. I am appreciative of all this assistance and of all the opportunities I have had to work on this fascinating project.

To be in the quiet of the Gethsemani Abbey library, to locate an obscure reference, and to go into the stacks and find the exact book that Merton had decades earlier held in his hands as he wrote some particular entry for this journal was a very satisfying feeling. It was as if the labor of Merton's keeping a systematic journal during these pivotal years and my work as editor leading toward this finished edited volume were together coalescing to form new enlightenment at those very moments. All this is possible because of the work of so many persons. Truly such an editing project as this has been a pleasure because it was a collective effort.

Translations of almost all of the foreign language passages here were facilitated by Robert Urekew of St. Catherine's College in Springfield, Kentucky. He fastidiously assisted with the French and Latin and also proved that his knowledge of Spanish, Italian, Greek, and German as well as knowledge of monastic usages could solve mysteries page by page. Sometimes, he could decipher Merton's handwriting when it seemed almost illegible.

Other persons who assisted in finding answers to many questions about language and translations were my wife, Dr. Dewey Weiss Kramer, and Dr. Umberto Delgado-Jenkins, her colleague at Dekalb College. Finally, Dr. Kathleen Doig, of Georgia State, and Dr. James Doig, of Clayton State

College, have provided considerable thorough, invaluable assistance with regard to many, sometimes vexing, questions about French and Latin spelling, phrasing, and translation as well as Thomistic nuances.

My thanks cannot be fully expressed to all the people, mentioned and unmentioned, who have made this project a success. Once again I simply indicate my gratitude.

Introduction: Toward Crisis and Mystery

This portion of Thomas Merton's private journals is intriguing for several reasons. Its three hundred handwritten pages document aspects of several crucial developments in his life. During these years Merton was finally moving toward the conclusion of his extended period of extremely close association with student monks and novices. He had served as Master of Students from 1951 to 1955, and then as Novice Master from 1955 to 1965. By the time of the years covered in this volume, 1960–1963, Father Louis, as he was known at the Abbey of Gethsemani, had already spent a decade immersed in the demanding duties of teaching and spiritual formation.

The 1960s began a new period in which Merton invested far more energy in questions about himself and his own spirituality and about monastic relationships to the world. This is also the time when his long-dreamt plans for a hermitage were being somewhat mysteriously fulfilled. A separate structure, about three-quarters of a mile from the monastery, built more as an ecumenical meeting center than as a place of solitary retreat exclusively for him, was constructed in 1960. Five years later this isolated cabin was to become his solitary dwelling place.

These decisive years, when Merton was in his late forties, were not, however, times that would allow Thomas Merton to separate himself from the world. Paradoxically, precisely when he longed for more solitude and often debated about how much he should continue to publish, he found himself asking complex questions about contemporary society, war, and the Church's role in the world. Thus, this monk/writer was being drawn much more frequently into confronting questions about Christian responsibility during a time of rapid, and often surprising, change in his culture. This volume of his private journals documents his engagement both with personal questions concerning the nature of solitude and questions about his more active relationship to society. The journal does so frequently by recording thoughts about particular items Merton was reading.

Thomas Merton was someone who literally had several books going at any one time. We can observe the record of his reading both throughout these journal pages and in his "Working Notebooks," which also exist for this period. He would frequently become fascinated with a topic – for example, the School of Chartres and William of Conches – and then such fascination would lead to an examination of many other related topics. During these particular years Merton was also becoming more and more interested in the earliest monastic writers, the desert fathers, and in monastic parallels in other religions.

One of the methods that Father Louis had much earlier developed, and that by 1960 was perfected as a relied-upon interpretive method for examining himself and culture, was this intense reading and his taking of elaborate notes so that he might later more easily draw comparisons. We see this already in his earliest journal, *Run to the Mountain* (1939–1941), and to a lesser, but significant, degree in the complete journals published under the titles *Entering the Silence* and *A Search for Solitude*, which follow chronologically and cover the almost two full decades from 1942 to 1960 that precede this particular holographic journal.

The entries at hand from Merton's complete private journal (transcribed from a bound ledger volume of three hundred lined pages) provide information about Merton's reading in great abundance. This documentary journal material is also evidence of his systematic drawing together and examination of many personal issues about his involvement in the world, along with varied questions about the complexity of modern and contemporary culture.

Merton's *Conjectures of a Guilty Bystander* (1966) comes out of this same opening-up period, and a large amount of the inspiration for that book, a vastly reworked "journal," is found buried in the journal entries presented here. Comparison of these two texts would be an exceedingly complicated, but rewarding task. It is worth observing that *The Secular Journal* (earlier derived from the holograph and typescripts related to *Run to the Mountain*) and *The Sign of Jonas* (derived from materials that make Volume 2, *Entering the Silence*) are books mainly constructed of passages simply selected, and thus often left largely unrevised, from the much larger holographic private journal. In the case of *Conjectures of a Guilty Bystander,* far more creative, imaginative reworkings and extensive expansion of the original journal entries were taking place.

Conjectures of a Guilty Bystander therefore demonstrates Merton's renewed creative energy in the early 1960s *and* his emergent openness to questions not just about himself, but about monastic relationships to other religious traditions, art, architecture, and the Church, as well as about society at large, especially issues concerning race, war, nuclear madness, and other basic threats to civilization as a whole. This fourth volume of the journals clearly provided much of the raw data that fed into *Conjectures*.

It was also during this exact period of the early 1960s (specifically October 1961–October 1962) that Merton felt compelled to circulate "underground" his unpublished "Cold War Letters." Those sometimes controversial documents also have a direct relationship to matters recorded here. Many of the same subjects are systematically entertained – questions about dialogue with the world, responsibility, action, and solitude. Merton's questioning was definitely leading him toward more involvement with the world. Maybe this was because he had more time for solitude.

Already in his May 1960 entries Merton several times records facts about the developing plans for his incipient "hermitage" and meeting center. In these entries he frequently mentions the several groups of visitors with whom he was by that time occasionally meeting, and then corresponding. As subsequent years unfolded, that modest place of dialogue and solitude (where he at first was not even allowed to spend the night) became of increasing importance and comfort to him. The year 1960 certainly saw his questioning about the nature of both the monastic life and the world take on an intensity that Merton had never before allowed himself to express.

The years 1961 and following, not surprisingly, reflect an accelerating pace of attention to related questions about the world as Merton became more fervently interested in raising, if not answering, questions about the nature of contemporary society. However, almost simultaneously Merton notes that perhaps he should not write so much for publication in the future: "The question of writing: definitely it has to be cut down, or changed" (January 19, 1961).

Paradoxically, throughout these years of journal entries Merton expresses a longing for quiet and simplicity *and* a realization that one must continue to confront one's innermost self along with broad cultural questions. On July 9, 1961, Merton records that he walked up the hill to the building that would eventually become his permanent hermitage to say the Divine Office and found the atmosphere there very valuable. Praying "the office is entirely different in its proper (natural) setting, out from under the fluorescent lights. There [in church] Lauds is torpor and vacuum." A bit later in 1961, on September 24, he quite explicitly and enthusiastically states, "There is nothing that makes sense to me or attracts me so much as living in the hermitage." This rhythm of often being alone and needing to be so more was becoming quite essential for him, and such solitude had to be cultivated.

Many of these same patterns of awareness about self and solitude continue in 1962, yet Merton is simultaneously becoming much more outspoken about contemporary issues. Thus, although he clearly wanted (in a sense) to remove himself more and more to the solitude of the hermitage, his journal entries frequently demonstrate a continuing keen awareness of a fragmented, maybe even demented, world that demanded compassion. On January 25 (while on retreat) he once again questioned the nature of his voluminous published writing and whether he should cut back. Humorously, he asks himself whether or not his "Guilty Bystander" should be published. He assumes "it will be execrated in the [Cistercian] Order and will get me shot by the John Birch Society. How serious is my need to be shot by the John Birch Society?" With that last quip he thereby reveals some ambivalence, but also a great deal of irony and wit, and acceptance of his dual role.

Without a doubt, during this pivotal period Father Louis allowed himself to be drawn in two directions. A report of a visit by Douglas Steere on February 5, 1962, seems to be emblematic of these years: ecumenism, involvement in the peace movement, contemporary issues – all these subjects were discussed at this historic meeting and are recorded in the journal. Merton clearly sensed he had to bring his perspective of quiet and solitude to these larger issues.

More and more, as these years evolved, Merton often seemed almost preoccupied with questions about peace and war, especially in 1962. Yet there is always another basic, and just as important, fundamental theme – a renewed awakening to nature, the beauty of the landscape, the wonder of a particular moment – a theme that becomes considerably more predominant as 1962 unfolds and leads into 1963. On January 21, 1963, recalling an early (3 A.M.) walk to the hermitage, he celebrates his recollection of that specific dawn: "Sunrise – an event that calls forth solemn music in the very depths of one's being, as if one's whole being had to attune itself to the cosmos, and praise God for a new day." Delight in a rainstorm, the landscape, the evening light, snowflakes, mauve hills, sunset, the whistling of titmice, morning, quail, calves, and the paradise of a cornfield are all examples of Merton's developing awe, celebration, and praise. What we see in the unfolding of these few years, then, is a new side of Thomas Merton that observes a world not so frequently celebrated before – one beheld both in nature and in other persons.

One of the most interesting patterns to be observed in the years 1960–1963, as Merton moves closer to giving up his duties as Novice Master (the period of 1964–1965, documented in the selection of journal entries published as *A Vow of Conversation* in 1988), is his developing ability to be far less critical of others while being more accepting of the mystery of God's plan for himself and all persons. He can even occasionally write quite positively of his abbot. It is as if the very keeping of the journal during this period (when he was truly longing for more solitude, finding ways to be apart from others, etc.) had an effect that is, if not quite the opposite, somewhat surprising.

The Merton of these years clearly becomes much more willing to accept mystery on many levels. This volume of his journals, therefore, is the basic documentary record of his movement from cloister toward world, from Novice Master to hermit, and from ironic critic of culture to compassionate singer of praise.

Editor's Note: Accuracy of transcription and assistance to the reader have been my primary concerns while editing this holographic journal. Fuller identification of significant names, places, and items and occasional necessary explanations of abbreviations have always been added in brackets. The only exception to this procedure is the addition of the year in the date of each entry, without brackets. For regularization, some punctuation has been added – especially when, for example, Merton, writing spontaneously and privately, omitted commas or placed no period at the end of an entry.

Two textual alterations have been introduced to conform to the uniform appearance of the preceding three volumes of the HarperCollins Merton journals. Two symbols that Merton used to indicate the beginning and end of entries do not appear here. First, his indentation following the dateline has been omitted; all initial entries are justified to the left. Second, the cross (" † ") separations in each entry are not used.

The Promise of a "Hermitage"

May 1960–December 1960

Awakening us gently when we have exhausted ourselves to night and to sleep. O Dawn of Wisdom!

July 2, 1960

May 25, 1960. Vigil of the Ascension

Said mass this morning for the Louisville Carmel. Wrote to Mons. [Loris] Capovilla[1] to thank him for the book on Italian Church architecture which has some very satisfying small churches. Some of the more ambitious projects do not impress me, but in general the plans are honest and straightforward. Some of them can give us some ideas for the Mount Olivet hermitage and retreat house. Jack Ford wrote about that today. I mean he wrote on the 18th and I got it today.

Had been waiting for an opportunity to say a Mass for Louis Massignon[2] and for his project, under the patronage of Bl. Charles Lwanga for African boys etc. I happened in a curious and almost arbitrary manner to pick on June 3rd and only today did I discover by surprise that this day is the Feast of Bl. C.L. and the Uganda martyrs! Louis Massignon wrote that non-violence is mocked in Paris and opposed by the French hierarchy.

Was annoyed at the farce of having to go to vote at the primaries yesterday, without having the slightest knowledge of the candidates. (Except that Johnson came here when he was governor and I remember Dom Frederic's speech.) But the ride turned out to be nice and all the kids were playing outside St. Catherine's school. The big ones at basketball, some younger ones in an arbitrary and rather hectic game of catch, others in quieter games, and behind the gymnasium the girls in blue uniforms, much quieter altogether.

Reading [Joseph Jean] Lanza del Vasto, *Le Pélérinage aux Sources* [Paris, 1945]. His account of Gandhi and Wardha is impressive. I am still not persuaded that the spinning wheels were so foolish. It is customary in the West to dismiss all that as absurd, and to assume that technological

---

[1] Pope John XXIII's private secretary.
[2] Louis Massignon was a French scholar of Islamic and Arabic studies.

progress is an unqualified good, as excellent as it is inevitable. But it becomes more and more passive, automatic – and the effects on "backward" people more and more terrible.

Today they proudly posted on the bulletin board in the small cloister the news about an American intercontinental missile fired from Florida and landing in the Indian Ocean. Something to be proud of! Have we lost all sense of proportion along with our faith?

May 26, 1960. Ascension Day

Remember 11 years ago, to the day, my ordination. Certainly these 11 years have been the best, and also the hardest, of my life. But they are the only years to which I can attach any real importance, years of genuine and full activity and being – not preparation. Everything else was a more or less appropriate preparation.

Even my sins, for a priest is not without a knowledge of human inferiority and it is good that I have a deep knowledge of it in myself. Otherwise my life and writing might have been even more preparation than they actually are.

May 29, 1960. Sunday after Ascension

[Boris] Pasternak is ill – perhaps dying – perhaps dead.

Yesterday, rain – I finished ms. on Liturgy and Personalism – in the afternoon, cleaned up the room. This, as [Jacques] Barzun says, is the age of white people.

Fragments of faded, dying paper used as markers in my copy of Denziger.[3] A dim yellow envelope from New Directions, postmarked 1952. Already ancient history, 1952! I threw it away, along with an Italian holy card that got there no one knows how – (one of the baser variety!).

Eyes still bad.

Dogma.

More and more the average Catholic and priest tends to think of dogma only as what has been dogmatically defined by a universal council or a Papal definition.

We are losing our respect for the ordinary magisterium of the Church, because we no longer fully understand what it is.

[3] The standard collection of defined doctrines, papal statements, etc.

Actually, it requires a greater and more enlightened spirit of faith to adhere faithfully, intelligently and with suppleness to the *ordinary teaching of the Church*, which is richer, more living, more nuanced, more detailed, more complete than the formal and extraordinary definitions. These are capsules, containing the *bare essentials*, and in an emergency form, to meet a special need.

To live on formal definitions rather than on the ordinary magisterium is like living on vitamin capsules rather than bread and meat and milk and eggs.

I was shocked, in *Collectanea [Cisterciensia]* to read a report from one of our monasteries which said that contemplatives should nourish their prayer above all on what *is defined*. This is a distortion. First it implies that there is *nothing* in between formally defined dogmas of the extraord[inary] magisterium and controverted opinions. Second it shows a complete lack of appreciation for the real sources of contemplative reflection – liturgy, the Fathers and the Scriptures as understood by monastic tradition.

May 30, 1960. St. Joan of Arc
Mardis de Dar-es-Salam.[4] Deeply moving prayer of Louis Massignon on the Desert, on the tears of Agar, on the Moslems, the *"point-vierge"* [the virgin point] of the Spirit seemingly in despair, encountering God. L.M. is a man with an unusual and important vocation: the dialogue with Islam. Not the prissy, dressed-up dialogue over teacups of a bunch of dilettantes, but a real understanding of the greatness of Islam and of the problems and sorrows of the peoples of Africa and the Near East.

Difficulty of our apostolate which bursts in without understanding and asks the Moslem, without further explanation, to betray the brightest conception he has of God and the Holy. For we do not present him with what seems to him to be better or more Holy. As long as he does not understand, we are wanting him to be, he thinks, a traitor to his truth.

June 1, 1960
Hannah Arendt writes of the Greek πολις[polis] –
"Before men began to act, a definite space had to be secured and a structure built where all subsequent actions could take place, the space being the public realm of the *polis* and its structure the law."

[The Human Condition *(Chicago, 1958)*]

---

[4] See pp. 135–36 of *Conjectures of a Guilty Bystander* (New York, 1966) for Merton's extensive revisions of this key passage. Mardis de Dar-es-Salam is a publication of a center in Cairo for Christian/Muslim understanding sent to Merton by Louis Massignon.

I am fascinated (in the light of this) by the quiet way the Mt. Olivet retreat house plan develops – so unexpectedly and *without* premeditation – a "space" for a certain kind of "action" and "speech"?

Jack Ford and Art Bec Var here yesterday, and we sat on the pine logs and talked about design and the thought of the place moved about and reached for actualization, in its landscape, and under that particular sky.

I am not eager to make statements about it, however.

Most of the growth must be without words, and I must not yet impose a shape on it.

Pasternak died Monday. His story is finished. It now remains to be understood.

Another intuition of H. Arendt confirmed in fact yesterday: that one is "real" in so far as one "appears" in the "space" created by confrontation with other free beings in the *Polis*.

Called New York yesterday (Farrar Straus) about a problem created by all the delays, confusions and stupidities here. The difficulty of *beginning* the call – the chaos of noises here and at Bardstown – the delays – the absurdities – then the speed at which things moved as soon as we got connected with New York.

Finally the soft, sane voice of a secretary in the New York office and while the operators were stumbling and struggling over my name, the secretary immediately cut in with:

"Oh of course! We know who it is!"

And set their conflicts at rest.

How nice to have an identity in the civilized world somewhere!

In a "space" created over the heads of Bardstown and New Haven [Kentucky] (where I also have a reasonable, but perhaps different, identity in a different "space." My deeds are perhaps . . . New York deeds? Yes and no! Not the wrong kind, I hope).

June 5, 1960. Pentecost

Yesterday, under pressure, finished the galleys of *Disputed Questions* with my eyes stinging. Hot, I took a cold shower and went out and read a little of Paul Landsperg on Personalism and Lanza del Vasto on his pilgrimage to the sources of the Ganges. (How much better and more serious than Paul Brunton – Del Vasto's seriousness springs from the fact that he is a

Christian, and this permits him to go deeper into yoga, get closer to it, and to the people who understand it. Del Vasto, as a religious man, is *one of them*. Brunton, an agnostic, remains comparatively a tourist.) Landsperg too is excellent.

With sore eyes, said office privately in novitiate – and thus had about two hours for meditation. This is the first Pentecost here I have fully appreciated. The office too was more illuminating. These quiet hours before and after dawn!

The other day (Thursday) – the *full meaning* of lauds, said against the background of waking birds and sunrise.

At 2:30 – no sounds except sometimes a bullfrog. Some mornings, he says Om – some days he is silent. The sounds are not every day the same. The whippoorwill who begins his mysterious whoop about 3 o'clock is not always near. Sometimes, like today, he is very far away in Linton's woods or beyond. Sometimes he is close, on Mount Olivet. Yesterday there were two, but both in the distance.

The first chirps of the waking birds – "*le point vierge* [the virgin point]" of the dawn, a moment of awe and inexpressible innocence, when the Father in silence opens their eyes and they speak to Him, wondering if it is time to "be"? And He tells them "Yes." Then they one by one wake and begin to sing. First the catbirds and cardinals and some others I do not recognize. Later, song sparrows, wrens, etc. Last of all doves, crows, . . .

With my hair almost on end and the eyes of the soul wide open I am present, without knowing it at all, in this unspeakable Paradise, and I behold this secret, this wide open secret which is there for everyone, free, and no one pays any attention ("One to his farm, another to his merchandise" [Luke 14:16–20]). Not even monks, shut up under fluorescent lights and face to face with the big books and the black notes and with one another, perhaps no longer seeing or hearing anything in the course of festive Lauds.

Oh paradise of simplicity, self-awareness – and self-forgetfulness – liberty, peace . . . In this I have realized how silly and unreal are my rebellions, and yet how unavoidable is the pressure and artificiality of certain situations which "have to be" because they are officially sacrosanct. Yet there is no need to rebel, only to ask *mercy*. And to trust in mercy. Which is what I have not done. (Except in this matter of the eyes – etc.)

———

Cf. p 101–102*.⁵

God is my Father and my superiors are his representatives. And if I live quietly in long suffering and humility and patience, and represent my needs to them, they will have mercy: they always have had mercy before, when I have not tried to take care of myself and "extort" things as a "right." I must be content to accept mercy from them and be humble. Not demand "rights" and thus in some way try to save face – as if what I was receiving were not a privilege!

But what is the participation of solitude in my position?

Not solitude for its own sake, as a withdrawal, a refuge: but for the sake of understanding, wisdom, widening necessarily a certain commitment. (This brought home to me forcefully by readings from Landsperg and – Brecht!)

I have a natural tendency to become an escapist, a snob, a narcissist. (And my problems arise largely from guilt and attempts to cover up this guilt from myself and others.) [Paul] Landsperg says:

> *"La fausse supériorité de ceux qui se mettent en dehors de tout est devenue une véritable peste dans notre monde, et la tolérance mensongère de ceux qui se contentent de tout expliquer paralyse l'esprit occidental."* ["The false superiority of those who place themselves outside everything has become a real plague in our world, and the deceitful tolerance of those who are satisfied with explaining everything paralyzes the Western spirit."]
>
> [Problèmes du personnalisme *(Paris, 1952)*] *p. 35*

Certainly my solitude has not been *tolerant* – nor has it been an intellectual refuge in which I seek to *explain* everything.

Honestly it is a search for perspective – and for commitment.

But it is also a symptom of confusion.

Question: [Merton circles the numbers that follow.] 1. Can the Gospel commitment, in Gospel terms, be considered enough, or must it be translated also into concrete, contemporary social terms?

2. Is my commitment by religious vows enough or must it be clarified by a further, more concrete commitment

　　　a – to a *monastic* policy

　　　b – to a *social* viewpoint for myself and the other monks?

---

⁵ See the entry for May 20, 1961, Pentecost the following year. In writing that entry, Merton turned back to this entry, for Pentecost 1960, and added this cross-reference.

3. Are the commitments of the church and the Order such today that they necessarily involve one in a "reactionary" social situation? Or is it of faith that to follow the church even in politics necessarily implies going in the direction of justice and truth, despite appearances to the contrary? Or is this question absurd? What are the church's politics exactly?

Commitment – to the point at least of reading and studying fully these questions not speculatively but in order to form my conscience and take such practical actions as I can.

This requires a certain perspective which necessarily implies a withdrawal "to see better," a stepping back from the machinery of daily monastic life, solitude for study and thought, and a more individual development. Part of my vocation!!

June 6, 1960. Whitsunday

To discover *all* the social implications of the Gospel not by studying them but by living them, and to unite myself explicitly with those who foresee and work for a social order – a transformation of the world – according to these principles: primacy of the *person* – (hence justice, liberty, ag[ain]st slavery, peace, control of technology etc.). Primacy of *wisdom and love* (hence ag[ain]st materialism, hedonism, pragmatism etc.).

"Des hommes comme Saint Seraphim, Saint François d'Assise et bien d'autres ont accompli dans leur vie l'union des Eglises." ["Men like St. Seraphim, St. Francis of Assisi and many others brought about the union of the churches in their time."]
    Metropolitan Eulogies. *Quoted in [Maurice] Villain*, L'Abbé Couturier *[Paris, 1957], p. 51*

This is exactly my ideal and my desire.

There were two or three protestants among the Martyrs of Uganda – they were all one in their witness and their sanctity! A great sign.

June 9, 1960

In the last week of May twice, while praying in the novitiate chapel, I felt or imagined I felt very slight earthquake tremors.

Today for the first time I heard of the full seriousness of the earthquakes that took place, at that time, in Chile.

I knew that Puerto Monit [Montt] had been destroyed – in town I saw a grey picture in a newspaper, one of those pictures that you do not look at because it is meaningless. It *cannot* have a meaning. Today I found out about the meaning (article read in refec[tory]).

June 10, 1960

Big scoop shovel working all week to dig out a reservoir in the mill bottom. Hot weather coming.

Finished Lanza del Vasto two evenings ago and am getting to the end of H. Arendt – *The Human Condition.*

There are only nine novices now, plus Fr. David who is solemnly professed.

Trying to recite the psalms by heart all through the Night Office makes me pay more attention and avoid automatism, which is a curse in choir. And it is rewarding – the meanings strike home as if I were seeing them for the first time.

June 12, 1960. Trinity Sunday

Late yesterday afternoon Alceu Amoroso Lima Jr. – the son of A.A.L. – came by here with his wife. They are young and just married and were here in 1951 – or rather he was, with his father and two of his brothers. I remember his gay face and the even gayer one of his little brother with black eyes who now realizes his ambition to be a truck driver. His wife a charming, simple Brazilian girl, earnest and intelligent, named poets eagerly when I asked who was writing poetry in Brazil now.

Ernesto Cardenal's book of poems about Gethsemani arrived.[6] Small, bare, but warm poems, austere annotations, like Haiku, one of the most elementally simple being the one about a dog barking behind this wood here and another replying behind that other wood further away. His allusions to Nicaragua, to the train by the lake of Managua, to the steamboat Victoria that sank – give them a special quality. But they do not need this reference to be already very personal, pure and sacred. The religious ones are often the most simple and direct of all. Simplicity = Sacredness. These poems prove the essential and deep connection.

South American poets who held a meeting at Concepción, Chile, last winter – considered the 2 Americans Ferlinghetti and Ginsberg as examples of "innocents," i.e. fools. Esp[ecially] Ginsberg who made a great fuss about how poets ought to have plenty *drugs* and women and was always the first to go to bed – alone.

---

[6] Cardenal, who had been Merton's novice, wrote poems that Merton later translated into English and published in *The Collected Poems of Thomas Merton* (New York, 1977).

———

Finished the *Human Condition* today.

It is the deepest and most important defense of the contemplative life that has been written in modern times. That covers a great deal of ground!

I have pages of notes, just brief references and page numbers, and I don't know how to start organizing all this material for my own use. I mean for *real* use: for it is not enough just to have been exposed to such a book and to absorb, as one naturally does, something of its language and attitudes so that at times one may "sound like" that.

Meanwhile – a few remarks.

It is so clearly and tightly developed that in the last pages (I was relieved to find) clear conclusions rise up one after another and stand permanently in their place. They are not to be moved.

1. *Vita Activa* [the active life] lost its point of reference in contemplation – thereby becoming purely active – i.e. degenerating from *political action* to *fabrication* to *laboring* and finally to that completely empty activity of *job holding*.

2. Being has been replaced by *process*. The process is everything. Mod[ern] man sees only how to fit without friction into productive process and in this he finds "happiness."

3. Importance of Cartesian Doubt and Galileo's Telescope in giving man an "Archimedian point" from outside the world. Man *alienated from the world* and from experience of the world.

This very true. To cultivate *vita contemplativa* [the contemplative life] as we do here on the assumption that man is *worldly* and immersed in deep experience of world and things is complete reversal of facts today. We detach him from that to which he is not attuned and reduce him to still further alienation.

4. Her deep intuitions, not always fully pro-Xtian [pro-Christian], on the role of Xtianity [Christianity]: which in its respect for sacredness of life and its emphasis on forgiveness – changed the active life as conceived in ancient world quite radically.

(I think we could go profitably from this to a reading of the *whole City of God*, which I have never read right through.)

How Xtianity in one sense destroyed ancient politics. These intuitions to be taken with reserve. Certainly destroyed ancient city as the frame, the stage for political action.

One thing to investigate – Achilles vs. the martyrs of the "Unknown Soldier" – "nobody," made the war (WWI).

Xtianity making the public realm the realm of worldlessness and charity.

xx. [June 20, 1960]

One of the chief personal conclusions I draw from this book. Mission and obligation of the Xtian contemplative *to renew and recreate, to some extent, the classical concept of the public realm which Xtianity itself destroyed* – even with the concept of nobility and fame (*sub magnificentio* in St. Thomas)[7] which was discarded as vanity by the Fathers – Xtianity needs to produce *great men*. Cf. St. Louis – *not successful men* – great in understanding, self-sacrifice, forgiveness, men of tragic stature. (De Gaulle's sense of this, though he may be to some extent a ham.) (*Risking* above all the danger of being made inevitably a ham by TV and all the instruments of the "process.")

To fight against the process and yet use its implements – to control them, not be controlled by them.

Great importance of her clear statement of the *public realm*, the *private realm*, both of which have disappeared, devoured by the social – not realm but *process*. Of course – the problem which she does not take up – in classic realm, appearance is the appearance of a *reality*. In ours, we are made more unreal by our appearances and more and more become servants of process.

Very incisive notions (these are sidelights) on *suffering* and the private realm. Suffering, at once most private, least communicable experience of private self. One is completely subjected to necessity (public action – cont[emplation] – help one to rise above necessity or rather begin when one has stepped out of the gloom of necessity into light of "Day") – freedom. Notes on torture, redeeming the slave to a condition when nature *must* speak (no freedom = no invention).

Much to develop here –

A. The totalitarian use of torture – to get a statement of the *process* from the inmost privacy of the individual. I think they are convinced that this

---

7   Aquinas defines *sub magnificentio* ("under magnificence") as "a certain greatness of generosity about great and appropriate works" in his *Commentary on the Ethics*.

somehow justifies and indicates the process as an embodiment of ultimate truth. Process *has* to destroy individual to assert itself. More and more of this, of course.

B. The Trappist idea of self-punishment – *process* of sanctification – she mentions Jansenist ideas of labor as self-punishment – and truth? *N.B.* an instinct to anticipate *canonical process* of sanctification. The Trappist life as a "non-canonical process" of sanctification – to be verified step by step in Rome later. "He went through all the steps technically demanded – *ergo* he is a saint. He left out nothing."

Xtian love of goodness and the insight that no man can be good. Cf. important remarks on dynamics of forgiveness.

The most disturbing news these days is what comes out of Latin America. Cuba and Bolivia especially at the moment.

Articles read in refectory reflect the growing anger and fear in the U.S. – fear of a Soviet beachhead in the hemisphere.

This is far more serious than the U2 business, because this, more than anything, seems to foreshadow some actual fighting. Not perhaps an atomic war but a kind of Korean affair in Latin America. If the U.S. wins or loses in such an affair, it can only lose Latin America for good. Or so it seems.

If only our foreign politics made sense! But we have nobody in it who knows what he is doing: or if one or two know, they are still impotent.

I hardly spoke of this with Lima.

Articles in the refectory today were most unpleasant. And of course what makes it most unpleasant of all is that the Church, naturally, is right in the middle of it. But this in turn may react in the opposite direction in this Presidential year.

The trouble is that Christian democracy of Xtian liberalism or socialism cannot stand alone in between capitalism and communism and when it comes to a showdown the Xtian left is always drawn over to the right.

The other trouble is that American political life is so drastic and absurd and immature that the U.S. is unable to be what it should be – a real leader in democracy for both Americas. Castro gave the U.S. first chance to assume this role, and the U.S. did not respond.

Consequently . . . Christian Latin American groups have no choice but to line up with the U.S. and Franco's Spain, against Soviet Russia! What a situation! It is impossible. How can any good come of it?

June 21, 1960

A Byzantine rite mass today in Basilica before Prime. Most of the novices received communion at this mass.

News that Dom Gregorio [Lemercier] has seen Fr. Paul Philippe (now Secretary of the [Sacred] Congregation [of Religious in Rome]) and wants to see me if possible about this conversation – as if the Mexican question were once again open. The situation now being very different, I do not quite know what to think. Evidently since December I have come to regard the case as settled definitively. The increase in my own personal solitude here, and the plan for the retreat house on Mount Olivet seem in a way to have opened up a new direction here. But this is of course not real solitude either.

If the question is reopened then perhaps it can only be in terms of a real hermit life as opposed to this apostolic kind of life that is opening up here. But will it be any different for me anywhere? And again I think that if the worst came to the worst they would let me live alone here, if I wanted to . . .

It seems to me that it is quietly working itself out in its own way.

Bishop Nanayakkara of Kandy in Ceylon here last week. A strong and ardent personality, who got to know St. John of the Cross when the books were sent to him by a poor working woman in the U.S. He says the Little Brothers of Jesus are in Ceylon. He told one of them who is a shoemaker that if the other shoemakers have a party and invite him, and he can't go to it, he is failing in his vocation.

Nelson Richardson, who is not yet fifteen, accepted as a postulant by the Camaldolese in California, has suddenly ended up here. They could not take care of his education – we will try to. A totally unusual situation – the complete exception. But he's an exceptional kid, demurely reading Teilhard de Chardin in the novitiate garden, obediently eating his eggs, when I visit showing me the beatnik verse he has brought in on scraps torn out of pocket books, and talking like mad when he gets going, about everything from the Confucian Odes to *Naked Lunch*. It is wonderful to have something like this happen and for once the place begins to seem to me real. All this means is that I have probably been needing someone to talk to all these years! And someone I can really *give* something to. God grant that I do not submerge him under all the nonsense that is pent up in my head after so much time. At any rate I can teach him a little yoga (not Zen, though) and, seriously, help him to find in the monastic life its wholesome simplicity and rudimentary elements he needs. He seems to know everything that is in fashion but one wonders if he knows anything useful. He does, though he is very good mannered and he even speaks decent English. For such a one I would make any sacrifice.

June 24, 1960. F[east] of Sacred Heart
Scenes of life at Gethsemani: Fr. Idesbald, in work blouse, with a very well developed paunch these days, standing on the milk road and holding up his spectacles like a lorgnette to observe the work that has been done on the new reservoir in the mill bottom.

Bro. Octavius (back from Rome months ago but still clinging to ancient observances) saying the old laybrothers' office of *Paters* and *Aves* with Bro. Boniface (who is deaf) – standing together in the bare, gutted room that used to be the brothers' novitiate when I first came. The room utterly bare, very beautiful in a grim way. That was yesterday. Today large sheets of tin being torn from the ceiling and you can see through it and see the sky, through the second floor windows.

The Chapter Room too, bare, gutted, without a ceiling, bricks lying around where we used to prostrate. For the first time the place looks perfectly *true* – not pretending to be anything else but a wreck![8]

We have chapter in the library. This is unbelievable. Reproductions of Picasso on the walls, and Van Gogh's "Starlit Night." And the old floor and the old benches you can hardly sit on – this too will go.

And the summer postulant from Boston who will not believe me when I tell him he is not called to be a monk here – and who nearly fell through the dormitory floor they were ripping up yesterday.

Fr. David (my latest professed) preached in Chapter simply and well – a true, monastic sacred devout sermon, if by monastic you mean "religious" with the 19th century tone.

Today three professors from Asbury (Methodist) seminary are to come on retreat. Who am I to be talking to them? I feel this too is false.

----

[8] The monastery buildings were being renovated. For an account of the renovated church by Thomas Merton and an overview of the renovations, see the articles by Merton and Matthew Kelty in *Liturgical Arts*, August 1968, pp. 100–103.

All the Jesuits who were here Wednesday – Fr. Mailleux who reminds me terribly of Prof. Jean Hering at Strasbourg, with his red beard. A great gentleness in him (in both of them). Then Fr. John Ford to whom I spoke briefly asking advice. Fr. John Courtney Murray to whom I would like to talk more. Fr. Mailleux came out with Fr. Macpherson of Louisville, and he later told, in detail, of gaining a private audience with Pius XII through the ministrations of Mother Pasqualina and no doubt with the help of some dollars. It was like listening to someone calmly describe how he had been in an earthquake or shipwreck – without knowing what it really was.

Yesterday I took Fr. Aelred (Richardson) for a walk to the old lake and we sat with our bare feet in the water and I told him the basic things about yoga: what is ignorance, what are the restraints, what are the observances, what is the perfect posture and what [is] *pranayama* [breath control]. And this, no doubt, to Fr. Macpherson would sound like a shipwreck.

The guns of Fort Knox prowl incessantly, more and more, louder and louder. I found out from *The Catholic Worker* why Pres. Eisenhower could not go to Japan. Not just that the wicked Reds had prevented him – it was the U.S. army that prevented him. We had been basing U2 planes in Japan without informing the government of what we were doing with them. The Russians violate agreements with their enemies, we violate them with our friends. But of course, the Russians do that also, so we are all equal.

When the war comes, whose fault will it have been, and who will be the criminals? Anyone who preaches hatred of anyone is a war criminal. So that category includes practically everybody.

June 26, 1960. III Sun. after Pent[ecost]

Yesterday beautiful, cool after violent storms (the other night lightning hit the crane outside the dormitory. We have been having to form the floor of the new lay brothers' dorm). Sat in the cool woods, bare feet in the wet grass, and my quails whirling near me for my comfort, and wrote a poem about a flower.

In the afternoon went with the three men from Asbury – Dr. Stanger, Dr. Shipps and Fr. Hallman, up to the woods behind the lake and we talked theology. Fr. [John] Eudes [Bamberger] and Fr. Hilarian [Schmock] came along. It was a good animated discussion in which no one tried to dictate anything to anyone and I had the feeling that the talk was not a matter of words or formulas but of really seeking truth.

This retreat and the one from the College of Bible[9] have been very promising and rewarding. I am convinced of the great value of such encounters and all that is needed is for *me* to do less talking. For all those who have come so far I feel a very deep respect and affection and I believe it is mutual. I value their friendship and this is not just a conventional phase: it is important for the wholeness of my own life – it enables me to be friends with a hidden part of myself, which I can only find if I give my friendship to *them*.

Everywhere, all Christians should be making this same discovery.

June 30, 1960

I am in St. Anthony's Hospital for X-rays. A quiet hot day, reading Chinese philosophy and a little book on the Etruscans – and Bert[olt] Brecht's "Trial of Heron Lucullus" [radio play, New York, 1943].

July 2, 1960. Visitation

At 5:30, as I was dreaming, in a very quiet hospital, the soft voice of the nurse awoke me gently from my dream – and it was like awakening for the first time from all the dreams of my life – as if the Blessed Virgin herself, as if Wisdom had awakened me.[10] We do not hear the soft voice, the gentle voice, the feminine voice, the voice of the Mother: yet she speaks everywhere and in everything. Wisdom cries out in the market place – "if anyone is little let him come to me."

Who is more little than the helpless man, asleep in bed, having entrusted himself gladly to sleep and to night? Him the gentle voice will awake, all that is sweet in woman will awaken him. Not for conquest and pleasure, but for the far deeper wisdom of love and joy and communion.

My heart is broken for all my sins and the sins of the whole world, for the rottenness of our spirit of gain that defiles wisdom in all beings – to rob and deflower wisdom as if there were only a little pleasure to be had, only a little joy, and it had to be stolen, violently taken and spoiled. When all

---

9 See p. 394 of volume 3 of Merton journals, *A Search for Solitude* (San Francisco: Harper-SanFrancisco, 1996).

10 This entry is apparently the inspiration for the poem "Hagia Sophia," published in *Emblems of a Season of Fury* in 1963 and in *The Collected Poems of Thomas Merton*.

the while the sweetness of the "Woman," her warmth, her exuberant silence, her acceptance, are infinite, infinite! Deep is the ocean, boundless sweetness, kindness, humility, silence of wisdom that is *not* abstract, disconnected, fleshless. Awakening us gently when we have exhausted ourselves to night and to sleep. O Dawn of wisdom!

July 4, 1960

Perhaps there is no good reason to disentangle the threads of thought that have been tied up together in these four or five days at St. Anthony's [Hospital]. What would have been very simple has been complicated by friends and my own reactions. The people who want to take you out – when you shouldn't go and don't want to. I have been definitely at fault in yielding to them and it has made me miserable. And of course no one is to blame but myself. I suppose I have a way of implicitly encouraging that kind of invitation and not seeing it until I can no longer gracefully say "no" – or think I do not want to say "No."

What business have I to be sitting around in Jim Wygal's house in Anchorage, listening to records, trying to talk about something?[11] I don't belong in that any more, still less in the place where I went with Fr. John Loftus and his friend, the other night to hear some Jazz. At least I have found out by experience that this just does not go. I am dead to it; it is finished long ago. You don't drag a corpse down to 4th street and set it up in a chair, at a table, and in polite society.

This just made the reading of Chuang Tzu all the better and more meaningful. Here I am not dead, because this is my life, and I am awake, and breathing, and listening with all I have got, and sinking to the root. There is no question that I am completely committed to interior solitude. Where – makes no difference. Not a question of "where." Not "tampering with my heart" or with the hearts of others. This is imperative. "The mind is a menace to wisdom." To be one who "though walking on dry land is as though he were at the bottom of a pool."

The trouble is this being a "writer" and one of the most absurd things I have got into is this business of dialogues and retreats. This has to be faced. I can't completely back out now, but certainly no more pushing.

If the days here have taught me this, they are good enough.

[11] James Wygal was psychologist for the Abbey of Gethsemani; Merton gained permission for a series of psychoanalytic sessions in 1960.

July 10, 1960. V. Sun. after Pent[ecost]

A quieter week, thank God. New postulants, most of whom look good. I have been able to take a little time for reading in the woods, but have been trying to do too much especially with Richards' *Mencius* (getting excited about the ideograms and literal translations in the Appendix). [D. H.] Lawrence's *Etruscan Places* [London, 1932] is a book with which I am in harmony – I remember the day I discovered the Etruscans in the Villa Giulia. Of course L. has his axe to grind. *Pax* came this week with my four translations from [César Abraham] Vallejo. Read Brecht "Private Life of the Master Race" under the pine trees the other day. Because it is good, one can see how it would be not thoroughly acceptable to the Party – the good things precisely would make it unacceptable! Which? Well, one obviously thinks of the same things which he condemned in Nazism flourishing in Communism. It is a good medium.

Mencius – "The Ox Mountain parable." Importance of "night-spirit" and "dawn-breath" in the restoration of the trees to life. Men cut them down, beasts browse on the new shoots, no night spirit and no dawn breath – no rest; no renewal – and then one is convinced at last that the mountain *never had* any trees on it.

Kao Tzu and the willow cups. Is this discipline that leads a man to love [indecipherable letter] and righteousness 義 injurious to his nature? From the way many people talk, one would think [it] is. Not Mencius – and not St. Bernard. An interesting comparison could be made between them, especially as regards the "four beginnings" – the four roots in nature from which love, righteousness, Li, 帀豐 – and wisdom can always spring provided they are not completely killed.

But I like Chuang Tzu better.

Fr. Aelred (Nelson R.) with his verbal panic, his flights, his protestations, and his sudden obediences. Some of his poems are very good. He is perhaps afraid of spiritual experience, drawn to it, terrified by it, afraid he will ruin himself, swears he was happy when he fought everyone in the seminary. The Camaldolese had the right idea – left him alone: yet he needs something positive. What?

I am going on the assumption that I do not have to be too conscious of what he needs. That the Spirit is there, and that I am somehow in contact with the roots from which his growth will come, and that I don't have to preach sermons.

July 12, 1960

Jack Ford and Msgr. [Raymond] Treece were here yesterday. After a long conversation with Bro. Clement [Dorsey] I think we settled on what is to be done for the Mt. Olivet retreat house. It is just as well that it is going to be cheap and that we are not going to try to get the Ford Foundation to pay for it. That, it seems to me, was "playing" – and it would have meant more identifications with this social system than I am comfortable with. I don't desire it. I am sick enough at my monastery's involvement, which is inevitable. It is the inevitability most of all that makes me sick.

Very bad news from Cuba. It seems the Castro government wants to turn the U.S. out of Guantánamo and take over the naval base which, as a matter of fact, they have a right to do. And it seems inevitable, again (always the same "inevitability") that this time there must be resistance – and with arms.

That Bro. Clement should sit back and say "Well, they just *can't* get away with that." Everybody admitting tacitly that we are wrong "technically," but "what can we do?"

No doubt Russia has very cleverly encouraged and engineered this situation, and has been able to do so by having a more efficient and serviceable political theory than we have – one that takes more account of realities in action. We have political *ideals* that are more and more removed from and in contradiction with what we intend to do, what we "must do," because we are bound above all and before all else to "make money" and to safeguard our profits.

We are being slowly strangled by our own economic system. Just as they are morally and spiritually suffocated by their stupid ideology and the bureaucracy they have to work with.

Our system makes for "better living" (i.e. comfort), but theirs is more efficient in war and foreign policy – though we can fight wars when we set our mind to it. And "inevitably" both our systems gravitate towards war. We for profit; they for power. I hate both. I don't want to be part of either "we" and yet I can't help it, I am. How can I struggle out of this and become more explicitly part of the greater "we," the overwhelming majority that wants peace? Really wants it? Is there such a majority? That is the question. Perhaps we ought to assume that nobody, in reality, seriously wants peace except for *himself.* Hang everybody else!

Everybody else distrusts peace. War – hang them all – in order to have peace!

What is worst in the world is the *apathy*, the helplessness, the despair of men, especially of the intellectuals. Others continue to fill the air with the noise of deceptive hopes – thus intensifying our despair.

Terrible things in the Congo, which, left to itself, cannot govern itself. The fruit of a century of benevolent, clear sighted, happy-making exploitation. We do not know. We are blinded by the myth of our good intentions, our good will to men.

Because A. Schweitzer is there in the jungle we are convinced that we are *all* benevolent and that we have *all* loved Africa. There is *one* Albert Schweitzer. Or perhaps there are half a dozen.

For the rest of us – Africa is only part of our own myth.

Continents do not take well to this role of being imaginary. They insist, if necessary with violence, on asserting what is *least* imaginary, what is least acceptable to our imagination. They do not really need to know much about the myths. There is an instinct that governs these things.

The inexorable, shattering irony with which we are forced to eat our words and ideals, one by one, in the bitterest way. This is the real punishment of American complacency. But it is a punishment that assumes, at least (and rightly) that we have a conscience. Perhaps we do not admit the contradictions that stare us in the face; yet we feel them. We who are going to keep Guantánamo by force have commemorated recently the Boston Tea Party and the Declaration of Independence. Or did anybody think of this? All that was remarked was that this year there were more deaths in auto accidents than ever before on the 4th.

I feel I ought to use my voice to say something, in public, and I don't know where to begin. By the time it got through the censors it would have lost most of its meaning.

July 19, 1960
Classic sentence from a book that was being read in the refectory (now discontinued, thank God!).

"After his two legged master, the pig is the most abundant large mammal on the face of the earth."

Salutary strain and struggle of these days. I realize I have pushed too far in a stupid direction – reading too widely about everything, trying to write too much again, trying to set myself up as an authority on everything in my own imagination. Slow down! Don't expect to learn Chinese all of a sudden! Still, I think I will write that article on Chinese thought. Finished paper on creativity for the Benedictine Academy.

+

Raïssa writing of Jacques Maritain:

"L'irruption de la foi dans son âme avait dispersé tous ses plans de travaux méthodiques, la foi et l'aiguillon de Dieu lui interdisaient une vie paisible ou le souci d'une oeuvre édifiée à loisir passait avant tout." ["The inrush of faith in his soul had dispelled all his plans for methodical works, faith and the goad of God prohibited him a peaceful life, a work constructed at leisure being of primary importance."]

July 23, 1960
Maritain has said:

"La lecture de Platon est toujours un bienfait même si vous n'êtes pas toujours d'accord avec les thèmes du platonisme." ["Reading Plato is always beneficial, even if you aren't always in agreement with the themes of Platonism."]

Will I finally . . . ?
On philosophies: distinction between the primary intuition, the inspiration, the root of wisdom, from the conceptual elaborations which go astray.

July 24, 1960. Sunday – VII Post Pent[ecost]
Dim blue cornflowers. Heat haze – bells (eight o'clock).

Last night a car horn woke me up – on the highway towards New Hope – and I thought it was the fire siren.

That the man who dug up the Apollo of Veïs (Etruscan), when he unexpectedly saw the head, the eyes, the intense and lusty face, showered it with tears and kisses.

That Veïs was on a rock honeycombed with primitive water works, and that the main temple was always loud with waterfalls, and that spray came up – in clouds out of holes.

The Romans penetrated this mysterious city through the water tunnel.

Caere-(Chisra) and the gay tombs.

Later, the sad and awful tombs. ([D. H.] Lawrence barely mentions these, but with a sound explanation – that it was Rome that brought in horrors, snakes and Hades where there had been gladness and the egg of resurrection. Yet that is not all. Those snakes came earlier from Asia. At the end, the Etruscans returned to a dark beginning from which they thought to have escaped in the clear hills of Italy.)

When they owned Corsica, and mined iron on Elba.

When they went beyond the Pillars of Hercules in ships to Madena.

To the Low Countries and to Norway.

Finished the two appendices for *Disputed Questions* and sent them yesterday. And a letter to Olivier Clément, brought up by atheist parents in Languedoc, converted to orthodoxy, writing for *Contacts* (which has printed my Athos article). Importance, he says, of *écuménisme contemplatif* [contemplative ecumenism]. – Gave me the address of Fr. Sophrony, an Anchorite who has a small community in England.

July 26, 1960. St. Anne

Lost many hours of sleep last night. Hot, exasperated, worried.

Worried mostly about Fr. Aelred (Richardson).

I knew he would turn out to be a problem but in many ways he is more of a problem than I can handle. Yes. I hate to admit it, because I like him. Chuang Tzu says "to show affection is not benevolence" and it seems to me that my liking for him is in the long run cruel and nefarious, because it constitutes a pressure, a demand for what is almost hopeless.

Hopeless? His vocation, maybe even his Christian faith. I don't think he has, or perhaps ever had, any kind of religious vocation. Yet he loves this monastery, aesthetically and psychologically, purely as a refuge in which he is not much disturbed. As soon as anything displeases or disturbs him there is immediate trouble, endless, absurd subtleties. He retreats into a kind of voluble daze and stares at you, glassy-eyed, out of a cloud of words.

But of all the absurdities in the world, I elected to give him a series of talks on Chinese philosophy. Hoping the Confucian would revive some sense of ethics, and especially of *Jên* (Humaneness). He likes them – but no "ethics." This because he is *too* conscientious.

Dilemma in ways he seems to like and depend on me. But he is manipulating me like mad to justify all his own refusals, and they are too enormous. Yet if I back away from him, that will precipitate everything.

Over this, in the long run, I have no control.

I can tell him "Either behave like a monk or go home," but that is what is going to happen anyway, eventually.

He is going to have to do the thing he and his mother fear worse than everything on earth – be an ordinary student in an ordinary high school.

Then, one day, he will write a devastating book about this monastery.

July 30, 1960

This morning before Prime, or during it, three antiquated monoplanes flew with much noise over the monastery followed by a great heron.

The Theological Conference in Chapter was so awful that it nearly made me ill (nothing unusual in this): "That it is impossible to know with certitude of faith that one is saved." Much meandering about moral certitude and not a word about – *hope*. Are we really in despair? It would seem so.

Finished [Giuseppe di Lampedusa's] *The Leopard* yesterday. A finely constructed novel which suddenly disintegrates, and yet the last two chapters, icebergs broken off a huge moraine, float independently away and are interesting. It is a humorous and moving book. Thoughtful and archetypal, about the disintegration of an old Europe. But dignified and sane.

Fr. Aelred's mother is supposed to be coming here today.

I had a good talk with him under the tall pine trees yesterday. Of course I am wrong to expect him to be in all things like a Trappist novice when this is in no sense his vocation. That of course is the problem. It is *my* problem: that I insisted eagerly on taking him in, as part of my own delusion and escape. To have a prospective hermit to talk to. But he is not that either. He is an artist.

I am certainly very fond of him, and he is very gifted and good, but when he is in one of his moods it hurts me all the more because I know how good he is and can be.

Anyway the case has been already decided, not by me but for me. Father Abbot absolutely wants him to go, as he has no vocation and therefore no reason to be in our novitiate. Is it that simple?

I can't just dismiss him and his problem.

Victor and Carolyn Hammer came over and we had lunch together in the woods, in a fine quiet place, where the moss is on the way up the Lake Knob. No difficulty getting there and running around in the small car they have. As usual it was most pleasant, and I told them that they are the only people I know whose acquaintance and company are constantly improving. It is not true that they are the *only* ones though, for there are also J[ames] Laughlin and [Robert] Lax etc. etc.

Apparently there were two Mexican priests who were here and tried to see me. They saw J. first. But could not get in. About six weeks ago. Said they were very disappointed I could not come to Mexico.

Still waiting for some communication about that.

Talked about [Johann Jacob] Bachofen. May do Mencius' Ox Mountain Parable for a broadside (merely a matter of adapting the literal word-for-word translations in the back of Richard's *Mencius*). Fenellosa on Chinese art. The new things on Crete, and the disputed theses of the new man who says he can invalidate all the main statements of Sir Arthur Evans.

Above all they talked about Edward [Edgar] Kaufmann's house near Pittsburgh, built by Frank Lloyd Wright, its cave-like quality, its low ceilings, its hanging out over a waterfall etc.

And the treasure house in Kyoto with the wonderful things stored in it since the 9th century which Kaufmann saw (it is opened once a year for airing and one can only see it by special invitation).

August 2, 1960

Chuang Tzu said:

"At the present time the whole world is under a delusion and though I wish to go in a certain direction, how can I succeed in doing so? Knowing that I cannot do so, if I were to force my way, that would be another delusion. Therefore my best course is to let my purpose go and no more pursue it. If I do not pursue it, whom shall I have to share in my sorrow?"   XII,14

August 5, 1960. F. of Our Lady of [the] Snow[s]

Very hot weather. Rain cooled the air a little last night.

On Monday Fr. Aelred left, which was wise and the only solution – he was getting no education here and would only get into complications. So now he is gone and has left no memorial other than a spot of wine on the altar cloth – and the little India rubber eraser on which he carved my name so that with our ink pad I can stamp it on books etc. I like the way it is done, rough and crude and simple. [Merton stamped the front page of this journal with it twice!]

Herbert Mason came down here and I had permission to see him – he arrived Tuesday night and I did not find out he had arrived until Thursday afternoon (yesterday).[12] Spoke to him a little last night – about France, Louis Massignon, Cavallari's paintings (of which he bought many small ones – brown, coherent, massive and anonymous "movements" about a hidden Christ in His Passion).

A passionate and convinced book by a Franciscan [Giulio Basetti-Saris, *Mohammed et Saint François*, Ottawa, 1959] on Mohammed and St. Francis, so far a survey of the *incapacity* for dialogue between Christians and Moslems – and pointing to the need for it.

Some good talks with Herbert M. today.

Question of my being here and whether I really belonged here arose, and I thought about it during evening meditation – especially in view of the fact that Dom G[regorio Lemercier] has been trying to get in touch with me, and because his bishop is now in Rome. Summary: [Merton circles the numbers that follow.]

1. I still believe that this is not really the "right place" for me, that I ought to try to live a more solitary and hidden life that seems to me more honest, less ambiguous than this – in a word, to try out the possibilities of primitive Benedictine life, to be a hermit at Cuernavaca. This of course if it were possible.

2. I am fully able to accept, and have accepted the decision that I should stay here, assuming that decision represents the "mind of the church" in my regard. The change seems "impossible."

3. I do not feel that it is for me to take any positive initiative, except to make known that my desires are still the same. Perhaps I should make this known to Fr. Paul Philippe, on the occasion of the Bishop of Cuernavaca's *ad limina* [appointed] visit.

4. And also declare that should the Bishop or someone present a strong argument in my favor and if the opinion of the S[acred] Congregation change I would still be willing to accept an indult and make a trial of a different life at Cuernavaca –

---

[12] In 1959, at age twenty-six, Herbert Mason had come under the influence of Louis Massignon and then interested Merton in Massignon. See *Witness to Freedom: Letters in Time of Crisis*, edited by William H. Shannon (New York, 1994).

All that concerns me is to know whether it is *really* the mind of the church that I stay here, or go there, or what. I do not mean merely what is expedient for my Order but what is really for the glory of God and His truth and for the good of souls.

Unquestionably I can and do admit that my mere presence here is important and that this seems to be the majority opinion.

August 6, 1960. F. of Transfiguration

After Prime today I wrote to Paul Philippe, simply stating the conclusions I had arrived at yesterday, but not asking "for" anything. But in short, I said I still believed I should be somewhere else – not only for the good of my own soul but for the church and the monastic movement.

My attitude this time is very different: I mean, it is *in*different. I am completely detached, without strong desires or yearnings one way or the other, without temptation to make any plans, without anticipation. I feel my hands are really *out* of it.

This is a real joy, and because of it . . . I think the outcome will be different.

Instead of making plans, anticipating and doing other futile things, I am really going to simplify my own life here.

Cut out curiosities and useless studies; cut out concerns with mere fashions in art and thought; avoid trying to "keep up" as I have subtly and innocently done in the last two years. And yet still know what one needs to know, especially in all that concerns war and peace.

Yet it is clear that a mere compromise solitude here is no good.

The way that opens up to me really depends on no man, not even on myself – except that I have to leave it. And I will. For the rest it is God's way.

It has been helpful to have such a perceptive person as Herbert Mason here. His simply being here and talking has brought a lot of this out, and he is being quietly helpful – and will help, I think, in several important ways.

A copy of the letter to P. Philippe is going to Louis Massignon.

L.M. I regard as a genuinely prophetic figure in our time!

A prophet is one who cuts through great tangled knots of lies.

The High Mass today was glorious. Sense that the Light of the Transfiguration perhaps strikes us when we admire and exalt in the glory of Christ as

Son of God surely for *His* sake, His glory for glory's sake, or for the sake of the Father, the Source. Anyway, very happy singing – a liberated song, irrespective of any temporal thing.

August 7, 1960. Day of Recollection

Hot. Storms during the night, much lightning and thunder, lightning seemed to be striking close to the monastery. Heavy rain.

Herbert Mason came to communion at the Novices' Mass and afterwards we said goodbye in whispers. He is a person who is very eager to help everybody and very devoted to his friends, esp. Louis Massignon. Above all I think he is a really promising poet and I hope New Directions can do something for him.

Rev. Father,[13] much against his own will, has been appointed to make the visitation at Spencer and leaves tomorrow.

Bells; locusts; eight o'clock.

Lord have mercy.

Have mercy on my darkness, my weakness, my confusion. Have mercy on my infidelity, my cowardice, my turning about in circles, my wandering, my evasions.

I do not ask anything but such mercy, always, in everything, mercy.

My life here – a little solidity and very much ashes.

Almost everything is ashes. What I have prized most is ashes. What I have attended to least is, perhaps, a little solid.

Lord have mercy. Guide me, make me want again to be holy, to be a man of God, even though in desperateness and confusion.

I do not necessarily ask for clarity, a plain way, but only to go according to your love, to follow your mercy, to trust in your mercy.

If I am to be condemned by men, make me strong and quiet under their condemnation and above all show me how not to condemn them in return, but to forget any harm they may have intended.

Or not even to question their intentions.

I do not go anywhere out of ambition – I seek nothing for myself.

(That is: I want to seek nothing for myself.)

Or perhaps I want to seek nothing at all if this be possible, but only to be led without looking and without seeking. For thus to seek is to find.

[13] Dom James Fox, abbot of Gethsemani.

———

What I wrote to Paul Philippe I wrote frankly, but too outspokenly perhaps. In saying I do not think this is the place for me I should not seem to condemn the Order or its spirit or its observance, or even to seem to criticize it.

I told Mason above all not to start a "movement" in my behalf – for he may want to be *too* helpful. I am glad to have someone or other speak for me, but not exert *pressure*. But when and if it gets to the level of people like Card. Montini I can certainly count on their wisdom. I am doing *nothing* to further this, I mean nothing to exert pull with any cardinals. But Massignon is a close friend of Montini. I don't know how prudent L. Massignon may be but Montini is certainly prudent.

I can confidently leave this whole affair in the hands of God's Church and forget about it.

"Parmi les lignes il y a les vaisseaux qui, sur la mer, sont comme dans le désert." ["Among the many vessels are boats that seem to be in the desert when they are on the open sea."] *(Koran Sour. XLII–31)*

A line from a French translation of the Koran! It reads surprisingly like St. John Perse.

Loneliness, dependence, confidence, isolated journeys of the ships, held in God's hand, on the water, as camels in the desert.

Appalled by the passage of time, the loss of perspectives.

Walking in the cemetery, appalled by the dates on the crosses.

Already four years since Bro. Albert died – eleven since Fr. Odo died.

And the dim past, 1942, after Fr. Bernard died, a different age, a different world. The old monks who were still almost medieval, still certainly 17th century Trappists, with just a touch of American foolishness . . . but who lived and died so seriously for the most part. Even their craziness was serious. Even their flippancy seems now to have been rooted in a kind of solidity. Yes, this too was not fully real, perhaps.

The dim past. Fr. Aelred, who was here and left last Monday, was not born when Fr. Alfred, in my theology class, dropped in the cloister at night and died, half starved by his asceticism (and now *completely* forgotten, one could not be more so!).

Shaken with the sense of meaninglessness and sin and emptiness, of pretense.

The growing(?) pretenses. Our efforts to convince ourselves of the validity of the life we have embraced, both our levity and our despair. Yet it *is* in
some way solid. Strangely, no one knows how. Better not to prove it. Leave
it to be taken on faith.

What I have thought was solid in my own life (the woods, aloneness) has
been levity and recreation – and despair. I have the feeling it has been *toler-
ated* by the mercy of God as a lesser despair than my awful gyrations and
struggles when I was a student: so "regular and fervent."

Ehou! Eia! Helas! [Alas! Woe is me!]

August 10, 1960. F. of St. Lawrence

[Jean] Steinmann's book on St. Jerome [*St. Jerome and His Times*, New
York, 1959] in the refectory is interesting and well done but I am sick of
Jerome, his querulous sensitivity, his rages, his politics – and I am tired of
Steinmann's anti-Origenism. It is too insistent. I am for Rufinus and St.
John Chrysostom.

L. Massignon believes that the "nocturnal ascension" of Mohammed
brought him to the threshold of mysticism but he would go no further, and
that therefore mysticism was barred, under pain of death to all other
Moslems. (Though some got away with it.) I think Fr. Giulio Basetti-Saris
is a little romantic when he asserts that St. Francis, having offered himself
for martyrdom at Damiette, became a substitute for Mohammed and went
the whole way on Mount Alvernia. Isn't this a bit arbitrary?

August 14, 1960. 10th Sunday after Pent[eco]st

Msgr. [Alfred J.] Horrigan was here yesterday afternoon talking over plans
for this Bellarmine [College] "workshop" in October. The whole thing
seems to me a little unreal, but of course it is no more and no less than it
pretends to be – I find it hard to attach importance to "getting together
and talking."

But I should make more effort to take it at its face value, and I intend to.
At this moment it seems empty and silly, but that is probably only because
it does not offer me anything special. It is not pride to believe that perhaps for the others, coming here, new experience *et al.*, it might well have
some value.

———

Music is being played to the cows in the milking barn. Rules have been made and confirmed, that the music must be sacred and not secular. Gregorian only, or at least religious music. It is not for the amusement of the brothers. It is to make the cows give more milk. Sacred music has been played for some time and the cows have not yet given more milk.

Finished article on Chinese Classic Thought[14] last week. Enjoyed writing it. There is no question that the activity of writing and the thinking that goes with it all is for me healthy and productive – because, I suppose, it is my most normal activity.

I will probably never fully give up writing, and no doubt I am not meant to. But there is a difference between *writing* and *publishing*. I ought, I think, to do less of both, especially less publishing. Easy to say, now that I have four or five books lined up and ready for the press, contracts signed, etc. Nor are they all good ones, either.

Letters and poems from Nels[on] R. this week. He did his poems over and wrote a new one. I am trying to find a good school for him in Europe though his parents can't afford Europe. Plans for the retreat house on the hill came yesterday brought by a young designer from G.E. who had his girl out in a car and was going to the *Stephen Foster Story* in Bardstown. They have been very good about all this, I mean, working at plans first in order to do me a favor, and yet am not happy with the whole thing. It has been pushed and pulled this way and that and seems to have lost any real character; it is another abnormal featureless product of Gethsemani, with our trademark of ugliness upon it.

Ugliness, stupidity, purposelessness, vanity, self-deception, baseless optimism, Dishonesty – pitiable hopes and good will. What emptiness.

Rev. Father is back for two days and goes Tuesday to continue the Visitation of Spencer, then Wrentham etc., etc.

August 16, 1960
Was in Louisville today and had dinner at the Little Sisters of the Poor.

The moral beauty of the place, the authentic beauty of Christianity, which has no equal. The beauty of the Church is the charity of her daughters.

[14] Published in *Jubilee*, 1961, and in *Mystics and Zen Masters*, 1967.

The Good Mother, whom I shall never forget. Her transparency, unearthliness, simplicity, of no age, a child, a mother, like the Bl. Virgin – as if no name could apply to her, that is, no name known to anyone but God. And yet more real than all the unreal people in the rest of the world.

The old people. The old man playing the piano and the old man dancing – or rather turning about stamping the floor with one foot, unaware that he was no longer able to move the muscles that would make for tap-dancing. And the old man at the piano after all playing something far more alive than rock 'n roll (though all askew).

The old negro people also, the sweet, dignified negro lady who had worked for Fr. Greenwell, the old, beat, heavy negro lady with wisps of white beard sunk in her dream, her blank [expression], slowly coming out of it when spoken to. The lady who had both legs cut off. The little girl lady who made the speech in the dining room, the old lady with the visor cap on.

And the golden wedding couple.

But the sisters above all, and the little girls in blue and white uniforms, the "auxiliaries" and their song about playing the piano, the viola and the triangle. The dark eyes of the girl going Thursday to be a postulant in Baltimore.

Sweet, good people.

Now I have the prayers of the poor, the strong, merciful, invincible prayers of the poor behind me, and in me, changing my whole life and my whole outlook on life . . .

The two little Columbian nuns, the more Indian one from Tunja and the pure Spanish one from Medellín.

I have no regrets at this visit having been thought significant by them. No one can even say how significant for me.

August 19, 1960

A more important thing the other day – news from Dom Gregorio about his conversation with Fr. Paul Philippe, who is now Secretary of the Congregation of Religious.

P.P. definitely said that the decision of Card. Valeri was not absolutely final, that it was a request rather than a command and that it would be against the mind of the church to force me to stay here. Dom G's advice was very definitely this. I should renounce the initiative and repeat my request, "obeying God rather than men."

He was very definite that I ought to do this. Fr. John of the Cross also in confession. So I sent off a letter to P.P. requesting that my plea be reconsidered, and that I be allowed to go to Cuernavaca. (This was on Aug. 17th.)

Although I felt a hesitation about it, I am beginning to see, as Dom G. says, that my passivity is not a virtue but simply a compromise, and that it really takes more courage and sacrifice to make the break than it does simply to accept, inertly, a rather unjust decision on the part of my abbot – (who simply exerts pressure to get Rome to support him. It is certainly fair enough for me to renew my appeal).

The truth is, my natural inertia inclines me to a compromise situation in which all responsibilities are more or less abdicated: to stay here, enjoy the "secondary gains" and gripe about the unsatisfactory situation thus purifying myself in my own eyes. Better to face real risk and difficulty in a new situation and find myself forced to make a more valid and healthy adjustment. My spiritual life is poor here, and the "exercises" that are supposed to help one I find _stultifying_. They leaden the mind and spirit. (Except man[ual] labor.)

It is clear that some kind of painful change needs to be made. A break through, a new start, and honest struggle. Above all a clear grasp of what I am trying to do. _Not_ simply accepting an established routine and going along passively with it.

I left P.P. to _advise_ me if he really thinks the step ought not to be made. I'll see what he answers. I think it has to be made, and I have to overcome my inertia to make it.

How many people would define this "inertia" as "stability." But it isn't.

August 20, 1960. F. St. Bernard

Rain. Two wrens have a nest under the tarpaulin covering the saw in the woodshed.

Finishing the little book on C[harles] de Foucauld that H. Mason left. The voice and message of C. de F. mean very much to me. I think it is the most hopeful and living kind of message in our time. We think it great, or strange, because there is so little else – in the west.

The great effort necessary to get out of the spiritual paralysis in which we find ourselves. Words are cheap but they don't help. They keep us paralyzed.

Wonderful book by [Acharya] Vinoba [Bhave], _Talks on the Gita_ [New York, 1960] – sent by Lax. Began it yesterday. Just what I need at the moment.

I am very grateful to be in contact with L. Massignon and through him, with C. de Foucauld. This a very great grace.

A fine statement from Vinoba (p. 32).

"The action of the person who acts without desire should be much better than that of the person who acts with desire. This is only proper; for the latter is attracted to the fruit, and a part, much or little, of his time and attention will be spent on thoughts and dreams of the fruit. But all the time and all the strength of the man who has no desire for the fruit is devoted to the action."

I can certainly apply this to my present case!

August 21, 1960

I cannot get away from the fact that some of the great moral problems of my life are ones I have never fully faced. (And yet in another sense they are not so great and not really problems. Do I really think I have something to *face* or *just* something to *tidy up* in my mind. Yet I am not inclined to tidiness.)

Great moral problem – my evasion and disaffection from XXth century society. My refusal of all political commitments as absurd. Loud bluster in early poems about the futility of "the world." These are just noises made for my own comfort.

Note – I have now rejected the absurd and formalistic pose of "the monks" which is in favor here: that we have "left the world" and have nothing more to do with it; its pomps and its politics.

On the contrary, it has become very clear that the monastery is deeply committed on a political level. We *have to vote;* our vote *counts* very appreciably (one of the biggest precincts in Nelson County is ours – or at any rate we turn in one of the biggest votes).

Here we are subjected to all the political clichés and prejudices favored by the Abbot (v.g. for Kennedy, ag[ain]st Castro, conviction that the Russians *only* are warmongers, etc.). I am therefore a tool of something against which I *must* protest.

An interior ordering of thoughts and opinions, a *mere judgment of conscience* is absolutely not enough.

Yet I do have to strike out a position. Here is the problem, for mere *thinking* is a delusion. The answer has to be worked out in action and I cannot act.

I am in effect a political prisoner at Gethesemani.

A prisoner of my own inability to act, which I have strengthened a million times over by putting my life in the hands of – this Abbot. He is committed before all else to the smothering of any least spark of freedom, of political conscience, of a socially productive spirituality. He is dedicated to evasion. (Until Catholic Kennedy came along he was 100% Republican.)

Do I want to act? I am afraid I am only too glad to let myself be "held" in a position where I am unable to move, and only complain weakly to conceal from myself the fact that I enjoy this inertia. If this is true, how can I claim to have any honesty left, or any honor?

Even such reflections are largely useless, if they lead nowhere.

They do lead nowhere.

Hence the need to consider my *svadharma* [way of life] and to doubt, first of all, whether it consists primarily in "thinking." And yet it does: in clarification, in the Confucian sense. But clarification through and by right action. And I can't act.

August 22, 1960

"*La salud es escandalosa en un sanatorio* [Health is scandalous in a sanatorium]," says Octavio Paz.

Also, "*Las verdaderas ideas de un poema no son las que se le occurren al poeta antès de escribir el poema sino las que despuès, con o sin su voluntad, se desprenden naturalmente de la obra.*" ["The real ideas of a poem are not those which occur to the poet before writing the poem, but rather those which, with or without the poet's intention, are inferred naturally from the work itself."]

"*Poetizar no es decir el mundo sino decir la Palabra sobre la cual el mundo reposa.*" ["To make poetry is not to say the world but to say the Word on which the world rests."]

"The modern sage is not to be simply an eccentric and if he is ever again to play a useful role in society, he must learn to be wise in action rather than in meditation." Everett Knight

A sentence from a book that one can easily quarrel with on many points. But this agrees with Vinoba, and it is something I have come to admit in spite of myself. Can that mean that meditation was once for me an evasion from action? I know it certainly is so here for many and that's why meditation is blank.

August 23, 1960

I like this sentence quoted from St. Alphonsus Rodriguez in the book on St. Peter Claver now being read in the refectory. And I read Hopkins' poem on St. A[lphonsus Rodriguez] to the novices Sunday.

"Answer nothing, nothing, nothing."

This is important even in our thoughts.

Our thinking should not end by being merely an *answer* to what someone else has said – and the opinions of men. Every event to be only a moon of someone else's dim sun? (We are each other's moon – hence our darkness.)

A child may begin by answering. Yet in the child too, as a matter of fact, we are struck by *primal* utterance. His own significations, in which he responds not to words, but *to being*. In admiration.

Later he comes to respond in the way he feels is "expected." He gives out the words that are asked of him – hence he begins to answer not to being but the opinions and prejudices of others, either to conform or to resist.

Psalms fine at Vigils and Prime today. I was able, by saying them largely by heart and living in *truth* – to enter deeply, to *discover* lines said hundreds of times and suddenly mysterious again.

Summer visiting postulants fill the choir: new ones and old ones. The incongruity of big Joe Lime and Little John McKillop who want to talk, who both talk engagingly and earnestly. With Andy Wright who will v[ery] likely be spoiled and babied by the monks (like Bedford Doucette who went back to Canada yesterday).

I have been tempted to think of this as a "bad" and intemperate year, yet it has also been a more temperate year – more fasting and selective, and with joy. And with struggle too – deeper than the struggle of mere fasting because the fasting has been easy. O I am involved in these damned books. And in intemperate activity. A little temperance in one area reveals all the deep intemperance everywhere in me. Weakness, need, evasion. Yet I need to *act* but wisely and temperately.

August 26, 1960

I have finished reading the proofs of the *Divine Milieu* of P[ère] Teilhard de Chardin which were sent to me by Harpers. Yesterday (my feast day) I half finished an article on it.

There is much to say. More than I can say in the article.

Certainly the world is to be loved, as he says it. For God loved the world and sent His Son into the world to save it.

Here the world means the cosmos and all is centered on God. All seek Him.

Christianity should make us "more visibly human" – passionately concerned with all the good, that is, that wants to grow in the world and *that cannot grow without our concern.*

The stoic indifference cultivated by a certain type of Xtian spirituality is then a diabolical temptation and an emptying of pity, of charity, of interest. A hardening of the heart, a regression and an isolation.

His concern is admirable. And his indignation that "Christians no longer expect anything." It is true. Nothing great. But we expect *everything trivial.*

Our indifference to the real values in the world justifies our petty attractiveness to its false values. When we forget the Parousia and the Kingdom of God *in the world* we can, we think, safely be businessmen and make money.

Those who love the world in its wrong sense love it for themselves, exploit it for themselves.

Those who truly love it, develop it, work in it for God, that God may reveal Himself in it.

Feast Day yesterday. Enormous map of France, representing hours of work, and many other foolish contrivances, but also a charming card done by Nels Richardson and sent from Minnesota – with a map of *Persia!!!* But a wonderful Persian horseman, representing St. Louis (perhaps not Persian. But what?). A tough, gaily clad king with a sword like a huge feather.

Chapel overflowed with postulants, some of them perfect strangers.

August 27, 1960

Kairos [the appropriate moment] – moment in which there can come to a man He who is already present (one thinks [of] Clément's interesting book on time acc[ording] to orthodox theology).

August 28, 1960. Sunday

In Chapter bored and resentful of platitudes. Thought how after Chapter I would get this or that book, would go to the woodshed and would read and that it was *all an act of desperation.* An arbitrary act of will to convince myself that my life here makes sense. This of course is a condemnation of my own emptiness first of all – or rather of my lack of understanding of it, my fear of it still. Who cares? Read your book!

There isn't a reason in the world why life in this monastery should be a game in which we all perpetually convince one another that we are doing well and should stay, that our life amounts to something etc. etc.

But we are intent on amounting to something. We want to justify ourselves. We want to appear reasonable and indeed more reasonable than other men and this is the whole trouble. Why should I, who appear to know the difference, still insist on being reasonable – or on being *right*? And more right than everybody else, just because they are convinced of their own rightness?

They have cultivated an unshakable confidence in the rightness of their own way. I unfortunately have neglected this fundamental duty. Yet I have not been able to renounce the folly by which it is dictated.

September 1, 1960

Mass of St. Giles. His day always makes me glad, and it is cool, misty.

Fr. Joseph gave a naively amusing conference in chapter in which missionaries were chased by hippies etc. etc. Not meant to be as funny as it was.

Yesterday and the day before Earl Loomis and Jack Gruenwald (?) were here from Union Theol[ogical] Seminary and we had some good conversations. At such times I am tempted to think there is more point to my being here than there actually is. A delusion of efficacy, meaningfulness, productivity. Earl L. was older, more irregular, more intense than when I first met him at St. John's.

Still many visiting postulants.

I am ashamed of myself for having been angry with the abbot the other day, for no better reason than that he is abbot.

And I am a little annoyed at a Cistercian abbess who did not give a conscience-matter letter of mine to one of her nuns because the nun got mildly enthusiastic over a previous direction letter.

Part of the annoyance is at my own situation: because I cannot speak my mind without upsetting some people in our Order – and in others like it. Threatening the complacent and raising wild vain hopes in the dissatisfied. But this is absurd, because it is only a matter of words anyway. And I am powerless to *do* anything to help anyone who wants something better.

How nice it would be to be perfectly reliable, a pillar of the Order. An Abbot: or one who could be abbatial material. I *must* not become such a being here. But yet I ought to be able to run a house of my own. I think I am not (I mean a different kind of thing – that "new monastery" in Ecuador!).

First I have to get straightened out myself. Here I have been in many ways wrong. Just staying around would not make it all right.

September 2, 1960

"Le Temps de l'Eglise culmine donc à la prise de conscience par chaque personne humaine que la Fin est déjà présente, que l'histoire, en Christ, est dès maintenant consommé. Car Parousie signifie non seulement avènement mais attente, non seulement attente mais présence. Le Temps de l'Eglise pour reprendre l'expression de Saint Seraphim, est celui de 'l'acquisition du Saint Esprit.'" ["Time in the Church therefore culminates in an awareness for each human person that the End is already present, that history, in Christ, is, from that time on, fulfilled. For Parousia means not only coming but waiting, not only waiting but presence. Time in the Church, to use the expression of St. Seraphim, is 'the reception of the Holy Spirit.'"]

O. Clément, Transfigurer les temps [Neuchâtel, 1959], p. 136

This book of O. Clément is really excellent. Only now that I am in the middle do I realize that I have missed much by not reading with very close attention. A book to read twice. Few books deserve two readings!

September 3, 1960

"Le Fils porte témoignage du Père, l'Esprit porte témoignage du Fils, mais qui portera témoignage de l'Esprit sinon la transparence des saints?" ["The Son bears witness to the Father, the Spirit bears witness to the Son, but who will bear witness to the Spirit, if not the transparency of the saints?"]

Ibid., p. 142

Those who like T. de Chardin are called "rationalists" – and I suppose many other things beside. Why? The *fear* of the unusual. Originality is offensive to pious ears. "The most misunderstood of Jesuits" someone said of him – the man, not the books.

Yet I do not think he has the full answer to anything. I respect his answer because it is his own. But it is only partly mine and there remains much more to be said that he left out: including much of the traditional.

But those who fell for him completely – are they perhaps more delighted that they can once more feel that a Catholic "belongs in the modern world"?? Pitiable, I think, if it is only this.

On the first, a copy of *Disputed Questions* arrived. The "Notes on Solitude" is perhaps the best thing of the sort I have ever written. One reason being that the censors made me do it over five times at least. But this is something I must myself read and follow, for in it my deeper self is talking and I am obliged to listen. As if it were someone else, a director. (And of course Fr. J[ohn of the Cross], my confessor, says the same things when he says anything at all.)

The fires on the hill, Mount Olivet, the place for the retreat house. Grass green enough not to burn fast. We turned the brushpiles without setting the whole pasture on fire as I feared we might. The roar and the heat and the great red wash of flame flapping and sheeting upward, and reaching strongly toward the cedars. Brown bloody flame, earthen flame from the dry cedar branches.

Through the fire and smoke, the shadows of the postulants, standing as if waiting and as if helpless. Jim McMurray in floppy coveralls, quiet, shy and holy. And Fr. Liam in the bushes with a can of water on his back. And Fr. Cuthbert smiling and grinning from hard work. And all the others. Fr. Aquinas with hay fever.

But I have talked Rev. Fr. out of the full project, for fear that having a great house there I might somehow be kept here by it, or lest it be a millstone or lest having it we might have to keep it full. There will be only a very simple shelter. If I go the novices can have it, and it will not be against poverty.

(Afternoon) – A letter from Paul Philippe, this morning, written at Lisieux. As I rather expected, he was strongly against my leaving Gethsemani. "*Je vous supplie de ne pas vous évader de Gethsemani. . . il faut accepter.*" ["I beg you not to escape from Gethsemani . . . you must accept."] Even stronger than I expected. He does not *order* me to stay, but only because he really cannot. On the other hand if I demand, or insist on getting an indult, it is clearly against his desires and I do not intend to do that.

Yet now I am also convinced that the case must be patiently and humbly carried on. This much seems to be God's will; that I present all the reasons and arguments to my superiors.

Still there is little else I can do. And I can't move. Maybe Fr. Gregorio can come up here.

Action however can and must be taken in my own life which has become confused, distracted, sloppy, off center.

Do not know where the trouble lies – in too much reading and curiosity – or what? Not enough discipline anyway. Disciplined prayer. The woods are not enough. Less activity (when have I said that before?). More obscurity, more purpose, more perseverance in the mystery of helpless prayer. More real trust in God.

September 4, 1960. Day of Rec[ollection]

Reading the prophets. Ought to work on Greek to read the *Philokalia* but do not intend to launch on *any* project, at the moment. Maybe later.

Perhaps what is required is blind faith that in spite of everything God works in His own time, [will] lead me to a more fruitful place, where I really belong, where I can serve Him more truly. Pig-headed conviction that I belong in Latin America. But cannot do anything unless Fr. Paul Philippe changes his mind. Much as I would like to insist I really don't see any honest way of doing so. Unless there is something I have utterly failed to understand about obedience!

During Chapter (in library) a kingfisher flew through the *préau* [courtyard in front of the monastery] – a blue flash outside a window, and then the rattle of his controlled excitement.

Ducks yesterday in the bottoms, where the alfalfa has been cut for the third time.

The Quenons are here (Fr. Anselm made profession last Sunday) and this morning after chapter I had to talk to Phil Mullin's mother (Protestant), who brought him up from Texas and does not want him to enter.

No day of recollection for me today.

"Après la Résurrection, l'Ascension et la Pentecôte il est impossible à l'homme de reproduire l'économie propre du Fils. Le Chrétien doit non imiter les actions du Verbe Incarné mais revêtir, à travers les vicissitudes du temps déchu, ces états kénotiques glorifiés, ces situations de notre déchéance que l'Ascension a introduite au sein même de la Trinité." ["After the Resurrection, Ascension and Pentecost, it is impossible for man to duplicate the economy of salvation that is proper to the Son. The Christian should not imitate the actions of the Incarnate Word, but rather adopt as his own, through the vicissitudes of our fallen state, *these kenotic and glorified states*, these situations of our

fallen condition that the Ascension has introduced into the very bosom of the Trinity."] *O. Clément, p. 163*

The heart of Clément's book – that "fallen Time" (*le temps déchu*) *has no present*. It is only the expression of an absence – the absence of God. Redeemed Time (*le temps sauvé*) is concentrated in a "present moment" and born of the presence of God even in our own misery, in so far as our misery does not despair but falls into the abyss of Time, the Divine love, *"une ouverture de l'humilité à la vie ressusciteé du Seigneur"* ["an opening of humility to the risen life of the Lord"]. Tremendous content of this. Interesting content with French – somewhat existentialist. Very deep and true of Max Picard's *Flight from God* [Washington, D.C., 1951] (which is far less deep).

Basis – this doctrine founded on remarkable spirituality of Sylvanus of Athos, d. 1938, who was told by Christ, "Hold thy spirit in hell and do not despair, for in condemning himself to hell and in this destroying all passion, man liberates his heart to receive the divine love."

This is great reading for a Sunday, an Easter, a renewal in Christ! I praise the Lord Christ for His great mercy!

And this superbly wise sentence –

> *"Quand l'eau des larmes rejoint, sous le sable des passions, l'eau vivifiante du baptême. . . la lumière d'une seule fête, d'un seul dimanche, d'une Pâque perpétuelle, la lumière du huitième jour illumine chacune de nos instants."* ["When the water of tears is united, under the sand of the passions, with the vivifying water of baptism . . . the light of only one feast, one Sunday, one perpetual Easter, the light of the eighth day illuminates each one of our moments."] *(167)*

September 8, 1960. Nativity of BV [Blessed Virgin]

Importance of being able to rethink thoughts that were fundamental to men of other ages, or *are* fundamental to men in other countries. For me, especially – contemp[orary] Latin America – Greek Patristic period – Mt. Athos – Confucian China – T'ang dynasty – Pre-Socratic Greece. Despair of ever beginning truly to know and understand, to communicate with these pasts and these distances, yet sense of obligation to do so, to live them and combine them in myself, to absorb, to digest, to "remember." *Memoria*. Have not yet begun. How will I ever begin to appreciate their problems, re-formulate the questions they tried to answer. Is it even necessary? Is it sane? For me it is an expression of love for man and for God. An expression without which my contemplative life would be senseless.

And to share this with my own contemporaries.

September 9, 1960 – Rain.

Heavy rain after a long dry spell. (I think perhaps I register all the rain in this book – solicitude for rain and for freshness, as if dying in the desert.)

Heavy rain while they (especially novices) poured concrete for the roof terrace on the dormitory wing. There was no conference this morning. Probably canning tomorrow (apples).

I am finishing the notes on the vows: ironically, on stability. I write nothing I do not believe. (Fr. [John] Lafarge has written a book on Toumliline, the primitive Benedictine place in Morocco. It pierces my heart. Why am I not allowed to be something worth while, instead of carrying on this pretense here?)

Sorrow. Sorrow for sin. No more fooling about this sorrow in silence. Mourning. Grief.

On 5th St., Louisville: broken down buildings. Gaps between them, empty lots, full of weeds and sumac, even wild trees growing. As though in the country. Two blocks away, tall buildings.

I went with a nail in my shoe. I rode in a poor broken down taxi driven by a Negro (springs busted, meter did not work, "Liberty Cab") to find the little Greek Orthodox church of the Assumption but it was locked. I could not find any priest's house. Negro women, drinking beer under a tree in a hot grassless yard did not know anything about it. "We would not know about it," they said.

Big red Massey-Harris combine here, half under the covering woodshed, half in the rain, with red gestures and dinosaur expressions.

What happened to the grey cat, with the white spot on her chest? The grey cat that got thinner and thinner this summer and rubbed desperately against your ankles at evening, in the novitiate garden?

———

Brought back from the library, for light reading, O[liver] St. John Gogarty's _Week End in the Middle of the Week_ and could not stand it. Empty, absurd, it antagonized me. That peculiar type of emptiness (which requires a peculiar type of snotty audience) I tend to label (perhaps unjustly) as fascist. So I turned to a paperback of E. M. Forster's, _Abinger Harvest_ [New York, 1953] and this, on the contrary, I find charming and alive. And I agree, and I delight in listening, and in agreeing. It is a voice that comforts me, it is a voice of a world to which I still belong and am proud to belong – of humanism and, culturally, of Catholicity. (Yet Gogarty is the Irishman of the two and Forster the English protestant.) I have to be humble to take serious thought in having to say Forster is my kind of person (I hope).

September 10, 1960

"For what, in that world of gigantic horror, was tolerable except the slighter gestures of dissent?"

So says E. M. Forster, discussing his satisfaction on reading the early Eliot during World War I.

We tend to think massive protest is all that is valid today. But the massive is also manipulated and doctored. It is false. The genuine dissent remains individual. At least that is my option. In my view it is saner and nobler to take the kind of view E. M. Forster takes, not line up with the manipulated group. But to the group this looks like defeat. It looks like futility.

What is likely to be wrong is the failure of action. This kind of dissent may never be anything but words, attitudes, ideas.

On the other side what seems to be "action" on the mass scale may be nothing more than a parade – or an organized disaster. A big, blown up expression of a puny idea which, by its very emptiness, leads to a cataclysm of destructiveness. This is the gigantic horror, against which even the slightest idea is of great value.

September 11, 1960. XIV Sun after Pent[ecost]

Today is the anniversary of the death of the holy Staretz Sylvan, at St. Panteleimon on Mount Athos – Sept. 11, 1938. Or rather, on their calendar, Sept. 25th. But this sudden confusion of perspectives makes me wonder about _all_ days. Who says this is Sept. 11th? Well, we do. We have elected to call this Sept. 11th. Actually it is just "a day." A rainy, grey one, with crows busy over the woods there and a cold wind in the grasses and bluejays behind me by the church. Rare cars on the road, going where? We have chosen to call this "a day." In order to imitate God's day on which everything is already complete, or in order to imagine that our days are leading somewhere? Like that car that passed going south toward the distillery. (But it will turn either right or left before reaching the distillery? Where then? As if anyone had to know yet, if we do not assume it is *known* of someone, we will grow anxious.)

Staretz Sylvan did not want to die in the infirmary because they would put him in a room with a clock which would disturb his prayer.

Sitting at a table with other stewards, he refused to join all the others in criticizing one of their number who had failed in some monastery business.

His combats and sorrows. The Lord said to him, "Keep your heart in hell and do not despair." This to me is one of the most enlightening and comforting of statements, lifting a weight from my heart, inexplicably. (Ten years ago it would have weighed me down with foreboding.)

In so far as hell means apparent rejection and darkness, some of us must elect it, as it is ours and Job's way to peace. The far end of nothing, the abyss of our own absurdity, in order to be humble, to be found and saved by God. In a way this sounds idiotic and even heretical. Yet no – I am one who is saved from hell *by God.*

Or rather that is my vocation and destiny.

If I spend my time saying "I *have been* saved," then I may have to resist the awful fear of falling back, of saying I have not fallen back, of denying that I have fallen back when I have . . . etc. And never knowing at any time where I am. Foolish concern.

To have the flames of hell around me like Sylvan and to hope I *shall* be saved. Thus I *am* saved, but no need to insist on myself. Jesus, Savior.

Quis mihi det ut in inferno protegas me? [Who will grant me that in the nether world you protect me?]

The book on Staretz Sylvan by Archimandrite Sophrony [*The Undistorted Image*, London, 1958] – monk of Athos now in England, has a small community at Maldon in Essex. I wrote to him about his book and then Friday I found we already had it in the library. This is remarkable. We really have good librarians now!! (Esp. Fr. Sylvanus. No doubt this explains it.)

General chapter this week. I told Rev. Father I thought the Order was obsessed with trivialities. He replied, "Oh no! The [Abbot] General is most broadminded. He allowed an Englishman to be Master of Students in Rome!"

Fr. Marie Louis at N[otre] D[ame] du Desert wrote about my (miserable) preface to the book on Joseph Cassant. Disturbed by my use of the word "Procrustean" in relation to spiritual directors in our Order. And in the first place did not understand it. Thought I meant only "severe." Fr. L. is *our postulator* for "the cause" – another triviality! I wonder how many in the Order are really interested in Jos. Cassant and in his canonization. Hardly anyone here exc[ept] Fr. Chrysogonus, maybe!

Yet walking to Prime in the grey cloister, realized that I have paid too little attention to a great reality – my love for my monastery and the love of the community for me. (I hate to admit it, for it may mean I must stay!) But not love for or interest in the stupid superficial concerns of the community as an official body.

That is it, though. What is said, what is planned, what is achieved, is not really the community's real concern, though many may think and hope it is.

Resentment toward those who try to convince themselves of the reality and significance of their lives by making the community adopt and carry out their plans.

I can honestly say I do not want the cty [community] to carry out any plan of mine.

I know too well with what lack of interest these plans are really carried out. Even those who are most involved do not really care for the plan – but they care for something the plan represents, and here the devil does his little bit, I imagine. Distinction between "action" and "acting out."

Of one thing I am certain.

My life must have meaning. This meaning springs from a creative and intelligent harmony between my will and the will of God – a clarification by right action.

But what is right action? What is the will of God?

What are the sources of all my confusion on these?

I can no longer accept the superficial verbalism (going in circles) which evades reality by simply saying the will of the Superior is the will of God and the will of God is the will of the Superior. I do not mean that the will of the Superior does not, or cannot, indicate where God's will may be for me – but the will of the Superior simply defines and points out the way in which I am to try to act intelligently and spiritually, and thus clarify the meaning of my own life ("giving glory to God").

Simply to go ahead blindly, muttering "the will of God, the will of God" clarifies nothing and it is making me mentally ill. Not because obedience is unhealthy – on the contrary! But our obedience *here*, or at least mine, is unhealthy because in the first place it is not real obedience. Whose fault? We are *all* to blame. For me to say I alone am to blame would be another lie. Too many lies already!

But "obedience" here tends to sanctify various lies like this one.

The sanctification of falsity by the magic will of the Superior – in order that the will of the Superior may continue to have its "magic power" which must never be questioned. Precisely this is the greatest lie, for the will of the Superior is not supposed to have any power but the power of Christ's humility and of His love. And this power is not derived from some secret magic source: it comes from – where? If the church is not love . . . But the church is the Body of Christ, and full of His love.

It is true that I have sinned by lack of trust in God Who can make even the mistakes and willfulness of Superiors fruitful for good. I should not question the decisions of Superiors as intently and resentfully as I have done. The fact remains that my obedience should bring clarity into my life, not confusion. Can I rightly say that *obedience* has brought confusion? Perhaps this is too much. It has not brought clarity.

September 14, 1960. Holy Cross

". . . Was it not a fearful thing, my reader, that the object of your seeking was so near you that you did not seek God, but God sought you?"

Kierkegaard ["On the Occasion of a Confession"]

A very pleasant afternoon, the tops of the apple trees, finding apples out of the bright September sky. Proofs of *Wisdom of the Desert* came, from [Giovanni] Mardersteig – beautiful typography, a few Italian errors. Moved and consoled by K. Barth's essays (homilies) on Christmas. (The gratuity of Agape, the helplessness and transiency of Eros.)

Dan Walsh from the guesthouse sent over an article by Morton White on philosophy – depressing inanity. Since we cannot really say anything about anything, let us be content to talk about the way in which we say nothing – the institutional viewpoint we take of nothing. A far more organized futility than atheist existentialism, which at least has the dignity of revolt and despair. The straight-faced *acceptance* of nothingness as if it were the content of life – this is ultimate degradation of the mind.

September 16, 1960

Fr. Cyprian [Carew], from Georgia (on the way back to the monastery from Rome), said his feast day mass in the Novitiate Chapel this morning.

From Karl Barth – *Christmas* 1931 [translated by Berhard Citron, London, 1959]. (That Christmas I was in Strasbourg, as also in 1930, and on one of these occasions I went to a Lutheran church where all was in German and did not understand.)

"Suppose a person living in Germany today had faith, then the comfort and direction he received (from the Christmas light) in all humility, *would consist in the permission and command to continue without those fixed ideas which at present he cannot avoid* . . . [Merton's emphasis]. Not only should man be able to live with principles but he must also be able to live without them. The eternal light which entered the world at Bethlehem, is, if its testimony can be trusted, certainly the most unprincipled reality one can imagine. The fact that God became man cannot be kept in a system. . . . It cannot be proved . . . but it is as true as the eternal light which differs from all other lights inasmuch as it requires neither fuel nor candlestick."

He goes on to say that what the German of the time needs is to learn to do without principles to which he is fanatically attached without "causes." "*Is perhaps unconditional faith in all sorts of principles* not *the typically German form of unbelief*?" [Merton's emphasis]. And because of them, he says, they inflict untold injury on themselves and others. How necessary, he says, would be a spiritual disarmament.

This is most true for Europe, for Germany – the truth would have to be stated differently for us – we are much more inclined to muddle along without principles, but that is not what he means either. He means – the eternal light to believe in the Gospel and not take *one's own convictions* quite so seriously.

To be, therefore, merciful.

"People cannot come together if they are so tied up in principles that they can only hit one another in the face. . . . While everyone's convictions are supposed to be sacred, everyone remains impractical."

And fine lines on Xtian humanism. Not something back into oneself and spinning out "the dream of his Ego in unfathomed, even though perhaps Christian profundity." But "The ideal humanity lies outside of us, and is represented by our fellow man *whom we can never see through the dark glasses of principles* . . ."

Love itself is not a principle, an act – of being interested not in "the good or useful" but in the "actual fellow man."

But if love becomes a "principle" and is then "authentically interpreted," one's fellow man is identified with class, race, or nation and the principle of love is used to destroy others – one sees the actual fellow man even less than before.

If we believed that the eternal light which entered the world was man, then we also would be really human?

Opposites: Karl Barth and Gemistus Pletho.[15] I do not mean to be facetious. Gemistus (who attended the Council of Florence, from Greece) also wanted to revive the Olympian gods – who anticipated the Positivist Pantheon of A[uguste] Comte, who will doubtless be loved by magicians since he sounds like one . . . Pitiful, symptomatic, symbolic figure of the humanist renaissance. But Barth with his earnest, reforming Christianity, and his insistence that the Incarnation makes it impossible to invent even a Christian god – or to reach into "the infinite" to select our own concepts (idols) of them. Two extremes, but Barth is salutary. There is so much truth there, so much of the Gospel.

"Revelation never has a recognizable form, its wisdom and power can never be proved, its triumph is never apparent, its success is not tangible and its benefit not for immediate enjoyment." Never? Never! Still, though, too absolute, acceptable.

"Divine revelation cannot be discovered in the same way as the beauty of a work of art or the genius of a man is discovered. . . . It is the opening of a door [that] can be unlocked only from the inside . . ." etc. I like Barth.

September 17, 1960

Karl Barth had a dream about Mozart. (Mozart a Catholic, and Barth is piqued by the fact that M. did not like Protestantism, for he said it was "all in the head" and that they didn't know the meaning of *Agnus Dei qui tollis peccata mundi* [Lamb of God who takes away the sins of the world].) Well Barth dreamt he had to "examine" Mozart in Dogma. He wanted to make it as favorable as possible and in his questions he alluded pointedly to Mozart's "Masses." But Mozart did not answer a word.[16]

---

[15] Pletho was a Byzantine philosopher, born ca. 1355 in Constantinople.
[16] This passage was reworked for Merton's manuscript "Barth's Dream," which eventually was published as *Conjectures of a Guilty Bystander* (New York, 1966).

I am tempted to write Barth a letter about this moving dream, which of course concerns his own salvation.

He says for years he has played Mozart every morning before going to work on dogma himself. (Just think! Dogma is his daily work!!)

The Mozart in himself is perhaps in some way the better, hidden, sophianic fact that grasps the "center" of cosmic music and is saved by love (yes Eros!). The other, the theologian, is seemingly more occupied with love, but it is a stern, actually more cerebral, agape . . . A love that is *not in us*, only in God.

I remember my own dream about "Protestants." (They are perhaps my *aggressive* side.)

Barth seeks perhaps to be saved by the Mozart in him.

He says, "It has been said that it is a child, even a 'divine' child, who speaks in his music to us." That some consider M. a "child" in practical affairs of life, and that Burckhardt "earnestly took exception" to this view. At the same time "Mozart never was allowed to be a child in the literal meaning of the word." (Infant prodigy – first concert tour at 6.)

But he was a child and in that other, higher meaning of the word.

September 18, 1960

How much I need clarity. I live in great darkness and weakness, occasionally getting some smell of the fresh air where light is outside my cellar.

The center of the problem – my own pride, the pride of others, the pride of my monastery. I enter into dialogue with the pride of others, and it is my own pride that speaks. Hence I have to see their pride and not my own.

Fury after Prime, or brief spasm of it, resentment, clearly seen. And the realization that the whole thing *can* someday break off like a cliff and fall into the sea, if I learn to *not* identify myself with my own angry, righteous, spiteful image.

My dependence on the community. First as to privileges. Upon which I depend for so many wrong reasons, but they give me some of the solitude "I need." But I rightly need it. This is the wrong way, an enslaving way, to avail myself of it. What other way? Leave here, of course. But my pride befouls and obscures *that* issue – if only there were more love in my heart. *Ahimsa* [Non-violence, Fundamental principle of Jainism. Also invoked by Gandhi]. *Agape* [Other-centered love].

I hate my wrong dependence and this makes all my protests foolish and spiteful.

Yet I should be able to say NO to all this. A real peaceful, but complete NO. I am in no position to do so.

September 23, 1960

Moving words of K. Barth preached on Good Friday 1948 in Hungary at Debrecen, the great Calvinist center.

"For in His meekness which we remember today, He achieved the mightiest of all deeds ever fulfilled on earth: In His own person He restored and re-established the violated law of God and the shattered law of man. In this meekness the grace of God appeared in His person, and the obedient man, at peace with God and in whom God has pleasure, was revealed. In this meekness of His, Jesus Christ, nailed to the cross as a criminal, created order in the realm of creation, the order in which man can live eternally as the redeemed, converted child of God."

Against the Stream [London, 1954], p. 55

Death of Fr. Lambert yesterday.

Fr. Peter, then Fr. Alphonse, came to choir at None to get the Infirmarian. (No one as yet knew what was going on.) After I had finished distributing work the church bell began to ring for the prayers of the agonizing. Fr. L. died in his chair, where he had a stroke. His face was very pale and most of the novices had no idea who it was that had died.

Long office of the dead after vespers, then the air compressor started up and they dug his grave with a machine, not that he cared one way or another.

A postulant said this morning, "How deep do they dig a grave? They have been at it all morning."

Yesterday I killed a big shiny black widow spider in its web, in a rotten tree stump. A beautiful spider, more beautiful than most other species. But I thought I had better kill it, for I nearly sat down next to the stump and someone could get bitten. Strange to be so close to something that can kill you and not be accompanied by some kind of a "desire" – as if desires were everything. (A car can kill you, too.)

———

Death. We think we understand it. That we know what it is. That we know what life is. That we know who we are.

Fr. Lambert – *Cum sapientes sapiat. Cum canentes canticum novum cantet!* [Let him be wise as wise men are. Let him sing a new song as singers do!]

September 25, 1960. Sunday

Yesterday – by surprise, during the morning work, a group of twenty foreign students from the University of Indiana showed up in the novitiate. I gave them a brief talk. They were all journalists, on some kind of project or other, and this was part of a tour (a non-journalistic part. Just recreation or uplift or something). But it was a fine group. Africans (a Nigerian in a fine comfortable looking costume, one from Kenya, one from Tanganyika.) A Pole, who remained invisible. Several from India, one from Pakistan, several from Korea, one from Norway, Sweden, Germany and one from the Argentine.

I spoke of the importance of spiritual values in the modern world and of the role of the East in this matter, and got a very fine response from especially the Hindus. Also the Koreans and the man from Jordan who cupped his hand behind his ear but was always smiling. The negroes seemed more perplexed. The Europeans acted as though they had heard this kind of thing before and were prepared to be tolerant about it. All in all everyone was very friendly. And I enjoyed it mightily. Everything took place on the spur of the moment, and left me bewildered.

Reading Lorca again – what a marvelous poet, so alive, so much strength and vividness and sound. I can think of no modern poet that gives me more genuine poetic satisfaction. Wholeness. Primitive and modern. Beauty. Toughness. Music. Substance. Variety. Originality. Character. Color. Andalusian weather.

Finished *Abinger Harvest*, embarrassed a little by the pageant but loved all the rest of it. Finished Isaias.

Not finished – Daniel the Stylite. But turned him in anyway.

Pussy's life of Dom Martène.[17] I'll keep at it.

And I want to read this about Toumliline, too.

[17] Merton may well be referring to the biography of Benedictine Dom Edmond Martène by Joseph Daoust, *Dom Martène, Un Géant de l'Erudition bénédictine* (Fontanelle, 1947).

September 29, 1960. F. of St. Michael and All Angels

My work as hebdomadary. But today some Byzantine rite priests are to concelebrate in the High Mass. Ray Parrish is, I hope, to start work on the Mount Olivet hermitage.

It has been a beautiful week except for a stupid quarrel with Fr. Tarcisius, who, with his usual willfulness and political wrangling tried to put over some ideas of his own as to how the novices' communion Mass was to be said. The thing that exasperates me is that he is typical of those liturgy movement people who take advantage of any and every "pronouncement" to impose their own ideas no matter how little they may be justified by the circumstances. In this case he wants the Mass of the Catechumens said out loud – the rest silent as another Mass will be going on at the side altar after that. I had refused to do anything about this before, knowing that only half measures or trivial adaptations were possible. He tried to go ahead on his own with this silly solution. But I should not have been angry with him. Another indication of the corruption and sinfulness of man! I am sick of myself but cannot change, only pray to be changed.

Politics – at last I think I am beginning to come out of my stupor. Excellent book on [Reinhold] Niebuhr (by G. Harland). A great and lucid mind and profoundly Christian. One of the most hopeful signs in America.

I must examine the superficiality of my European prejudices. There is a great deal wrong with my instinctive tendency to think in a French way about America. Certainly it is the _easiest_ way. It gives me the impression of being independent, but it is only another form of passivity.

The sentimental, out of date moralism and shallow self-righteousness of most American thought is too self-evident for comment. It is a tragedy of great dimensions. But for me to repeat _all_ American ideas would be another tragedy. We _know_ we need something better. The courageous thing is not to be negative but to seek, like Niebuhr, to build something solid. Even to fail in this would be nobler than a total rejection.

This is _most important_ for my vocation and my spiritual life. It all affects the Mexico proposition.

September 30, 1960

Is it a temptation for me to want to form judgments and enumerate them, judgments about the situation of many today? Sometimes I imagine that this is pride and megalomania – as if I were an authority. Who am I? The point is that I have acquired the power to be heard, and there is every evidence that I should use it discreetly and modestly, when it seems that I have something to say. The humble and prudent solution is then to accept the responsibilities this entails, to mistrust my own observations and limitations but to study and think and, when opportune or fitting, to speak. There is no megalomania in this if I don't delude myself that I am a prophet or a doctor of the church – and this delusion, objectively speaking, should not be too hard to avoid since it cannot leave any visible or factual basis. Who am I? A priest and a writer, and one who has the gift of speaking intelligently I hope. Hence I must also think clearly, and pray, and meditate and when circumstances require it, speak. And speak to as many as will listen to me. About things concerning their happiness and their destiny – along with my own. In a word, about salvation.

October 2, 1960

Yesterday took Dan Walsh over to Loretto to see if they could use him as a philosophy professor, and it appears that they can.

Very impressed with the place. The country is already a little different from here – they are in the rolling land beyond Rohan's Knob. It reminds me in a way of Shakertown: a village of old brick buildings on a hilltop, everything neat and well ordered, lovely trees. The old "Academy" building is very picturesque – built in 1858 – gingerbread and high windows, but quiet and sedate. It gripped me. I could feel the hundred Kentucky summers that had been lived in that building by nuns and the winters also, just like our summers and our winters. As if I shared with them a secret that someone like Dan could never quite understand, being a layman and not from Kentucky – not from *silent* Kentucky.

Mother Luke [Tobin], energetic, bright, capable, warm, a wonderful person: the Mother General of Loretto. One likes her immediately. Then the others whose names I did not remember. But all bright and sensible and solid people.

Later met one or two postulants and novices, including the twins, one of whom I had met in St. Anthony's hospital last fall. The novices wore charming white coifs and were for the most part very ethereal – but when a whole procession of them came trooping down the stairs we took flight.

Nine of the nuns start for Bolivia Tuesday – they will take a freighter from New Orleans. Making a foundation in La Paz. Mother Luke very insistent that we should go there. Shocked by the poverty.

I have heard that Rev. Fr. had an hour long private audience with the Holy Father in Rome and all day this fact (?) has filled me with foreboding. It is so easy to come back and declare that our Pope has simply said everything you want. No doubt. The Holy Father will have said everything Rev. Father has been saying himself for years, thus communicating his infallibility to our abbot's policies. I am sure there must have been questions of my dialogues. My "ecumenism" as Rev. Father apparently calls it. I learned from Dan that he is really very keen on it although he says little about it to me. I am afraid of it becoming some kind of a silly, organized racket to bring publicity to Gethsemani. More glory! I am not in it for my glory or for the glory of the house – but for the good that comes of simple and charitable conversation. This needs no publicity and no attention. It is good in itself and does not need to be used to prove anything. If we leave it be what it is, it will give glory to God.

Again, this talk with the Holy Father may well have been momentarily concerned with my desire to go to Mexico. "Holy Father, you surely don't want Father Merton to be a hermit in Mexico, *do you?*" "I most certainly do *not!!*" Another infallible decision, settled for all eternity.

Saying my Mass after Chapter. This morning, clear sun, quiet chapel, and a whole new outlook. Happy!

October 3, 1960. F. of St. Thérèse
After night office, long quiet interval, reading [André Marie Jean] Festugière on Plato. And that life of Dom Martène. In a way I admire Saint-Germain-des-Prés and in a way I don't. I admire their scholarship, not their rigidity.

After High Mass I went out with Mr. Parrish, the contractor from Bardstown, to stake out the place on the hill – let's be frank: the hermitage.

It is nothing like the plan made by Art Bec Var and the G.E. people after all. It has been cut down by so many people, including myself, and is no longer a shiny, smart little pavilion but just a plain cottage with two rooms and a porch. Clearly it is a hermitage rather than a place for conferences.

The thing about it I like best is the improvising that goes on between me and Mr. Parrish, the decisions we made on the spur of the moment, dictated by the situation. It got smaller, then larger, and now it is in a better place than I had anticipated, more hidden, but with the same wonderful view over the valley.

I and three novices (Timothy, Sebastian and Cuthbert) went out and helped dig the foundations in the afternoon. It was hot work but friendly and pleasant. Parrish's men were glad of the help and seemed to be cheered by it and I was certainly gratified and grateful. Sang in secret to myself "*Bene fundata est Domus Domini, supra firmam petram* [The house of the Lord is well founded, on a strong rock]."

The soil is good. During collation I thought of planting some fruit trees on the east side, where there is now a pasture.

October 9, 1960. Sunday (18th after Pent[ecost])
It has been a busy and in some ways exhausting week. Have begun to say Mass after Chapter as a regular daily thing. This means I get a half can of black coffee after the night office and settle down to about two hours of study. One thing I have been working on is the longer edition of Tobias (not the one in the Vulgate or the trans[lation] from Greek).

Bob MacGregor was here. Eloise Spaeth and Marna were here. Fr. Tarcisius was busy on the schola that was recording for Columbia (people from Columbia records were here). A man who wants to translate *No Man Is an Island* into Polish was (is) here. Dan Walsh of course is still here and will be for a year (?). All these I saw and spoke to. Bob MacGregor had many interesting things to say about Japan, and Buddhist rites, and about some young lama refugees who are to come from Tibet. Victor and Carolyn Hammer came over and with Bob MacGregor we ate some sandwiches in the tobacco barn.

All week we feared rain. Much would stop work on the hermitage, but it did not rain. At last, on Saturday (the men worked overtime). There were showers but in the morning I looked over at the hill and a great truckful of ready-mixed concrete was roaring up to the top behind the trees.

So the slab was poured and the foundation was finished. This is the essential thing . . .

Then suddenly in the evening Rev. Father started berating me for "changing the plans" – a tissue of misunderstandings but I was annoyed at it.

And he came back from Rome full of cagey political statements and repeating over and over that the Pope had said we must "pray for the

Ecumenical Council." Obviously he has talked to various people about things concerning me and will not tell me what was said but will interpret it to suit himself and "use it against me" – so to speak. I found it very trying.

But I have to use it, as best I can, to liberate myself still more, interiorly. To be less dependent on approval and support – not to need to ask for encouragement, comprehension, and tokens of trust.

October 10, 1960

After the Night Office. The superb moral and positive beauty of the *Phaedo*. One does not have to *agree* with Plato, but one must hear him. Not to listen to such a voice is unpardonable, it is like not listening to conscience or to nature. I repent, and I love this great poem, this "music." It is a purifying music of which I have great need.

And Gandhi – how I need to understand and practice non-violence in every way. It is because my life is not firmly based on the truth that I am morally in confusion and in captivity – under the half truths and prejudices that rule others and rule me through them.

October 12, 1960

"A person who realizes a particular evil of his time and finds that it overwhelms him dives deep in his own breast for inspiration and when he gets it he presents it to others." *Gandhi*, Non-V[iolence], *p. 191*

October 13, 1960

Moved and delighted by the lines of the book of Wisdom about ships (14:1–7), especially the one ". . . so that even if a man lacks skill he may put to sea." Profound implications, especially for me at this moment. The necessity of risk and its place in the context of Providence and wisdom. A desire for gain plans the vessel (not necessarily reproved here); wisdom builds it; Providence guides it and the navigator needs not long experience but trust and good sense.

The beautiful awareness of the divine seeing in Wisdom (not utterly condemning the Greek philosophers, see 13:6–7 – including Heraklitus). (13:2). Another line that moves me much:

For even if we sin we are thine, knowing thy power; but we will not sin, because we know that we are accounted thine. *15:2*

October 16, 1960

The hermitage grows, but I find that anxiety grows with it because Rev. Father keeps intimating that it is something he does not want me to have or even use except in a very restricted way. I mean, he is very clear about my not *living* in it, or sleeping in it, or saying Mass there.

It is exceptionally frustrating to have such a beautiful place as this one is getting to be – tucked away among the pines – and to have to stay away from it. Along with this, the conviction that the abbot has no interest in how I might feel about this, and is sure that my desires are absurd, and even fears them. But in that case why did he do something that would manifestly encourage them? I did not really ask for this, far rather I showed a great deal of hesitation and gave him five or six chances to reverse his decision and call the whole thing off. This by now he will have completely forgotten.

Meanwhile I have a hard time appearing cheerful and sociable. I can't say I have tried too hard, either. Complete disgust with the stupid mentality we cultivate in our monasteries. Deliberate cult of frustration and nonsense. Professional absurdity.

Isn't life absurd enough already without our adding to it our own fantastic frustrations and stupidities?

Yet as soon as I set foot in the woods and climb to the place where the house is being built, I can forget all this. But as soon as I come back I am in it worse than ever.

Frank Kacmarcik[18] and Bob Rambusch were here. K. is grossly overworked and I don't think his work or his thought are gaining by it. I am usually a little suspicious of the intense activation and restlessness of some of these liturgical enthusiasts. (Nothing against liturgy.) And I suspect their clichés about "visual theology" etc. But Rambusch gave a good talk on the theology of light.

R. brought a wonderful paperback of Ben Shalur! The forms in the drawings!

The best book on yoga so far is the synthesis of Sri Aurobindo – I got it last week from the Louisville Library and am the first to have taken it out.

[18] A liturgical artist.

October 24, 1960

Coffee after night office and the good long silence until Prime. *Deliciae meae.* [My delights.] This is something wonderful, and in this silence, reading Festugière, I have finally come to admit to what extent I have always been a Platonist. My reservations about Plato have gone, since the *Phaedo* (understanding of course always that one is not obliged to agree with every theory!).

Finishing life of Dom Martène – the curious condition at Saint-Germain-des-Prés at beginning of 18th cent. – something like Gethsemani – analogous to our state – for we are certainly not students.

The Bellarmine conferences last week. These busy but rewarding days, talking on wisdom, talking boldly, offending pious ears (that wanted to be offended) urging a broadening of horizons in every direction – political leftism, peace (Gandhi), study of the Orient, creative work, writing, publishing and whatever else I could think of. Impression that it was a warm and responsive group. Drank tea. Novitiate still smells of cigarettes. Fr. Abbot did not like it. Impression that he is worried and suspicious. Too much life for him. He likes silent, passive conformity. Fr. Damasus, novice master from St. Meinrad, was here yesterday. What a life he leads! Works like mad. I had a talk with him and only afterward discovered that he was not supposed to see me.

Msgr. Horrigan, who brought the Bellarmine group here, is, I am told, a possibility as the new bishop of Owensboro.

Khrushchev who pounded with his shoe on a table at the UN. The election coming, interminable and stupid articles read in refectory about "protestant bigotry" ag[ain]st Kennedy. And inflammatory stuff against Castro. And Michener's book on the Hungarian revolt. Too much of this – can have a very unhealthy effect! Symptomatic of the real underlying political temper of the monastery – or of its abbot! His attachments, commitments and anxieties. What are my own obligations? To avoid entanglement in *his* commitments at all costs.

October 28, 1960. SS. Simon and Jude

After my class, wrestling quietly with the circumstances of my life. There is an attitude to be taken, there are decisions to be made. There is a radical refusal demanded of me somewhere and I do not know where it begins and ends and how to approach it.

Fragments of unrelated thought.

If I invite people, esp[ecially] Protestants, here, I am in part inviting them to view the monastic façade we have constructed. It would be better not to do this perhaps. Not that they will necessarily be deceived, but it is simply useless and illusory. *Divertissement* [amusement or distraction].

The curiously unformulated, ambiguous attitude taken by the abbot towards retreats anyway. And towards all my "contacts."

How do I know that if I tell someone they can come, they will be actually allowed to see me when they *do* come?

Do I have to worry about this?

Writing: surely no need to continue writing for *Sponsa Regis*.

In so far as my writing is part of the Gethsemani façade, it is undesirable and should be stopped.

Refuse to be part of this façade.

In a way – it a very right for me *to be as if I were no longer here.*

But there is so much I am yet incapable of grasping, about this. Because of course I am still too involved.

I ought to be writing poetry and doing creative work. Or nothing.

Tried some abstract-looking art this week. This no relevance to problem.

I have to re-think ["reformulate" written first, then canceled] my whole attitude towards "contacts" with people outside monastery. What am I doing? What am I saying? Who do they think I am, and who am I? Who do I think they are? What do I think they want?

In practice, I seek a kind of obscure support from them: agreement. Agreement with my own peculiar attitudes, which are *not* those of the monastery. Yet if they think me liberal, I may be creating a façade for a monastery. That is – simply confused, obscurantistic, pragmatic and which lacks all depth. So what?

Is it a question of living in complete spiritual independence, silence, detachment, freedom? Of course this sounds nice. But what does it really mean? This is my job, to find out the meaning of this.

Went to Cincinnati Wednesday to get reproductions of prints in Honiber Collection at the Art Museum.[19] Enormously impressed, deeply moved, by

---

[19] For his book on art and liturgy, never published.

Persian and Indian things, above all by the tomb cover of Inman Riza with its paradise motifs and its Sufi poem. Sacred and wonderful, enigmatic, innocent, alone, by itself. Saying nothing to the uncomprehending people. Also Sivas and Mother Goddesses; the inscrutability of the smiles of the liberated ones all the more inscrutable and even a little sardonic, in a museum. They are very patient with the joke that has brought them there, and put them in our foolish midst, and in our century.

St. John Perse has the Nobel Prize.

Nixon promises a man in space by 1966.

We saw the confetti and streamers left by his passing in Cincinnati.

I renew my respect for the beauty and character of Cincinnati, its wide river, its hills, its misty views, its sudden corners. It is a good and real city, not a shadow of a city like Louisville.

People at the museum were kind and eager to help.

Liked the action paintings – deeply impressed by them.

October 29, 1960

The other day we returned from Cincinnati through Lexington and had supper at Victor Hammer's. A pleasant evening. Rain on the shining streets, under the thick trees by the library. The warm lights of the house, and after supper, brandy in front of an open fire. Spoke of getting some furniture for the hermitage. He knows someone who will copy the table he made for himself in his print shop. Carolyn is busy with a group of people who want to buy Shakertown and make it a place for quiet and study. Renfrow, at the Inn, is holding out for a high price (for which no one can blame him), but this project is a very good one and it *must* succeed sometime. I am very interested in it. Want to help by writing something but don't know where to begin.

Cincinnati. The Jewish girl sitting on top of the filing cabinets with her shoes off in the office of the Director of the Museum, while he was out lecturing to the ladies of the garden club. She gave me a top secret photo of the Spanish tomb figure whom they call Don Sancho. An impressive head.

Dan Walsh v[ery] interesting on Plotinus last evening. His affinities with modern existentialism. Evil – a being without an essence.

Abraham Heschel wrote an amiable and humble letter and sent three books. I am happy and consoled. He is the most significant spiritual (religious) writer in this country at the moment. I like his depth and his realism. He knows God! Is writing now on the prophets, and is worthy to do it.

Happy in the wet woods yesterday for a short while. The roof is beginning to appear on the hermitage, St. Mary of Carmel.

October 30, 1960. XXI Sunday Post Pent[ecost]. Day of Rec[ollection]
After Mass. It seems to me that the most honest thing for me to do is to more or less abandon any initiative or effort to bring Protestants or others here for "dialogue." It is not a question of what "I want" or what anybody else wants, but a question of honesty and fundamental Christian decency.

The issue is too involved with false motivations – the Gethsemani façade, the abbot's interest in the façade, the "movement" that is in fashion at the moment, my own desire for conversation and friendship. The fact that it is approved by John XXIII makes no difference, does not make it relevant. Certainly no indication that I am "bound" to continue with it.

The abbot *wants* it to continue, but will not say anything positive or definite to that effect and consequently the whole project remains so vague and uncertain that it is unworkable. Hence if I am to take on conversation with any group or individual the invitation must be *his*. He will probably do little or nothing about it anyway.

Hence I will plan *no* retreats for 1961 and will not invite anyone for anything.

And I will decently abstain from any further references of the matter to Rome.

As for letters – I might as well refrain from making new contacts, except for necessity.

Aurobindo's excellent analysis in chapter on personification of intelligence. First distinguishes *manas* (sense-mind) and *buddhi* [enlightenment].
And in *buddhi* –
1. a level of "customary understanding" – reflex thinking, prejudice – ready made opinions – based on manas.
2. a level of creative understanding, enlarging experience, by creative interpretation not of pure truth but of "the truth of the moment." Words to fall back on (1) when uninspired.
3. spiritual understanding of pure truth.

Important – exercise of cutting off the "customary understanding," withholding from it the sanction of the higher reason which remains free, observing and silent. "The current understanding begins to run about in a futile circle reflecting all its formed opinions . . . until it begins to distrust itself, fail and fall silent."

Not his special aim – not escape from nature but to education and spiritualization.

November 1, 1960. All Saints

Yesterday, in the morning, during squalls of rain, they poured the floor of the Chapter Room and after Mass there was another false alarm – everybody running and the fire engine out. Nothing. Some wires crossed in the cannery.

This evening, after Office of the Dead, sat on the porch of the hermitage and watched the sunlight fade in the valley, and saw the moon rise over the little maple saplings we planted on the east side yesterday. Extraordinary peace and silence. If I have any desire left in the world it is to live there and die there.

November 7, 1960

Grey cold days lately. Today the sun is out; hard frost. Temperature about 28 early this morning. No heat, the furnace is dismantled.

Fr. Alfonse's jubilee Saturday. Dom Vital [Klinski] – jubilee of profession a week or so ago. Redoubled articles on Kennedy in refectory – election day is tomorrow. I hear Rev. Father has already invited him here for a pre-inauguration retreat.

75 seminarians from Southern Baptist are to come today.

Read sermons of St. Faustus of Rieg the other day, and liked them. Curious about the monks of Lérins. Reading Heschel, *God in Search of Man* [New York, 1955] and [C. H.] Dodd (very good), *The Bible Today* [Cambridge, 1956].

November 9, 1960

Yesterday was election day. At about 10:30 I went out to the gate, after spending some work time on abstract drawings for a possible experimental book.

Sun out. Few people there, first Bro. Bruno and Fr. Idesbald and a couple of brothers. Someone had stuck a "Vote Democrat" sticker on a wheelbarrow that was standing there. At about 11 a car showed up. Rode over with Bernard Fox. Kids in blue dresses playing around the school. Went in to the gymnasium and voted a split ticket – Kennedy-Johnson, Cooper for Senator, Chelf for Representative.

This morning early rumors were already going around that the Cellarer had sat up all night listening to the radio and that Kennedy was in. This was a bit premature, but by Chapter time the California returns cinched it for Kennedy. I am not surprised and not especially impressed either. But he ought to make a reasonably good president – with the aid of his brothers, sisters, cousins, aunts, uncles etc. And that old turkey his father. If I had known yesterday something of his history in finance I would have been even more hesitant to vote than I actually was. The story was read in refectory today but have had nothing but Kennedy for days, with occasional interludes of Nixon.

November 14, 1960

It was a very close election. Even now it is not clear how California voted. Absentee ballots may change the result. It was Minnesota cinched it for Kennedy. Glad the South went for him, though Kentucky did not. A curious election, symptomatic of the conflicts, ambiguities and confusions of this country.

How I hate what I see of the magazine *Life*. It looks like a parody of American existence. If it wanted to be a deliberate satire, it could not do better. Or has the parody now become completely real? I have not yet reached the point where my despair would believe this.

Dom Gabriel [Sortais, the Abbot General], after consulting a professor in Rome, has refused permission to print an article I wrote on Teilhard de Chardin's *Divine Milieu*. A book in itself "harmless" they admit. But one must not say anything in favor of T. de C. One must "make the silence" regarding T. de C.

The decision means little to me one way or the other, and I can accept it without difficulty. Less easily the stuffy authoritarianism of Dom Gabriel, who cannot help being an autocrat, even while multiplying protestations of love. I rebel against being treated as a "property," as an "instrument" and as a "thing" by the Superiors of this Order. He definitely insists that I think as he thinks, for to think with him is to "think with the church." To many this would seem quite obvious. Is it not the formula they follow in Moscow?

Where I draw the line is this: I have *no obligation* to form my thought or my conscience along the rigid lines of Dom Gabriel. I will certainly accept and obey his decision, but I reserve the right to disagree with him on T. de C. By the way, I do not "disagree." It may be quite correct that T. is a theological screwball. But I refuse to form part of an indignant chorus against him, and I refuse even to form part of a silently disapproving or hostile assembly of righteous critics. I refuse to draw back from him shaking my garments. I have nothing but sympathy for his attempt to take a new view of things. I have not read anything but the *Divine Milieu,* but as far as I am concerned the book is generally healthier and more deeply, genuinely *spiritual* than anything that has ever emanated from the authoritarian mind of Dom Gabriel.

Dom G. is now in Canada. Dom James leaves today to consult with him about "something important" at some Canadian monastery. The Spencer affair – about which nothing is known. It is said Spencer wants to break off from the O.C.S.O., and if they do, I can see their point to a great extent.

The O.C.S.O. has become a big, pompous, self-righteous, autocratic body of monastic politicians, very conscious of its prestige, and ready to exploit that prestige to the limit. The Order has begun to rate, and wants to. Yet there are some good tendencies in the new generation in Europe, to judge by the *Collectanea* – not all in the direction of pomposity and self-importance, but of monastic spirituality.

Struggling with the question whether I ought to drop writing, or rather publishing – altogether or temporarily. (Excepting of course the books that have been turned over to publisher.)

Whatever is decided must be decided on a non-political basis. I.e. not attempting to manipulate superiors one way or another by means of my decisions.

C. H. Dodd – in a remarkable book (*The Bible Today*):

"We shall get at the truth of our present situation only by exposing *ourselves* to the judgement of God in it. . . . I mean (by) an effort to recognize our own behaviour as contributory to the corporate actions and reactions which have brought us to this pass, and to assess it by given moral standards." *p. 137*

Important for me at this moment!! if what is said above about O.C.S.O.

November 15, 1960. F. of Dedication of Church
At the heart of Heschel's splendid book – *God in Search of Man* – the consistent emphasis on the importance of time, the *event* in revealed religion, Biblical, prophetic religion.

Event, not process. The unique event, not repeated.

The realm of the event is the realm of the person. Liberation from the process by decisions, by free act, unique, irreplaceable. The encounter with God.

Contrast Buddhism. Yet of Zen – the event of enlightenment. But this is not an encounter. Part of a well-ordered process?

"An event is a happening that cannot be reduced to a part of a process."
[Heschel] p. 210

"To speak of events is to imply that there are happenings in the world that are beyond the reach of our explanation." *[Heschel]*

See early chapters of St. John – the encounter of the Apostles and of John with Jesus. Emphasis on the words to *see*, to *find*, and the naming of names, the designations of persons.

And in the feast of the Dedication, Jacob's dream and his awakening. "This is the house of God." It became *so* by reason of the encounter, the ladder.

By virtue of great events – relived and remembered – the past becomes present and one transcends the process.

"Such understanding of time is not peculiar to historians. It is shared unknowingly by all men and is essential to inspired [the Heschel text reads "civilized"] living."

After Mass.

During Mass I was distracted and troubled by the attitude of the authorities of the Order – or what I imagine to be their attitude.

(In the little cloister is posted a color-photograph of Dom James with the Holy Father. A *bad* color picture. Dom J.'s face is blueish pink, and wears a sugary expression.)

(This picture reminds me of my resentment and helplessness over that visit to the Pope which was due in large measure to the respect that is felt, rightly or wrongly, for me in the Vatican. I know it is atrocious even to admit such a thought to one's mind, since it implies conviction of superiors for being complacently arbitrary and high-handed under the guise of the purest piety. But the fact is that Dom J. has used *against* me my own "prestige," such as it is, and this is a very dirty trick. And he has further exploited it to enhance his own prestige. Never letting his left hand see what his right hand is doing, naturally.

(I do not say: "If I were a saint I would keep my mouth shut about it." I *have* kept my mouth shut about it, but I want to put it down *here*. And it is put down. Fiat.)

They are "in good faith," but that does not help matters much.

It is the presuppositions in which they base themselves that are wrong – the placid assumption that since "the will of the superior is always the will of God," it matters little how arbitrary, selfish, prejudiced and interested they are; they are always infallible and sacrosanct. The subject has no appeal. His voice should not even be heard, and as far as possible it should be kept silent. Except of course to manifest his passive submission to the superiors who ignore his needs and his rights. ("You have no rights. By your vows you renounced all your rights!") ("*We* will take care of your rights.")

This does not apply to Pope John of course. He knows only what he is told and I don't know what they have told him. Obviously *something*.

However, after Mass I prayed earnestly to know what to do – in all truth. "The truth shall make you free."

And doubtless the truth is that all of us are wrong in one way or another. And the ways in which we are "right" are so illusory as to be non-existent. The truth is somewhere outside and above the spider's web that they have woven – with "the best of intentions." Why get caught in it? What I need above all is to be liberated from my own imagination and from theirs. But I do seek liberation, at all costs.

November 20, 1960. XXIV. Sunday after Pentecost

Yesterday, a meeting of the Building committee – what to do about finishing the Chapter room, dormitories etc. And whether to take the South wing next. The (written) suggestions of Kacmarcik and Rambusch did not even get a hearing. There was practically no discussion of them. We had begun with the idea that the bar joists were to be concealed and it is obviously too late now to change. No one except me is interested in leaving the old brick walls bare. They want new buff brick. I did not bother to argue, it would have been hopeless. We will have a new, shiny, vacuous, secular hall without character or meaning. The dormitory sounds better – but will be *heated*, so that when there is a 'flu epidemic everyone can stay in the dormitory and give each other plenty of 'flu.

I am helpless in articulating anything when I come in contact with the mind and convictions of our community – practical, unimaginative, pragmatic, communal, obsessed with the new, the straight, the slick, and in love with a kind of secure definiteness, a pretense of order, at the expense of anything savoring of spirit or of character.

Where I am most helpless is that I do not know the names and natures of new materials, what they are, what they are for, what they cost, what one does to them, what they do to people. I have no technical language, only a few hopeless spiritual intuitions.

November 22, 1960. (Day of Rec[ollection])
Woods. Dead leaves, grey sky, noise of the corn picker in St. Benedict's field. Just came by St. Mary's hermitage: they have finished the chimney and are working on the fireplace.

Sunday went to Jim Wygal's first communion (he came into the church by conditional baptism Saturday). Chapel at Bellarmine College. Drove in with Bernard Fox and John Eudes [Bamberger] through mist, but it cleared later. All had dinner together at Owl Creek Country Club. An event with a proper celebration, yet I prefer non-celebrations. Today, fasting is more of a celebration for me. There is an interior silence, a clear-headedness you do not get except by fasting. We are a society of gluttons.

Impressed by Dom Bonaventure of St. Meinrad's saying mass assisted by two of his young priests (Fr. Kieran, Fr. Camillus). A meaningful and Benedictine act. All very clear about what they were doing. And no sentimentality – nothing starry eyed about it, no gush.

Must take better advantage of woods and solitude.

It is rare I get out in the morning like this – but I could take Saturday mornings as well as Tuesdays. On the other days I have conferences.

Mail is one of the things that holds me up. But it is *necessary* to write some letters, even long ones. For instance last week to Czeslaw Milosz who is now teaching at Berkeley (U. of California), or Abdul Aziz, the writer on Sufism in Karachi whom L. Massignon referred to me for something. And will write to Heschel soon. Many short necessary letters can be written quickly at odd moments that are now wasted.

Fr. Abbot keeps talking about "not having contact with the world." I notice that in reality the people he does not want me to have contact with are other monks, particularly those who are working for a more intelligent and living form of monasticism. P. Francis Mahieu and Dom Bede Griffiths in India, for instance, or Toumliline in Morocco, and Dom Damasus [Winzen], and Dom Gregorio [Lemercier] (of course, now) and even ones who are no threat like Dom Hubert Van Zeller or Dom [Jean] Leclercq. Let alone Carthusians, Camaldolese etc. etc. And above all Dom Alexis Presse. Deliberate policy of stifling real aspirations and substituting conformity to the policies of confused, inert, businesslike, middle-class monasticism which is ours.

Gathering texts from Gandhi on non-violence.

Sense of obscure struggle to find a genuinely true and honest position in this world and its belligerent affairs. I wish I knew where to stand. I think I stand with a Gandhi more than with anyone else. But how to transpose his principles to suit my own situation? . . . A growing obscure conviction that this country, having been weighed in the balance and found wanting, faces a dreadful judgment.

Yet I am always ready to feel this and don't know how to interpret such ideas after all. The whole world is judged.

November 28, 1960. (Advent)

Advent has begun, but having had a touch of 'flu, I have not yet sung any of the Advent hymns in choir and I feel lost. Though I was in choir for the Mass of the First Sunday yesterday. Today it is warm – 65 – and finally they have the furnace out and the heat off. It has been stifling in choir, one reason why I have had to stay out, because after I am in there ten minutes I am pouring with sweat, and then get a new attack of 'flu as soon as I get out.

The Hammers and Wygals here Saturday, but it was too much of a party. I don't need all this social life – better without it. Prefer when just Victor and Carolyn come alone. Victor is more of a monk than anybody I know, because he is rooted in his own solitude, his integrity and his work which receives no publicity. And he does not rebel uselessly, he is content; yet maintains his true honor in simplicity. There's therefore in him a humility and honor together, a kind of monastic silence. Not a passive self-effacement but a quietness that speaks to anyone who can listen for it is full of honest reality.

Before that, the two boys from Jewish Seminary in Cincinnati, and Fr. Anselm's sister Carolyn with her husband, an organic chemist at the U. of Michigan, whom I like very much. They too are simple and honest.

———

Struggle in my heart all week. My own moral conflict never ceases. Knowing I *cannot* and *must not* simply submit to the standards imposed on me, and merely conform as "they" would like. This I am convinced is wrong – but the pressure never ceases. It takes every possible form. But it is not obedience. I will do what they tell me, but I will not and cannot think as they think. If I did I would be untrue to God, to myself and to all those who for some reason or other have a kind of confidence in me.

Yet I do not know where I stand myself. As though I were standing on "nothing." And perhaps that is the only position possible.

My fears – fears of the peculiar solitude willed for me, of *not* being exactly a monk in the conventional sense that is respected here. (I mean now by the *community*. The Superiors ask only conformity and submission to *their ideas* – which can be very lax. The community still respects a more austere and faithful "regularity").

There is nothing here to which I can assent without reserve except the barest essentials.

And I do not even assent to my own way of life – only to the rare afternoons among the trees when I have nothing but a flute and a couple of books under my arm. Or the early mornings, reading in the silence while everyone else says Mass –

Beautiful notes on the ascetic life from Archimandrite Sophrony and a heart-warming letter from him. An old monk of Athos starting a small, unknown, orthodox community in England. At Tolleshunt Knights, Essex. No publicity, no concern with trivialities. Six of them. Solitude. They seem very real. Fr. Sophrony (who wrote the book on Staretz Sylvan) knows what he is about. I wish I could really lay all my problems before him. But it is my destiny to be without that kind of guidance!

Dom James has gone to Argentina to make a visitation of the foundation at Azul – more to do with the secret trouble at Spencer, which no one really knows anything about. A symptom of what is really happening in the Order. No one must see symptoms! Too dangerous.

November 29, 1960. Weekly Day of Rec[ollection]
J[acques] Maritain, since Raïssa's death on Nov. 4th, is planning to retire to Kolbsheim and live with Alexeis Grunelius. He will spend part of his time teaching philosophy to the Little Brothers in Toulouse. And he speaks as if

he were in fact accepted as one of the Little Brothers. A marvelous grace and one which I envy him. As if there were a reward for one who had been so good and so honest. And indeed there is.

Walked in the woods and thought about my life in the Order. Suddenly rediscovering that I am after all periodically a member of it! Well, what about it? Making a problem out of nothing. Strange, though, that I should have come so completely, in my own mind, to dissociate myself from the Order and its aspirations and its present life. In a way this is a weakness and in another way it is a certain strength. One perhaps does not enter fully with the life of any institution until he is "in" it without really being "of" it. But this is not advice I would preach to all in public and it would require plenty of careful explanation.

December 1, 1960
Some poems of Peter the Venerable, and a lovely letter to hermits.

Yesterday the workmen finished their job on St. Mary's hermitage. There only remains for them to remove their planks and scaffolding.

But the building that was begun on the Feast of St. Thérèse is finished on the Feast of St. Andrew and in the first week of Advent, and let's hope it will not be closed down or dynamited by the Abbot General in January.

Need to distinguish more clearly my disassociation from the abstract and formal "image" of the Cistercian life willed by publicists and managers of the Order, from the real "Order," i.e. the men who are in it, with their desires, their aspirations and their sorrows. These I have not loved enough, nor have I recognized my indebtedness to them or my obligations toward them – even my own novices whom I imagine I love.

December 2, 1960
Came to St. Mary of Carmel and built a pretty fire in the fireplace and got settled down to read: and opening the book (Boisinard – *Du Baptême à Cana* [Paris, 1956]) picked up where I had left off this morning before Prime. These were the first words I read in the finished house (after a brief introduction to explain why they are quoted). From Proverbs: 9:1–15.

"La Sagesse a bâti sa maison, elle a dressé ses sept colonnes, elle a abattu ses bêtes, préparé son vin, elle dépêche ses servantes pour proclamer sur les hauteurs de la cité: Venez, manger de mon pain, buvez du vin que j'ai préparé! Quittez la folie et vous vivrez. Marchez dans la voie de la Vérité." ["Wisdom has built her house, she has set it up with seven pillars, she has slaughtered her beasts, prepared her wine, she sends her servants to proclaim from the heights of the city: Come eat of my bread, drink of the wine I have prepared. Desist from folly and you will live. Walk in the way of Truth."]

And then one of my oldest favorites from Isaiah – "All you who thirst come to the waters etc." *55:1–2.*

O God, that I may listen and believe and see things in their true perspective, and trust in wisdom.

The place is not cleaned out yet. I must do that this afternoon.

Not to be moved by guilt at having such a fine place to go! Not to take out my guilt on the community, suspecting that they envy me (which probably many do) and above all remember, whatever may be the foolishness that goes on, whatever the limitations of the abbot. There is no harm in being grateful – in having the *courage* to be grateful, and not fearing I am laying myself open to some manipulation by expressing gratitude.

How much better and healthier a wood fire than steam heat. Good smell of burning pine and cedar!

December 5, 1960

Magnificent light in the lapidary sentences of Isaac of Stella. Fire struck from stone: but how marvelous!

His Easter sermon – deep, deep intuition of faith as a resurrection because it is an act of obedience to God considered as supreme life. What matters is the act of submission to infinite life, to the authority of Creative and Redemptive Life, the Living God. Faith is this submission. The interior surrender of faith cannot have its full meaning except as an act of *obedience.* I.e. self-commitment in submission to God's truth in its power to give life; and *to command one to live.*

Hence faith is not simply an act of choice, an option for a certain solution to the problem of existence etc. It is a birth to a higher life, by obedience to the giver of life, *obedience to the source of life.*

To believe is to consent to a creative command that raises us from the dead.

December 10, 1960

Totally new perspectives on solitude. Afternoons at St. Mary of Carmel. It is true, places and situations are not supposed to matter. This one makes a tremendous difference. Real silence. Real solitude. Peace. Getting acclimated to the surroundings. The valley in front. The tall, separated pines to the west, the heavy, close-set denser pine wood to the north east, the sweep of pasture and the line of bare oaks on the east, various clumps of pine and poplar between east and south, bright sky through bare trunks of ash, elm and oak to the southwest, when a shoulder of hill hides the abbey. And a great dance of sky overhead. And a fire murmuring in the fireplace. Room smells faintly of pine smoke. Silent.

After having thought for ten years of building a hermitage, and thought of the ten places where one might be built, now _having built_ one in the best place, I cannot believe it. It is nevertheless real – if anything is real. In it everything becomes unreal. Just silence, sky, trees.

Worried that the Abbot General may close it down. But I say "_Nihil solliciti sitis_ [Be anxious about nothing]."

Not to fear feelings of guilt, not to justify myself, not to wonder what this or that person may think. Or what I myself may think. It is not thoughts that matter, but hours of silence and the precious dimension of existence which is otherwise completely unknown, certainly unknown when one thinks, or mentally speaks . . . or even writes. It must simply be seen, and is not seen until one has been sitting still, alone, in its own utter obviousness.

December 13, 1960. St. Lucy

White smoke rising up in the valley, against the light, slowly taking animal forms, with a dark background of wooded hills behind. Menacing and peaceful, probably brush fires, maybe a house, probably not a house. Cold, quiet morning, watch ticks on the desk. Produce nothing.

Perhaps I am stronger than I think. Perhaps I am afraid of my strength and turn it against myself to make myself weak. Perhaps I am most afraid of the strength of God in me.

———

Yesterday, F. of Our Lady of Guadalupe, Vol. I of the *Obras Completas*[20] arrived from Buenos Aries, with the preface I had written (in 1958). I mean that preface. The day emphasized my meaning of it. Had to revise for Image Books, preface to *The Soul of the Apostolate* [by Dom Chautard] written when I was a different person fifteen years ago. I am not concerned now with the same things in the same way.

Work. To be a solitary and not an individualist. Not concerned with mere perfecting of my own life. This, as Marxists see, is an indecent luxury (because there is so much illusion in it). My solitude belongs to society and to God. Are these just works? Solitude for its special work, deepening of thought and awareness. The struggle against alienation. The danger of a solitude that is the worst alienation. *Not* a matter of holding the community at arm's length. Important that I continue to be Novice Master for the time being (and he wants me to anyway). But I think at night of St. Mary of Carmel. I go to sleep thinking of the quiet hermitage and wishing I were there in bed (there is no bed) in the silent woods where the owl cries. "Self-love" they would say.

It is simply time that I must pray intently for the needs of the whole world and not be concerned with other, seemingly "more effective" forms of action. For me prayer comes first, the other forms of action follow, if they have their place. And they no doubt do to some extent. Prayer (yesterday Mass) for Latin America, for all of America, for this Hemisphere – sorrow for the dolts, for the idiot civilization that is going down to ruin and dragging everything with it.

December 18, 1960. IV Sunday of Advent

Several professed brothers have left in the last months and especially in the last weeks. Including solemnly professed. A fact which points up the situation in the house: or reminds us that there *is* a "situation," whatever the situation might be.

And people discuss it here and there, with Superiors, with Confessors.

The Prior had become "too broad minded" and people had pinned more and more confidence in his advice – and finally he would agree with them that they ought to leave.

[20] *Obras Completas I [The Complete Works of Thomas Merton]* (Buenos Aires, 1960) is the first volume of a still unfinished Spanish-language edition of Merton's writings.

The real "problem" and what worries the Abbot, is probably the fact that so many have suddenly followed the Prior's advice and not his. So doubtless we are going to have a new Prior; next year.

But what actually is "the trouble"? God alone knows, and I am not the one to try to answer such a question. It is sufficient for me that the novices who leave do so with good reason – because they do not adapt well to our life and apparently do not have vocations.

Those others, on the contrary, may once have appeared to have vocations. Yet there are some certainly whose vocations I have always doubted.

In any case they have been frustrated and miserable here. Could they have been anything else? Who knows? Doubtless they blame their failures on the community and the community blames it on them.

There is a lot of subdued animosity against the Abbot. It seems to grow as the years go on and probably for no other reason than that he is Abbot for life and has now been in office twelve years and seems utterly strong and healthy. He realizes this no doubt, and resents it in his turn. So that life in the community is to some extent a continual, but subdued, cold war between the Abbot and (some of) the monks. This is all the more irritating to all concerned because of the Abbot's official sweetness and loving concern for all, and the community's formal, "good Joe" front. But behind this is all the bitterness of a vestigial and suppressed jungle war with poisoned arrows and stone hatchets. Only the arrows and hatchets are words, slogans, programs, or just manual signs.

How much of what goes on is really a question of evening the score, of justifying oneself, putting oneself in a psychologically secure position and putting everyone else out of commission. It never works. The enemy is always there, as large as life, with his punishing reminder, his critical innuendo, his hostile admonition.

And because I (through my own fault) assert my own independent views and stress the individuality of my position, I make them all insecure (except those who seek security from imitation of me and they make it all worse!). Hence I am a plane to be brought down. And I fly constantly surrounded by a cloud of ethical *Flak!*

The Abbot is in a favored position not only because he has all the almost unlimited powers of his office, but because for him the glory of the community is in fact his personal glory (his achievement) and he can have all his glory under the guise of altruism. He can cut down individuals with good conscience, to protect them against "pride." He wins in every way. But because he "has to" win like this, all the time, he is perpetually insecure. *Là recommence toujours*. [There it always begins again.]

Hence the guarded belligerence of his pious clichés, the tension and intensity of his hiddenly furious insistence on obedience, his fervor in creating an atmosphere of optimism and success, of painting his business ventures with the bright colors of "family cooperation" and "recollection." It is the contemplative life that flourishes most on the assembly line in the farm building. (No harm in that, if only the propaganda were spared us.) Those who seek deeper forms of contemplation are reminded that all is illusion save "just doing the will of God." True. But one realizes, after so many repetitions, that there is a big void in the argument. The plea for obedience and cooperation – certainly legitimate – is not presented for what it really is. There's always a façade of spirituality and disinterestedness – it is always "for *your* greater sanctification – not for dollars."

Most people cannot love sanely or comfortably under the shadow of such self-contradictions and evasions.

But when they are seen for what they are they must be – accepted. There is much more trouble when they are *not* seen. When they are recognized, the affair is relatively easy.

December 19, 1960

Yesterday in refectory – a tape recording of a Boston psychiatrist who also sings in a choir and who declared that those who resist lay participation in the Liturgy usually do so out of psychological fears and compulsions. Well and good. But one of the community politicians had made sure that Rev. Father previously, in the morning chapter, emphasized how much and how well this talk could "*apply to our situation here*" – which I would say it does not at all. After all, we participate in the liturgy for several *hours* [double underlined] daily – and participate as fully as any liturgist might desire, at least *de jure* [by law].

Why the insistence on all this?

Perhaps some do not like the Brothers' dialogue mass.

Perhaps Fr. Chrysogonus, the choir master, and Fr. Tarcisius, my undermaster, are still pressing for a dialogue mass in the choir novitiate right after the night office (which most of them do not want, as they are tired by that time).

And in part it is an attack on those few (like myself) who will always personally prefer silent and meditative prayer to anything else, even while respecting the liturgy and granting it all its rights.

(Certainly the liturgical mysteries are the "highest" and most valuable and most Christian worship. But when it comes to personal tastes and preference, solitary contemplative prayer is to me the source of the greatest joy and hope and strength, and I *like* it. I think I have a right to – and to spend as much time in it as I like outside of choir. But this *preference*, even though it is nobody's business but my own, seems to be something they resent intensely.)

According to [Étienne] Gilson – Duns Scotus says of God that he is free to set up any moral code He pleases *so long as it deals with rules of human conduct whose relation to His own essence are not necessary ones.*

As opposed to those who at least implicitly conceive morality as an entering into a relation with God *in which there is no longer any spontaneity or choice.*

For such it is not sin alone that is to be reproved, but *choice*, preference, any form of spontaneous movement, any personal act of will. Since for them obedience becomes a matter of compulsion, and no longer a question of free choice. Souls are stifled by this conception and then obedience, instead of giving life and liberating them, stifles and bores them.

December 22, 1960

This morning, because it is the longest Advent, the full four weeks – we sang a Benedictus Antiphon we rarely sing, *"Leve Jerusalem"* – wonderfully solemn and mysterious melody in which the 1st tone, remarkably, rises to the level of the 4th tone.

A terrible book in refectory. Jim Bishop – a Hearst reporter – *The Day Christ Was Born*. Every possible inanity, cliché, platitude. It is a pure burlesque. The fact that such a book can be proposed here and accepted almost without comment tends to explain the weakness and deficiencies of the community.

In fact, in these last weeks there has been a regular exodus of professed, simple and solemn, leaving the Order. Almost all brothers. Though now I hear Fr. Hilary, over 20 years here, who was with me in the novitiate, is getting a dispensation. (However, he did not, but is out to Vina.) [This last sentence was added later in smaller hand.]

For the brothers who have gone I have no special explanation – Finnian, Theophane, Austin, Leopold etc. They formed a kind of clique surrounding the prior (Fr. Baldwin). They were all very immature, all had hankerings after a kind of pseudo-intellectual life, were dissatisfied, restless, had entered too young; ironically they were the ones (esp. Finnian, the Abbot's secretary) who were suggesting so many changes that they would have completely done away with the lay brotherhood in the end. Changes which those with genuine brothers' vocations were the last to desire.

And now the ones for whose sake the changes were made have left and the others are holding the bag.

Very cold. Zero this morning. Snow two nights ago, after the rainy day when David Rowland came from Lexington with the redwood table for St. Mary of Carmel and got stuck in the mud behind the sheep barn.

Yesterday I would have loved to go to St. Mary of C. in the snow but had no time. The Bloodmobile was here.

Have been reading about the Incarnation. How much my theology needs deepening and broadening. Dissatisfied with Thomist explanations which are too neat. Note – liturgical struggles around the 4 great councils. Mystery of conflict and tensions in the 4th–5th centuries, from which the brevity and conciseness of those definitions issued. Has this ever really been studied, meditated on? It is crucial.

December 24, 1960

Fr. Hilary is not getting a dispensation but, driven to distraction by his secretarial job, is getting a leave of absence to go to the monastery in California for a change. But he does not want to leave the Order nevertheless.

Snow is melting a little. Quiet afternoon of Christmas Eve. Read a book of Newman's romantic but fundamentally sound essay on St. Benedict. Finished first volume of *Paideia* this morning. Must read Thucydides. All I can remember of it is the general with nephritis in Sicily. The total lack of perspective with which we read Greek authors, word by word, at school.

December 26, 1960

After a feast day dinner, my hands smell sweetly of oranges.

Christmas Night – all the fuss and ceremony in the stuffy Church meant little. I had to make an effort to penetrate *through* all that and find the Mass.

Christmas Day – (Novitiate cluttered with decorations) – Dan came to my three Masses. After sunrise everything began to make more sense.

The absurdity of this cloister, all the fun, all the tinsel and confusion. Unreal. Bro. Wilfrid with his toys in the infirmary kitchen. The payoff is a Panda bear that smokes a pipe and shines his shoes with a busy mechanical clatter. We all want to be Panda bears, cuddly, busy, mechanical, full of energetic and pointless fun. Shining shoes and smoking pipes which are impossible and have nothing to do with our concrete existence, if any.

Everything has to be a "production."

I deliberately avoided the carol singing in the library, though at moments I was tempted to give in and "please" the community people. It would have been a silly weakness. I have got to cling to some principles somewhere. My principles are principles of solitude, and God knows I am weak enough with *any* principle, even the kind I like.

After None – in the pretty pine wood of young pines by St. Teresa's field (I still call it now St. Teresa's wood) – where I have gone many times a week for four years, especially four summers, since 1957. The time has come for a kind of summing up of all this silence and sunlight and of those similar afternoons. Attached and at peace in this wood because it knows me so well now and I have no house there, and nothing has ever been said or declared to indicate that I was there always. Nothing said it was "my place."

There I discovered Paraguay and for a while this wood was Paraguay (1957). I read a thing of Kierkegaard with a lovely paragraph on solitude – a bit of Henry Miller on Big Sur (in another place), much Suzuki, Vinoba Bhave. It is an oriental wood. I taught Nels Richardson a little yoga there, walked and planned with Dom Gregorio anxiously there. There walked one winter afternoon after discovering some lyrics in the *I Ching*. Read *The Leopard* and Ungaretti there. Above all prayed and meditated there and will again.

But St. Mary of Carmel (after Vespers) this is tremendous: with the tall pines, the silence, the moon and stars above the pines as dark falls, the patterns of shadow, the vast valley and hills everything speaks of a more mature and more complete solitude. The pines are tall and not low. There is frankly a house, demanding not attachment but responsibility. A silence for dedication and not for escape. Lit candles in the dusk. *Haec requies mea in saeculum saeculi* [This is my resting place forever] – the sense of a journey ended, of wandering at an end. *The first time in my life* I ever really felt I had come home and that my waiting and looking were ended.

A burst of sun through the window. Wind in the pines. Fire in the grate. Silence over the whole valley.

In [Ananda] Coomaraswamy – a footnote to his Hinduism: "The forerunners can be traced by their spoor as far as the Sundoor, Janua well, the end of the road; beyond that they cannot be tracked!"

December 27, 1960. F. of St. John Evangelist

Incomparable richness of Coomaraswamy! His book on Hinduism and Buddhism. I am giving it a first reading in which I do not expect to understand and appreciate everything.

One point – already familiar – driven home more: Whatever is done naturally may be either sacred or profane according to our own degree of awareness, but whatever is done unnaturally is essentially and irrevocably profane! (p. 25).

One of the great problems of monastic life here, today, with machines, noise, etc., and commercialism, is that the *unnatural* is taken for the *supernatural*. No concern at all for natural and for natural process leads to perversion and degradation of the spiritual life.

For instance the abbot said today with incomparable gusto and satisfaction that it was "Jesus who threw St. John into the boiling oil." In a sense, yes: but when it is said with such facility and utterly without awareness of any values, purely as an arbitrary declaration that is supposed to answer all questions (or rather to silence all questions), then it is merely a bad job.

December 31, 1960

End of 1960. Still decorated. The tinfoil bell, the cedar wreaths, the drying pine boughs, the colored lights.

I was wondering at the beginning of morning meditation if it would be given me to see another twelve years – to come to New Year's, say, 1973. To live to be fifty-seven and nearly fifty-eight. Can such an age be possible? What foolish perspectives we get onto, by believing in our calendars. As if numbers were the great reality, the sure thing, the gods of life and death. The numbers, good old numbers, faceless, voiceless, will surely be there with nothing to say.

What is likely to happen in twelve more years? Is the final war so feared and so expected that it cannot after all happen – as if what everyone expected was by that very fact excluded?

Is this inanity of man's world finally going to work itself out to its ultimate absurdity?

Fr. Kilian McDonnell came last night.

I am rewriting *Seeds of Contemplation*.

Thinking of a story and "Momotombo's Lucky Day" and the murder of Somoza.

PART II

The Continuing Need to Question

January 1961–December 1961

Determined to write less, to gradually vanish. Do not know how and do not pretend it is easy.

March 7, 1961

The New Year: frozen snow, in a thin layer, crackling under my shoes as I cross the dark *préau* after Lauds to get hot coffee in the refectory. Mist, damp air, no sun, the excitement of an imaginary new year. The changes in the officers of the monastery. New Prior (Callistus), New Master of Brothers (Philip), New Master of Bro. Novices (Hubert), etc.

I have a new undermaster, Fr. Felix, still studying Pastoral theology and not yet ordained. After three years with my quiet, definite, ambitious, and yet good and likeable Fr. Tarcisius. He knows what he wants. He will get it smoothly. He will do good. He is a future Prior. At the moment he is Master of Students.

Fr. Kilian McDonnell was here over the weekend, talked to the novices New Year's afternoon on the ecumenical movement. I got a good letter from Roscoe Pierson at the College of the Bible (Catholic Christmas cards repel him, he will send me a book of Söderblom – will talk about their faculty men coming on retreat – likes the Mencius broadside).

The chief joy of the Christmas season was the warm and cordial letter from Abdul Aziz, Moslem scholar, student of mysticism, at Karachi.

January 8, 1961. Sunday within Octave of Epiphany

Monthly day of recollection. The usual depression and guilt because I am not an ascetic. Usual failure to distinguish between what I *can* do and what I *can't*. Certainly, since doctors keep putting me on this infirmary diet, I might as well regard it as God's will – but I could eat less of the infirmary food since I certainly eat far more than I need, though in the last months I have often gone without breakfast (and made up for it at dinner!).

Should I try to fight my way out of the infirmary? This, in me, would be weakness and insincerity. At least so I think. It is better to lose face than to try and save it.

What I do need to do is to become compassionate and merciful and not resent others or judge them, but to accept criticism peacefully, or rather not even to be so sensitive to the thought that I am perhaps not approved of.

Nor to be so quick to resent all the frictions of community life, but accept them peacefully. Nor are they all such frictions. And they have their place. I do not waste time comparing community and solitude (though there is such an immense difference!).

Distinguish *solitude* and *privacy*. I resent invasions of my privacy. I am too insular. It is my English nature. I must be glad to give up privacy when the novices need me, or even when they don't need me: but when I am there. In this I am very weak.

God the compassionate and merciful!

Reading Schmon[1] on Moslem angels. Have brought [Anselmo] Giabbani's *Eremo* here this evening. Sunset – quiet hills. Nothing.

January 18, 1961. Retreat begins this evening.
Moved by S. N. Behrman's beautiful book on Max Beerbohm [*Portrait of Max*, New York, 1960]. That is important for me – the lost side of my life. Note Brecht loved Kipling and Beerbohm hated him. I think this is very significant. Brecht – something of the self I wanted briefly to become when I immigrated (I ceased to want to be Beerbohm).

The other day in rain and mist, the Hammers were here. Victor and I ploughed through mud to the hermitage to discuss shelves for an alcove.

Meditating on Hiroshima.

Articles read in refectory, one on El Salvador. The usual communist menace stuff and it is a menace. So is almost everything.

January 19, 1961
To be freed from involvements – on all sides. To work for the solitude that one has to keep preaching: not as a luxury but as a necessity. How my ideas have changed on that, over the course of years. It is no longer a question of "sanctification" but of pure survival, I mean, survival in the integrity God gave me.

To know when, how and to whom to say no! Considerable notes and difficulties. Not to want to hurt people certainly, but not being too anxious to placate them.

People are constantly trying to use you to help them create an illusion by which they live. Especially various collective illusions. Through my own

[1] Merton may be referring to Gershom Scholem.

fault I have become a part of too many collective illusions, and have wanted to.

A distinction in the order of love. I have been satisfied to be "thought of kindly" by many, and to think of them kindly. A diluted benevolence, that keeps us all secure.

I must sacrifice this diffuse aura of benevolence, and pay attention only to the _genuine care_ for individuals that are brought to me by God. This care _is_ an involvement, and a vital one. But it is good and right, since it is specific, personal. It is not a "movement." It is not diffuse, foggy, consuming, absurd.

The question of writing: definitely it has to be cut down, or changed.

Someone accused me of being a "high priest" of creativity. Or at least of allowing people to regard me as one. This is perhaps true.

The sin of _wanting to be a pontiff_, of wanting to be heard, of wanting converts, disciples. Being in a cloister, I thought I did not want this. Of course I did and everyone knows it.

St. William, says the Breviary this night, when death approached, took off his pontifical vestments (what he was doing with them on in bed I can't imagine) and by his own efforts got to the floor and died.

So I am like him, in bed with a mitre on. What am I going to do about it?

One thing from which I must free myself is the popular Catholic image in this country. I am not at all that kind of a Catholic and why should I be giving all these people the idea that I am an inspiration to them? I am not. And the clergy that have opposed me will realize it. There is an abyss between us.

At the same time, the subtler temptation, the temptation of the French avant-garde Catholic, to want to be on good terms with the proletarian left. To want to be "part of the future." But that is another myth. In many ways a worse one. The temptation is pragmatic, for that myth is likely to be the more successful.

I have got to face the fact that there is in me a desire for survival as pontiff, prophet and writer, and this has to be renounced before I can be myself at last.

January 20, 1961

In the refectory we are being boomed at by a liturgical tape – that is, by a tape-recorded talk on the liturgy. A harangue, ardent, deafening, blasting everybody's head off. The material in itself is fair – the usual, not too bad, present-day emphasis on the theology on the mysteries of Xt in the liturgy. All standard since *Mediator Dei* [Encyclical letter by Pius XII, November 20, 1947] – and certainly nothing beyond or besides *Mediator Dei*.

But the blasting, the emphasis – (*everything* is emphasized) – the impassioned pointing to the "Ca-ROSS!" . . .

Fr. Idesbald in the infirm[ary] refectory was mimicking it under his breath and finally got tired and walked out, first kicking the door and then slamming it. Not exactly "virtuous" but in some sense understandable.

Pontiffs! Pontiffs! We are all pontiffs, surrounding and haranguing one another.

It occurs to me seriously to wonder at the close parallel between our organized life, spiritual though it be, and certain other forms of social organization . . . The factory workers of say, Czechoslovakia, listening to a loudspeaker booming the approved ideals and goals at them . . .

The comparison need not be labored. I do not intend it as a deliberate irreverence.

One thing that went through my mind during this tape: the resolution never to publish my book on the liturgy: I mean the novitiate liturgy conferences.

More and more understanding and sympathy for those who, like [Charles] Péguy and Simone Weil, felt it necessary to choose to be, so to speak, marginal Christians, that is, not right in the middle of the Catholic approved and censored page.

Question marks in the margin.

So clear that they did not question Christ, but certain Christians or "just Christianity" in Kierkegaard's sense.

If this were the real issue I had to face in this retreat!

If it is, of course. I have already faced it, and my life will not be any easier for it. I stay put. But a whole series of hidden, obscure, changes are to be made. And it will mean *real* loneliness.

January 21, 1961

F. of St. Agnes in the infirmary. There is a plague going around. Kind of intestinal 'flu and I have it. Got it badly yesterday afternoon: miserable in the evening, awful fever, chills. It got better during a long night's sleep. This afternoon it has reached the pleasant stage, where one sits up in bed and reads.

That Behrman book on Beerbohm is not always admirable. Sometimes his admiration makes him sound like something Beerbohm himself would have parodied. He foolishly says too much.

You can make of your life what you want. There are various ways of being happy. Why do we drive ourselves on with illusory demands? Happy only when we conform to something that is *said* to be a legitimate happiness? An approved happiness?

God gives us the freedom to create our own lives, according to His will, that is to say in the circumstances in which He has placed us. That we refuse to be content unless we realized in ourselves a "universal" standard, a happiness hypothetically prescribed and approved for all men of all time. Not just our own happiness. This, at least, is what I do. I am a happy person, and God has given me happiness, but I am guilty about it – as if being happy were not quite allowed, as if everybody didn't have it within reach somehow or other – and as if I had to justify God Himself by being zealous for something I do not and cannot have – because I am not happy in the same way as Pericles – or Khrushchev.

That is the thing that strikes me in reading about Beerbohm. He belonged to his clan and his time and was content to do so – for after all there was little else he could be.

January 22, 1961. III Sun after Epiphany
Kennedy's inauguration speech was read in refectory today. Clear and intelligent enough. The country has a good president – it remains to see what the country will do about it. I suspect our standard gestures of cooperation – they are not quite enough.

Getting tired of Max – after all he is a little arid spiritually, though there is an implied spirituality in his cultured detachment.

Still in infirmary – got up for Mass and meals, but am soon tired. Have not yet got rid of my bug.

Raided the library and came out with, among other things, Ansari.[2]

> "On this faith argument is of no avail,
> He whom Thou killest doth not smell of blood

[2] Persian mystic, 1006–1089.

He whom Thou burnest doth not smell of fire. . . .
O Lord, better for me to be dust
And my name effaced from the records of the world than
that Thou forget me."

An overwhelming statement of P[aul] Evdokimov.

"Pour l'orthodoxie il ne s'agit jamais d'une soumission à une institution historique, encore moins à un pouvoir, sauf celui de l'amour. Il s'agit – et c'est ici que l'orthodoxie est absolument originale et fidèle à la Tradition apostolique – pour toute aspiration sincère à la Vérité de l'embrasser et c'est cette participation à la Vérité apostolique dans sa plénitude qui introduit ipso facto à la communion de l'Eglise, orthodoxe." ["With regard to Orthodoxy, it is never a question of mere submission to an historical institution, much the less to any power, except that of love. It is rather a question of – and it is here that Orthodoxy is absolutely original and faithful to the Apostolic Tradition – embracing every sincere aspiration to the truth, and it is this participation in the Apostolic Truth in its fullness that inserts by that very fact someone into the communion of the Orthodox Church."]

[L'Orthodoxie *(Paris, 1957), p. 74]*

I know what really annoys me about the Behrman book – he is finally, completely, dedicated to the illusion that Max was to be treated as some kind of *ultimate* reality, as an *ens per se* [being existing by itself]. The total acceptance of shadow for substance, the conservation of accident for its own sake. One can and should enjoy Beerbohm's humor, his comments on his time and on his contemporaries, but to solidify him into something eternal, just in what was precisely transient about him, this is sentimental and idolatrous and therefore it is very boring.

Just the opposite to Coomaraswamy, who made so much good sense in everything. But this is the trouble with America and our confusion of the individual nature with the person. I have a feeling he tries to fix this in the last sentence.

January 24, 1961

Out of infirmary but still feel knocked out.

While I was getting my tonsure this morning I watched the novices milling around getting ready for work – standing in their patched coveralls and their funny hoods, some being very recollected, some very efficient, mostly quite happy. I was moved by the sight of them and the awareness of how much we all impede ourselves with useless spiritual baggage. And how difficult it is to try to help them without adding to the baggage instead of relieving them of it.

I can at least love them and thus create, or keep alive, the climate in which the Holy Spirit does the work. I do love them, but what are they getting into? At least let me not give them illusions.

January 26, 1961

Retreat ending.

Long quiet interval in dark hours. Evdokimov on orthodoxy – once again, as I have so many times recently, I meet the concept of *natura naturans* [nature acting according to its nature] – the divine wisdom in ideal nature, the ikon of wisdom, the dancing ikon – the summit reached by so many non-Christian contemplatives (would that it were reached by a few Christians!) Summit of Vedanta? –

Faith in Sophia, *natura naturans*, the great stabilizer today – for peace.

The basic hope that people have that man will somehow not be completely destroyed is hope in *natura naturans*.

– The dark face, the "night face" of Sophia – pain, trouble, pestilence.

– [Salvatore] Quasimodo's wonderful poem on Auschwitz [*Complete Poems*, New York, 1984] sees this.

I am deeply influenced by Quasimodo, richness, firmness of his imagery, sober, spiritual. He is no Marxist poet even though his political sympathies may be that way. He is of my country.

January 28, 1961

I respect more and more the intelligence and integrity of Reinhold Niebuhr. His is one of the few authentically Christian voices that have something to say that is relevant for our time. And also an American voice, with a clarity, a sobriety, an objectivity, a lack of despair that *should* be ours. We do not have to speak with sick voices, as France does.

"There is so little health in the whole of our modern civilization that one cannot find the island of order from which to proceed against disorder."

(Xtian Realism and Polit[ical] Problems [*New York, 1953*], p. *117*)

February 3, 1961

Ice storm, followed by light snow, cold wind. Paths and roads are like glass, that is putting it mildly: glass is not so slippery. Ed Rice[3] is supposed to be driving from here to New York – I don't know how he is getting along.

---

[3] Columbia University friend and Merton's baptismal sponsor.

He and Eloise Spaeth were here and we worked together on *Art and Worship*.[4] Most of the work we did on Tuesday, which happened to be my 46th birthday. Went over the text and made selections from a pile of new pictures.

On my 46th birthday they put an ape into space. In fact they shot him too far. But they recovered him alive. He flew through "space" at some fabulous rate of speed, pressing buttons and pulling levers, signalling with faultless regularity, as he had been trained to do. They picked him up out of the Atlantic and he shook hands with the Navy.

Ed Rice talked about the death of R. Hoguet, suddenly, with Maritain there. Another shock for poor Jacques! And of Lax and his beat friends; and how Kerouac is not really beat. (His poems about Mexico City, or *in* Mexico City, seem to me to be sloppy and disorganized – Effusions.)

This afternoon I took one look at the MS of *The New Man* intending to read it, or at least make the censors' corrections, but it filled me with revulsion.

Ed Rice works very hard on *Jubilee*, has two bright kids. Did not really have an awful lot to say. Complained of the [Bishop Fulton J.] Sheen tape, in guest house (still!!).

Every time President Kennedy sneezes or blows his nose an article about it is read in our refectory.

February 4, 1961

Tremendous discovery. The *Brihad-Aranyaka Upanishad!*

Kairos! Everything for a long time has been slowly leading up to this, and with this reading – sudden convergence of roads, tendencies, lights, in unity!

A new door. (Looked at it without comprehension 9 months ago.)

Yesterday's disgust with the trivial, shallow contemporary stuff I am tempted to read! No time for that.

---

4 This book was never published. David Cooper offers an extensive study of the manuscript in *Thomas Merton's Art of Denial: The Evolution of a Radical Humanist* (Athens, 1989), pp. 89–129.

Scriptures. Greek patrology. Oriental thought. This enough to fill every free corner of the day not given to prayer, meditation, duties.

February 5, 1961

> "Spirit, go thy way"
> Love called again
> "And I shall be ever nigh thee
> As thy neck vein"
>
> _(Rumi)_

February 14, 1961. Bl. Conrad

Today, feast of the Cistercian hermit whom no one in the Order loves – at least I think I am right in saying this. I myself obviously _do_ love him very much and have more and more devotion to him. Though when I was a novice [and] I wrote those absurd lives of saints of the order, he bothered me and I don't think I ever included him. He seemed like an odd ball and a failure. His life seemed to end somewhere in mid air, making no sense – he was a hermit on his way home, as the Breviary reassures us, to his monastery? As if to give his life a semblance of security. As if at last he had repented of his folly, seen the light, hot-footed it back to the cenobium. And above all because he heard Our Father St. Bernard was "gravely ill." (St. B. was gravely ill ever since the foundation of Clairvaux thirty years before!!!) And there is a note of anxiety: he did not make it back to France! Was he perhaps punished for his madness? Yet he died in a "grotto dedicated to the Mother of God" . . .

This morning, splendor of my Mass! Sun pouring in on the altar, and in glory of reflected lights from the hammered silver chalice splashed all over the corporal and all around the Host. Deep quiet. The Gospel – _Nolite timere pusillus grex_ [Do not fear little flock]. Where your treasure is, there your heart is also. May I learn the lessons of detachment, even from the little white house of St. Mary of Carmel. But no nonsense about not desiring solitude. On the contrary, to desire it in perfection and in truth. Interior and exterior.

I have been for the past few days anxious and disturbed because the Abbot General is on his way – supposed to arrive tomorrow, Ash Wednesday, in the evening. There will necessarily be "_les explications_ [the explanations]." What I "fear" is the arduous labor of trying to bridge the gap between us without simply pretending that I agree with him. To obey at once him and my own conscience, without being either disobedient or servile. Uncommonly difficult, I have no idea where the "middle" is found.

Certainly I must begin by not entirely disturbing him. Or at least I must trust God and not resist authority even when it is authoritarian. Yet not simply grovel either. He has his viewpoint and his reasons for acting as he does. I owe him at least some indication of my own convictions; yet I do not intend to simply present them for him to squash without ceremony. Hence I will listen more than I speak – I hope. And in the light of grace try to discover what is really God's will.

Distinguish the account I owe him as a subject, a member of the Order and a Novice Master, and personal matters of conscience which are really none of his business. In the former – I must be frank and truthful. In the latter – discreet.

February 16, 1961

Sun warm. Buds on one of the little dogwoods we transplanted 2 yrs. ago (but not on the other four), clear sky. Spring – yet not quite, either.

Ash Wednesday, yesterday. In the evening I was called to be one of the party of "seniors" to greet the Abbot General at the gate on his arrival in the Oldsmobile.

We stood among the mail bags (by which he was eventually mildly scandalized). At least the headlights were seen, right there, approaching very slowly and very close, as if to push us right up against the wall.

He was affable and not as thin as I expected.

This morning in Chapter, after a polished speech of twenty-five or thirty minutes in baby-talk, interpreted with gusto by Fr. Nicholas of Georgia, he said he was not going to make a regular visitation but would receive "all who wanted to see him" after having first called in the Abbot and "those whose problems I know."

It was clear that he was going to act and speak with all the unshakeable firmness of the author of the long letter against those who attempt to leave the monastery and it is also clear that Fr. Gerald might as well have got his hair cut with the rest of us last week.

For my part, I have no desire to leave or go anywhere unless there are difficulties about the moderate and unorthodox opportunities for solitude which have been conceded here lately. And I haven't much that I want to discuss, though he probably has.

It does not make sense to try and say where I stand or what I think about it, as I have stopped thinking much about it. And about whether or not I shall continue writing. I have no intention of asking him for explicit permission to live in St. Mary of Carmel, which would be useless and in my case absurd as the permission is not his to give (it is in the hands of Dom James, really – but they like to pass the buck back and forth and I see no reason to waste time in this kind of amusement).

In fact it seems absurd to talk much about anything that concerns me closely because all that seems to have been settled. There is no more to be said – except of course by our standards, for we say over and over what we have already said enough long ago.

One thing I would like to talk about – the question of the Chinese monks of Lan Tao [Peng Chau, Hong Kong] (where a young priest of Vina is going as novice master) and whether it would make sense for them to come here for part of their formations –

February 20, 1961. 1st Sunday of Lent

This Sunday always moves me with joy. The liturgy is strong and appeals directly to monks. I wish my life were more genuinely ascetic. I am caught in confusions which continue and continue, to await clarification. And perhaps I am the one who resists their clarification. Meanwhile . . . yet in the bottom of my heart and in my conscience I know that the answer is *not* merely a question of conforming to approved and well-accepted standards . . . or at least not merely a question of getting in line with the others (who in any case are by no means in line with each other).

It is true that a certain laziness and lack of generosity have always marked my life, and my attempts to do anything about this are always too feeble and sporadic. *Ecce nunc tempus acceptabile.* [Behold, now is the acceptable time.]

Dom Gabriel called me in after he was through with Dom James. In a sense this was a kindness and even an honor. He spoke kindly and understandingly and we touched on various subjects but not on the one which he obviously intended me to discuss – the Cuernavaca question.

His spiritual conferences in Chapter have been solid, but one is irked by the fact that it all has to be translated.

Yesterday afternoon – going over the censored ms. of *The New Man*.[5] It is fair, but I am embarrassed by more and more words of my own. I have a feeling that it is not really worth publishing and yet because they want it I will (weakly?) allow it to be published. Of the *Behavior of Titans*, which came Friday, I have other thoughts. I am pleased with it, especially with Atlas.

February 21, 1961

Dom Gabriel's tremendously earnest, energetic, even powerful talks in Chapter, solid, utterly sincere. Emphasis on discipline, on ascetic *effort*, on striving and – here it comes out – on *activity*, on *conscious control* on mastery, on domination. "Keep busy." "Work. Avoid idleness!"

I agree with some of it, but the rest of it . . . No. There is something wrong, something destructive. Certainly we must be detached, pure in heart. Certainly too here is a very living and spontaneous person; but there is a rigidity and a "rationalism" in his thought that kills spontaneity. That represses and crushes interior life in its most delicate forms. Or at least would seem to do so in me if I followed that line, with that mentality.

Certainly there is something great about his strength – it pulled him through great difficulties in the prison camp . . . yet . . . ! He is an "active." His way must be *left* before one can enter into the way of contemplation.

Or rather, I think I must not follow his strenuous path. Obviously *he* must.

Contemplative life, he said, is clinging by main force to an idea one had on entering novitiate.

And "though contemplation is a gift of God" he speaks of "forcing God" to give it to us. If that means forcing God to give us what we imagine to be the kind of contemplation we want . . . well.

February 22, 1961

Much rain. Today arrived from Mexico Ernesto Cardenal's translations of my poems and again I feel that in some way they are better in Spanish than in English. The first part of "Elias," for example, is perfect in Spanish. Ernesto is a fine poet and translator. Armando Morales' black, coarse, difficult prints are superb. One likes immediately some of the distinct heavy birdlike calligraphic forms, yet perhaps the best of all are the earlier ones

[5] Eventually published by Farrar, Straus, & Cudahy in 1961.

he did, cramped, obscure, confused but powerfully impressive. Each one is a small, hard chaos with forms either about to be created or past having been destroyed.

Rain, Rain. In yesterday's rain I sent off, with a bad conscience, the finally, largely corrected ms. of *The New Man*. Never write another like that, or like the aberrant parts of it. Adam all right.

And in today's rain? Not take Dom Gabriel to see the hermitage, probably. But I am to interpret for him as he talks to the novices.

March 3, 1961

The rains of these days have waned, and it was bright afterward and now there will be more rain.

Dom Gabriel came to the hermitage that Wednesday [February 22] (it was Washington's birthday and the 19th anniversary of my taking the habit). And he sat in the chair by the redwood table and told me of a hermitess in the Dept. [*département*, county] of Var, and her life. All to convince me not to leave to be a hermit alone, but that "this was a kind of solution." Namely having a hermitage to come to during the day. He seemed glad of it, eager for me to have it, not to live in it, "for you are the novice master." But all his logic (and he is after all very logical) was that this was right for me. He was very kind.

We spent the whole afternoon walking about the woods. He was really very kind. But he lost his glasses. I went to look for them and did not find them. He went to Louisville. I went to Louisville. He talked about [the Abbey of] Spencer in the car, about their chairs, chests; tapestries, Virgins, crucifixes. 15th century. 16th century. I got off at the university and read some Coomaraswamy in the art library. He got a new pair of glasses from Dr. Kesselring.

The visit ended with his saying the monastery was getting lax, and he meant too much talking and other things particularly among the brothers.

I started the mystical theology class Wednesday (Mar. 1).[6] I continued today A.M. reading the ms. of Benet of Canfield sent by Mrs. [Etta] Gullick, from Oxford, and it has come from God. Essential will.

---

[6] Merton's lecture notes for this series of classes on ascetical and mystical theology remain unpublished. See my article "Patterns in Thomas Merton's 'Introduction to Ascetical and Mystical Theology,'" *Cistercian Studies*, Vol. 24 (1989), pp. 338–54.

Like the finished Eckhart sermon from Claude Fredericks in Vermont. The *Wisdom of the Desert* came today.

Gregory Palamas defence of the Hesychasts for a Lenten book.

The hermitage is right, even though to some it might be wrong. More right and less right. It is God's way of being right in my life in spite of everything, and not for me or anyone to talk about, or to discuss. He is greater than all possible blame.

A good loneliness, a good insecurity. Stone room, pines. His will, His mercy. An imperfection to say it, and to insist: lack of faith.

Do not explain.

March 7, 1961. F. of St. Thomas Aquinas

Quiet humor and shyness of Fr. Robert in the (student) conference in Chapter – St. Thomas on "patience." Probably the last feast of St. Thomas we will celebrate now [that] we have a new calendar with so few feasts.

Determined to write less, to gradually vanish. Do not know how and do not pretend it is easy. Vanish from popularity into insecurity and anguish of my own decision to be alone, which is dangerous and arbitrary. Yet this must be done. I must begin to do what I must do. Not insisting on it as a preference, which perhaps after all it really is not.

Great distaste for the idea of finishing *Art and Worship*. Wish I could finally drop it but cannot since Ed Rice and Eloise Speath are involved. But I do want to get together a little collection of Coomaraswamy's sayings, to be printed by Victor Hammer.

My motives are mired and confused but the time has come to straighten them out if I can and to "die" as an author, or as a popular and celebrated one. Certainly if people read, really read, my most recent work, my popularity is done with.

The last things I will give up writing will be this journal, and notebooks, and poems. No more books of piety.

Finished reading the MS of Pt. III of Canfield's *Rule of Perfection*. It is really very fine.

"Plato maintains that one who is *in earnest* will not write; and that if a wise man writes at all, it will either be only for amusement – mere *belles lettres* – or to provide reminders for himself when his memory is weakened by old age."

(Coomaraswamy)

That is it: the question of being *in earnest*. Perhaps what I have lacked is the faith that one can be in earnest and yet silent; i.e., in earnest without convincing anybody else of the fact.

March 8, 1961

Audite et intelligite traditiones quas deus dedit vobis – [Hear and understand the instructions which God gave you –]

Moved by this Benedictus antiphon [Lauds]. At a time when all the healthy traditions are vanishing or being corrupted or destroyed. We have no memory (as Coomaraswamy says – and as Plato said); instead of traditions we have neuroses. The loss of tradition is an important factor in the loss of contemplation – in the fact that contemplation is blocked and sidetracked by neurosis. Neurosis as false religion and false contemplation.

March 11, 1961

The Negroes and their struggle for integration into American society: not only do they have to face the enormity of the whites who are completely unsettled by their irrational fears, but they have to face fear, guilt and passivity in themselves: one of the most difficult things is for them to admit completely in their hearts what they know intellectually: that they are in the right. It is fine that they have a leader who can direct them in the way of non-violence. But the situation is so ambivalent that there remains danger of violence – as the less rational whites seem to sense intuitively. Great admiration and compassion for the Negroes.

I am still a 14th century man: the century of Eckhart, Ruysbroeck, Tauler, the English recluses, the author of the *Cloud*, Langland and Chaucer – more an independent and a hermit than a community man, by no means an ascetic, interested in psychology, a lover of the dark cloud in which God is found by love. This is what I am: I cannot consent to be it and not be ashamed that I am not something more fashionable.

But I must watch my silly tongue.

Who? Whose tongue? What do you mean "watch"?

Afternoons are for nothing. For cutting away all that is practical.

Learn to wash your cup and give rise to nothing.

What house? No house could possibly make a difference.

It is a house for nothing. It has no purpose. Do not give it one, and the whole universe will be thankful.

March 15, 1961

Scheles points out: those who criticize out of resentment do not really want anything to be changed, bettered or reformed. They pretend to want an improvement. But when they are put in a position to collaborate in making things better they are impotent and frustrated – deprived of what they really want; an opportunity to criticize.

March 16, 1961

The saints of the 15th century – are among those who most move me. The collapse of medieval society, corruption of the clergy, decadence of conventual life – and there emerge men and women of the laity *supremely obedient to God*. Especially Nicholas of Flue and Joan of Arc. Complete and simple signs of contradiction to worldliness and system and convention and prejudiced interest. *Not* rebels at all, but completely meek and submissive instruments of God. In them you see clearly and movingly revealed what it is *not* to be a mere rebel but to be obedient to God as a sign to men, a sign of mercy, a revelation of truth and of power. I am drawn to these "signs" of God with all the love of my heart, trusting above all in their love and their intercession, for they live in the glory of God, and I would not love them if God had not made them "sacraments" to me. St. Catherine of Genoa also, whom Natasha Spender loves (she keeps wanting me to write about C. of G.).

Note especially the fabulous supernatural providence with which St. Joan remained obedient to the *church* while resisting her judges who seemed to be and claimed to be speaking entirely for the Church.

Frank Sheed talked here on Laetare Sunday about his street preaching. I enjoyed his talk and enjoyed meeting him. A healthy Catholicism, not inbred with nonsense or servility or pretense. He looks a lot like W. C. Fields. Likes Ed Rice and *Jubilee*. Spoke of reissuing [Charles] Journet's *Dark Knowledge of God*, although it "did not do well" (thirty years ago).

March 19, 1961. Passion Sunday

Finishing [Arthur] Koestler's book on Asia, *The Lotus and the Robot* [London, 1960]. Though there are plenty of passages where one has the feeling that he did not catch on, still I think the book is important and offers a basically healthy corrective for the Western intellectual's guilt complex toward Asia. What he says of Asia's spirituality vs. Western materialism is pert[inent], but perhaps has truth in it.

"A saint who lets herself be seduced willingly and asks for more cannot be much of a saint." Look at China and Japan. Note Western influences on Gandhi.

March 22, 1961. F. of St. Joseph (transferred)

Continual rain.

Yesterday, the afternoon being partly clear (though I did not expect it to be), had a novitiate conference in St. Mary of Carmel. Very pleasant and peaceful. An altogether new atmosphere of light and peace (though there is plenty of both already in the novitiate). Sense of not being immersed in a fluid medium but out in the air.

Fr. John of the Cross said I would have less resentment in me if I were more concentrated on doing whatever it is God wills for me and not considering the defects of this institution.

One thing very clear after Mass: the "return to the Father."

The nonentity and insufficiency of all other concerns.

A going clear out of the midst of all that is transitory and inconclusive. The return to the Immense, the Primordial, the Unknown, to Him who loves, to the Silent, to the Holy, to the Merciful, to Him Who is All.

The misdirectedness, the folly, the inanity of all that seeks anything but this great return, the whole meaning and heart of all existence.

The absurdity of movements, of the goals that are not ultimate, the purposes that are "ends of the line" and therefore do not even begin.

To return is not to "go back" in time, but a going forward, a going beyond to retrace one's steps is nothing on top of nothing, vanity of vanities, a renewal of the same absurdity twice over, in reverse.

To go beyond everything, to leave everything and press forward to the End and to the Beginning, to the ever new Beginning that is without End.

To obey Him on the way in order to reach Him in Whom I have begun, Who is the Way and the End – (the Beginning).

March 24, 1961. F. of Our Lady of Sorrows (last time this feast of the year)
Wednesday afternoon (rain). The Pastoral Theology group and others
came to St. Mary of Carmel – conference on the Spiritual Senses and general discussion. A very happy atmosphere and I think everything was prof-
itable – a kind of opening up. Have never had so much of a sense of the
need and the *hunger* of the priests in the monastery for mysticism and contemplation – in a very simple way. It is true that a large part of our difficulties comes from frustration of this deep need and a kind of inarticulate
temptation to despair that takes refuge in activities without too much sense.

Yesterday (rain) discovered Po Chü-i – in the stacks of the U. of Louisville
library, leafed through other things. They have the Legge trans. of Mencius there. Well, I have it here too. What struck me most of all I looked at
was Léon Bloy's diary. The intensity, the vehemence, the seriousness of his
denunciation of clerical complacency and *impiety*. Really the atheism of the
believers!! The sense that among so many books, with so many words
in them, here was at least one living voice, a prophetic voice demanding to
be *heard*. (The others could be taken or left alone.) And I thought of the
Maritains.

When I got back, there was a superb letter from Dr. John Wu in answer to
one I had written to him about collaborating on some selections from
Chuang Tzu. A letter of great humility and nobility, from the depths of a
great heart, of one who loves deeply his Chinese heritage and knows well
the depths of that wisdom. I know once again we are touching something
real that cries out for a hearing (*Sapientia in plateis clamitat* [Wisdom cries
out in the marketplace]). I can see no other way to be honest before God
than to *hear* the premonitions of His wisdom in one like Chuang Tzu. Dr.
Wu had much to say about the Confucian and Taoist traditions that opened
up exciting horizons. I think this will be a fine work, even though it may
"accomplish nothing." (Why read Chuang Tzu and want to accomplish
something? Wisdom takes care of herself. Tao knows what she is about.
She has already "accomplished" it . . . And I have had the first glimpse of a
reservoir that is already full to the edges. It remains only for us to drink.)

March 28, 1961. Tuesday in Holy Week
Once again I dimly realize the enormous proportions of the ambiguities in
myself. And I cannot expect to resolve them. Nor should I be surprised at

the ambiguities in others. The great ambiguity of the whole monastery, on the question of "contemplation." We travel at all times in two opposite directions, and do so quite serenely. As if it were enough to have some kind of ideal of contemplation in one's mind, and then *do* anything one is impelled to do by latent activism, to allay one's guilt feelings at being, perhaps "unproductive." It is a peculiar problem of our time when we come from a world that is completely opposed to our ideal and do not really "come from" it, but only bring it along with us.

At such a time the break should be more complete – more thorough. But being "drastic" is no answer. There is a kind of violence which does not take heaven by storm, but serves only to justify our internal contradictions, and this is an illusion.

The liberalism of the Thirties is dead and has been judged and it is most important to realize this, for an attempt to recapture its atmosphere now could be the most dangerous weakness and illusion. The optimism of F.D.R., who was fooled by Stalin.

Deeply impressed by this statement of Robert McAfee Brown:

> "All of the great movements of reform and renewal in the history of the Church have grown out of a rediscovery of the Bible, and there is every reason to believe that the present [contemporary] rediscovery of the Bible (both by Catholics and Protestants) may create a situation full of possibilities beyond our power to predict."
>
> [The American Dialogue: A Protestant Looks at Catholicism *(New York, 1960), p. 80]*

Wrote two letters to Czeslaw Milosz. He is a terrific correspondent, full of wise insights, shrewd judge of the sickness of America, wants me to campaign against TV. It is 4 months since he wrote. I waited too long to answer him, thinking I will have something more adequate to say.

Letter from an American monk, student at the *Maison Généralice* [Abbot General's House, Rome]. About the Order, problem of solitude etc. What should he and his group do? There may be several planning transfers. Is there anything that can be done *within* the Order? I doubt it. Yet it should be possible. [Merton circles the numbers that follow.]

1. What *must* come: (a) The Superiors will have to stop evading the issue with clichés and half-truths, and will have to stop pretending that the

desire for a really contemplative life is not real or is not there. (b) Someone is going to have to admit that the accepted formula for the contemplative life in the Order is, or easily becomes, a mere evasion: or at least it is sufficient only for (good) novices and for very active types of contemplative whose whole horizon is bounded satisfactorily by the liturgy. (c) Some solution, permission for a more solitary life is going to be necessary and this has got to be found.

2. It won't hurt if a few go to Monte Corona. It will keep the issue alive and wake people up.

3. It is a shame that in my own life, which has become symbolic, there have had to be such ambiguities, e.g. I wrote to a great extent to get solitude. The hermitage is "for Protestant retreats."

In the Order, solutions will not be clear cut and satisfactory.

The confusion caused by the desire for *official and permanent* solutions that everyone can see and admire. Some of these students will one day be American abbots.

4. Possibility of an American hermitage? In connection with one of our monasteries.

April 1, 1961. Holy Saturday

The power of the Easter Vigil liturgy in part stems from the fact that so many vestiges of primitive nature rites are included and sanctified in it. Mystery of fire and mystery of water. Mystery of spring. *Ver sacrum* [Mystery of spring]. Fire, water and spring made sacred and meaningful theologically by the Resurrection of Christ, the new creation. Instead of stamping down the force of new life rising in us (and turning it into a dragon), let it be sweetened, sanctified and exalted, a figure of the life of the Spirit which is made present in our heart's love by the Resurrection.

Baffled and beat by the rejection of Christ – *our* rejection of Him – the *official* preference, by the Pontiffs, of Caesar over Christ as King – by the people of Barabbas as "their Boy" – i.e. as the hero with whom they wanted to be identified. Choice of the Barabbas type of liberation – guilty but absolved by popular acclaim. "We want *you*, Barabbas!" This the mentality of America today. Its response to sin – get around it by letting the criminal be popular. Note – crime itself thus becomes vicarious. We do not want to be fully vicious ourselves, by our own act: we do not have the courage. It would be too much trouble. Easier to watch it on TV. Question of a fully accepted "complicity" does not even arise. But we want Barabbas.

———

Temporarily solving, or putting off the problem of the hideous tabernacle in the novitiate chapel by hiding it with a veil. Trying to get rid of the square, night-clubbish candle holders. Frank Kacmarcik is right, the altar *does* look like a bar. Perhaps the new veil is a bit jazzy too, with its Matisse leafage (in brown). Bro. Olaf [Lavrans Nielsen] and I were in collusion, in its design.

One unquestionable improvement in the liturgy of Holy Week is the re- covery of the more ancient tone for the singing of the Passion. I do not know if this is the primitive Cistercian one, or Gallican, or what, but it is splendidly austere and noble. Tremendously moving, like great tolling Flemish bells stirring whole populations in medieval cities, or like the stone sides of the Cistercian churches of the 12th century which echoed to those tones. The chant was a mighty and living presence, binding us to- gether in mystery. Great eloquence and sobriety that has almost been lost from the world and has been recovered. This eloquence, though, is stub- born, it is in man, it will not go, Christ preserves it, as He preserves us, from our own vulgarity.

Fr. Marion has formed a pair of fairly presentable candlesticks.

April 2, 1961. Easter Sunday

A gay, bright, glorious day and a very fine Easter such as I do not remem- ber for a long time. The Vigil was tremendous for me and the glory of Christ was in it. There has been splendor in everything (including the emptiness of Good Friday morning when rain came down in torrents and I stayed in the hermitage).

Yesterday – reading bits of Dame Julian of Norwich and today I began Gregory of Nyssa's homilies on the Canticle.

"There is not a more dangerous tendency in history than that of repre- senting the past as if it were a rational whole and dictated by clearly de- fined interests," says [J.] Huizunga. What about the present? An even greater error.

Fr. Sylvanus was in town to the doctor and brought back a newspaper story about a man in the Ky. mountains, a former coal miner, who for 13 years has been living as a hermit, with a dog, in a pitiful little shack without even a chimney and with an old car seat for a bed. "Because of all these wars." A real desert father, and probably not too sure why.

April 7, 1961. Easter Friday

The hills are suddenly dark blue. Very green alfalfa in the bottoms. Yellow or mustard or siena sage grass in my own field. Here there is no impatience. I am a submerged dragon. The peace of the Alleluias. Another fine letter from John Wu and today I received from him the Giles translation of Chuang Tzu.

Trying to finish Nicholas of Cusa's *Vision of God*, but he verbalizes too much. Influence of Augustine.

April 8, 1961. Low Saturday

Bright noon sun and warmth. I left the refectory early and as I was hurrying across the Night Pasture I could hear the echo of Fr. Raymond's urgent shouts (he is reader in the refectory) relayed over a loudspeaker in the empty barns and in the farm building. It is characteristic of us that all our noise has to be heard *everywhere*.

Nels Richardson wrote with appalling glee about the John Birch society, which for some reason he admires. Principally because of the discomfiture it causes to "Red Professors." So now he has in his mind some image of Red Professors. He also seems to have caught some of the nasty diseases that go along with that, including a phobia about Jews and Negroes. I wonder if this is something they have in his private school.

This morning on the other hand I got a letter from a (Catholic) graduate student at Loyola who knows the editors of *New University Thought*, a fairly good independent radical magazine: I won't say quarterly, it comes out when it can. He says the Communists have already started making overtures to them. And no doubt some of their stuff *will* be written by Communists. I had written them a letter about a subscription.

I am sympathetic in so far as they represent a rebirth of the healthy leftism of the Thirties – it was to some extent healthy, or was healthier than what was bred in the '50s. What will come of it, however? Will it only aggravate the overwhelming trend to Fascism?

To what extent is it simply a temptation for me to want to take some political position, as distinct from an ethical one? Are the two separable, for instance where war is concerned? One thing is sure – it is beginning to be clear that opposition to nuclear war is something else than being simply a "pacifist." Also, opposition on the moral level demands some kind of open expression of one's position.

The question is – how to clearly, definitely and openly make such a stand without lending oneself to exploitation by one or other of the big power groups.

The editors of *New Univ. Thought* are not out to distribute bouquets to Catholics. Dorothy Day and *CW* [*Catholic Worker*] came in for a brief mention in connection with Peace demonstrations in N.Y. – as if they had not taken their stand alone and without encouragement for years. As though Dorothy had not been jailed five times – and more, for refusing to "take cover" during [air raid] alerts.

Reading Chuang Tzu at this time. I wonder seriously if the answer, the only possible answer, does not lie hid far below the political and ethical levels. Ethics, and politics, certainly, but only in passing, only as a "night's lodging"? When all action has somehow become absurd, shall one act merely because at some other times action was once expected and significant? Like setting the dinner table in time of starvation when you have no food, but setting it anyway, out of habit.

April 15, 1961

The Russians had a "man in space" the other day, that is, they had him in orbit around the earth in a satellite and apparently recovered him.

We are reading John Wu's delightful biography in the refectory. What a completely wonderful person he is.

Dom Leclercq will quite probably be down here at the end of June, at least I received permission to invite him to give three or four lectures to the novices. And perhaps Fr. [Jean] Daniélou will be here in July. He is coming over to give a course at Summer School at Notre Dame and Mother Luke has invited him to speak at Loretto.

Quiet, grey afternoon. It is warmer. Birds sing. There will be more rain. Cocks crowing in the afternoon silence, very distant.

Thunderstorm. The first I have sat through in the hermitage. Here you really can *watch* a storm. White snakes of lightning suddenly stand in the sky and vanish.

The valley is clouded with rain as white as milk. All the hills vanish.

The thunder cracks and beats. Rain comes flooding down from the roof eaves and the grass looks twice as green as before.

Not to be known, not to be seen.

April 16, 1961. Good Shepherd Sunday
In announcing to the community in Chapter that the Russians had put a man in space, Rev. Father included a lot of dire innuendos to the effect that no one knew "how many had been killed" in previous attempts. It is of course possible that the mystery of the big 6½ ton satellite back in January or February had something to do with that.

There was some suppressed laughing at pious Fr. Basil when the name of the "cosmonaut" was announced: Galganin. For Fr. B. has tender devotion to St. Gemma Galgani. Such are the incidents of monastic life that arouse attention.

Fr. Gabriel Sweeney, the little white-haired Passionist who is in the novitiate, who asked to leave before Easter and was dissuaded by Rev. Father, stands with a piteous expression in the novitiate library reading "Relax and Live." Sooner or later they come to that.

[F. X.] Durrwells's book on the *Resurrection*, sent by Frank Sheed, is excellent when you get into it. A remarkable insight into the visible and institutional aspect of the Church as something provisional, belonging along with death and suffering to the time of imperfection. A necessary corrective. Too many evils are excused by a passionate and one-sided attachment to the Church as a juridical institution. Pius XII says truly that the evils of the Church's history are to be blamed on men, not on the institution. But men *use* the institutional framework of the Church as the scene and the refuge of certain injustices and inequities, and bend it at times to serve their purposes. It would even seem that the framework lends itself to this – at least in its present complex condition. It is not new to remark [on] our perpetual need of reform.

(St. M. of C[armel])
The evening sky over the valley. Long lines of clouds travelling in strong cold wind toward the east.

Janua Coeli [Gate of Heaven]. How different prayer is here. Clarity – direction – to Christ the Lord for the great gift – the passage out of this world to the Father, entry into the kingdom. I know what I am here for.

May I be faithful to this awareness. "*Le project initial?*" ["The initial project?"]

April 18, 1961

A talkative fire in the fireplace. Loud watch on the table.

Letter from the American Cistercian student in Rome that he – and the "others" like himself, will probably transfer in a group to the Camaldolese of Monte Corona. Fr. André Louf, editor of the *Collectanea*, is thinking of doing the same. The *Collectanea* has been very good lately – good "*Bulletins Monastiques.*" Certainly with this movement in the Order I must think of my own part. This hermitage should be sufficient answer. More of it.

A good group from the Southern Baptist Seminary here yesterday. Very good rapport. I liked them very much. An atmosphere of sincerity and understanding. Differences between us not, I think, minimized. Dr. [Glenn] Hinson, the Church history man, a good and sincere person, with some of the other faculty members, will come down again. We will talk, perhaps, about the Church. I am glad they will come. Yet each time some new arrangement like this is made, I wonder if I have not committed myself again too much. The hermitage is "for" that. (Really it is "for nothing.") It seems to be part of the game to have people come to the hermitage. A strange, humorous game of God that I cannot quite take seriously. A mystifying game, in which, no doubt, He will make all things well and very well. But I must not play it too madly, or become too engrossed in it. It is the game of another, not mine.

Yesterday in the Building Committee meeting they all suddenly started talking about the landing of revolutionaries to fight Castro in Cuba, and that the Russians were pulling out, that someone had dropped bombs on Havana, that Castro was laying curses upon the head of Kennedy. They seemed pleased. But this only complicates a matter made complicated already by America's muddled foreign policies. It will not solve anything.

April 22, 1961

Important article on Dom Lambert Baudouin (d. Jan. 14, 1959) by O. Rousseau. Once he stayed at (*un court séjour* [a short stay]) a Trappist monastery. It repelled him.

"*Dom B. entrevoyait difficilement la vie du moine au XXe Siècle autrement qu'engagé d'une certaine manière dans un dialogue*"

["Dom B. imagined with some difficulty the life of the monk in the Twentieth Century *without some kind of participation in dialogue*"

"*. . . le rayonnement devait s'exercer à partir de la prière, plus que par une simple présence.*"

". . . the radiance would manifest itself through prayer, rather than by presence alone."]

However, I disagree with his conception that this solitude of the first monks was something transient and provisional, to remain only as an ideal for the cenobite to look back on.

His reaction to the romanticism of Mont César [Louvain, Belgium].

To the timetable of the big monastery – its recreations, devotions, manias, amateurishness, hobbies, pettinesses. Disliked Pontifical ceremonies and the pomp of Abbots. Did not like exemption.

In his foundation – encouraged by Met[ropolitan] Saepticky[7] and his Studite foundation.

Read *Equidem Verba* of Pius XI to Ab[bot] Primate March 21, 1924.

In 1925 L.B. visited Galicia, the Studite foundations and the Laura of Potchasew 1925. Takes over the Carmel of Amay [Chevetogne, Belgium].

Special emphasis on mass, labor and on twofold liturgy: oriental and western. This – I don't know. It is *his* way, not for others.

Prime and Compline half ceased to exist, were said behind curtains "*à mi voix* [at half voice]."

In the beginning the day hours were said, as in a charterhouse. Lauds and Vespers were solemnized. I like his Sundays – in theory at any rate.

This – yes: "*Il fallait chercher à l'orient son secret pour un labeur continu et une application sans relâche, et l'intégrer dans notre culture.*" ["One would have had to search the East for its secret of a continuous toil and an application without respite, and integrate it into our own culture."] But are energy and doggedness enough?

Other things – interest in the problem of brothers – would level all off as monks.

Etc.

April 23, 1961. III Sun After Easter

Modicum . . . [Second lesson (Gospel), John 16: "A little while, and you see me no more . . ."] I love this mysterious and joyful Sunday. The responses

---

[7] Merton refers here to Andrew Sheptysky.

about the Heavenly Jerusalem and the Gospel about the joy which "no man shall take from you." Remember twenty-one years ago in Havana: the Sunday of the great joy in San Francisco Church. (That was April 29 that year.)

And now the sorrow of Cuba, the confusion, the bungling and the evil. The Reds quickly using Fidel's dumb zeal to grab everything. The Americans fomenting a revolution that will not quite be decisive enough . . . Poor Cuba! Poor wisdom used! What lies ahead for all of us? *Vos autem contristabimini, sed tristitia vestra vertetur in gaudium.* [You will be made sad, but your sorrow will be turned into joy.]

John Beecher and his wife were here yesterday.

English prof. at Arizona State U. He resigned a couple of months ago to join the Peace March from San Francisco tomorrow and left it at Chicago because he could not get along with the younger ones who have "no discipline." Telling fact that the group bickered and argued all the time, bitterness, no real peace among themselves, no spiritual roots. They claim to be Gandhians, but you cannot practice Gandhian non-violence without deep spiritual roots in prayer and abandonment to God.

Their eagerness to cover ground, to make time, to be everywhere on schedule. Their tendency to measure their own value by the amount of space they get in the press. This is the root of delusion.

He said they were often welcomed by Protestant ministers, nowhere had any contact with Catholics, esp. priests.

The place in Oklahoma where they were received with hostility but changed the attitude of local college students, talking far into the night.

Everywhere – U.S. is an armed camp.

Card. Cushing has come out in favor of the John Birch Society. One portent after another!

While the rain poured down we had lunch together in the Beechers' small, compact-trailer.

Spoke of Koinonia, in Georgia,[8] etc.

They will probably go on to Mexico.

April 27, 1961

On the 24th I just noticed green worms of the pine saw fly on the pine saplings around St. Mary of Carmel. Sprayed some of them yesterday, a

---

[8] A Protestant community, founded 1941.

bright afternoon. It seems to have done some good. Another bright day today. One redbud in full blossom, what there is of it. It seems those we planted on the way up to the hermitage will do well. The valley is filling with the clear soft green of spring buds.

April 29, 1961. F. of St. Robert

Fr. Michael, who is renewing his temporary vows today and plans finally to make his solemn profession, wrote me a touching and surprising note – or at any rate it surprised me. He said I had very much helped him "by word and example" to see that the monastic life is livable. By example!! Aware as I am of my interior depressions, gloom, rebellions, bitterness – of my very real inadaptability to the rigid form of cenobitic life which is here conceived as an ideal (and yet certainly not accepted by all) – I can hardly believe such a statement. Evidently people consider me a happy man. And I suppose in a way I really am. But I spoil it for myself by my stubborn, interior refusal of happiness.

What a sad and silly thing! God has been constantly and incessantly good to me in everything, and I refuse to be content. Incapable of contentment, really. I *cannot* be content, or admit contentment, because perhaps I think that if I do it is a sign of defeat, an admission of something I don't want to admit. But surely it implies no admission that the official statements we make about ourselves are true.

We are so intent on proclaiming ourselves happy in words that are patently false or insufficient, that we cannot admit our *real* happiness for fear of submitting to our own official lie. Where *is* the truth? It is there, and we must see it where it is. It is not we who have made ourselves happy. God keeps me in His mercy and I am capable of happiness in spite of my own folly and the falsity of our community slogans. And indeed one of the great realities and goods is precisely the community: not in its lies and fantasies, but in the hearts of its members who suffer, as I do, because of those lies.

I can and must dare to live through this contradiction, not for myself only but for them. This is the responsibility I come more and more to see, and it can at times be a bitter, galling one, but it must be assumed.

A fine sentence in a mediocre article (part of that on the Church in *DS* [*Dictionnaire de Spiritualité*]):

> "*Édifier c'est se rendre pleinment docile au Seigneur au point d'être un instrument capable d'aider les autres à se laisser prendre, tailler et polir pour entrer*

dans la construction de la Maison de Dieu." ["To edify is to put oneself completely at the service of the Lord, to the point of being an instrument who
can help others to let themselves be taken, cut and polished in order to be
part of the building up of the House of God."]

The very real temptation, the worst temptation and the most difficult,
comes from the fact that we seem to be leading one another into a trap. As
if I were caught myself and were leading others to be caught in a net of
hypocrisies. Can it really be God that is behind all our official nonsense?
All our trumpery and circumstance and pontifical verbosity? All our laws
and decrees and statutes and rites and observances ... The mind groans
and cracks under the immense burden of complications we have created
for ourselves. And yet it is certainly simpler than the awful confusion of
"The world" – and look at the monumental, and self-evident hypocrisy of
the communist states and *their* unbearable burdens!
Wherever you look, on that level, you find confusion.
There is the level of faith, on which nothing is seen, and yet there peace
is evident, and it is no self-delusion to say "all manner of thing shall be
well" because experience has repeatedly proved it.
If only faith can survive the choking complications of our judicial and
spiritual red tape.

My basic trouble: it is a strictly *unchristian* refusal, I regret it, but this is
true. *The refusal to love those I do not consider worthy of love.* The refusal of
happiness goes with this – for if I admit to being happy and content, it
seems to me (falsely) that I am admitting the *worthiness* of all and the *rightness* of this special claim as opposed to *all other claims*. In other words I am
supposed to be saying, "Our group alone is supremely worthy."
To refuse this is perfectly right. The claim is preposterous.
Yet I cannot refuse my love, even where the claim is preposterous, because as a Christian I am not supposed to demand that my brother be worthy of love.
(The claim, on the part of a group, to special or exclusive worthiness can
indeed be very unchristian.)
God is asking of me, the unworthy, to forget my unworthiness and that
of my brothers and to dare to advance in the love which has redeemed and
renewed us in the divine likeness. And to laugh, after all, at everything preposterous. To laugh at our pseudo-worthiness – for it is a cosmic joke.

May 1, 1961

It started by pouring rain. Protestants were coming, and they were here. Two groups of them, one early, one late. In the rain I went to the hermitage in the morning and ten or so from Asbury came up in the rain – we spoke briefly together and it was simple and charming. But had to come down quickly for high Mass.

After dinner – the large group, some thirty or forty from Vanderbilt Divinity School (and still those from Asbury). A good lively session, which continued after None and got too long, degenerated a bit into a kind of relaxed silliness in which they tended to bicker among themselves. The Vanderbilt group is always in general good and mature. I am sorry the more serious and profound of them did not come in a smaller party.

Contest between the sweet earnestness of Methodists, the polish and sophistication of Anglicans (or rather Episcopalians) – the sometimes rather taut fervor of the Baptists – though I don't know exactly who was what. There was a general laugh of surprise when one of them made a derogatory remark about Baptists (and rather silly too) and there turned out to be two in the group, which evidently the others did not know about.

The sun came out brightly in the afternoon, and I left them to their tour of the monastery, came to the hermitage to reflect and wish I were more a True Man or Mountain Man of Chuang Tzu. Talking exhausts me because I imagine I have something to say.

May 2, 1961

Brilliant afternoon. It is the day when everything finally opens out and the green woods on the hills turns definitively into foliage. The most marvelous time of the year. After this comes summer, very quickly. But it is still cool.

I have read this afternoon the chapter on the Battle of Britain in [William] Shirer. It needs to be read, it needed to be read by me. For first of all I had almost forgotten it, and second I never really knew how close Hitler came to the invasion, *or what would have happened to England after the invasion* and how much depended purely and simply on the R.A.F.

There is no question possible of absolute, unqualified pacifism in the light of this. The Nazis had to be fought and were fought very bravely by my people and I wish I were worthy of them. I would still make the same decision for myself as I made then – to be a non-combatant, e.g. in ambulance corps. But now the decisions are no longer the same. There is a new kind of war, and no less ruthless an ememy, though perhaps less pathological – but a war which either advances widely on a political front or promises total destruction.

There is no question *Dictatorship must be fought*, if possible non-violently. But if that is not possible, then violently.

Abdul Aziz has sent some books on Islam, including first of all a powerful and concise little volume on Sufism by one Titus Burckhardt, of whom I had not yet heard. Certainly the very finest thing on the subject I have yet touched, marked with a hardness (solidity) and sureness one rarely finds in western studies of oriental mysticism.

Also A. Aziz's own essay on Islam with two tremendous quotes at the end. This is for me only a first reading of the Burckhardt, which I will go over again more intently.

Here a frankly intellectual mysticism – with real roots. The Truth Itself smashing vanity: and with *no* separation of knowledge and love.

May 4, 1961

Today, St. Francis of Paula. First time interested in him since reading Huizunga. Mention of his being called to France by Louis XI in the 3rd lesson, but could not remember what had seemed so amusing about it – except that he was exhibited like a rare captured beast: or a "saint."

Last evening at Vespers – singing the Magnificat antiphon with great joy in the splendor of the Gregorian setting, its rhythm, its verve, solidity and "*entrain* [liveliness]." When we were singing the last alleluia I suddenly realized that this was the last time the antiphon would ever be sung, quite probably, as the Feast of the Invention of the H[oly] Cross has been abolished. In memory of this day I will translate the antiphon:

O Cross more splendid than all the stars
Glorious to the world
Greatly to be loved by men
More holy than all things that exist,
Thou who alone wast worthy to weigh the gold of the
world's ransom   (*portare talentum mundi*
                                                 [to carry the worth of the world])
Sweet tree, beloved nails

Bearing the Love-burden
Save us who have come together here, this day,
In choirs for thy praise.
Alleluia, Alleluia, Alleluia.

May 7, 1961. V Sunday after Easter

In the Night Office – St. Ambrose: all *must* rise from the dead. Resurrection is our lot. Life is our destiny whether we want it or not. But to be risen and not want it, to hate life is the resurrection of judgement. Man is not, and cannot be, a merely ephemeral thing. But if he wills to be evanescent, to remain in what is *not*, he is a living contradiction.

Thunder, lightning and rain all night. Heaviest rain for a long time. Floods in the bottoms. Water bubbling in under the basement wall into the washroom. Novitiate garden flooded in the NW corner. (One day the whole retaining wall will go if this keeps up.) Sound of waters in the valley.

My love is
The fragrance of the orchid
And the sound of waters

says the Haiku on my lovely Zen calendar.

America got a man 115 miles up out of the air in space last Friday and I am glad everything went so well. The beauty of the whole shot was that everything was near perfect and clicked off according to plan. There is a monstrous absurdity about the whole space business, but if we are going to do it we might as well succeed at it. And above all it is good for America to do something well for once, because after all, for all our faults, we represent a better and more decent life than Russia and China ever can. Reading Shirer is a sobering experience. What a tragedy to forget Hitler and Stalin and their total corruption of the moral sense. The complete and systematic inhumanity of Hitler's whole plan, and the way his generals, many of whom must have been "good Christians," accepted it. What a commentary on obedience! We have become so docile that we no longer obey God.

The inexorable succession of Hitler's mistakes, dictated by his folly. How clear it seems now. One is tempted to wonder how easily he could have been master of the world if he had first a little more humility. If he had been really humble, of course, he never would have started, or thought of being master of the world. The madness of his armies that let themselves be destroyed for the sake of his pride!

O God how blind we all are! Not to see these things, and the appalling irony of them!

And then the temptation to embrace Marxism, which seems wise, seems more efficacious because it is not built on individual folly. Not on the folly of the leader but on the anonymous obsession of a Party which, because collective and anonymous, seems to be quasi-divine. *This* is the real temptation!

Hitler regarded the power of his madness as a divine power, because he felt inspired. The Reds regard the power of their collective obsession as a divine power, or a power of destiny, because it is *not* [double underlined] inspired, and therefore seems to have an even higher inevitability. "It is written . . ."

Wrote an essay on the English Mystics this week (review of Knowles and a new anthology).

Must get to know Hilton. Have been put off by the *Guard of Love*, which is not really his.

Novices tore out the ceiling of their dormitory. The floors are finished in the north wing and cells are being put in the Brothers' Dormitory.

Rev. Father away in the East seeing the [Abbot] General before he returns to Europe. Discussing, no doubt, the stuff he has been writing up as material for an Encyclical.

In Refectory – a discouraging book on the Church Councils by P. Hughes. Severe test of faith!

Have finally after five – no, seven, years got down to work on the remarkable little book of Dom [Jean-Baptiste] Porion on Hadewijch. The introduction is full of information and of sagacious remarks. A really new and clear perspective. I am more and more fascinated by the mysticism of the late Middle Ages, with its defects and its qualities. The whole scope of the vast movement going back to the Cistercians, Joachim [de Fione], St. Francis, the Béguines, the Cathari, the Spirituals, *assimilated* fully by the Church in the great Rhenish mystics . . . We have not even begun to understand all this, or appreciate its purport.

———

In all this rain – I have left a work blouse, scapular and T shirt out on the line and a letter from Dom Leclercq in a pocket of the work blouse saying he is to come here early in June.

Fr. Felix in the infirmary, got himself banged up falling through a hole in the dormitory attic in the dark. I had a row with him ten days or so ago about the crazy scaffolding 40 feet high on which he was sending up novices to clear the ceiling of the church.

May 10, 1961. Vigil of Ascension
Bright day after much rain (more). Quails whistling loudly in the bushes around the edge of the woods. They live all around the hermitage.

May 15, 1961
Touching, very courageous letter from the wife of a man taken prisoner in the "Cuban landing" and from the *novia* [girlfriend] of Manuel Artime, who led the "invasion" and was captured. A very sad, hopeless business, engineered by some fools who thought they knew what they were doing. A great waste of lives and effort. The Midas touch is not magic, after all. American money can't do everything. When will we learn it?

Last Friday – a good bright morning – stopped in at the Baptist seminary in Louisville. A good visit and a short discussion which I think was worth while.

May 16, 1961
It is like an English summer day, cool and cloudy, with deep green grass all around the hermitage and trees heavy with foliage. Occasional slow bursts of gentle sunlight that imperceptibly pass by. Shafts of light and great rooms of shadow in the tall tree-church beyond the cedar cross. The path of creek gravel leads into the shadows and beyond them to the monastery, out of sight, down the hill, across fields and a road and a dirty stream. All such things as roads and sewers are far from this place.

All through the Hughes book are the Councils, especially the 8th, I find myself looking at everything from the viewpoint of Byzantium . . . How much trouble has come to us from the association of Patriarchs with Superiors, and of Patriarchal Sees with imperial capitals. Is there not in this the most solemn of lessons?

Reading Martin Luther King [Jr.] and the simple, moving story of the Montgomery Bus boycott. Especially interested not only in the main actions but in the story of his own spiritual development. Certainly here is something Christian in the history of our time.

May 19, 1961

Knowing when you do not need any more. Acting just enough. Saying enough. Stopping when there is enough. Some may be wasted, nature is prodigal. Harmony is not bought with parsimoniousness.

Yet stopping is "going on." To cling to something and want more of it, to _use_ it more, to squeeze enjoyment out of it. This is to "stop" and not "go on." But to leave it alone at the right time, this is the right stopping, the right going on. To leave a thing alone before you have had anything to do with it, if it is for your use, to leave it without use, is not "stopping," it is not even beginning. Use it to go on.

> To be great is to go on
> To go on is to be far
> To be far is to return.

Nonsense of autographs. Dan Walsh is always after me for them. Nonsense of recreation – of the wasted kind. Jim Wygal is after me for that. And he is perhaps right. I need to be properly social, yet it is wasteful and absurd too. A little is good. Enough is too much.

Cool day. Grass wet. New mower, the old kind, that you push.

Useless letters. And the censors of the Order have forbidden the Atom bomb piece. Behind this foolishness, this instant resolve not to let anyone protest!

Msgr. [Joseph] Chatham, here last evening, a good priest, convinced the Church is in a full movement of reform, because that is what he hopes for. I admire and respect his hope. If I share it guardedly it is because of my greater temptation to fear this inefficacy of our actions for social reasons.

We are bound by our commitment to wealth. Shame and frustration. He realizes this also. So many do.

Today, St. Peter Celestine. Yes and no.

Enjoy Clement of Alexandria. He is underrated and ignored. A great mind and a great Christian, noble and broad and belonging to antiquity, yet new.

⸙ Finished the official mystical theology course today. Some extra classes to be fitted in where I can. The Italians shout in the chapter room, laying down terrazzo floors. Work on novices' dormitory, new ceiling.

May 20, 1961

A PRAYER TO GOD MY FATHER ON THE VIGIL OF PENTECOST

Today, Father, this blue sky praises you. The delicate green and orange flowers of the tulip poplar praise you. The distant blue hills praise you, with the sweet smelling air that is full of brilliant light. The bickering fly-catchers praise you, with the lowing bulls and the quails that whistle over there, and I too, Father, praise you, with these creatures my brothers. You have made us all together and you have placed me here this morning in the midst of them. And here I am.

For a long time I prayed, in the years that are past, and I was in darkness and sorrow and confusion. And no doubt the confusion was my own fault. No doubt my own will was the root of my sorrow, and I regret it, O merciful Father. But whatever may have been my sin, the prayer of Your friends for me and my own prayers were answered, and I am here in this hermitage before You, and here You see me. Here You love me. Here You ask the response of my own love, and of my confidence. Here You ask me to be nothing else than Your friend.

To be Your Friend is simply to accept Your friendship because it is Your Friendship. And this Friendship is your life, the Spirit of Your Son. You have called me here to be Your Son: to be born over again, repeatedly, in Your light, and in knowledge, and consideration, and gratitude, and poverty, and praise.

Here I will learn from the words of Your Friends to be Your Friend and here I will be a friend to those in whom You send me Your Son.

If I have any choice to make, it is to live and even die here. But in any case, it is to speak Your name with confidence here in this place, to say it by being here and by having You in my heart, as long as I can be here.

And now Father I beg You to teach me to be a man of peace and to help bring peace to the world. To study here truth and non-violence, and patience and the courage to suffer for truth.

Send me Your Holy Spirit, and unite me with Your divine Son and make me one with You in Him, for Your great glory, Amen.

[This is not what I first asked for but it is what the Father has given me, *against* my own striving. It is better than what I asked for. Above all it is far simpler. But I am guilty about it since it is easier and not heroic, and not worthy of any wonder. And it is accepted by the church as right and fitting, without this much comment – at least it is gladly granted me on a "take it and shut up" basis. This is enough.] [Merton's brackets]

[See what was written last Pentecost under the same kind of peace and certitude as this today. The paragraph "God is my Father," on page 5.[9] I was not wrong in my trust. What is important, I was not wrong in trusting the church and my Superiors. Surely this ought to be a lesson! I have indeed received mercy, but am still restless because I want everything to come to me as my *Just due! Miserere mei.* (Have mercy on me.)] [Merton's brackets]

May 27, 1961. Ember Saturday of Pentecost
Here ends Paschal time, and beautifully.

There was more rain and cold wind. In the east there were storms. Now as the week ends it is bright and cool with an untamed sky and fair green grass standing high – except where I have cut it with the small new mower (it is not a power mower).

Have not had much time alone at the hermitage until today.

Tom McDonnell came down. He is editing an anthology (*Reader*)[10] of my work. Has an interesting idea but it needs work on my part. Was busy with that for two days. He is a Thoreau man, quiet. We sat in the woods and talked of Walden pond, saved. No longer a bathing beach there.

This morning Wm. Congdon, sent by Frank Sheed, was here, and left this afternoon. He is an abstract expressionist converted to the faith and the conversion is lived out in his painting, remarkably. I had seen a newspaper reproduction of one of his crucifixions without being especially impressed, but looking at the transparencies I was delighted with their

[9] See the June 5, 1960, entry.
[10] *A Thomas Merton Reader*, edited by Thomas P. McDonnell, published in 1962.

spiritual quality, sometimes like Reichenau Mss., sometimes like Blake, strong and delicate, wonderful colors. The most popular of his crucifixions is not the most powerful and most subtle. His Christ in Gethsemani in a silver cloud is tremendous. Silver is for him an ominous color. And gold is a saving color, but before he was converted he could not penetrate the gold in his painting. It was a hard door, like St. Mark's for instance.

Very fine painter. (Victor Hammer would not like this.) He left me the use of a book of his Reynal is to do.

May 30, 1961. F. of St. Joan of Arc

Trinity Sunday after the Night Office I realized I had plenty of time to go to the hermitage and went as the sun rose. I wonder why I had not thought of it before – perhaps too obsessed with the reading I have been doing at that time, and in which to a great extent I have been fruitlessly lost.

This morning I came up again, and I am doing my best to take, as far as possible, the whole day here, going down of course for exercises. Which is possible, as I have no conference or direction.

This morning at four. Great full moon over Nally's hill, pale and clear. A faint mist hanging over the wet grass of the bottoms.

More and more I appreciate the beauty and solemnity of the "Way" up through the woods, past the bull barn, up the stony rise, into the grove of tall, straight oaks and hickories, and around through the pines on top of the hill, to the cottage.

Sunrise. Hidden by pines and cedars on the east side of the house. Saw the red flame of it glaring through the cedars not like sunrise but like a forest fire. From the window of the front room, then, he, the Sun (can hardly be conceived as other than he) shone silently with solemn power through the pine branches.

Now after High Mass the whole valley is glorious with morning light and with the song of birds.

It is essential to experience all the times and moods of this place. No one will know or be able to say *how* essential. Almost the first and most important element of a truly spiritual life, lost in the constant, formal routine of Divine offices under the fluorescent lights in choir – practically no change between night and day.

May 31, 1961

Gandhi once asked, "How can he who thinks he possesses absolute truth be fraternal?" Let us be frank about it: the history of Christianity raises this question again and again. Doubtless Gandhi implies an answer that is too simple and leads to vague indifferentism. The problem. God has revealed Himself to men in Christ. He has revealed Himself as love first of all. But this is inseparable from the truth of the gospel message. Only he who loves has really grasped the truth of the message . . . And in that case he is humble about it, and wise also. *Scientia inflat.* [Knowledge puffs one up.] He who is absolutely sure he *knows* absolute truth which is withheld from others: how can he "love" those others except by subjecting them to what he knows, imposing it on them? This is the temptation.

The great work of sunrise again today.

The awful solemnity of it. The sacredness. Unbearable without prayer and worship. I mean unbearable if you really put everything else aside and see what is happening! Many, no doubt, are vaguely aware that it is dawn: but they are protected from the solemnity of it by the neutralizing worship of their own society, their own world, in which the sun no longer rises and sets.

Again, sense of the importance, the urgency of seeing, fully aware, experiencing what is *here*: not what is given by men, by society, but what is given by God and hidden by (even monastic) society. Clear realization that I must begin with these first elements. That it is absurd to inquire after my function in the world, or whether I have one, as long as I am not first of all alive and awake. And if that, and no more, is my job (for it is certainly every man's job), then I am grateful for it. The vanity of all false missions, when no one is sent. All the universal outcry of people who have not been told to cry out, but who are driven to this noise by their fear, their lack of what is right in front of their noses.

June 6, 1961. In the Orthodox calendar, Bessarion the Great, of Egypt
It is said that I am being awarded today a medal, at Columbia and that Mark Van Doren[11] is receiving it for me. I do not know for what. But I am glad of it.

Dom Leclercq came last Wednesday afternoon, before Corpus Christi, stayed three days and gave some conferences, and we had some talks together.

---

[11] Merton's teacher at Columbia University.

In conferences – mention of various Benedictine and Cistercian writers, on an introductory level. A good talk on Monastic Tradi*tions* and tradi*tion*, both necessary. Recent theories about St. Benedict and the Rule. (What seems to have stirred people most is the hypothesis that St. B. never existed. By this Dom L.'s visit will be most remembered.) A good quote from Hildeman on contemplation. What I gathered mostly, for myself, was the repeated assurance of the traditional value and real need for such exceptions as my own, in view of solitude. This I think should be the most important thing about it for me.

He also told me I was a pessimist, and too anxious, and too negative.

Actually I also had a feeling of an underlying disharmony between us, a kind of opposition and *méfiance* [mistrust] under the surface cordiality and agreement.

He is certainly one of those, one of the very many, who accept any writing I have done only with great reservations. And that I can certainly understand. As a theologian I have always been a pure amateur and the professionals resent an amateur making so much noise. Though he is friendly to a book like *Thoughts in Solitude*, I know he is not happy with something like [*The Sign of*] *Jonas*, which would obviously disturb most Europeans, most European monks. He protests he is not against journals as such. As for *Ascent to Truth* – all right, I know this was a foolish experiment, a false start and a mistake. I am ashamed of it. Perhaps it is not as bad as I feel, in my guilt. So too some of the other rather fatuous didacticism I have got into.

He told me with very evident satisfaction of the "cruelty" with which a certain Mother Dore had taken me apart in some Italian magazine (1951). I can imagine it. But who is Mother Dore, and who gives two hoots about what *she* thinks?

I have no doubt she is right on many points; it would not be hard for her to be so. But what of it? The whole issue is trivial anyway. What difference does it make that I have written superficially? So long as I stop now when I see there is no point to it.

Yet here I am confronted with the galleys of *The New Man*. Sometimes clever, generally superficial, and a waste of time.

Did I really *have* to say what is said there?

Was it really needed?

The things I have said fairly well are things I needed to say: I stand by them. Most of the *Seven Storey Mtn.*, and *Jonas*, and anything on solitude, esp. the notes in *Disputed Questions,* a lot of the poems, *Seeds of Contemplation* and *New Seeds* (I think), a good part of the *Silent Life.* Perhaps a few pages of *No Man Is an Island,* a good bit of *Secular Journal,* and most of the recent work: *Behavior of Titans* especially. And the stuff on Herakleitos and Chinese thought? Maybe.

What hurts me most is to have been inexorably trapped by my own folly. Wanting to prove myself a Catholic – and of course not perfectly succeeding.

They all admit and commend my good will, but frankly, I am not one of the bunch, am I?

For my comfort a squirrel just ran across the porch.

June 10, 1961

I am less disappointed in the galleys of *The New Man* than I thought I was the other day. There is some fairly good material in it. Much of it is poorly written, and in a hurry.

Rain again, yesterday, on the Feast of the Sacred Heart. And a pretty snake doubled up on the top of the jakes door here in the woods. A young kingsnake, after the mice that have their nest there, up under the roof.

Wrote a couple of pages for Bill Congdon's book the other day. He deserves a statement. He needed the transparency of *Christ Walking on the Waters* and I hated to part with it. It is really beautiful. A delight.

In the refectory, a tendentious book about Communism, its insidiousness, how we should hate it. But the basic presupposition is that we ourselves have perfect freedom and justice. Too much of this political hate. Hate Castro. Hate Khrushchev. Hate Mao. All in the same breath as "God is love" and the "beatings of the Sacred Heart"? There is another dimension we have not discovered.

Cistercian history: a new dimension there too. I am studying the 13th–14th centuries, about which I thought I knew at least a little and literally knew nothing. I assume I have knowledge I do not have.

This for novitiate conferences on the decline of the Order.

Interesting book of J. B. Mahn on Benedict XII and the Cistercians. And the question of studies (The College of St. Bernard was not a cause of the decline or even one of its symptoms). Yet one wonders at all the expense and effort put into this, and for what? Perhaps it contributed to the general stultification of the Order, or perhaps on the contrary it was necessary to hold the Order together in the lean years . . . Two aspects of inertia. From one point of view it can be regarded as stability. Yet it would perhaps be a myth to say the Order was ever really inert. There must have been also a real underlying faithfulness, as in the Benedictines also, witness Knowles' sketch of Thomas de la Mare, abbot of St. Alban's.

A Trappist formation makes it very hard to understand properly the history of the decline. Too many prejudices and myths of our own.

June 11, 1961

This is the last time the F. of St. Barnabas will be celebrated on a Sunday and with three nocturns. I was especially interested in the office and even more so in the Office of the Sacred Heart the other day, about which I say nothing for the moment.

Chrysostom in the III Nocturn, about sheep and wolves. "Let us blush that we are wolves rather than sheep, and rush upon our adversaries." A fine text for Christian non-violence.

Nam quamdiu oves fuerimus, vincimus; etiam si multi circumstant lupi, superamus et victores sumus: quoad si lupi fuerimus, vincimur. Tunc enim a nobis pastoris auxilium recedit, qui non lupos sed oves pascit! [For as long as we are sheep, we will conquer; even if many wolves surround us, we will win and be victorious: but insofar as we are wolves, we will lose. For then the help of the Shepherd, who feeds sheep, not wolves, will disappear.]

(from Hom[ily] 34 in Matth.)

This is true of my own wolf-nature, I am afraid! How angry I am and resentful interiorly, and spiteful in my criticisms. Even to people who have been kind to me: because there is a certain kindness which I at once accept, take for granted, refuse to acknowledge and even actively resent. And this is the source of many sorrows. I remember all the injustices these persons may have appeared to do me, and perhaps some of these are real, even though they were meant kindly. It is true that I am too quick to see evil, and want to see it, and this is a great failing. May God pardon me.

At Mass, thinking of how many delusions there have been in my life, and how I have resented having to admit them, and yet been forced to (which is a good thing!). When will I become a Christian? When will I begin to work for this, instead of taking it all for granted?

Charmed by fragments of a letter of Arturo de Guevara. Would like to read more of him.

June 15, 1961

Well, another torrent of Rain.

We have five or six gardenias, sent from Mepkin last year, growing in big cans. They have to be taken in for the winter. They were put out but not in the ground. I picked one and put it in a little bottle that once had vitamin pills in it and set it in front of the wooden Soledad[12] from Oaxaca and the room smells sweet with it. The pure white, the dark green leaves with beautiful forms, against the dark wood and gold of the image. The scent is heady but delicate. The smallness of the flowers. I am grateful.

Began the other day reading Romain Rolland's *Inde*. Wide awake and all there when I read this (I cannot say as much for Nels Ferré, whom nevertheless I like). Much more myself, much more awake, reading this than when reading some of the long chapters, in proof, of my own *New Man*, which is a failure.

The thing that keeps me awake in Rolland is *truth*. I don't mean dogmatic truth, but the truth of life. He is a lover of India but not a zealot or an enthusiast and he sees the weaknesses, the vanities, the blindnesses. He does not just take Gandhi blindly. He sees the element of despotism in Gandhi. He likes Tagore and now so do I. I really want to read Tagore. Victoria Ocampo sent me a picture of him. I sent her Mencius.

Some time ago received a (second) letter from Evora [Arca] de Sardiña, wife of one of the men who participated in (led) the Cuban landing. Friend of Manuel Artime, whose *novia* [girlfriend] also wrote me. De Sardiña, after twelve days in the marshes eating lizards and crabs, was caught and put in a truck that was practically useless with twenty-one other men. Seventeen were dead when they reached Havana. He survived. Is in prison in good spirits. Tragedy of the Castro revolution, which still thinks itself something new, and is being completely absorbed by the Communists.

There has to be a politics without opportunism, to escape fatal entanglements: is such a thing possible? Politicians sell their soul for the next immediate gain, and the result is hell for everybody.

Where is Lax? Athos? Cards came from Vienna and Ravenna.

[12] Statue of Our Lady of Solitude.

———

Last night. Talking to Fr. Cuthbert (Rietdorf) in direction. He was going on about Parish life at home, and the things that excite the people there and I thought how infinitely alien and strange it all sounded. In reality it is a world about which I know nothing and in which, to tell the truth, I find it hard to see anything very significant. And that is (part of) the trouble!!

June 16, 1961

St. Lutgarde today. The High Mass was fine. I thought of all the Béguines . . .

Yesterday all day that small gardenia was a great consolation. Since it rained I stayed in and wrote the review of the "Two Chinese Classics" sent by Paul Sih (*Tao Te Ching* and *Hsiao Ching*).

In the evening Rev. Father gave me the medal I was awarded by Columbia – a huge golden penny with the head only of Britannia (Columbia of course!) and around her "*In lumine tuo videbimus lumen* [In your light we will see the light]." Grayson Kirk had a cordial little statement. I was glad, and wrote to thank him this morning.

Shortness of breath, and palpitations of the heart enough to be noticed, quite prolonged. Not that I care. In any event it could be something merely psychological! But I stayed long looking at a goldfinch and walked slowly up through the woods, gazing at the tall straight oaks that are before you reach the stile. Everything is beautiful and I am grateful for all of it. And maybe now I begin to be old, and walk slowly, like Victor Hammer.

When the Dalai Lama was young, still a boy, he was lonely in the Potala and would walk on the roof looking through field glasses down upon the houses of his subjects to see if they were having parties and to watch their enjoyment. But they in turn would hide themselves so as not to sadden him still more.

Sweet afternoon! Cool breezes and a clear sky! This day will not come again.

The bulls lie under the tree in the corner of their field.

Quiet afternoon! The blue hills, the day lilies in the wind. This day will not come again.

June 20, 1961

Bruno [Scott] James sent a copy of a review of *Disputed Questions* he did for the *Tablet*. Partly very favorable and in part reproves me for being bitter and critical, trying to sound like a prophet in the lands of Sinai. I think he certainly exaggerates and in any case he referred to the Pasternak article. There is no doubt that the problems of our time call for some strong protests and declarations.

However, it is really less sensitivity reaching to the element of harshness, of impatience and violence that are in me. My reprisals, my resentments. Really he is right. I have got to stop making negative statements dictated by these sick drives. If I can. At least I must try more than I have. It has spoiled all my work from the beginning, a basic defect, deep in my character. Such a defect one must fight, especially in a monastery, and I have tended not to, but rather justified myself about it.

No need to overemphasize the importance of spiritual direction but one thing I have certainly lacked is a director.

Fr. John [of the Cross] is capable but says nothing.

June 21, 1961

Summer solstice. Rain and cool.

On Monday there were three Baptists who came out from the Seminary with Fr. John Loftus. Spent the afternoon at the hermitage. We talked of the Church. There were two Methodists Sunday evening with them, ministers in Louisville, but these had to leave.

These three are getting to be good friends now: Glenn Hinson, Dale Moody and Les Garrett. Great simplicity and goodness: we get along very well together and the hermitage is a fine place for free and uninhibited discussion.

For instance, the difficulties of the Southern Baptist minister who might want to support integration, and his conflict with his congregation and its prejudices. They spoke of the meetings of the Negroes in Louisville and the wonderful Christian atmosphere there. It sounds very moving. Here is one of the few indications of a deep and genuine Christianity in this country. More and more I see the validity of Protestantism and its spirit: though the weaknesses are also enormous, much greater than ours, in a way.

This is not "official dialogue" and that is a blessing. It is purely and simply a Christian contact of persons who are "in Christ" according to His mercy and the sincere good will of each. But one is certainly aware of the reality and life of *the Church* in a contact like this – much more so than in formalized and stereotyped gatherings for the celebration of clichés. I mean that in these conversations I have a fuller awareness and certainty of *fulfilling my function in the Church* than I have, for example, when I sit in the monastic refectory and listen to tirades from Catholic papers against Castro. (N.B. of course the refectory is a good and holy place, and a centre of my monastic community life. I am referring to the low level of the mental nourishment that is shared there.)

Romain Rolland's *Inde* is detailed and interesting – besides being very important – in the objectivity with which he treats Tagore. The conflict in Tagore between the poet and the prophet. He is too seldom able to rise to the "prophetic" (or shall we simply say political) level. Analysis of his struggles over Fascism – how easily he was duped and used and how much trouble his friends had to go to [to] wake him up. We are travelling toward an age in which consciences are no longer troubled over such things!

> *Que penser d'une époque où les fêtes du centenaire de St-François d'Assise sont patronées par un Mussolini! Et l'Église Romaine, bien loin de protester, y trouve son profit!* [What can be thought of an age when festivals celebrating the anniversary of St. Francis of Assisi are presided over by a Mussolini! And the Roman Church, instead of mounting a protest, profits from the occasion!]
>
> Inde, *p. 167*

Same page. That the basic conflict is between Conscience = Christ in us, and the state.

June 22, 1961

Two great men who impress themselves more and more upon my heart, whom I revere deeply, though formerly I ignored them or could not understand them. They are Newman and Fénelon.

Descriptions of Fénelon in exile at Cambrai. No doubt some exaggerations (as those of Pater).

What moves me is their greatness, the polish of "finished" men who because they are perfect beyond the ordinary seem to have reached a *stasis*. They are no longer ahead of their time, or of it, or behind it. They are above it, and seem therefore old, or of the past. Yet they survive indefinitely. Newman is always young and Faber, on the other hand . . . compared with the disgraced Newman and his fineness there; coarseness in the popular and effective Faber.

I think Fénelon and Newman look alike, even. And they both have, above all, *style*.

June 25, 1961. V Sun after Pentecost

There has hardly been a night this summer when I have slept without a blanket and the days are rarely hotter than 70 or 75, perhaps 80. But it continues to be a very cool summer, cooler than anyone can remember, so much so that last Sunday I thought I ought to say something to the novices about weather cycles, the jet stream, etc., on all of which I am no authority.

Instead of the usual accidents, overturned trucks, burned convents, and crashed planes which adorn the cloister notice board, we have this week the mummified bodies of Lenin and Stalin, doubtless because Rev. Father is exercised about the book he has chosen for the refectory – still Schwartz on Communism.

Today in Chapter it was made clear to me that Communism was purely and simply diabolical, and that its chief, if only purpose is the destruction of the Church.

Once again this brings up a serious problem of conscience, and a difficult one to disentangle. Mostly because so much is *implied*.

The situation as I see it is this.

1. We are involved in a cold war, which is a war to the death. Between capitalism and communism.

2. Most Catholics, obligingly for the communists, do exactly what the communists expect and desire them to do: line up with Capitalism.

3. Hence it is easy to equate the one with the other, and *de facto* the two are now inextricably intertwined. A war to the death against capitalism is also *ipso facto* a war against religion and vice versa.

4. It happens that the communists are *winning* the cold war. It is not to their interest then to have a costly and disastrous hot war on a large scale.

5. On the other hand, when America really gets hard pressed and this will be soon, the reaction will be a resort to hot war, probably nuclear war.

6. This hot war may doubtless be justified by some as a crusade against atheism and the devil. It will be a "holy war."

7. But such a war has *no justification*. It *cannot* be a holy war, it cannot be even ethical in any sense of the word. Such a war of aggression can only

go down in history as a crime. *Non sunt facienda mala ut eveniant bona.*
[Evil is not to be done so that good can come of it.]
8. How great are the *mala,* how uncertain the *bona!* We assume that we
have freedom and anticipation. But what is our freedom? This requires a
detailed study. It still has its advantages, but it is full of illusion and corruption. Freedom for TV, for the pulp press, for advertising, to ruin the
souls of men indiscriminately. Cultural prostitution . . .

June 26, 1961
The above notes on war are not finished. Indeed hardly begun.

Excerpts of a letter from Dom Jacques Winandy to Fr. S.
1. *"Vous ne trouverez ni chez les chartreux ni chez les camaldoles ce que vous
cherchez. Ces religieux disent volontiers que leurs saints fondateurs ont dû fon-
dre dans une heureuse harmonie les avantages de la vie solitaire et ceux de la vie
commune. Sauf le respect que je leur donne et qui est grand, je suis forcé à croire
qu'au bout d'un certain temps on doit s'apercevoir qu'ils ont aussi gardé les in-
convénients trop réels de la vie cénobitique sans réaliser ce qui fait vraiment la
vie de l'ermite. La vie solitaire ne se mène pas à plusieurs, du moins pas avec des
réunions fréquentes, ni sous un même règlement.* Elle demande une simple
adaptation aux besoins de chacun, avec un silence et une solitude aussi
rarement rompus que possible." ["You won't find what you're looking for
in the Carthusians or the Camaldolese. These monks freely say that their
holy founders had in mind a harmonious balance between the benefits of
community life and solitary life. I have a great respect for them, but I do
believe that, in the last analysis, one could say that they have retained
many of the all-too-real inconveniences of the common life without really bringing about the true solitary life. The solitary life is not led in
groups, at least not found with frequent (community) meetings, or under
the same rule. *It requires a simple adaptation to the needs of each one, with a
silence and a solitude that are interrupted as little as possible."*]
2. Ways: a) living with permission in dependence on one's own
monastery. b) Secularization living as a forester or in a small parish
(France). c) Exclaustration *ad nutum sanctae sedis* [according to the Holy
See's good pleasure], which does not separate from Order but which presupposes cooperation of Superiors.
The only one of these left for me is (a). How possibly? Dom L. suggested "educating your Superiors"!

June 27, 1961

Realization that I need to turn a corner, to slough off a skin.

Need for moral effort, in the midst of *engourdissement* [growing dull and boring] and confusion. There is probably something sick about the mental numbness and anguish.

It is hard to see exactly what is to be left, to be thrown overboard.

But once again, at the risk of getting involved in hopeless confusions, I try to face the incomprehensible problem (for me) of writing. Incomprehensible because I am too involved and committed. That is the bad thing. It is so true that I have to continue being a writer that I do not know where to begin to think about not being one. Where to make the divisions. I feel it is useless even to make them, though I know what they are in my own mind. Certainly I can write something, and write, if possible, creatively. But not to *preach*, not to dogmatize, not to be a pseudo-prophet, not to declare my opinions. And yet it is essential to take a moral stand on some points – like atomic war. Am I so far gone that I can't do this without putting a brazier on my head and running about like Solomon Eagle in the London fire?

There has got to be something, at a time like this, for which I am willing to be shot – and probably for which I actually do get shot. This must, no doubt, be something that involves loyalty to *persons* even more than to principles. I think here is a concrete truth I can hang on to – if I remember it. If I get shot for it without remembering what it could have been there is no harm done.

A statement of Brendan Behan – it reached me in a roundabout way through the *Revista de la Universidad* [*University Review*] (Mexico). It is summed up in "Let the whole world go to the devil." This is a bit naive and certainly not in the face of it Christian, yet there was, it seemed to me, a great deal to respect in this declaration. Very genuine *contemptus mundi* [rejection of the world] – a refusal to take *any* respectable formalities into account. A point-blank refusal to take them seriously.

Marta Elena R. – the *novia* of Artime who is in jail in Cuba: what she needs is perhaps not to go and argue with radicals in Brazil, but a little *contemptus mundi* herself. Maybe she is clinging to a niche on the cliff where the rockslide just happened.

———

Possibly what is required of some of us, and chiefly of *me*, is a solitary and personal response in the form of *non-acquiescence*, but quiet, definite and pure. I am not capable of this purity because I am frankly and simply clinging to life, to my physical life of course and to my life as a writer and a personage. To save myself I have got to lose at least this attachment.

June 28, 1961

Last evening Tashi Tshering, a Tibetan, came here. He left this morning, going to the state of Washington. One brother of the Dalai Lama is in Seattle, and one is in New York. Lobesauh Sauter is I believe a student at NYU.

Tshering told me his life story – how he was brought to Lhasa by the government with other boys to learn to dance. How he hated it and tried to run away. How he made some money in business and escaped to India on a pilgrimage after the Reds came. His obsession with education (he has had a year on a scholarship at Williams College and is going now to the U. of Washington).

He spoke of the monks of Tibet, good and bad, and of the monasteries. Of the hermits, who renounced all and are "the best." Of the philosophy students. Of the Mongolian monk now in New Jersey. Of those who may come from India.

The Dalai Lama is very intelligent and enlightened and is working for a complete religious reform and renewal. A nucleus of 1,500 of the best monks are gathered around him in India. 60,000 Tibetan refugees, mostly in India.

There is a possibility that the Dalai Lama might send one or two of his monks here to learn about Christianity and Christian monasticism.

June 29, 1961

By the end of the long night office of Sts. Peter and Paul I was utterly exasperated. Not that there is necessarily anything wrong with the office (which has never interested me, in contrast to St. John Baptist and especially the Visitation which I love). But many things have come to a head. So many things cling to me like burrs, "alien forms," excrescences, things in no way proper to me, things that have nothing to do with my spiritual life, bloodsuckers and barnacles. In the end I become aware that I am covered with them and my whole being revolts not against them but against everything, in exasperation and near despair.

For when I am not fully free, everything weighs on me.

Dom Leclercq's advice to accept and like all this is very far from the truth. That may be his vocation but it is not mine. This explains my uneasiness with him – his eagerness to be interested and busy with a million things and people, his careful construction of a better monastic mentality, his erudition . . . He is simple and kindly and a great man but that is all utterly alien to me. I have a feeling that, when there comes a slight lull in his million pursuits, he is bored and restless. And I am only fully at peace, on the contrary, when everything stops, or drops off my shoulders, and I am busy only with pure nothing.

Don Giovanni Rossi – head of Pro Civitate Christiana – writes a pleasant breezy note asking for an article on the holiness of the church just like that! Great God, what have I done to make everyone believe I secrete articles like perspiration! This is clearly not his fault, and clearly *mine*. It has really got to stop. I shall politely decline, and I guess I should have declined the encyclopedia articles too.

New Cath. Encycl. has repeated its request for one article. I am convinced they do it very unwillingly, merely to get my name on their list. I refused before a ludicrous request to do 300 words on Dom Edmond Obrecht (!!) and now they have asked for 5,000 on spiritual direction and I feel utterly foul for having accepted.

This is the kind of quandary I am in.

My whole position as a Catholic writer is to me extremely oppressive. I repeat it is all my own fault. But the time has come to draw the line somewhere. I guess I have to do something for the Poor Clares of Toulouse – unless Fr. Abbot is convinced I should refuse them also. Preface to some life of St. Clare. What nonsense!

It all cleared up after High Mass when I saw my only solution is to do what I have always wanted to do, always known I should do, always been called to do: follow the way of emptiness and nothingness, read more of the "nothing" books than those of the others, forget my preoccupations with ten thousand absurdities, to know without wanting to be an authority, or else I will forever be a lackey of pious journalists and editors; the right-thinking rabbit who gives birth to litters of editorials every morning before breakfast.

July 3, 1961

Hot yesterday, rain in the night, a brilliant hot day.

Blasting in the creek bed in the mill bottom. Work slowly moving to the south wing of the building. Work creeping very slowly toward some kind of completion in the new dormitories.

Wm. Clancy, formerly of *Commonweal*, was here Saturday with a bad cold. He is to be one of the first members of the new Pittsburgh Oratory, and Fr. Reinhold also, he says. Also James Kirtzeck.

Two Anglican youths, one a postulant for St. Gregory's, are to come up to the hermitage this afternoon.

All the articles read in the refectory about Cuba, giving us the impression we understand what is going on. At least we are definitely "concerned." I think this is going to do something to change the attitude of the U.S., maybe towards an ultimate totalitarianism of our own. There is a general atmosphere of anger, confusion, frustration and humiliation everywhere, even though a lot of people apparently "don't care" what is happening. This can get to be a rather bad atmosphere – generating hatred, intolerance, fascism.

There is a general inability to face the fact that Cuba and Latin America generally are likely to be very happy with the new trend – because it gives people a sense that they are at best doing something and getting somewhere.

We are unable to conceive the basic truth that men feel better when they are making sacrifices for a cause, even though the cause and the sacrifices have to some extent been forced on them.

The "world" with its funny pants, of which I do not know the name, its sandals and sunglasses, its fat arses, its raped [?] bellies, its nerves (my nerves too, my belly too), its hair, its teeth. And its talk. I do not have words for the world. I do not understand my fear of it, which includes fascination and a sick feeling in the pit of the stomach, since I am also part of it. The smell of its lotions is already in our front wing and in our offices and the little printed pieces of paper we send out are responses to its sly intimations of complicity. I don't care what Bruno James says, I must write about this, not perhaps with the overtones of a preacher or of a prophet. Write about the sick feeling I get, about the plague, the suntanned death. First I must collect all the words I do not know: the names of the plastics, the drugs, the oils, the lubricants, that make it smell so and move so. I do feel, I do feel like a child that lives in a whorehouse, or right next door to one, and guesses what goes on, *feels* what goes on as if the whole place were impregnated with a sly fun for which you pay. Sex is after all what has gone wrong perhaps in everything; but that too is the temptation – that I too might indulge in my own way by raising a chorus of exacerbated protest . . .

July 4, 1961

I am becoming entranced with Eckhart: I have been won by the brevity, the incisiveness of his sermons, his way of piercing straight to the heart of the inner life, the awakened spark, the creative and redeeming word, God born in us. He is a great man who was pulled down by little men who thought they could destroy him. Who thought they could take him to Avignon and have him ruined and indeed he was ruined in 28 propositions which did not altogether resemble his joy and his energy and his freedom, but which could be brought to coincide with words he had uttered.

The two Protestants, Sterling Rayburn and Carl Cundliffe. Both from the university at Sewanee, but the former going to an Anglican seminary near Milwaukee (Nashoda House) to prepare for St. Gregory's and the latter to the Sorbonne to study political science. I like them both. They are intelligent and have a good background and a good future, particularly Carl I think. Sterling – seems to be mostly preoccupied, at least on the surface, with the absolute *identity* between the Anglo-Catholic liturgy and ours. He showed me Missal and Ordo and indeed they have even adopted *all* the latest changes made by the Congregation of Rites with a too exemplary duality.

He showed me a photograph of a Dom at St. Gregory's standing at the altar, and the only thing Anglican, this giveaway, was the old *sarum antependium* [cloth in front of the altar] and the twelve candles.

As for Carl Cundliffe, it gradually came out that he had lived in Japan, the Near East, and had been to school in Switzerland. He spoke of the monastery on the Mountain of the Temptation, and I gave him the names of monasteries to see in France, particularly St. Jean de Bourices.

It was pleasant to have someone sit in the front room and quote Montesquieu.

I hear Fr. Abbot announced that Hemingway had died.

We must adjust our attitude. We are living in a world that used to be Christian – and Hindu, Moslem, Buddhist. In the west we are in the post-Christian age – and all over the world it will soon be the same. The religions will be for the minority. The world as a whole is going to be not pagan but irreligious.

Hence we are already living, and will live more and more, in a world that we cannot look upon precisely as "ours" in any external and obvious sense. Certainly we shall "inherit the earth," but not to build an earthly kingdom in it, I am bold to think! Nor to have a genuinely Christian society in it, nor to have, in any manifest way, an *accepted place* in it. We will be lucky to submit at all. We will certainly survive, but as genuine aliens and exiles. And perhaps this is as it should be. Yet we should not for all that become inert and inactive. But our activity must take into account this new dimension of a humility that has at last come to check our illusion of a politically successful Christendom. This sounds like defeatism and I am ready to revise and qualify it. But I confess it looks to me like the sober truth. It does not make one any less a Christian. On the contrary, it confirms me in my dependence on the Gospel message and in my dedication to Christ!

July 7, 1961

What I wrote above, though not quite what I wanted, I still stick to in principle in spite of what K[arl] Rahner says in *The Prospect for Christianity*. He holds it not only unlikely but impossible for the world as a whole to become irreligious, and states that since "Christianity has no serious rival," it is in effect impossible for the world to cease to be Christian. He assumes that it has been Christian at one time or other, and still is so. Of course he has to preserve a semblance of sanity by admitting we are going through a crisis, but it is just an "adolescent crisis" like that of a boy with a new bicycle who "rides his bicycle rather than going to church on Sunday."

Such statements annoy and confound me. I have hitherto respected the wisdom of people like Rahner. I certainly do not deny that it is a matter of faith that the church will not be destroyed by her enemies – but it is quite another thing to assert that the world will always be "Christian." He puts it in another way – the church "will remain as a stumbling block." Perhaps.

But I wonder if he is not just making comforting noises in the dark, and I wonder if the noises have much meaning.

I resent the fact that I am apparently required, by this argument, to believe not only in the indestructibility of the mystical Body, but also in the indestructibility of the *Civitas Christiana* [Christian city]. Maybe that is really an important issue I have not yet faced. As a matter of fact I am not and never have been too sanguine about the *Civitas Christiana* as I see it. Does any such entity really exist? Has it ever really existed? What is it – the Spain of Philip II (and his Americas)? The France of Richelieu? or the France of de Gaulle? (I give him credit for being one of the most competent of today's Presidents.) Even the France of St. Louis – is this enough? I admit I do not fully know the problem and the questions at issue; but speaking as one less wise, I find it hard to take seriously even the best of realizations of the *Civitas Christiana* even in the "ages of faith," and even the least of our dreams for one now. Too easily one starts with a beautiful ideal and ends up with a prissy, rigid, unjust and paternalistic dictatorship like that of Franco in Spain. Show me, please, the *Civitas Christiana*, which is at once perfect, indestructible and a real political entity. Is this not a contradiction in terms?

July 8, 1961

Building committee. I sit in silence in the meetings, with nothing more to say.

The new dormitories: dead white walls – dead white ceiling – no form of blinds or shutters in the windows (and none provided for) – and from July 23rd on we go on Eastern Standard Time. Hence the community will be going to bed at 6 p.m. by the sun, with at least two hours of daylight remaining in this season. And everything to make the dormitory as bright as possible.

It occurred to me why our buildings look the way they do. Bro. Clement is a cattle man pure and simple and everything he builds ends up looking like a dairy barn. He plans accommodations not for people but for cows!

We *could* of course continue to go to bed by the sun, and ignore the fiction that has been adopted by the people around us. But this would mean *on paper* that we went to bed at 8 and rose at 3. This the abbot cannot accept. Above all, even if the world comes to an end, the postulants' guide has to be able to declare that we "get up at two in the morning." (*Not* that we get 7 hours sleep.)

In effect we are alienated from true natural surroundings and completely dependent on the reaction procured by our publicity. We are living according to an image of ourselves we have created for our "public."

Two letters from Lawrence Ferlinghetti. He is very anxious to have "Original Child Bomb" in a new *Journal for the Protection of All Beings*. Bob Lax has already sent layouts done by Antonucci which are very handsome. So also, and especially, the pictures by Antonucci.

An understanding of why I am so taken with Romain Rolland, why he speaks to me with such warmth of conviction: a chance phrase. "*Tout m'est fermé en France; et je n'ai pas où aller* [All is closed to me in France, and I have nowhere to go]" (*Inde*, p. 282). That is the condition for penetrating *everywhere* – but to a few.

July 9, 1961

Dawn at the hermitage.

I slept until 3 and came up here to say the office – the long way round by the road. Very thin end of a moon in the morning sky. Crows bothering an owl.

Once again – the office is entirely different in its proper (natural) setting, out from under the fluorescent lights. There Lauds is torpor and vacuum. Here it is in harmony with all the singing birds under the bright sky. Everything you have on your lips in praising God is there before you – hills, dew, light, birds, growing things . . . Nothing in the liturgy of light is lost.

I saw in the middle of the Benedicite the great presence of the sun that had just risen behind the cedars (same time and place as Trinity Sunday). And now under the pines the sun has made a great golden basilica of fire and water.

Perspective: crows making a racket in the east, dogs making a racket in the south, and yet over all the majestic peace of Sunday. Is that, after all, the true picture of our world?

Deus cuius Providentia in sui dispositione non fallitur . . . [O God, whose Providence never fails to accomplish its ends . . .] This is the great truth. Christ has indeed conquered and the world does indeed belong to Him alone. This cannot help but be reflected in society. Society cannot be left entirely to the forces of evil. But that does not mean of course that we must naively expect the triumph of the *civitas christiana* as we imagine and plan it, still less that we must believe in some kind of clerical fascism.

Points from Gandhi on non-cooperation (R. Rolland, *Inde*, p. 327)

1. To refuse military service when the time has come for it is to act *after* the time to combat. The evil has run out. Mil[itary] service is only a symptom of a deeper evil. All who support the state in other ways besides this are equally guilty. (I mean support a state organizing for war.)

2. *All* cooperation must be withdrawn from a state organizing for war. The precise way of going about it varies. Means refusal of privileges and advantages as well as of service.

July 11, 1961

Essential soundness of the principles in *Divini Redemptoris* – Pius XI's Encyclical against atheistic communism. It is an old one, 1937, but it has lost none of its value today. On the contrary.

In this, besides everything else, he says clearly:

"Every other enterprise, however attractive and helpful, must yield before the vital need of protecting the very foundation of faith and *of Christian civilization.*"

This assumes – and I think not incorrectly – that Xtian civilization has not yet been completely undermined.

But yet where we see the means he suggests, and see how they have been neglected . . . It is certain that Christian civilization and the capitalist economy are by no means the same thing, and the confusion of the two is what has done more than anything else to promote communism and corrupt Christian civilization.

He later speaks of the mission confided to the Church of Christ of "constructing a Christian society" and the duty of the state to help the Church in this. But this is not necessarily the *American* outlook on the question! Perhaps it should be – but in fact it is not.

Here of course he is not considering whether the ideal of Christian civilization has in any given case been realized. But certainly I admit that to abandon this ideal is supremely dangerous, no matter how critical one may be of existing social systems.

Hence it is quite definite now, in my mind, that clinging to the faith of Christ is in practice without too much meaning unless one also clings to the ideal of a Christian civilization. This corrects what I wrote the other day (July 7).

July 12, 1961

Now I see one of the roots of the temptation to false optimism.

Christianity, face to face with Marxism, confronts the accusation that religion divides and alienates man, makes him miserable because "lost" and divided.

Hence at all costs angst and dark night must be done away with. We are happy, happy, happy! *Epanouissement!* [Fulfillment!]

But the misery of our alienation is not due to religion, it is due to technology and to the collapse of capitalist society . . .

July 18, 1961

I did not have time to finish the above. No matter, I have thought and spoken of it, or of things close to it, with Père Daniélou whom, as theologian, I consider my director and who was here over the weekend.

I had planned to go over the whole subject of the *civitas Christiana* but did not formally and expressly do so. But much was said that really covered that subject.

1. The obligation to maintain a will for survival in a social sense. We discussed this and the ambiguities of capitalism. Careful to distinguish western civilization, Xtian culture, Catholic society, the Church. Daniélou's book good on this. I will finish it and make more notes.

2. He is preoccupied by the pessimism and defeatism of the French intellectual, esp. the Xtian intellectual. Laments the poverty and the practical collapse of French Catholic intellectual life at least as regards literature, social thought, etc. He wants to start a literary magazine. Liked my "Hagia Sophia" and the "Elegy for Hemingway" but not the Auschwitz poem.

3. He is very concerned with the condition of America, the ignorance and confusion of the country in the presence of the highly organized and concentrated advance of communism.

4. I am in agreement with his idea of optimism. He finds in T. de Chardin one of the most salutary influences in this respect. I should have spoken of [Emmanuel] Mounier, but the occasion slipped by. (He had only a shrug for *Esprit*.)

5. From the point of view of direction the most important was his full encouragement to go on in the study and meditation of oriental wisdoms. Here the true optimism came clear. The *contempt* of the cynic, the Zen master and the Desert Father for the politician. Not being in servile

submission to those who wield social power. Having full freedom to speak out and declare the truth in defiance of all, e.g. Léon Bloy.

The Paradisiacal life. These are not like the trees of Paradise, they *are* the trees of Paradise.

But not narcissistic regression to the freshness of childhood. On the contrary a new birth, the divine birth in us, the new life.

6. Recommended [Placide] Temples on Bantu philosophy, new novel of J[ulien] Green (we wrote Green a card in the car returning from Loretto), Corbin and the gnostics. Gnostics angry at Yaweh who deceived them.

7. Excellent talk at Loretto on missionary problem, true ecumenism. He says the great question today is really the question of Xtian humanism and I agree.

July 21, 1961

I agree with these propositions in C[hristopher] Dawson's excellent book, *The Historic Reality of Christian Culture* [New York, 1960].

"Christians stand to gain more in the long run by accepting their minority position and looking for quality rather than quantity." *p. 89*

Importance of religious education, especially Christian university education.

For –

a) Recovery of the rich Christian cultural inheritance (I would add all religious wisdom).

b) Communication of this to a sub-religious or neo-pagan world.

That these sub-rational and rational (cultural) levels of social life need to be coordinated and brought to a force in spiritual experience which transcends them both and is lacking in secularist culture (see esp. pp. 92–93).

Recovery of spiritual vision is the real task of Xtian education.

July 23, 1961. 9th Sunday after Pentecost

Jerusalem, and Christ's tears. The Holy City. Thou hast not known the time of thy visitation.

I will stop making any kind of effort to justify myself to anybody. To prepare a place for myself anywhere, among any group. It is this that I have to face. This and the necessity to give up any activity that leaves the slightest (intended) impression upon the surface of the world. This and the necessity to renounce all surreptitious reaching for human immortality – that is, for being remembered.

Peace is impossible until I fully and totally realize, and embrace the realization, that I am already forgotten. Not that I can help wanting to be remembered. But daily I am confronted with the price that would have to be paid!! I shrink from it, yet want to pay it. And this is what must not be done. Render unto God the things that are God's.

Fr. Paul [Bourne] was here from Georgia. I know what I say "No" to most in the Order. He spoke of this problem. I am lucky to be more or less out of it here, or only on the fringe of it.

Fine letters from Etta Gullick, wife of the Senior Tutor at St. Edmund's Hall, Oxford. I say I will not make friends and yet I do, I have friends, and it is true that on them I depend for support and recognition. She is becoming one of them. Like John Wu and J. Laughlin (one of the most solid) and of course Rice, Lax, Ad [Reinhardt]. And Mark V. Doren. Etta Gullick is the one who is editing Benet of Canfield. Works of Eckhart. And of C. F. Kelley who used to be Dom Placid at Downside.

A letter from Pasternak's sister at Oxford. Same warmth as B.P.

July 24, 1961
Another ranting liturgical tape. The impression of ranting is of course the result of circumstances – the contrast between monastic refectory in which it is heard and the hall in which it was delivered – the mass meeting. Actually this is sober and solid, by B. P. Waters, except for a completely nonsensical theory that racial injustice (ag[ain]st negroes) is a manifestation of *individualism!* Individualism is a scapegoat for everything with these people. I suppose Nazism was the result of *individualism*. I am sure they have maintained this somewhere. On the contrary!

"Race pride is revealed today as man's primary *collective* [double underlined] sin." – *R. Niebuhr*

July 26, 1961. F. of St. Anne
Fr. Ray Ryland, an Anglican minister from Oklahoma City, was here Monday and over Monday and Tuesday Zalmon Schacter, Rabbi and friend of Heschel. Great warmth and openness. Spoke of lots of things, of Rabbi Nachman especially. Is not too sold on Buber. He said that in Hasidism

when one seeks direction, one hands in a card with one's name and the _mother's name_, then a manifestation of conscience or a statement of a difficulty. The purpose of the direction is to help one find one's special path or task. Why the mother's name? In confronting the law one comes forward with the Father's name. In Hasidism it is the Name of the Mother that is relevant, for the mother gives the soul its character. And the Father is the source of the body.

The gardenias, of which there have been plenty, are running out. But now one stands before the face of this Angel on the cover of the new Rublev book which came today from Bob Rambusch.

One of the fairest gardenias was a large one which I picked for Our Lady on her feast of Mt. Carmel, and it had raindrops on it which stayed most of the morning.

Moved deeply and to tears by Pierre van der Meer de Walcheren's book _Rencontres_, which he kindly sent, saying rightly in the dedication that we are "close" – and it is certainly true, for I am somehow of the family of Bloy. The section on Bloy is fine and even more moving is the one on Raïssa Maritain.

Proofs of _Hagia Sophia_ came today from Victor.
And yesterday the superb lovely book on Eckhart.
Wrote to Arthur Hays Sulzberger, in reply to his letter. Suggested articles on Marx in _Times_ Sunday Magazine and using Marx against the Marxists. One of the most powerful intellectual forces today is Marxist revisionism.

"I will stop making any kind of effort to justify myself to anybody . . ."
To exist in society is to exist in contradiction. And this is not because of Marx's alienation but because it is the nature of society.
Mater et Magister is being read in the refectory and is one of the greatest Encyclicals of the modern papacy from the point of view of Christian humanism.

July 27, 1961
Lovely poem on Chagall by Raïssa Maritain in P. Van der Meer's _Rencontres_. Like to translate it in _Jubilee_ with a note on her and perhaps some Chagall picture.

In any case the woodshed is again full of French angels the way it was the summer I read Julien Green's *Journals*. And coming back again, by the willow (going with the empty shadow of the path, after bright sun), all the angels of Montauban and of Chartres also (poor Chartres, where someone set off a bomb in the door of the Cathedral!).

July 28, 1961

Looked over notes on Sophocles' *Antigone*.

Must read it again and again. How great are the Greeks, how much we owe them, how foolish to set them aside in silly contrasts with the Bible. Sophocles throws light on his contemporaries Isaiah and Jeremiah.

Especially the problem of true obedience – to God, and false obedience – to tyrants who confound the upper and the nether world, try to hold them apart by force of will, and declare heaven to be hell, and hell heaven. They demand obedience as justification of their pride and violence and by their logic disobedience is the greatest sin.

July 31, 1961

Very hot.

During night office and morning meditation, seeing that my whole life is a struggle to seek the truth (at least I want it to be so) and that the truth is found in the reality of my own life as it is given to me, and that it is found by complete consent and acceptance. Not at all by defeat; by mere passive resignation, by mere inert acceptance of evil and falsity (which are nevertheless unavoidable) but by "creative" consent, in my deepest self to the will of God which is expressed in my own self and my own life. And indeed there is a sense in which my own deepest self is in God and even expresses Him, as "word." (Such is the deep meaning of our Sonship.)

Gradually I will come more and more to transcend the limitations of the world and of the society to which I belong – while fully accepting my own little moment in history such as it is.

I have a great love and compassion for China, for the people of Red China with their fabulous sacrifices and sufferings, in order to industrialize their country. The system is terrible, but the work has to be done, and there is no doubt that capitalism was helpless to do it. I hope they will become a great nation and recover the wisdom of their ancient traditions in a new and living context.

To be detached from all systems, and without rancor towards them, but with insight and compassion. To be truly "Catholic" is to be able to enter into everybody's problem and joys and be all things to all men.

August 3, 1961

Impressive record by Fr. Basil Kazan, orthodox priest in Louisville, in Arabic – of Joseph of Arimathea pleading for the Body of "this stranger – who has always been a stranger and has had nowhere to lay His Head – who will become the guest of death – ." The sin of rejecting God as a stranger sins against hospitality. L. Massignon would like and understand this. Fr. Kazan came out with Fr. J. Raza, a dynamic Lebanese uniate priest with a wonderfully practical sense of Liturgy, who had everyone participating gladly (I think) in his Byzantine (St. Chrysostom) liturgy today. I was the one to come out and read the (Thursday) Epistle and was deeply moved in the midst of it when I realized I was announcing that *all power and authority were to be overthrown* by the Risen Christ. We do not know what we are reading or hearing.

Element of spontaneity in the Eastern Rite.

Curious that after I had tried in vain to find someone at the church of St. Michael last year, now the priest should come by surprise himself. I think he is to be Bishop in Mexico. His stay in L'ville is provisional. Ancient Byzantine chants tremendous. First direct contact with the *Great Church of Antioch*, and its own superb character, warmth and seriousness. Its richness and fluency and subtlety. It means far more to me than Constantinople. When will I meet Alexandria and hear its voice?

Brilliant warm afternoon with a cool breeze. Refuge in hermitage from much talking. The Eckhart book is difficult. Quails whistle in the hot field.

Aug. 6, 1961. F. of Transfiguration and Day of Recollection

I had to give the Conference in chapter – on the Good Samaritan, and the "*chesed*" [loving faithfulness] of God. Fr. Bartholomew from O[ur] L[ady of the] Genesee here, on his way back from Rome, fat enough to be a little Italian cardinal and Fr. Tarcisius from the Georgia monastery here studying the organ – he was in the novitiate with me twenty years ago.

Thought much today of the tone and value of my own interior world, which is after all important, at least relatively. And culture, of a sort, has given it much of its tone. Christian and European culture, Christian spirituality, monastic life, occidental mysticism, plus a certain openness to other cultures and spiritualities, especially I think the Chinese. All this is not only relevant to my life and salvation but has crucial significance in my whole vocation.

That I have known the hill town of Cordes; that I have walked from Caylus to Puylagarde and know Caussade and Cahors and the church of Saint Jacques by the bridge in Montauban. That I have stood in the ruined castles of Penne and Najac and waited under the high bluff of Beziers among the wine barrels – or passed by the walls of Carcassonne.

That the quarterboys of Rye never cease to ring in my ears and that I know the silence of the broad marsh between Rye and Winchelsea, and listen to it forever . . . or the fens at Ely, or the backs behind Clare and Kings and Trinity . . . or the bell in the cloister tower of St. John's as heard by night in Bridge Street, Cambridge.

The tower of Oakham Church, and the vale.

The Surrey Downs, and the ruins of Waverly in the meadow on a September evening.

The high roofs of Strasbourg, Tauler's city, and streets known to Meister Eckhart.

Today I read the wonderful sermon on the divine truth in which Eckhart says that as a person about to be struck by a thunderbolt turns toward it, and all the leaves of a tree about to be struck turn toward it, so one in whom the divine birth is to take place turns, without realizing, completely toward it.

The village church at West Horsley and the other one at Ripley. And Newark Priory where Christopher Pierce knew all about the drains.

I must not cease to read David Knowles, but get the book back again and continue.

High Street, Guildford. And St. Albans, as I passed by in the LMS. And Limoges also. All this is important, for it has all been in some sort sacramental. And now I am in a world which is to a great extent without such *experiences* and *symbols*. Yet I have come to a place that has, or once had, something of that spiritual climate. I resent the lack of it, yet create it always for myself.

The point is: I need not be ashamed of this world because the communists want to build another. Let them build anything they can, for something has to be done. For my part, my vocation includes fidelity to all that is spiritual, and noble, and fine, and deep. This I will keep alive in myself and hand on to anyone who is capable of receiving it.

August 7, 1961

Both Newman and Fénelon loved Clement of Alexandria, which is not at all surprising. To Newman he was "like music." This may look like a cliché but it is profound. For there are people one meets – in books and in life – with whom a deep resonance is at once established.

For a long time I had no "resonance" with Newman (*cor ad cor loquitur* [heart speaks to heart]). I was suspicious of letting him enter my heart. Clement the same. Now I want all the music of Clement, and am only with difficulty restrained from taking new books on Newman from the library while I have so many other things to read and finish.

Resonances: one of the "choirs." Maritain, Van der Meer de Walcheren, Bloy, Green, Chagall, Satie – or a string sextet!

Another earlier music: Blake, Eckhart, Tauler (Maritain got in here too), Coomaraswamy . . . etc.

Music: the marvelous opening of the *Protreptikos* [of Clement of Alexandria] – the "new song" – the splendid image of the cricket flying to replace by his song the broken string in the Lyre of Eunomos at Delphi. Though he repudiates the myth he uses it splendidly. Humanity a musical instrument for God.

August 8, 1961

Dream of being lost in a great city, and walking "toward the center" without quite knowing where I was, and suddenly coming to a road's end on a height overlooking a great bay, an arm of the harbor, and seeing a whole section of the city spread out before me on hills, covered with light snow, and realizing that, though I had far to go, I knew where I was because in this city there are two arms of the sea which one always encounters, and by this one can get his orientation.

Then, in a library of this city, speaking with some strangers, I suddenly realize there is a charterhouse here and that I have promised myself to visit and speak to the Prior about "my vocation." I ask someone "where is the charterhouse" and he says "I am just going to drive that way, I go right by it and I will take you." I accept this offer realizing that it is providential.

I think frequently that I may soon die, but I don't know what kind of conviction this thought carries with it. Rather that I *may* die, and that if it is God's will I am glad. *Exite obviam ei.* [Go out to meet him.] And I realize the futility of my attachments, particularly the big one – my work as a writer. I do not feel inordinately guilty about this, but it is a nuisance and an obstacle. I feel hampered by it. Not fully free. But the love of God, I hope, will free me. And this important thing is simply turning to Him daily and often, and preferring His will and His mystery to anything that is tangibly "mine."

August 11, 1961

When I thought the gardenias were all done I found a splendid one this morning in the dark with a flashlight. It budded yesterday afternoon in the rainstorm while I was writing up mystical theology notes.

Terrence Phillips, the Canadian postulant whom they nearly sent back and who seems to me to be a very good kid, showed up this morning with an enormously swollen lip where a mosquito bit him in the dormitory.

Utter hatred of the book in the refectory which is a novel about Carmel, where all cells are austere, all nuns severe, and where sanctity consists in finding fault. The abbot loves it for the coy laughs at tripping postulants and veils falling off. This is an immoral book – except to those who can relish it with a good conscience, because for those the only immorality is sex. Here it is sado-masochism that is offered for our "enjoyment."

The other morning I translated a bit from Clement of Alex. about Zeus being dead as swan, dead as eagle, dead as δρακων [dragon, serpent].

Will send the Good Samaritan to Claude Fredericks today. What lovely things he prints at Pawlet. What perfection! And no question that it has a special grace and nobility which you can't get with a machine.

August 13, 1961

Reading Mircea Eliade.

Astonished by the extent to which I regard the monastery as secular and its activities as spiritually inefficacious, because they are "secular activities." And this because I am sensitive to the fact . . . or not fact, but possibility that the "myth" of Dom James and of a lot of the others is to me secular and cheap and it is this myth that has crept in to the sacred world of the liturgy etc. Or at least I have come to think it has. Certainly the American myth dominates monastic labor, which is seldom "sacred" (but is mechanized, to provide escape into *something else* regarded as sacred).

Really we are dominated (if not crushed) by the abbot's completely secular concept of Time (as in this business of getting on Eastern Standard Time, to be coordinated with what the seculars are doing, and hence going to bed in the afternoon instead of at night).

As soon as the choir in fact is considered more as a musical production than as anything else, it becomes secularized. This of course is never faced, because the office is claimed to be prayer in proportion as it is musically perfect.

But *Kabod* [Glory] (the glory of God) is present in liturgical worship. Worship establishes in type the "future" situation in which the *Kabod* will shine upon all men.

Eliade stresses that the "Great Time" is in the primordial past. But it is also in the eschatological future – this the mark of the Biblical Religious.

August 16, 1961

The biggest and most perfect of all the gardenias bloomed yesterday for the Assumption. I wish I could describe its shape, its freshness, as it was half open yesterday morning.

Solemn Professions. Letters from Ferlinghetti and from *Catholic Worker* (a mix-up on the Auschwitz poem). Erich Fromm has sent his new book on Marx, which is revealing. I see more and more clearly the Biblical roots of Marx, of which he himself was perhaps unaware. And not only in the messianic myth of the Proletariat either. Much more fundamentally in his view of man and work, and alienation. Fromm rightly points out the similarity of alienation and idol worship. (They are in fact two modes of the same passivity and defeat.)

It is certainly true that man is most human, and proves his humanity, by the quality of his relationship with woman. (This, in Marx, surprised me.) How much more true than I realized in the past! Here in the monastery with our chastity, we are ideally supposed to go still further, in this dimension of humanism and love. This is one of the keys to our problems: how can one go further than that to which one has not yet attained?

Not that virginity cannot be deeply and purely human. But it has to be spiritual and positive. And this spiritual character of chastity and virginity is *not* found in alienation. It is *not* found in sentimentality, in a "thought" of pure love for Jesus.

[Here Merton deletes a passage of two lines.]

Another letter from Ferlinghetti. Again about the Auschwitz poem, which he wants to print in the first issue of his "Journal" since he thinks that by the second issue we may "all be floating around full of irradiated particles."

Fr. Basil's brother – driving out of Louisville seeing a sign "Evacuation Route."

– "To where?" Nobody thought of that.

Everyone is anxious because last week the Russians *really* got a man in space – he went around the earth 17 times. And then Khrushchev started shouting and threatening to rain down H-bombs on America.

First of all, no matter how much we may be at fault ourselves, this alone is a criminal act.

All the people who are exploiting atomic weapons in any way for political ends are, to my mind, already war criminals. As if it made any difference what you called them. (The very *act* of calling someone a "war criminal" tends to involve one in the great web of lies and hatreds and illusions.)

The absurdity of American civil defense propaganda – for a shelter in the cellar – "come out in two weeks and resume the American way of life."

Inexorably life moves on towards crisis and mystery.

Everyone must struggle to adjust himself to this, to face the situation for "now is the judgement of the world." In a way, each one judges himself merely by what he does. Does, not says. Yet let us not completely dismiss words. They do have meaning. They are related to action. They spring from action and they prepare for it, they clarify it, they direct it. They are not, by themselves, enough. Yet united with action they constitute *testimony* and therefore decision, judgement.

In the first place I see no reason why I should go out of my way to try to survive a thermonuclear attack on the U.S.A. It seems to me perhaps nobler and simpler to share, with all consent and love, in what is bound to be the lot of the majority: but with an acceptance that seeks in no way to avoid this. Only one modification – if possible I would like to spend my last days alone in the hermitage. This, I admit, comes under the heading of luxury.

———

Meanwhile, until then, I need to *meditate* on what comforts us all and find some way of saying NO to the warmakers, and saying no, if possible, not merely as a feeble gesture, but with meaning and even with some effect. To say no in a way that unmasks falsehood and speaks the truth and articulates the desire of the vast majority of men in the world for peace. All those who are confused and helpless and are driven on to their death by the leaders.

It is not enough to hope that the fallout will find me "doing my duty" and conforming to one or other of the great systems.

On the contrary, the problem – or the temptation – seems to be to stand above the water level in which all minds drown. Precisely – to escape the flood of falsehood.

August 19, 1961

And yet one must not be too quickly preoccupied with professing definitively what is true and what is false. Not that true and false do not matter. But if at every instant one wants to grasp the whole and perfect truth of a situation, particularly a concrete and limited situation in history or in politics, he only deceives and blinds himself. Such judgements are only rarely and fleetingly possible and sometimes when we think we see what is most significant, it has very little meaning at all.

So it is possible that the moment of my death may turn out to be, from a human and "economic" point of view, the most meaningless of all.

Meanwhile, I do not have to stop the flow of events in order to understand them. On the contrary, I must move with them or else what I think I understand will be no more than an image in my own mind.

So, the flow of events: Terry Phillips with a wrecking bar smashing the plaster off the walls of the room in the old guest house where, twenty years ago, I first came on retreat, that moonlit night in Lent! He – our youngest postulant – was not even born then.

They are finally getting around to the ceiling of the Chapter Room – in an odd and complicated way, which I do not understand.

The library has bought a copy of the *Theologia Germanica*, which I began today. I am ending my week as hebdomadary.

Having finished the *Protreptikos* of Clement, began the *Pedagogue*. He is certainly one of the Fathers I like best, and with whom I feel the closest affinity.

August 22, 1961

Yesterday in Louisville. Sadness of George Reiter as we drove in, fatalism about "the war." This seems to be general and significant – a weakness of the whole country, a symptom that things have got beyond us. A symptom of alienation.

However, after Mass at Carmel read the paper Msgr. Horrigan had left, and found the "Berlin crisis" (another one) had begun to subside.

What absurdity! Purely symbolic actions for purely symbolic issues, and some of the symbolisms very poor.

A symbolic "task force" of 1,500 American troops covers 660 miles of road to reach Berlin, courteously assisted by Soviets.

Vice President Johnson comes to West Berlin and goes around making speeches and giving out ball-point pens.

An Englishwoman watching the thing on TV sees Johnson land in West Berlin and hitch up his pants like the Texas sheriff "in a town where there has been trouble." This was "exactly right," said the watcher.

So it is all in the head. It is all a TV show. It is all meaningless.

Meanwhile the same paper carried a report that American contracts to supply Russia with all kinds of things had rocketed up in the last weeks. The American business man may scream about war and freedom but what he really wants is a fast buck. That is what comes first.

Why shouldn't George be sad, and I with him?

Will write elsewhere about the missile technician I found in the files of the university library.

In the *Nation* – a good article on Nicaragua: a poisonous critique of Miller's *Tropic of Cancer* by [Kenneth] Rexroth (which may have some truth in it – well written, but very nasty) and a poem I liked, about George Fox. I certainly don't accept Miller as a prophet, though he has good things to say in *The Colossus of Maroussi* [Norfolk, 1941].

A character in Chicago (?) has (like a million others) built himself a fallout shelter in his cellar, and has declared that he and his family will occupy it keeping everyone else out, if necessary, with a machine gun. This I think is the final exaltation of the American way of life: individualism, comfort, security, and to hell with everybody else. If he wants to bake underground he can have it, as far as I'm concerned. I'll fry in the woods.

I finished [Christopher] Dawson's _Understanding Europe_ [New York, 1952]. It is a fine book. He is completely right about the central importance of Christian culture, the danger of the theological dualism à la Barth playing into the hands of secularism. Whether or not he came too late, who can say? In any case I have a clear obligation to participate, as long as I can, and to the extent of my abilities, in every effort to help a spiritual and cultural renewal of our time. This is the task that has been given me, and hitherto I have not been clear about it, in all its aspects and dimensions.

To emphasize, clarify the living content of spiritual traditions, especially the Xtian, but also the Oriental, by entering myself deeply into their disciplines and experience, not for myself only but for all my contemporaries who may be interested and inclined to listen. This for the restoration of man's sanity and balance, that he may return to the ways of freedom and of peace, if not in my time, at least some day soon.

August 26, 1961

Letters to Fr. S[ylvanus] from the hermits in Martinique, very touching. An American (?) and Dom Winandy. The American has finished building a hermitage for Dom W. Says he eats fruits which can be had for the picking. The poor people share vegetables with him – one does not "insult these good people by offering dirty mammon in exchange."

"If you are in a financial predicament, just come as you are with nothing in hand but Bible and breviary and count on unfailing Providence."

Evidently the American hermit is going to work and to study and Fr. S. will have his hermitage, clothes and blanket (they sleep with a blanket as the nights are cool).

Dom W. says to him:

"Prenez tous les livres dont vous jugerez avoir besoin. L'anti-intellectualisme érigé en principe absolu est une folie et n'a rien à faire avec la vraie tradition monastique. L'idéal est cependent de rapporter toutes les études à la Bible.

"Il y a trois ans que je suis ici et je suis toujours plus heureux d'y être venu. Vous ne sauriez croire combien peut être sanctifiant l'éloignement réel de son pays, de sa famille, de tout ce qu'on a connu et aimé."

["Take all the books that you think you need. Anti-intellectualism as an absolute principle is foolishness and has nothing to do with authentic monastic tradition. The goal is rather to connect all these studies with the Scriptures.

"I've been here three years and every day I'm glad that I came here. You wouldn't believe just how sanctifying it can be to distance yourself from your country, your family, from all that you have known and loved."]

J. Laughlin is here on his way back East from San Francisco. Talking about [Robert] Hutchins and [W. H. Ping] Ferry at Santa Barbara. Their concern for peace – the saber-shaking recorded speeches of B[isho]p Sheen in the guest house dining room, – and other things like that. Is it possible to found a Third Party that would be a Peace party? Would it be completely trivial? I said that at least it would be a way to help a person commit himself morally for peace. Only a gesture?

With Laughlin in the hermitage – talked of the state of the world and of the state of Henry Miller (another wife got away from him – Eve) and his running from city to city in Europe, disconcerted. And his convictions that America would invade France at the time of the Algerian Putsch. Bro. Antoninus's [William Everson's] Psalter and how he does not finish his printing jobs (which I think is significant and symptomatic and says more about the condition of the artist in religious life than his article last year did). Talked of China, and of primitive people. And he told me about all the double talk of politicians, of "new frontiers," and how he was summoned to the State Dept. in Washington for a conference on "cultural weapons." From which I conclude that this country is no wiser than I have hitherto imagined.

Finally, three wonderful chapters in the *Cloud of Unknowing* on Martha and Mary, ending with this, which is everything:

"Therefore you who set out to be a contemplative as Mary was, choose rather to be humbled by the unimaginable greatness and incomparable perfection of God than by your own wretchedness and imperfections. In other words look more to God's worthiness than to your own worthlessness. To the perfectly humble there is nothing lacking, spiritual or physical. For they have God in whom is all abundance and whoever has Him needs nothing else in this life." *(ch. 23)*

August 27, 1961

A good biography of Lincoln in the refectory. But America in those days was a different country.

Laughlin talked of the despair of Kenneth Patchen, and to some extent (the despair) of Ferlinghetti and of so many others like that. I mean of sensitive and reflective people.

Theologia Germanica on the heaven and hell we carry about within us, and how it is good to experience within one or the other of these, for there one is in God's hands. But when one has neither a heaven or hell, one is alone in indifference of the lessons of the II Nocturn today (IV Sun. of Aug.) from St. Gregory.

August 29, 1961

Decollation [Beheading] of St. John Baptist. Last time we celebrate the feast. For the first time really liked the rhetoric of St. Ambrose in the II Nocturn. The responses are artfully constructed and the whole office has a solid dramatic quality about it that the men of the 12th century must really have enjoyed. The hymn melodies – all of them, but especially of martyrs, begin to mean more and more to me, when I apprehend their "European" quality – thinking of Xtian and medieval culture as opposed to what develops now. Not in any hostile senses. But no longer seeing the tradition I am used to as the only valid one – yet valuing it more as my tradition.

The Mennonites in Kansas want to reprint the Auschwitz poem.

I have been considering the possibility of writing a kind of statement – "Where I stand," as a declaration of my position as a Christian, a writer and a Priest in the present war crisis. There seems to be little I can do other than this. There is *no other activity* available to me. Going to the schoolhouse in New Haven twice a year to vote is ridiculous and means nothing. If I can say something clear and positive it may be of some use to others as well as to myself.

This statement would be for the *Catholic Worker*.

As a moral decision, I think this might possibly be a valid step towards fulfilling my obligations as a human being in the present crisis.

Not only can such a statement be very meaningful – but there is no question that they are taken seriously by everyone. The Reds will brainwash you in order to get a declaration – and Madison Ave. will sell you your grandmother's wig and then publish to the world your complete satisfaction with the deal.

September 5, 1961

Yesterday having received a note from Ethel Kennedy (wife of the Attorney General and sister-in-law of the President), I wrote her an explicit statement of objection to the resumption of nuclear testing. At least this much I can do. Yet there is something very unsatisfactory, something not quite true, about this whole moral question. This idea that it is important to take a "stand" as an individual. As if by mere gestures and statements one could satisfy conscience. And as if the satisfaction of one's conscience (emphasis on *satisfaction*) were the great thing. It can become a mere substitute for responsibility and for love.

Mao Tse Tung said there would be no love until the Revolution had triumphed. There is a grain of truth in this – in this very great and misleading lie. Yet that one grain is what I lack.

Confucius said: "The higher type of man is not like a vessel which is designed for some special use." He was wiser than we monks are.

Fr. Illtud Evans was here last week, among many others. His visit and conversation I enjoyed most. He spoke in Chapter of Fr. Vincent McNabb. We talked together of Cambridge, of Bede Griffiths, and Caldey. He told me the story of Archbishop Roberts of Bombay and his forthright work for peace and the opposition to him. He was delated [summoned] to Rome and silenced. Archbsp. O'Hara, the American apostolic delegate in London, had much to do with this. Another visitor. Merlon Green, a negro and a remarkable person. He is fighting for the right to be hired as a pilot by the passenger air-lines, which said they would hire negroes but in fact refuse to.

September 8, 1961. Nativity of Our Lady

Interior struggle because of the bitterness and selfishness that are in me, and the lack of love. I know what I should do, what I am perhaps capable of doing, that God perhaps wants of me and yet I can't do it. It seems I "have to" refuse, as if it were impossible not to refuse. This is terrible. My only hope is that while refusing I still try doggedly to do it. Is this a deception?

I should love my abbot, my order, my community. But really I doubt if I do, I doubt if I *can* love them spontaneously. I am too obsessed by the unfairness, the injustice that was done me in Rome by the Abbot, and above all embittered and frustrated by the fact that he was able to do this with a good conscience, subjectively, thinking himself perfectly right. And he does the same to everybody. His deviousness, his ambivalence, his trickery, his business manipulations are to him pure guileless simplicity because, while he does these things, he does them "with a pure intention."

Yesterday he was talking of "poor Dom Edmund [Futterer]" (his collapsed rival, who overdid it with his South American foundations). Dom E. has cracked up completely and is in the Mayo Clinic after being practically deposed (he was advised to resign). Dom James was talking of the lovely monastery of Snowmass in Colorado, and he anticipates (with the greatest satisfaction) that it will be closed down because "it cannot make any money." It was founded especially for a group that wanted real silence and solitude. Can't Dom J. see that he really hates monks who desire that kind of thing, that he resents them and does not understand them? Yet he thinks of himself as a great solitary. I cannot make him out. Contrast Snowmass with the prune farm he founded in California, and you have Dom James. And of course he is perfectly "*right*" – according to all standards except those of the Gospel.

Such are my thoughts. They are "uncharitable." Yet I cannot not have them.

And he is kind to me, very considerate in many ways. That makes it worse. Perhaps worst of all is the realization that I need "his kindness" in some sense. That I need him to be considerate of my deficiencies and limitations. This he is. But all the time I cannot help feeling he is so for business reasons. I cannot forget the letter he wrote to Montini, and that someone saw. Incredible!

This I have to live with. This I have to absorb in an abundance of love that I don't have. All I can do with the man is smile and be courteous and obedient and try not to argue, and simply carry out his wishes in the work he has given me. And of course I must understand and forgive; I think I do understand that he is made that way and there is absolutely nothing he can do about it. I can try to be sorry for him – but without success, for I am afraid I want all his chickens to come home and roost all over him, so that he will *see* [underlined twice] himself . . . This is a rather general, hopeless desire in the community and a luxury which we have renounced by our vows.

Still, I hate to see myself covered with my own loveless chickens.

And the community. I really don't do my full part in it. There are functions, simple in themselves, that I practically can't face, can't handle without extreme difficulty. I have to beg to be let off – which nobody minds, there are plenty of others who like to do these jobs, especially when they involve singing. I feel I have to make up in other ways. So I teach and teach, not only novices. This mystical theology class drags on and on. The young priests now want some sort of seminar, and I think it is foolish, a waste of time, yet to please them and soothe my guilt feelings – and perhaps to satisfy my vanity – I suppose I will do it. I wish I could call it love.

The normal thing would be to explain this frankly to the Abbot himself. Impossible. For twelve years I have failed to establish a real rapport, an understanding in which these things can be faced. There is just *no* meeting of minds; except on a superficial level. Only our "well-meaning" efforts to communicate, which break down because we speak different languages. The only meeting is in the realm of perfectly acceptable clichés. Not cliché words but cliché *ideas*. A real idea has to be emptied of its content and turned into a stereotype before one can use it in a conversation with him. And yet he is so earnest about all those stereotypes!

As soon as you say anything that does not fit with a completely commonplace and familiar category, he goes on the defensive, and retreats with a suspicious silence; he no longer thinks you are "practical."

September 9, 1961

The story of the tiger cub brought up among goats and confronted one day by a strong tiger who reeducates him and teaches him who he is.

Strong tiger inside me says "choose!" and cuffs me into the bargain.

Papers from Mexico. Cardenal translated my Hemingway elegy. Its *first* publication is in *Mexico en la Cultura*. Moving quotes from Bernanos in *Revista de la Universidad*. Analysis – one-sided but perceptive – of fascist trends in U.S.

I fear the ignorance and power of the U.S.

And the fact that it has quite suddenly become one of the most decadent societies on the face of the earth. The body of a great dead candied child. Yet not dead, full of immense, uncontrolled power. Crazy.

If somebody doesn't understand the U.S. pretty soon – and communicate some of that understanding to the U.S. – the results will be terrible. It is no accident that the U.S. endowed the world with the Bomb.

The mixture of immaturity, size, apparent innocence and depravity, with occasional spasms of guilt, power, self-hate, pugnacity, lapsing into wildness and then apathy, hopped up and wild-eyed and inarticulate and wanting to be popular. You need a doctor, Uncle!

The exasperation of the other nations of the world who know the U.S. thinks them *jealous* – for what they don't want and yet what fascinates them. Exasperation that such fools should be momentarily kings of the world. Exasperation at them for missing their great chance – this every one finds unforgivable, including America itself. And yet what held the U.S. back was a spasm of that vestigial organ called conscience. Unfortunately not a sufficiently educated conscience. The conscience of a ten-year-old boy, unsure of his parents' standards – not knowing where approval or disapproval might come from!

September 10, 1961

In refectory today – the Lincoln book told of the first casualty, Lincoln's friend Ellsworth, killed in Alexandria. They were *human* in those days! Lincoln's emotion and his letter to Ellsworth's parents! No such articulateness is found today except perhaps in France. But I doubt it.

All day (Day of Recollection), at twenty or thirty minute intervals, a big bomber would pass flying low over the monastery, and as I write here comes another one.

Magnificat antiphon "*Amice, ascende superius* [Friend, take a higher place]" – and I thought that perhaps soon I might die after all. Not that I desire either life or death, but only to be united with God's will. And *ascendere superius* when He decides it is time to do so. *I'm sure he did*

September 12, 1961

A dream last night that was in many ways beautiful and moving – hieratic dream.

I am invited to a party. I meet some of the women going to the party, but there is estrangement. I am alone by the waterfront of a small town. A man says for five dollars I can get across on a yacht to where I want to go. I have five dollars and more than five dollars, hundreds of dollars and also francs. I am conscious of my clerical garb. The yacht is a small schooner, a workaday schooner and no yacht. It does not move from the shore – we make it move a little pushing it from the inside, then I am out swimming ahead in the beautiful water, magic water, from the depths of which comes a wonderful life to which I am not entitled, a life and strength that I fear. I know that by diving in this water I can find something marvelous but that it is not fitting or right for me to dive as I am going to the further shore, with the strength that has come from the water, immortality.

Then in the summer house on the other side, where I have arrived first of all, I play with the dog and the child brings me two pieces of buttered white bread, which I am to eat on arrival.

A magenta-colored stamp from Haiti with the picture of Claudrette Bouchard – Miss Haiti – *Reine Mondiale du Sucre 1960 [World Sugar Queen 1960]* – in queen's robes, her crown at a rakish angle, pointing with her scepter to an ox-cart in a cane field. *Vive la Reine du Sucre!* [Long live the Sugar Queen!]

(Some nuns in Port-au-Prince wrote, stimulated by the passage in *Sign of Jonas*, about a dream of being sent to Haiti.)

September 19, 1961

The letter to Pablo Antonio Cuadra which I wrote last week is bitter and unjust.[13] It lacks perspective. It cannot do much good to anyone in its present shape, and yet I have mailed it off to him and it may get published (though only in Nicaragua) before I have time to make any serious changes.

How did it get to be so violent and unfair?

The root is my own fear, my own desperate desire to survive even if only as a voice uttering an angry protest, while the waters of death close over the whole continent.

Why am I so willing to believe that the country will be destroyed? It is certainly possible, and in some sense it may even be likely. But this is a case where, in spite of evidence, one must continue to hope. One must not give in to defeatism and despair: just as one must hope for life in a mortal illness which has been declared incurable.

This is the point. This weakness and petulancy, rooted in egoism, and which I have in common with other intellectuals in this country. Even after years in the monastery I have not toughened up and got the kind of fibre that is bred only by humility and self-forgetfulness. Or rather, though I had begun to get it, this writing job and my awareness of myself as a personage with definite opinions and with a voice, has kept me sensitive and afraid on a level on which most monks long ago became indifferent. Yet

---

[13] This letter was subsequently published as "A Letter to Pablo Antonio Cuadra Concerning Giants" in *Emblems of a Season of Fury* (1963) and in *The Collected Poems of Thomas Merton*.

also it is not good to be indifferent to the fate of the world on a simply human level.

So I am concerned, humanly, politically, yet not wisely.

Nor am I really pure enough and humble enough to make a Christian protest. However, I do not know if I have the right to keep silent – and my Superiors do not oblige me to do so; they leave me the power to express myself in writing, and in personal contacts with men from the outside world. I am always too vehement. Bitterness can do no good at a time like this. There is too much senseless bitterness, too much hatred justified by a "just cause," too much hatred in the service of truth, even in the service of God. This is the great lie which the West seems unable to see and now the East is learning to be far more blind and fanatical in their attachment to this lie than we have been.

September 23, 1961

Bright hot weather. A Coast Guard jet plane flew low over the hermitage and monastery after dinner and circled and came back and finally took off at great speed into a white cloud to the north. No denying the beauty of it, though I am finishing, and with complete agreement, Lewis Mumford's *Art and Technics* [New York, 1952].

They are finishing in refectory the reading of Jerome Frank's article, "Breaking the Thought Barrier." I got the offprints from him and it was at my suggestion that it was read. Of course a lot of people don't like it. A lot simply will not face the possibility of such a thing happening – and from a certain viewpoint it seems incredible. All the more reason for trying to face the situation and understand it. This is one of the very rare occasions on which a suggestion of mine for refectory reading has been taken. I discovered the article quite providentially – my Auschwitz poem was in the middle of a reprint of it in *The Catholic Worker* and the poem itself was only printed there by "mistake."

The last two or three days – great seriousness in prayer, sense of the meaning and value of vigils, of self-stripping and going in poverty "to the Father." Orientation out of this world, sense of its transiency and provisional character.

Silent afternoon at the hermitage – wind soughing in the hot pines, crickets in the yellow grass.

This week – finished quickly the galley proofs of *New Seeds of Contemplation*. This is one of the books with which I am more or less content. I am not sorry to have written it and I think it is an improvement on the original. Sent some bits of it to *Catholic Worker* (the war chapter with a little addition) and *Jubilee* (The general dance). The Hemingway Elegy was in the *Commonweal*, and Eloise Spaeth wrote a letter about it just before taking off on a KLM plane for Amsterdam to see museums. I sent the Cuadra letter to Carrera Andrade in Caracas. Still have not corrected it.

I heard today of the death of Père François de St. Marie by drowning. A sad thing. His book is supposed to be appearing in English with my preface. Though I seldom wrote to him I felt close to him, and he helped me much with the French edition of *The Ascent to Truth*.

September 24, 1961

Vanaprantha! [Knowledge!] There is nothing that makes sense to me or attracts me so much as living in the hermitage. I dread the politics of the permission, and the time has not come for that. But to take advantage of the present situation and use it as fully as possible.

I am determined now to embrace the long task of unweaving the garment of *artha*, my writer-self, my official business being, so as at last to step out of it. Have to finish article for *Catholic Encyclopedia*. And a few more things to do on the art book (which I would gladly drop, but others are involved and I am obligated). A preface to the selections from Gandhi . . . Then for the time being I can taper off with minor translations and allow poems to come when they will. But not to write books. And to disappear after the *Reader* is out.

It is complicated because I am complicated, but this is the right direction.

September 25, 1961

One of the people I most enjoy getting letters from is Doña Luisa Coomaraswamy. I am growing very fond of her and she has been most generous – writes long letters full of all sorts of interesting things and sends offprints of A.K.C.'s articles. She is very much a recluse and remains generally suspicious of scholars and publishers, but I am happy that she accepts me so completely. It is a friendship in which, it seems, we both recognize correlative needs and potentialities in one another and are grateful. This is good and consoling, and is from God. Or at least I hope so, and why should it not be? One is happy for the mystery of mutual recognitions in this great, confused, silent and anonymous sea which is our world.

Finished Mumford's *Art and Technics* yesterday. His last pages on the interior life are very good. He is another for whom I feel great sympathy.

September 29, 1961

St. Michael. Weary from trip to Louisville yesterday to see some professors at the Baptist seminary. Principally Eric Rust whose ideas on Old Testament theology and on history seem to me to be very solid and alive. A group of us had lunch in one of their cafeterias – the campus is enormous. This cafeteria was in a women's dormitory. Some rather pretty girls studying to be Baptist ministers! But the group I met were very fine, five or six professors, many of whom I met before. They have come to Gethsemani with classes or for retreats. A new acquaintance was Dr. Mueller (?) who had studied a year with Barth and also at Duke with Ray C. Petrie, who edited a very good anthology of late medieval mysticism in the Xtian classics series. Rust is an atomic scientist who became a minister and theologian after the war. His view of history is eschatological and in agreement with Daniélou. Mueller was talking about K. Barth's more recent position on man and nature in which he has become less intransigent.

In Louisville the municipal authorities are determining what buildings provide a relative protection against fallout, and a Jesuit theologian, writing in *America,* has declared that it is perfectly legitimate to shoot your neighbor if he tries to break into your private shelter. Such is the climate of the world. And there is some fighting in Syria.

Aidan Nally, who has worked for the monastery well over 50 years, came up with an expression of concern and said, "Father, they're mobilizing in No Man's Land." This is probably a very astute summary of the world situation!

September 30, 1961

Perhaps what Aidan was talking about was outer space. For Kennedy's speech at the UN, after the death of Dag Hammarskjöld, was read in the refectory. An admirable speech, fully recognizing the realities of the situation and coping with them, I think, sanely. That we must disarm or perish – yet no question of sentimentality or "appeasement." The eerie thing about the speech was the matter-of-factness with which he discussed the possibility of wars in outer space! We have caught up with the comic strips – and they have perhaps meant more than we thought. Buck Rogers was our prophet. We should be paying attention to Superman, Superboy and Superbaby.

A gardenia bloomed even for the Feast of St. Michael.

Of course the reactions to the Kennedy speech show the full complexity of the affair.

Its main value was apparently to encourage America and our allies.

And to take a stand against a complete blockade of West Berlin.

From the political viewpoint there remain grave ambiguities, due to the fact that apparently Kennedy knows what is really being planned by USSR for Berlin, as opposed to the conciliatory protestations of Gromyko that no harm is intended to Berlin or West Germany.

Evidently the crux of the matter is really the power of West Germany and the threat to Russia of a reunited Germany, having in it many ex-Nazis seeking revenge.

So once again we come around to war and the source of the war is after all Germany.

Not Germany alone, but the U.S. which, as I wrote 20 years ago, has in overcoming Germany taken over the German position for herself. And of course Russia. It is to a great extent the same basic situation that has been producing all the wars in Europe since the Reformation.

This is not what Kennedy is thinking by any means.

For my own part, I have one task left. To pray, to meditate, to enter into truth, to sit before the abyss, to be educated in the word of Christ and thus to make my contribution to world peace. There is not much left to be said.

W. H. Ferry, according to a clipping sent by Laughlin, advocates a "shelter-for-things" (as opposed to people) in Santa Barbara, to show that shelters are "credible." It is too straight-faced for a joke, yet I cannot believe it is serious! It is exactly the same grisly joke with which I end my letter to Cuadra!

October 1, 1961

A wet, cold, murky Sunday after a stormy night in which the lights failed in choir during the Third Nocturn. We had just enough light to get through Lauds, and I read afterwards with the help of a candle.

The first book of Buber that has really gripped me is the one on the *Origins and Meaning of Hasidism* [New York, 1960]. The point about the seriousness of the Hasidic reaction against Sabbatian Messianism is very convincing. The whole question of the Gnostic trend and temptation. The question of gnosticism is an important one. I am at the same time much taken with H[enry] Corbin's book on Ibn al' Arabi [*L'Imagination Créatrice dans Le Soufisme D'Ibn Arabi*, Paris, 1958], and his gnostic sufism, this from a favorable viewpoint.

The question is – is there an ineradicable opposition between gnostic and prophetic religion? This is stoutly maintained by Buber of course and by Protestants like H. Kraemer. It raises no doubt in the mind of staunch and staid Catholics (who oppose *both* prophecy and gnosticism). But I am not so sure after all. It is a big question, and the Corbin book shows it is not a simple one.

October 3, 1961

Yesterday, Feast of the Guardian Angels, a bright, cool afternoon, a fine half day of meditation at the hermitage. The Corbin book on Ibn al' Arabi is in ways tremendous. The plays and changes on the theme of the divine compassion, on the "sympathy" of the spirit and God, on God seeking to manifest Himself in the spirit that responds to a "Name" which it is meant to embody in its life. Compare the medieval Cistercians with their births of Christ in us. Need for compassion and tenderness towards the infinite fragility of the divine life in us which is *real* and not an idea or an image (as is our conception of God as "object").

This could and should lead me more and more to a new turning, a new attitude, an inner change, a liberation from all futile concerns to let Him emerge in His mystery and compassion within me. Yielding to the inexplicable demand of His presence in weakness. To be very careful and timid now about those innumerable self-affirmations that tend to destroy His weakness and littleness in me – fortunately indestructible. This mustard seed, His kingdom in me. The struggle of the very small to survive and change my self-affirmations.

October 5, 1961

Yesterday was memorable for a visit to Loretto, and what a visit! I had been invited to their Sesquicentennial celebration and begged off, as I should not be at such things. Otherwise the invitations would never end. And the Sisters well understand. This time I went over privately, but to my surprise it turned into a celebration nevertheless. But one from which I think we all derived joy.

The novices and postulants sang for me a musical program on the history of Loretto and it was really charming, moving and well done. It was perfectly right and straight and simple. There was a great deal of spirit in it. And all their hearts were in it! The wide-eyed, disoriented look of the new postulants, a little wild with their black uniforms and hair out of order. The angelic voices and the praise of the novices in their white veils. I felt especially sympathetic towards the postulants, some of them so young.

They sang about Loretto, and about going out in wagons to found Indian schools in the western plains and New Mexico, a hundred years ago. The community has a wonderfully simple and sane spirit, the first completely American congregation of Sisters.

So I spoke a little to the novices and postulants, disarmed by their simplicity and their avidity. And I think they believed more in God's love after I had spoken: I certainly did.

Spoke also in the Infirmary and then had a meeting with Mother Luke and, I suppose, her council at which questions of policy and various problems of formation were discussed. I enjoyed it and this too seemed very simple and practical.

Finally we all dined together in the Guest House and laughed a great deal and told many stories about our communities and about people we knew, and about everything. It was utterly wonderful, and I am completely grateful for their love. Never anywhere, even at the Louisville Carmel, have I felt so much at home, so much with real friends with whom there could be a complete and unreserved understanding, at least about the religious life and its problems. The wonderful, salutary honesty of Loretto and of Mother Luke! This is a treasure beyond estimation, and it manifests something that is absolutely dear to me about Kentucky – this part where I am – and shows me really why I am here. This is something of the real mystery of my vocation here and something that is in the silence and in the bricks of the old buildings, something inherited no doubt from the days of Father Badin and Father Nerni[c]x.

Letter from Ernesto Cardenal: he likes the Letter to P.A. Cuadra. Speaks of the way the intellectuals of Latin America are more and more pro-

Very special Thought

didn't
Hype

Russian. Disastrous American policies. Somoza fraternally present at the sendoff of the Cuban invasion etc. The important thing is to keep alive the concept of a Third World, genuinely free and peaceful and not committed to power politics based on a nuclear threat.

October 10, 1961

Sunny morning.

What earthly reason is there for taking color photographs? It is absurd. This I have thought, after taking half a roll of Kodacolor at the hermitage. Or any photographs at all. Well – to send pictures to Loretto and to the Carmelites. Mother Luke cannot come to the place and see it herself. From a certain point of view it is reasonable and charitable. Yet from that viewpoint every folly becomes reasonable.

The other day I finally finished the article "Direction, Spiritual" for the *New Catholic Encyclopedia*. I should have finished it in August (Deadline Nov. 1, but I wanted to get it done in August).

This is the last thing that was hanging over me.

Still one or two pieces I may or may not do. For instance the little essay on Gandhi and non-violence, to go with the texts I selected. Similarly for Benet of Canfield and Coomaraswamy. About Benet I am most doubtful.

An American poet has translated Ernesto's Gethsemani poems. They are fabulously good, wonderfully simple. Very Franciscan. So pure I can't imagine the eye of anyone here ever setting on them for more than ten seconds. We have an image of ourselves, and it is by no means so simple. It is "enriched" with all kinds of synthetic colors. It is full of spiritual plastics. It is . . . Kodacolor.

The Critic has now become a self-consciously "Catholic" culture magazine. Not bad in its way. Sister Maura in it, James Bank, Fr. Roseliep, etc. etc. Tom McDonnell. Article on e.e. cummings. You see we dare to be interested, at this late date, in e.e. cummings. OK. It is still just another way of being Catholic with a capital "C." But it would be silly and unkind to even mention it. Dear people. They will suddenly get very good, perhaps, one morning. Now they are earnest about not being tied to clerical apron-strings – much. Half the writers are nevertheless priests. *Jubilee* better.

October 15, 1961

Nothing of St. Theresa [of Avila] today – it is Sunday.

Still, a last gardenia came out for her feast, and a big one too. The warm afternoons brought it out. But this night is cold and dry. The stars are bright and the pump is loud over by the lake.

I have been reading Henry Miller's *Remember to Remember* [Norfolk, 1947] especially for the part about war, written twenty years ago. Some of it is very much like what I myself wrote at the same time. And it is exactly what one could write now. *No peace now – Roosevelt* was the headline in the evening paper. One night he will say *No Peace Now – Kennedy*. For Kennedy is not letting anyone get any illusions about the Berlin crisis "dying down." In Miller's words, of twenty years ago, "The vast majority of people know deep down that the day is drawing near. . . . They are dumb and silent, more or less reconciled to their lot because it seems inevitable." This time there is more confusion about it. Last time – Pearl Harbor made everything very simple. The Berlin issue is still, whether you like it or not, relatively technical. Most people are not easily convinced that it is worth a world war of the proportions war might now assume.

October 17, 1961
Bright hot sun on the bronze trees.

The Tricenary ends, and this morning I said a requiem Mass for Fr. François de Sainte Marie, who drowned in France between retreats preached to nuns. The last I heard from him he sent me a postcard from Mistassini, one of our monasteries in Canada. That must have been this spring, or perhaps at the beginning of summer.

Lowell's *Imitations*, a fascinating book. He has developed the vein I liked least in *Lord Weary's Castle* of taking liberties with the language and experience of foreign poets. It is no longer they – no longer Baudelaire, but something fascinating, a picture of Baudelaire's idea with the solidity of Hogarth, for Lowell's is an 18th century idiom.

He cannot imitate Valéry, no one can. He is good at Rimbaud and Pasternak.

October 19, 1961
The offices at night have been fine. I have slept more and have a clearer head to attend to the Word of God with. Also have been reading more Bib-

lical theology – esp. G. E. Wright, *God Who Acts* [Chicago, 1952], a book given to me by Eric Rust, the Baptist theologian. And a very fine book too.

Yet it is surprising I do not lose more sleep as there is a bulldozer *working day and night* in the cornfields, the bottom lands, and I sleep next to the window right over those fields. What are they doing? Can't they be content to let the creek wind as it always did? Does it have to be straight? Really we monks are madmen, bitten by an awful folly, an obsession with useless and expensive improvements.

To the east, then, the bulldozer day and night. The noise never stops. To the west, the dehydrator. The noise stops perhaps at midnight. A layman drives the bulldozer, brothers work at the dehydrator.

To the northwest – a pump, day and night. Never stops. There is nothing making any noise to the south – but then to the south the monks' property soon comes to an end, and there are only lay people, whose lives are generally silent. They only speak. We make signs, but drown everything in the noise of our machines. One would think our real reason for making signs might be that it is not always easy to be heard.

October 20, 1961

Cold rainy afternoon. First time I have had fire in the fireplace at the hermitage. Yesterday we were cutting wood. Today, typed some pages from the "Guilty Bystander," which seems at the moment to be pressing. Worked a little this morning on Clement of Alexandria – the selections and preface.[14] This is satisfying work, because of my love for him.

After dinner – in the cold woodshed – have discovered a marvelous book by [Jean] Giono – of ancient vintage: *Regain* [Paris, 1930 and 1950] – in a bunch of books sent over from the library of the university. This is perfect writing.

In the morning, after Mass, realization how true it is that prayer really "has power" over the heart of God, really reaches the sanctuary of His heart – starting from the sanctuary of my own: and they are one sanctuary.

October 21, 1961

Perhaps the last time we celebrate the Feast of St. Ursula in our calendar. Not that the same Mass texts will not be used over and over again in other

[14] *Selections from the Protreptikos*, published with an essay and translations (New York, 1962).

Masses of Virgins. Special joy in listening to the Epistle and Gospel. To *be-come* attention from head to foot, to become all joy in hearing the Word of God. A deep pleasure of monks and, by rights, of all Christians.

Pleasure of fire in the grate at St. Mary of Carmel. The only talkative be-ing, this child, this fire. The only one speaking in the quiet room outside – cold, damp, foggy day. Barely see the hills across the valley. You could not guess their presence unless you knew beforehand where to look.

Letter from Jim Forest at the *Catholic Worker* – that my article on the War Madness is published and that there will be controversy about it. That everyone has gone crazy, building fallout shelters and preparing to shoot their neighbors. Whole towns preparing to defend themselves against neighboring towns. What do the Russians need with bombs at all? Just get a false alarm going and we will all shoot each other up without giving them further trouble! A nice testimony to democracy and individualism!

October 23, 1961

I am perhaps at a turning point in my spiritual life: perhaps slowly coming to a point of maturation and the resolution of doubts – and the forgetting of fears. Walking in to a known and definite battle. May God protect me in it. *The Catholic Worker* sent out a press release about my article, which may have many reactions – or may have none. At any rate it appears that I am one of the few Catholic priests in the country who has come out unequiv-ocally for a completely intransigent fight for the abolition of war, for the use of non-violent means to settle international conflicts. Hence by impli-cation not only against the bomb, against nuclear testing, against Polaris submarines but against all violence. This I will inevitably have to explain in due course. Non-violent *action*, not mere passivity. How I am going to ex-plain myself and defend a definite position in a timely manner when it takes at least two months to get even a short article through the censors of the Order, is a question I cannot attempt to answer.

In a way I think the position of the Order is in fact unrealistic and absurd. That at a time like this *no one* in the Order should seem to be concerned with the realities of the world situation in a practical way – that monks in general, even those (O.S.B.) who can speak out fully – are immersed in lit-tle scholarly questions about medieval writers and texts of minor impor-tance even to scholars, and this in the greatest moral crisis in the history of man: this seems to me incomprehensible. Especially when it is the definite policy of the Cistercian Order to impede and obstruct every expression of concern, every opinion, in published written form, that has reference to the crisis. This seems to me extremely grave. The futility of taking the issue up and solving it is evident; I talked to Fr. Clément, the [Abbot] General's secretary about it and it was like talking to a wall. Total incomprehension and lack of sympathy. The General himself is more understanding and Dom James too sees the point somewhat (they surprisingly released *Original Child Bomb* after the censors had definitively blocked it).

And the Jesuit who condoned – even apparently encouraged – the business of sitting in your fallout shelter with a machine gun to keep others out! This is the best Catholic theology has had to offer in this country, so it appears.

At least I feel clean for having stated what is certainly the true Christian position. Not that self-defense is not legitimate, but there are wider perspectives than that and we have to see them. It is not possible to solve our problems on the basis of "every man for himself" and saving your own skin by killing the first person who threatens it.

Etta Gullick – along with wonderful letters from the Adriatic, for she was at Istanbul to see the Patriarch and at Patmos also – sent Watkins' book *Poets and Mystics*. She wants me to read especially the Essay on [Augustine] Baker. I have begun instead with Julian of Norwich, because all this year I have been more and more attracted to her. Now the immense wonder of her is opening up fully. The doctrine on sin. The parable of the servant. Tremendous! How great a joy and gift!

W. H. Ferry wrote from Santa Barbara. He too is impressed with the exceptional gravity of the hour. Feels that the Institute for the Study of Democratic Institutions there, though good, has come too late and has occupied itself with superficial symptoms of decay and not with the real roots. He and Hutchins are to go to Athens and Israel and he will perhaps stop here on his return journey.

I am happy that I have turned a corner, perhaps the last corner in my life. The sense of abandon and homegoing joy, love for the novices, whom I see as though dwelling in light and in God's blessing – as we go home together. And the thought is not negative or destructive – for it is a fulfillment, and whatever happens to the world, its infinitely varied dance of epiphanies continues: or is perhaps finally transfigured and perfected forever.

October 27, 1961

Tom McDonnell was here this week, working on the *Reader*. It was a distraction. It brought me again into the realm of doubt and uncertainty. It seems to be necessary and right and then at moments I glimpse all the possibilities of dishonesty and self-deception it brings with it. The creation of another image of myself – fixation on the idea that I am a "writer who has arrived" – which I am. But what does it mean? Arrived where? Void. Has there been anything else in my life but the construction of this immense illusion? And the guilt that goes with it, what is this? A justification for it, a second illusion? Certainly I can have no peace in this kind of nonsense. My home is elsewhere.

Calmed down to some extent this morning in the "sacred silence," reading, at peace. G. Ernest Wright on Biblical Theology. E. F. Osborn on Clement of Alexandria (dry). [Jules] Monchanin . . .

Was up late last night with Fr. Urban (Goolsby) and his worries about his vocation, then got up accidentally at 1:30 and couldn't get back to sleep after getting dressed etc. Bulldozers still in the bottoms, interminably, at night. Absurd.

But work yesterday was fine. Bright afternoon, fall colors everywhere. Fr. Cuthbert sawing a log simply radiant with peace and happiness – and Fr. Urban at the other end of the saw miserable!!

Absurd contradictions. Where do the books come from? I think of myself as stopping writing, yet two books are coming out this winter, two more sometime in 1962 . . . and there is "just a little typing to do . . ." on this or that. The short job on non-violence seems really necessary.

October 29, 1961. 23rd Sunday after Pentecost

"The key to the interpretation of history is historical activity," says Tillich. One of the statements that reflects a Marxist influence. But I agree.

Yesterday I finished an article on Peace: Christian duties and perspectives. Discussed it a little with the novices, which was a good idea. It will certainly not please many people. I am disturbed by the development of things in this country where so many people get their living from war industries and are consequently not disposed to see or understand a real need for disarmament. It is to their interest to believe that the way to peace is the accumulation of nuclear weapons. This is disastrous.

Someone (Fr. Alberic) wisely remarked that if the Russians wanted to ruin America, all they would have to do would be to agree to all disarmament plans and go ahead with them. The American economy would collapse.

It is a frightful thing to live in such an economy. Everyone who participates in it runs the risk of being guilty.

Again I am faced with the fact that people in general do not want to face all this, do not want to talk about it, or think about it. As a result, when things suddenly become hot, they run around in desperation building fallout shelters.

October 30, 1961

The anchor in the window at the Old Zion church,[15] before it burned in 1924 or 1925 . . . This is the earliest symbol of which I remember being conscious. I was struck by it, aged perhaps seven or eight, but could not see why it was in a church window. Perhaps I did not know what it was. Yet I must have seen the symbol somewhere in crossing the ocean (and I desired to be a sailor). Anyway there was an anchor in the window, and I was aware of it. I have forgotten almost every other detail of the church except perhaps the Eagle on whose outspread wings the Bible rested and even of this I am not sure. Was there really such an eagle?

Whether or not it is relevant that the anchor is symbol of hope: but hope is what I most need. And what the world most needs.

Glenn Hinson brought his Church History students out from the Baptist seminary and I spoke to them briefly after dinner about peace. We had a good conversation, and felt we understood each other completely. At the end we all said the Our Father together – it was about a year since the first group came from the Southern Baptist Seminary.

Letter from the Fellowship of Reconciliation. They want to reprint "The Root of War" as a pamphlet. And a letter from John Wu – who has been ill as a result of his trip to Taipei. He sent some translations of Chinese poems.

Convinced again that I must set everything aside to work for the abolition of war. Primarily of course by prayer. I remain a contemplative, but as

---

[15] Episcopal church in Douglaston, New York, where Merton's father was organist.

for writing, contacts, letters, that kind of effort: here it seems to me everything should yield first place to the struggle against war. This means first of all getting into contact with the others most concerned. The Pax Movement in England especially, deepening the contact with F.O.R. [Fellowship of Reconciliation] and the *Catholic Worker*. It seems there is *no peace movement to speak of* in this country, except the F.O.R.

I noticed among some of the Baptist students at least a surprising frankness in questioning the ultimate validity of so many assumptions made today about the "American way of life," especially as to whether it has anything particularly Christian about it. I believe there is an immense doubt moving through the nation, and because of this doubt, indecision and guilt. We do not really believe that we are what we say we are and we are honest enough to be disturbed by this: a weakness which evidently the Russians do not share. (Yet they *do*. The de-Stalinisation campaign is bringing this out.)

A monk said to Joshua – "What is the way?"
   He replied: "Outside the fence."
   The monk said, "I mean the great way: what is the great way?"
   Joshua replied, "The great way is that which leads to the Capital."
   Remember this in this war business, please. Stay on the way where you now are and don't get off it to run all over the countryside shouting "peace! peace!" But stay on the great way which leads to the Capital.

Perhaps peace is after all not something you "work for." It either is or it isn't. You have it or not. If you are at peace there is peace in the world. Then share your peace with everyone and the world will be at peace.

November 4, 1961
Aunt Kit is here on her way back to New Zealand, delighted at having hopped over New York in a helicopter. It rained yesterday. We sat in the gatehouse and made tea and talked about the family. She had already written to me about it, but I will try to put down the essentials as I remember them.

James Merton – from Stoke by Nailsby (?) Naseby (?) in Suffolk. Bailiff of the Torless family. The Mertons were apparently the only ones in the village who could write. Was James' son Charles already schoolmaster there?

In 1856, with the Torlesses, James Merton, Charles, his son, and their families went to New Zealand to settle (or did James stay in England?). Charles – musical precentor in St. John's Church (Christchurch? Rangiora?). Taught school. His wife – melancholy and silent. Alfred, my grandfather, his son, was born in New Zealand. Music master at Christ's College, Christchurch.

My grandmother – a Grierson – born in Wales of a Scotch father. Her mother's family Welsh, the Birds. Miniature of a Lieut. Bird in the Navy, was once over the mantle at Burston House. Don't remember. It is from the Bird family that comes our face – the one Father had and I have and Kit has and Dick Trier has. The look, the grin, the brow.

Granny lived in Cardiff and as a child had infantile paralysis. They did not think she would live. She lived to be 101. When she came to Flushing with Kit in 1919, I was four. I remember her very well. The reason: her affection. Kit said Granny and my mother didn't get along. Mother said Granny was being too indulgent with me and that I ought to be made to obey. I remember Mother as strict, stoical and determined. Granny believed children ought to be brought up by love.

Mother's integrity, directness, sincerity. She was "artistic but not an intellectual." And she was practical, more so than Father. The Mertons were all eminently impractical. It was Granny who bought the house in Christchurch and kept everything together.

Granny in London would meet people "by the Elgin Marbles in the British Museum." Was greatly interested in architecture, history, etc. Kit was a history teacher. I told her to read Christopher Dawson.

November 5, 1961

My father was born in 1887 in Christchurch – left school about 16 to work in Bank of N.Z., but left for England about 1904, studied art – returned to N.Z. and then back to England, with money he had made in an exhibition in N.Z. Came steerage, his overcoat was stolen, reached England cold and penniless. Had an allowance from Aunt Maud. Studied in Paris, worked also for Tudor Hart in his studio. My mother, whom he met in Paris, was studying interior decorating. They married hoping to sell pictures to tourists who came through south of France, but the war stopped that. They married about March 1914 – came to U.S. about April 1916. My mother was strongly pacifist and opposed further going to war, saying it would be murder. She also was strong on poverty and did not want to have many possessions. Whatever asceticism I have in me seems to have to do with her and my problems about asceticism are inseparable from my problems about her. Certainly I understand my vocation a bit better.

Sad to see Aunt Kit go. Forty-two years since I last saw her and will probably never see her again. The only blood relative I have seen for twenty years. Lots of lines in her face, but much animation. Thin and energetic, she reminds me of Aunt Maud.

November 7, 1961

After a long cold and gloomy weekend it is bright again. There was a very hard frost this morning. Yesterday Edward Deming Andrews, who has written several books on the Shakers and has a wonderful collection of furniture, drawings etc., was here with his wife and Ralph McCallister, who is in charge of the project for the restoration of the Pleasant Hill Shaker Colony. We had a short but pleasant visit. Andrews was interested in some of the benches in the library and in the old refectory tables. They are also restoring the Shaker Community at Hancock, Mass. This will be a stricter restoration. The Pleasant Hill project will include "educational facilities" – i.e. there will be courses, conferences, etc. And the papers are sanguine about its possibilities as a "tourist attraction." They want to make it sound as if there is a fast buck in it for somebody, then it will make sense in American terms. This is evidently not McCallister's idea – but perhaps the fast buck group will after all prevail. Really, I am interested, and would like it to be as good as it actually can be. And I still hope Shirley Burden will come and take pictures.

Some copies of *Pax Bulletin* came today from *CW*. Impressed. We realize too little the actual substance of the Church's ideas about war. In being "obedient" we submit to the prejudices of fat men with vested interests, assuming that this is what a Catholic has to believe. And we humbly try to put forward a little "truth" that will fit this scandal and be acceptable to all.

Like Cardinal Spellman talking at a supposed Peace rally in Washington and ranting against the aggressive designs of Russia.

"I am known by no one but thee, just as thou existest only by Me. He who knows thee, knows Me – although no one knows Me. And thus thou also art known to no one."

Sublime theory of prayer of Ibn al' Arabi.

November 12, 1961. Day of Recollection

I must pray more and more for courage, as I certainly have neither the courage nor the strength to follow the path that is certainly my duty now.

With the fears and rages that possess so many confused people, if I say things that seem to threaten their interests or conflict with their obsessions, then I will surely get it.

It is shocking that so many are convinced that the Communists are about to invade or destroy America: "Christians" who think the only remedy is to destroy them first. Who thinks seriously of disarming? For whom is it more than a pious wish, beyond the bounds of practicality?

I need patience to listen, to learn, to try to understand, and courage to take all the consequences and be really faithful. This alone is a full time job. I dread it but it must be done, and I don't quite know how. To save my soul by trying to be one of those who spoke and worked for peace, not for madness and destruction.

I am slightly ill. Very bad throat since Wednesday or Thursday. Then a cough that keeps me awake half the night. (Slept late this morning.)

Today a headache and upset stomach, which are probably psychosomatic or perhaps come from too many useless medicines.

November 14, 1961

The sanity of Eichmann! Such sanity is not sanity. Such health is not health. On the other hand the true sanity of Clement of Alexandria. His beautiful, clear, clean doctrines full of peace and light. That we are planted in Christ as in Paradise. His realization of hope in Christ, Life in the Spirit. There is no other true sanity. *Epistemonike Theosebeia* [Understanding fear of God].

November 17, 1961

Lovely, cold, lonely afternoon, winter afternoon, rich winter silence and loneliness and fullness into which I entered nearly twenty years ago! These afternoons contain all the inexplicable meaning of my vocation. I am happy at having at least a few precious moments in the hermitage. Yet if I have been busy, it was also with rich and rewarding things.

Victor Hammer came over. Brought the beginning of the woodcut for *Hagia Sophia* and some proofs of his new thing on *Mnemosyne*, which is excellent. (I finally apprehend the very simple thing that Fiedler is getting at: that the work of art is to be *seen* – not imagined, worked over intellectually by the viewer. Central is the experience of seeing.)

V. H. worked on a sketch for a portrait of me, and this (contrary to what one might say according to prejudice) makes at least some sense. The patient, human work of sitting and talking and being understood on paper. How different from the camera! I am incurably camera shy! The awful instantaneous snapshot of pose, of falsity, eternalized. Like the pessimistic, anguished view of judgment that so many mad Christians have – the cruel candid shot of you when you have just done something transient but hateful. As if this could be truth. Judgment really a patient, organic, long-suffering understanding of the man's whole life, of *everything* in it, all in context.

However, it is good to be a little in the woods and alone.

Yesterday (I hate the Brown Hotel, and its noise and confusion, and the rednecked business men crowding to the bar, fat assed and arrogant and yet humiliated, frustrated, confused . . .). Why eat in such a place? Why go near such a place?

Spoke at length in the evening to Terrell Dickey, in his house. He is dying of lung cancer. Looks haggard, but is a fine, sensitive person, a person of quality, a good friend. Thinking of all the work we have done together in the past on monastery booklets etc. This has been precious and good and its value will never be lost. A bond in Christ. He feels this, I know. Neither of us could say it.

The great preciousness of the deep, disinterested recognition of value in one man by another. The unspoken, deep mutual recognition of what has *absolute* worth, because it is "in God." This recognition is so great, so precious, beyond estimation.

For instance, in a letter from Alceu Amoroso Lima . . . and all my other friends – Ernesto Cardenal, J. Laughlin, Lax and Rice, Mark of course. And some of those in the monastery who are of such value, yet in a different way. *One must have excessive love* for this inestimable worth in good and special men. An ordinary appreciation will not do. It is an imposture.

Affection too for the people in the Louisville Library whom I had not seen for a long time.

And Mother Luke and the nuns at Loretto also: there is in them this wonderful worth.

Not many here at Gethsemani have this special value – that is, they are fine, I love them, but they are strangers: and so irrevocably alien at times. There is no penetrating the barrier. But there is a different love, in spite of the barrier.

November 19, 1961. 26th Sunday after Pentecost

At the end of Lauds, coming over to novitiate, saw snow on the dim trees in the garden, and on the ground, lighted from the windows. This is to be a hard winter, we are told.

Reading Clement, the *Stromateis*, with comfort and consolation. I see no problem at all in his "esotericism." Obviously one cannot tell everybody everything, and there are certain truths for which the vast majority are not and never will be prepared. I cannot talk to the novices about the things which are central in my own spiritual life – or not about many of them, and about none of them directly.

November 20, 1961

Dark and cold. Busy. Confusion of letters and novitiate work, was glad to get a quiet hour or so in the afternoon, with the wood fire and the silence at St. Mary of Carmel. To meditate on longsuffering. "There is no guilt equal to hatred, no mortification equal to longsuffering" (Sántideva). Added a page to the Red or Dead article for the FOR [Fellowship of Reconciliation]. Letters – from Jim Forest about progress of Pax Movement. No bishops are to be among the sponsors (I am one. Lax and Rice and Fr. Hovda and some others I know). Letters – again – from Lax, from Archbishop Roberts – his difficulties after having been denounced to the H[oly] See by Archbishop O'Hara. If you want to espouse the cause of peace it is not just a matter of speaking out, but also of exhausting yourself uselessly in endless political maneuvers. Does this make sense? No, but it may be necessary and inevitable. Dorothy Day – talking desperately and meeting only indifference.

November 21, 1961. F. of the Presentation

Clear again. Went up to the hermitage in the afternoon. Clearly meditation is the main thing. And then reading with prayer.

But noise everywhere. There is still a bulldozer in the bottoms, and another in the still half finished reservoir in the mill bottom. The Chapter Room is coming along.

Across the valley they are building what purports to be a "cheese cellar." There is much blasting, with great dirty clouds of yellow smoke. And a jackhammer can be heard across the valley. I secretly suspect it is a fallout shelter for the Cellarer and his friends.

A hawk circled higher and higher until he was almost out of sight over the sheep barn. I read Laurens van der Post's *Heart of the Hunter* [New York, 1961]. Dangerous secrets to reveal. Once again I am in favor of the esoteric principles of Clement of Alexandria. Yet I would not want to be deprived of such a book.

November 25, 1961

Tomorrow is the last Sunday after Pentecost. "Let he who is in Judea flee to the hills." Always the same deep awe and compunction at this Gospel. It has been with me every year since my conversion, and its repetition has not robbed it of significance or turned it into a dead, routine affair. On the contrary, I see more and more how central this is in my life.

Yesterday afternoon at the hermitage, surely a decisive clarity came. That I must definitely commit myself to opposition to, and non-cooperation with, nuclear war. That this includes refusing to vote for those who favor the policy of deterrence, and going forward in trying to make this kind of position and its obligation increasingly clear. Not that I did not mean this before – but never so wholly and so definitely.

Last evening, a note from Louis Massignon about fasting for the Algerians recently slaughtered in Paris. I have often skipped frustulum but this time skipped collation. Very good. Slept better, much more clarity at the Night Office and meditation. Also my Mass – too dark to read the Epistle and Gospel without a light but after the offertory only the dawn light. Splendor of the first, dim, holy light of the day. Much meaning.

Yesterday, also, letter from Abdul Aziz and today a fine letter from Dan Berrigan about the apathy of Catholics in U.S. and the things that are to be done.

From Ferry – copy of a talk given by Gerard Rice, publisher of the *Scientific American* – on nuclear attack. He says, "The kind of society that would emerge from the shelters may be guessed from the kind of society that is preparing to go into shelters now." Not that he expects shelters to be of much use, except far from the "hard target" where a groundburst kicks up a lot of radiated fragments of buildings – and people.

November 27, 1961

Last night was on the night watch. (Last Sunday after Pentecost.)

Wasted time, brooded. The cloud that hangs over everything is more than a mood now. It is difficult to realize that the sort of thing that has always been just a kind of pretending is now suddenly fitted out with objectivity. One may say, "Men have always expected a universal cataclysm and it has never come." Now that it is quite possible, and within man's own power, one begins to think that man has always expected it because it was coming as the result of a self-fulfilling prophecy. Now, since he *can* destroy everything and *cannot* stand the tension of waiting or face the labor of patient reconciliation . . . Fortunately one thinks such a thought without understanding it, as a child thinks of death.

But on the night watch, hurrying by, I pushed open the door of the novices' scriptorium, and flashed the light over all the empty desks. It was as if the empty room were wholly full of their hearts and their love, as if their goodness had made the place wholly good and rich with love. The loveliness of humanity which God has taken to Himself in love, and the wonder of each individual person among them. This is of final and eternal significance. To have been appointed by God to be their Father, to have received them from God as my children, to have loved them and been loved by them with such simplicity and sincerity, without nonsense or flattery or sentimentality; this is completely wonderful and is a revelation, a parousia, of the Lord of History. That history may now end is not so relevant.

From this kind of love necessarily springs hope, hope even for political action, for here paradoxically hope is most necessary. Hope is always most necessary precisely where everything, spiritually, seems hopeless. And this is precisely in the confusion of politics. Hope against hope that man can gradually disarm and cease preparing for destruction and learn at last that he *must* live at peace with his brother. Never have we been less disposed to do this. It must be learned, it must be done and everything else is secondary to this supremely urgent need of man.

December 4, 1961

Mark Van Doren was here yesterday, 1st Sunday of Advent. We had a good quiet talk walking up to the hermitage and back. He said a lot about animals and about God loving them. This was what I liked best. It seemed to me to be a most fitting subject of talk for the porch up there. It was a warm day, so I could not build a fire. He spoke of Ferry at Santa Barbara (who has been sending all sorts of documents and helping with the paperback on peace I am doing for New Directions), of Scott Buchanan, who must come here. Of the conference with some Russian generals and scientists there. Certainly they sincerely want disarmament and peace – at least those who are not politicians. Mark of course highly respects Lewis Mumford who has consented gladly to write for the peace book (I wrote to him at Berkeley). The *Nation* has asked me to consider writing an article. Began one that might be a possibility for them today.

Reading Clement still, and the *Scala Claustralium* (for the novices) and began today *The Causes of World War III* by C. Wright Mills. Clear and forthright, one of the best of the good books on peace that are being written, for this country truly has a conscience and I am inspired by the fact.

Life of Fr. Joseph Metzger, executed by the Nazis for his peace efforts. It is deeply moving, and suggests many reflections, as I myself may end up that way, and I can think of worse ways of dying. I do not account myself worthy of such a death.

Steve Rus, a Czechoslovakian postulant from Canada, is entering. He escaped from Czechoslovakia when the Reds took over in 1948. Was a Basilian in Canada.

December 11, 1961

Yesterday, day of recollection, realized again above all my need for profound and total humility – especially in relation to any work I may do for peace. Humility is more important than zeal. Descent into nothingness and dependence on God. Otherwise I am just fighting the world with its own weapons and there the world is unbeatable. Indeed it does not even have to fight back, for I will exhaust myself and that will be the end of my stupid efforts.

To seek strength in God, especially in the Passion of Christ.

The mysterious, unknown power of the Cross. Preachers of the Cross hide its power and distort its meaning by their own image of the Crucified.

The crucifixion is literally the *destruction* of the "Image" of God.

An "image" is presented and then taken away from man (and restored if man follows into the night). There is no adequate image. Preachers preserve an image, often a very faulty one. Meaning of the stress on the resurrection here.

But to descend into the Night of the Passion, the Night of Christ's death, baptism in His sufferings, without image.

Fr. Placide Deseille of Bellefontaine, who is rewriting the Directory, sent some excellent offprints of articles by him – one on Monastic Spirituality is quite perfect in its simplicity, though not complete. He has a good grasp of it. I wish he would write more about his visit to the Coptic monks in Egypt (he went to Scete).

December 12, 1961. (Our Lady of Guadalupe)
Looking at "facts" – if there are clear comprehensible facts to look at, and not delusions:
1. It is hardly likely that either America or Russia will disarm now.
2. It is very likely that other countries, esp. China, will "get the bomb" soon.
3. The situation between America and Russia is most unstable, and will continue to be so, perhaps increasingly, during the next six or seven years. At this time both countries will build up enormously complex and complete weapons systems.
4. There will be great, and even acute danger of nuclear war between now and 1967.
5. After that? If we can hold out that long, the relations with Russia may well become stabilized or stalemated. What will be the new problems?
6. Is there any likelihood of anyone disarming? Is America psychologically capable of standing an indefinite stalemate *in which nothing is solved?*

From Al Hujswírí [*The Kashf Al-Mahjub*]
"It is glorious for man to bear the burden of trouble laid upon him by his Beloved."
"Purity is the attribute of those who love, and the lover is he that is dead in his own attributes and living in the attributes of his Beloved." *[p. 32]*
"He that is purified by love is pure, and he that is absorbed in the Beloved and has abandoned all else is a Sufi." *(p. 34)*

"The Sufi is he that is dead to self and lives by the truth; he has escaped from the grip of human faculties and has attained. . . ." *(p. 35)*

"Renunciation of pleasure is the act of Man but the annihilation of pleasure is the act of God. The act of Man is formal and metaphorical while the act of God is real." *(p. 37)*

"The Sufi is he that has nothing in his possession, nor is possessed by anything." *(37)*

"Sufism is essence without form." *[p. 37]*

"The Sufi is he whose thought keeps pace with his foot." *(39)*

December 18, 1961

Yesterday afternoon, out by the lake where I planted the loblolly pines (they are doing well) there was a small goose in the lake, with some ducks. Could not identify it by the bird book, but it was closer to the snow goose than anything else. That lake was an awfully dangerous place for it! I could hear the natives whooping in the woods, and gun shots in the rain.

Fr. Barnabas [Ahern], C.P., gave one of his finest talks, on the Infancy narrations in the Gospel of Luke. The much controverted approach. Very clear and conclusive and above all it seemed to me this *midrash* concept is actually very well apt to bring out the fullest revealed content of the text.

December 20, 1961. Ember Wednesday

In this morning's nocturn: *Clama in fortitudine qui annuntias pacem in Jerusalem* [Cry out loud, who announces peace to Jerusalem]. To announce peace is something quite other than to preach it – it is not to exhort men to be peaceable, but to announce that the Lord has broken through the wickedness and confusion of the world to establish His kingdom of peace. My vocation seems to be only to preach peace, and perhaps only as a voice in the desert preparing the way for those who will "announce" it.

December 22, 1961

Or rather, it is even doubtful whether my vocation is to preach peace. More and more the conviction haunts me, that I shall sooner or later be silenced.

A letter from Fr. Ford, S.J., who is nevertheless one of the *minority* of U.S. Catholic moralists who are against the nuclear bombing of cities, assures me that I *cannot* deduce from the statements of Pius XII against nuclear war that the nuclear bombing of cities is "condemned." There are always "escape clauses." And he says that if I urge Catholics not to work in armament plants etc., I am urging them to be "more Catholic than the Pope and bishops."

He strongly advises against trying to help Abraham Heschel to get published in Italy, by making any statement in his praise.

If I am to write an article asked for by the *Nation* it must be super-cagey, censored by the Cardinal in N.Y. (or some other ordinary acceptable to the Canons).

Then yesterday a letter from the Papal Secretary of State to Rev. Father urges a "diminution of contacts with Protestant ministers and scholars." My inference is that I have been delated [from the Latin, to carry information] in the H[oly] See by somebody and the whole thing is regarded with disfavor and suspicion. Which may well be, for I am not always prudent in speech and am perhaps not the man for this kind of work. [Merton adds in the margin: "What was the absurd wording? I forget."]

About peace. Maybe the best is to say quickly and wisely and fully all that I have to say, all at once, and then let the blow fall. But it may be a premature and insufficient statement. No point in saving up the ammunition for later, there may be no later – I mean no opportunity to speak, because of protests and condemnation.

What obsesses me most is the grim condition of the Church, committed in great part to the "escape clauses" that "justify" the brutalities of the secular solution, and which enable the moral theologian to hand over the ordinary Christian, bound hard and fast, to the power of the militarist.

In the early days of Christianity, to be a soldier was *abnormal*, to refuse war was *normal*.

Today, when war is beyond all reason, is utterly murderous and suicidal, we are told that the Christian who fails to participate is not a good Christian, he is evading his duty, rejecting the *Cross!!!*

This is to me one of the most abominable and terrifying of signs. And one of the most convincingly awful indications that the end is near.

In a word – that it may indeed be vitally necessary for us to be better Christians than our theologians, and *that our very salvation may depend on this!*

December 24, 1961. Christmas Eve, and Sunday

Cold. There was a light snow during the night. Yesterday sleet and slush all day. The novices worked quietly at their decorations. The decorations are restrained and simple. Two small trees. The Notre Dame valedictorian has left. There is one postulant, a Mexican architect, who doubts his vocation. Fr. Boris, the Czech engineer, seems to be doing well.

In the offices lately I have been struck by the word *majestas* [majesty].

The anguish of the word "peace" in our offices. And the realization that it is totally serious, and perfectly simple. Above all our confusions, our violence, our sin, God established His kingdom no matter what "the world" may do about it. He sends the Prince of Peace. The message of Christians is not that the kingdom "might come, that peace might be established, but that the kingdom *is* come, and that there *will* be peace for those who seek it."

Multiplicabitur eius imperium et pacis non erit finis. [His reign shall increase, and there will be no end to peace.]

And this morning I was particularly struck by the 8th Responsory.

Intuemini qui natus sit iste qui ingreditur ad salvandas gentes: ipse est Rex iustitiae cuius generatio non habet finem. [Behold who is born, who comes to save the peoples: he is the King of Justice, whose line will have no end.]

Who He is, that comes to save the world! I have not known Him. I have not realized the meaning and power of His presence in the world, nor sufficiently believed in His message of salvation. Endlessness, power above and beyond times *majestas* – peace in the light of that all powerful and tranquil majesty.

The *Patria caelestis* [heavenly country] – a monk is one who hastens to his homeland, there to find Christ whom he has loved and served on earth. *Quisquis ad patriam calestem festinas.* [Who are hastening toward the heavenly country.] More and more I must lighten the weight of the baggage.

Opposition between the *militia mundi* [soldier of the world] and the *militia christi* [soldier of Christ].

Christmas Day

Many times yesterday and today it has occurred to me, irrationally, "what if this were your last Christmas?" A thought not to be toyed with, because of the temptation to *accept* war and destruction with fatalism and indifference. I can indeed be indifferent for myself but I must not be indifferent for the rest of the world, and for the children, and for all who have a right to live in happiness and peace. To live and say to all who would destroy peace –

"You are scoundrels!" and yet recognize them to be like myself, in confusion, and in many ways good men. Perhaps in many ways better than I, but blinded and deceived. For we cannot keep peace by calling one another scoundrels. On the contrary, the main thought of my heart (it has been a thought of the heart and not of the head) is that while Christ is given to me as my life, I also am given to Him as His joy and His crown (Julian of Norwich) and that he wills to take delight in saving and loving me. And this is all for me.

December 27, 1961. St. John

It rained at first but now the day has turned softly bright in the afternoon, and there is a little, cutting wind, and the sun is out, though it is pale. Most sit in the monastery writing their letters, though I saw Fr. Denis (Phillips) bobbing along the back road in his white hood, and Fr. Robert (De Sutter) taking off into the woods with a mysterious sack, and Fr. Martin (Gulliver) going off with sober joy in coveralls.

This morning I was praying much for a wise heart, and I think the gift of this Christmas has been the real discovery of Julian of Norwich. I have long been around her, and hovered at her door, and known that she was one of my best friends, and just because I was so sure of her wise friendship I did not make haste to seek what I now find.

She seems to me a true theologian, with a greater clarity and organization and depth even than St. Theresa. I mean she really elaborates the content of revelation as deeply experienced. It is first experienced, then thought, and the thought deepens again into life, so that all her life the content of her vision was penetrating her through and through.

And one of the central convictions is her eschatological orientation to the central, dynamic secret act "by which all shall be made well" at the last day, our *"great deed"* [underlined twice] ordained by Our Lord from without beginning.

Especially the first paradox – she must "believe" and accept the doctrine that there are some damned, yet *also* the "word" of Christ shall be "saved in all things" – and "all manner of thing shall be well." The heart of her theology is this apparent contradiction, in which she must remain steadfastly. And I believe that this "wise heart" I have prayed for is precisely in this – to stay in this hope and this contradiction, fixed on the certainty of the "great deed" – which alone gives the Christian and spiritual life its true, full dimension.

December 31, 1961

Quiet, early morning, dark. Distress and confusion of this year. Foreboding at 1962. What will it bring? Yet I think the foolish business about shelters, with all its enormous stupidities – down to the plastic burial suit for $50 – has got people "roused" as the saying is, and there is a lot of protest. The same ones have been too passive, and they are beginning to be forced to react. But perhaps it is too late.

Life is madder and madder, except that the woods and the fields are always a relief. Bright sun on the big sycamore by the mill yesterday, and light snow underfoot. And silence. Silence now also, and the night.

I still haven't ploughed through the pile of Christmas mail, not all of it. It appalls me. I haven't read enough of the things I should be reading and want to read: Clement, Gregory of Nyssa (whose relic came from S[ister] Thérèse [Lentfoehr] at Christmas). Then again I have worked myself into an equivocal and silly position with *curiositas* [curiosity]. By now that should be familiar. Disgust. Drop it. Return to the sources and to silence. Yet one *must* speak and act now. But I pray I may some day learn how rightly. I feel there is not much time left for one to be learning the most important things, and I will have to trust to God for all that I lack, and will continue to lack.

PART III

Seeking the Right Balance

January 1962–December 1962

The need for ripeness – for the slow finishing of the work of God in me.

February 14, 1962

January 2, 1962

"... Not much could be published, but up to his final arrest Metzger worked hard through personal correspondence."

(from the Life of Fr. Metzger lent to me by John Heidbrink of the FOR)

January 3, 1962

A warm sunny day, like spring, full of many small joys.

Talking to the novices about craftsmanship in the Rule, and [Eric] Gill, and "Good Work" and Shaker furniture. All subjects that are dear to me. And the sunny quiet room. Their presence and their love.

Talking for ten minutes before None to Bro. Gerard, who is teaching Frs. Basil and Isaias to make baskets, and this afternoon is out with them getting willows.

Finished a short piece on Fr. Metzger, and finished also the "Song for the Death of Averroes"[1] – from Ibn al' Arabi, as given in *Asin Palacios*.

Fr. Alberic said you can get bison from the National Parks that have too many. How lovely it would be to have some bison on this hillside.

But now I have gone too far! Return to reality! This is the age of nuclear war!

January 9, 1962

"... *ut placeam coram Deo in lumine viventium.*" ["... that I may be pleasing to God in the light of the living" (Psalm 55:14).][2]

Deeply moved by this psalm in particular, in the night office. As if I have never seen it before (Ps. 55). Sometimes you get the impression a psalm is being given to you brand new, to be your own, by God. This is one I may soon need, and need badly!

The O[ld] T[estament] idea that God grants us knowledge of His being inasmuch as He moulds one according to His will – as members of the People of the Covenant.

---

[1]   Published in *Emblems of a Season of Fury* (New York, 1963).
[2]   Merton's numbering is from the Greek Septuagint. In the Hebrew and Authorized Versions, Psalm 55 is 56.

January 12, 1962

Zero weather. Good work yesterday afternoon with the novices, cutting wood at the hermitage. Bright and cold.

On Wednesday I went over to the Methodist Seminary at Asbury – again on a bright, fiercely cold day. It was an experience being there, eating lunch with the faculty after a service in their chapel, talking to some of the students. Howard Shipps is a very fine person and I like them all – a great atmosphere of warmth and friendliness, good, grass-roots American people. Wilmore is a very small place off in a small corner of the country. The Seminary seems prosperous. They are to build a new library. The chapel, big and bright. I think of it, I don't know what I feel about it, my emotions are too deep and confused. Everything depends, I suppose, on their understanding of the prayer-community. I find it hard to get oriented without any altar of sacrifice. It seems to me a "synagogue" rather than a "temple." They sang a good hymn, which I remembered, and sang it with power and joy. And there was a longish informal report from one of the professors who had been in Asia on a sabbatical and had attended the World Council of Churches at New Delhi. A non-committal objective talk. Problem in the World Council: as at Athos in the 19th century, sudden danger of Russians controlling the votes. This had been obviated, no doubt. He spoke of Nelson's address to the Council – all about peace. But the Indian troops were already moving to take over Goa. About which I cannot get too excited, except that it was a bad gesture, an evil sign. India has meant much since Gandhi, and it is important to live up to such meanings.

On the way over and back stopped to take pictures at Shakertown. Marvelous, silent, vast spaces around the old buildings. Cold, pure light, and some grand trees. So cold my finger could no longer feel the shutter release. Some marvelous subjects. How the blank side of a frame house can be so completely beautiful I cannot imagine. A completely miraculous achievement of forms.

The moments of eloquent silence and emptiness in Shakertown stayed with me more than anything else – like a vision.

January 19, 1962

Dark. Snow.

Fr. Paschal Botz, O.S.B., arrived to give the retreat, which begins tonight. Rumor said that the preacher was to be [Hubert] Van Zeller.

Tired of war, tired of letters, tired of books. Shaving today, saw new lines under the eyes, a new hollowness, a beginning of weariness. Well. So it is good.

What matters most is secret, not said. This begins to be the most real and the most certain dimension.

I had been secretly worried about my writing, especially on peace, getting condemned. Nothing to worry about. Whenever I am *really* wrong, it will be easy enough to change. But it is strange that such things should be regarded with suspicion. I know this is wrong. Weary of blindness, of this blindness that afflicts all men, but most of all of the blindness afflicting those who ought to see.

J. Laughlin was here Tuesday and Wednesday and we worked on the Peace paperback. He will also do the little book on Clement and the *Protreptikos*, which is a project I like.

January 21, 1962. III Sunday after Epiphany
The snow remains.

From the night office:

Afflicti pro peccatis nostris quotidie cum lacrymis expectemus finem nostrum. Dolor cordis nostri ascendet ad te Domine, et eruas nos a malis quae innovantur in nobis. [Afflicted for our sins, daily with tears we await our end. May the sorrow of our hearts rise to you, Lord, and may you deliver us from the evils which have come upon us.]

The struggle against pessimism and desperation. How can we believe that the tragedy that is being prepared can be avoided? Everything contributes to the inexorable preparation. The weapons systems dictate their own policies and men obey their machines which demand a war of annihilation.

An H bomb costs $250,000. Was there ever such a bargain? In an age obsessed with bargains, this one will undoubtedly prove irresistible!

In the Gospel – "Many shall come from the East and West . . . but the children of the kingdom shall be cast out."

How can we evade the clarity with which this points not only to Jews but to all "children of the kingdom" who are not faithful to their deep vocation?

See Romans 2:9–16.

"A day when God through Jesus Christ will pass judgment on the hidden thoughts of men."

Rain pelting down on the remains of the snow. Slush and mud. I sit on my bed and look out at the garage, the farm building, the mud. The hills are invisible. Fr. P[aschal] preached a nice sermon on the Holy Name.

Amakuki Sessan in his commentary on Hakuin's "Song of Meditation" (conferences given on the radio in 1934!!) has a beautiful passage on the right use of all things – close to the very heart of Benedict's idea of poverty and also close to Shaker simplicity. Advantageous use (not wasting), loving use, living use, pure use, spiritual use.

And then this: "The madman runs to the east, and his keeper runs to the east. Equally to the east, but their purposes are different."[3]

January 24, 1962

Retreat still continues. I have liked all Fr. Paschal's simple and excellent conferences. It is good to have a Benedictine for a change!

Reading the *Tales of Rabbi Nachman* – some are a bit too drawn out, but the one about the Clever Man and the Simple Man was sobering. I was deeply moved by the one about the Rabbi and his son: the conventional and strict Rabbi going by the books and the son who tries his best to stick to the books and is led away by the interim voice. His desire to meet the holy Zaddik, and the way his Father half complied, and how the devil used his Father's superstition to prevent the meeting which would have meant "the coming of the Messiah." It is a profound story.

And in that connection: I am also reading the article on Conscience in the *Dict[ionnaire] de Spiritualité*.

Intense interior struggle in the past few days.

How I need interior freedom, and have blocked myself by false independence and indeed by all kinds of acting out and futility. This futility gets into everything oppressed by the peace writings and the implicit falsity in them, in spite of my good intentions.

[3] Merton used this Zen proverb as an epigraph in *Conjectures of a Guilty Bystander.*

I have not handled the community situation properly. Undoubtedly I have shirked sacrifices that would have helped me to be truly free.

What blocks me, however, is I think a genuine sensibility to wrong motives and emphasis in the community itself and in the Abbot. These are inevitable, and perhaps quite small, but I make too much of them, as if God could not use them precisely to free me.

Hence the infinite ways in which I permit myself to protest and complain – without being obvious to anyone. At least so I think, because I do not see it myself.

Yet all that "thinking" is, I know, absurd: both theirs and mine. It is not a question of working something out but of getting on another level, and this I can't do by myself.

It remains to be seen that this is probably as it should be!

January 25, 1962

Gratiam supernae benedictionis expostulet nobis sanctus Paulus vas electionis. [Let St. Paul, the "vessel of election," pray urgently for us for the grace of heavenly blessing.]

My problems are false problems. I would be a fool to write of them, and am a fool even to think of them. Yet I cannot prevent the absurd and wearying thoughts. Retreat has brought them on, not because of more solitude but because of less, for I haven't taken time to myself in the woods all week. I have been utterly regular and devoted to the ordinary common life, and hence I am feeling starved and strained, though it has been good in many ways. But really – have I any other satisfaction from this than the satisfaction of having done what I did not want to do? And is this fruitful? I cannot believe that this *alone* is fruitful and makes up for the lack of all other fruit.

In any case I have worried again about stopping writing, which is confused and absurd.

I *cannot* leave this decision to someone else, e.g. Father Abbot, who is in many ways indifferent.

I can perhaps withdraw from publication and write only what I deeply need to write. What is that? The little Clement of Alex. book is not it, I think. Not the way it stands. But it is to be published.

And the *Guilty Bystander?* Perhaps. But it will be execrated in the Order and will get me shot by the John Birch Society.

How serious is my need to be shot by the John Birch Society?

———

In concluding this retreat:

1. There can be no doubt, no compromise, in my decision to be completely faithful to God's will and truth, and hence I must seek always and in everything to act for His will and in His truth, and thus to seek with His grace to be "a saint."

Truth

2. There must be no doubt, no compromise in my efforts to avoid falsifying this work of truth by considering too much what others approve of and regard as "holy." In a word, it may happen (or it may not) that what God demands of me may make me look less perfect to others, and that it may rob me of their support, their affection, their respect. To become a saint therefore may mean the anguish of looking like and in a real sense "being" a sinner, an outcast. It may mean apparent conflict with certain standards which may be wrongly understood by me or by others or by all of us.

3. The thing is to cling to God's will and truth in their purity and try to be sincere and to act in all the things out of genuine love, in so far as I can.

January 30, 1962

Grey day.

Novices burnt up a huge pile of stumps in front of the sheep barn.

Afternoon at the hermitage – wrote the poem for the Ladies' Jail.[4]

Silence, semi-anguish. Grey blue hills.

Deeply moved by the story on Claude Eatherly – the pilot of the "Straight Flush" who cracked up after Hiroshima, who went around trying to get himself condemned for a crime, and the army kept getting him off because he was a "war hero."

He is in an institution somewhere now.

We have got to see. We have got to see what we are doing. We have got to see who we are in with – who makes our ideals meaningless, our decisions meaningless, our hopes for justice and innocence meaningless. The vast, vast corruption of the world, with America deeply involved – our ambivalence. The many who want the things we have always said to be true – the few who make them "true" only in a very special way.

---

4 "There Has to be a Jail for Ladies," published in *Emblems of a Season of Fury* (New York, 1963).

Names. A litany, a poem of magic African names. Power names. Names for which people die.

Sociéte Générale de Belgique

Fouminière	Diamonds	Kasai
Géomines	Tin	North Katanga
Bécéka	Railroads	Katanga, Kasai
Cottonco	Cotton	Katanga?

Union Minière

Metalkat	Coal, Zinc	Katanga
Sopolec	Hydroelectric power	Katanga
Sogechim	Chemicals	
Sopefor	Agriculture	

Monsieur E. Van Stracten. Monsieur H. Robiliart. Monsieur A. de Spirlet (retreatants at Orval? Readers of my pious volumes?). Charles Waterhouse. Harry Oppenheimer . . . Admiral Kirk.

And so Katanga operates independently and the armies of the big corporations backed by the U.S. kill off the UN soldiers and wear down the meaning and last semblance of UN authority.

(The Fathers of Woodstock will tell us of course that since there is no international authority of any significance, to control armaments, we must arm for war.)

British South Africa Company
Anglo-American Corp. of South Africa
De Beers Consolidated Mines etc. etc.

It is clearer than ever that the theological position in this country is *for* [double underlined] nuclear war. And with such self-assurance, such self-righteous complacency!

February 5, 1962

Douglas Steere and his wife were here this morning and I had a pleasant chat with them.[5] I liked them both and she especially struck me as a very spiritual person and a very typical Quaker, or what one imagines to be so. Very simple, direct, earnest, completely good.

---

[5] See *The Merton Annual* (Collegeville, 1994), Vol. 6 (1993), pp. 23–28, for Douglas V. Steere's account of this historic meeting.

He spoke of Dom Bede Griffiths, whom he likes and admires. Their Ashram is now a stone building with a pleasant chapel, in a very remote place, on a mountainside where the wind is so strong it almost blows all the vegetables out of the garden. Dom B. thinking primarily in terms of dialogue with Hindus, Buddhists etc., but nothing special has got under way.

He has been for a long time a member of Una Sancta. I forgot to ask if he had known Fr. Metzger. John Heidbrink wrote about starting Una Sancta in America. We discussed possibilities and I spoke of my total distrust of all movements and organizations. I said I thought we should simply do what Una Sancta does without making any declarations or statements, or drawing up constitutions etc.

Speaking of peace: John Bennett's inability to get loose from "deterrence." D.S. said there were men in the Pentagon who had a much more sober and prudent view of nuclear war than some of the theologians. This struck me as very significant.

He is a good friend of Dom Damasus Winzen and spoke of having met him at Marialaach years ago. Also said that in 1933 at Marialaach they were strong for Hitler. This confirms my impression that the liturgy people tend to lean towards totalitarianism.

He has spoken with a Carmelite (Fr. William [McNamara]) about their spiritual life movement and seems to think it a good one. And we were talking about possibilities for monasticism today. I was frank in saying I did not think Gethsemani had the answer to anything. It is good, but has nothing special to offer.

The most important thing that was said was concerned with Al[bert] Schweitzer's idea that the women of the world might possibly be the most effective force resisting war.

They spoke of the recent peace walks and demonstrations (strikes last week, which I heard of from the *Catholic Worker*).

"Who would think of lying down to sleep undisturbed when the whole living world is like a house on fire, blazing with the flames of death, disease, and old age?" *(Ashvagosha)*

Worse still with war, lust, lies, murder, greed . . .

February 6, 1962

A very important letter from Milosz, in reaction to the articles on peace I sent him. It touches me deeply because I respect his judgment more than that of anyone I know, on this question. For he has been through it. And we have not.

And yet, merely "having been through it" is not enough either.

The history of the last twenty years has been one immense brainwashing of everybody. And he is a graduate.

1. In particular he questions the validity of a moral examination of the question. Says it is irrelevant. The moralist multiplies noble principles but they have nothing to do with the facts. That this is merely "utopian," which I will accept, coming from him, as it is based on Polish disillusionment with the peace movements of 1939, and 1948 (Stalin).

2. That it is harping on the obvious because nobody would deny the evil of atomic war (but H. Kahn and Co. do and so do the theologians).

3. The *exasperation* caused by peace movements multiplies extremists on the right. This is the most weighty statement as far as I am concerned. There are awful ambiguities in this peace talk and I do not want to end up by simply crystallizing the opinion I think is immoral.

He judges on a sliding scale. On the one hand, the political crimes of the Totalitarians, on the other the (lesser) war crimes, which may have a "justification."

The Peace Walkers in Poland seemed to him to have made a ridiculous impression. He would hear from those who knew.

I seriously wonder about the letter I sent to *Liberation*. Perhaps this above all was noble nonsense.

Jim Forest wrote about civil disobedience at the AEC [Atomic Energy Commission]. Yes and no. I do not know to what extent this makes real sense. As a moral luxury for the participant, yes. But are things as simple as that?

> *Quoniam eripuisti animam meam de morte*
> *Et pedes meos de lapide*
> *Ut placeam coram Deo in lumine viventium.*
> [Because you delivered my soul from death
> and my feet from stumbling
> that I may be pleasing before God in the light of the living.]

These words of the psalm [55] are to me substantial and holy food, this cold afternoon, as they were in the night office this morning.

The reality of my life is the reality of interior prayer, always, and above all.

There is a large amount of delusion in all inordinate concern with action. Yet there must be the right action.

February 9, 1962

A very intelligent essay by Fr. [George] Tavard on Xtian culture was sent down here by Prof. Schlesinger at St. Mary's.

On the need of "openness" and contact with other cultures. Xtianity (which should be obvious) thrives on dialogue. No use being closed up and obsessed with a dead past. Xtian culture embraces its whole world and is larger than this world. Its facility is self-criticism.

I agree with his statement "Christian culture today is a problem rather than a fact." Why? Because the question is raised as to its ability to survive when "Christendom" (Xtian social order) is a thing of the past. Hence problem of rebuilding Xtian culture on the cosmic scale in cooperation with non-Christians . . . a cooperation he believes can become possible if post-Christian technological world realizes, in time, the need for Xtian wisdom.

February 13, 1962

Warm, spring like afternoon. Quiet.

Finished the *Last of the Just* [André Schwartz-Bart, New York, 1960], which is a tremendously moving thing, and says a great deal. Compassion in the midst of the inexorable absurdity and violence and madness of Nazism. Pity is the center. Pity as an absolute, more central than truth ("There is no place for truth here," says the Just man on the way to Auschwitz).

And that Christians have come in the end to hate Christ.

And that the Jews are Christ.

Letters from Rabbi Schwarzschild. Impressive generosity and warmth. He is the one who, alone, had a religious answer in a symposium, to the consecrated secularism of John Courtney Murray's war position. And yet J. C. Murray is a great and good man. But there are things he cannot grasp.

Letter from Jim Forest. The crazies, the Marxists, the psychotics in the Peace Movement.

Everybody says to me: "*You* speak! Everybody respects *you*! Everybody will listen to *you!*"

A man wanted to take my Peace Article in the *Commonweal* and buy space and run it as an ad in the *N.Y. Times*.

A John Bircher writes asking me to defend the John Birch Society, "which is being heaped with ridicule."

Everybody wants me now to say something, except the censors who want me to shut up.

It is when everybody wants you to say something that you are on the skids for real, like the river the kid saw in Stillenstadt [in *The Last of the Just*], revolving away from under all the people.

February 14, 1962

Blessed Conrad again.

The need for ripeness – for the slow finishing of the work of God in me. It needs my desire, my consecrated attention, my submission, my withdrawal from noise and confusion. Still many doubts about action, even in regard to war. To what extent is it significant?

And all these letters. But in the tension with Farrar Straus and Cudahy, about the *Reader*, I am also realizing that the time has perhaps finally ripened for less publishing.

I have nothing for them to publish except *Art and Worship*, which I do not want to finish, and the silly text on Perfection, which is a pure waste of time and which I am holding back.

But there is always of course *Conjectures of a Guilty Bystander*, which may not even get through the censor.

Milarepa's prayer in solitude – austere and beautiful. Something to meditate on – like the *Fiery Arrow*.

February 17, 1962

I have heard that in the Abbot's office, photostatic copies of the letters I send out are taken and kept. I almost believe it.

Fr. John Eudes has already left Rome after three months of study there, saying the course is of no value.

One of the boys at *Catholic Worker* wrote me a taunting letter saying that in speaking for this community, I spoke as the mouth of a dead body. But is it true to say I speak for this community? I hope not!

It is certain I do not speak for the Abbot and it is good of him to let me speak at all when I often say things he disagrees with – or *probably* disagrees with, for he says nothing. It is certain I do not speak for the seniors in the choir (only a few are senior to me now, however). It is certain I do not speak for most of the brothers, especially for those in the farm building. It is certain I do not speak for most of the young priests who were in the scholasticate when I was Master, though they are for the most part glad to have me speak as I do. In fact, I doubt if I "speak for" anyone here, though I scarcely speak against them either. Neither statement would be true or even relevant. I am here and I write, and most of them accept the fact without losing their composure.

Wm. Congdon is supposed to be coming for most of next week and I feel uneasy about it. Great fanfare over his conversion. Trouble with his Secular Institute, the Pro Civitate Xtiana; he is too great a speaker. Having an exhibition in the Betty Parson's gallery, to be attended by many uncomprehending Monsignors and even Bishops. This is the kind of Catholic activity that makes me a little sick by its phoniness.

At the Carmelites: dear things. But few of them have any sense. They *might* preserve some of their life; did not discourage it. Yet Mother Angela retains her balance and depth. She is a good one!

February 20, 1962

When was it – the 14th perhaps – that the New Sengai Calendar arrived? I think it is the best. Three of them.

One in the Fr. Master's room, which is the January Tiger (and this is the year of the Tiger, I am told), one here in the hermitage, which is the wild horse of May – and he is pawing toward the front door, so that I must think of his unruly dispositions when I propose to go out.

A very funny and also serious letter from Ad Reinhardt, mocking and reproving me for the piece I wrote about Congdon and which is splashed all over the back of his big book. Ad is perfectly right. Congdon not yet here.

Big group of Protestants here yesterday – Episcopalians, Methodists, Disciples of Xt.

A very encouraging letter from Justus Lawler on the Peace article in the *Commonweal*. He wants it for a book for Herder. Macmillan wants me to do a book . . . etc.

February 21, 1962

Admiration for the superbly written note from an old beekeeper in a village of Normandy, 30 km. from La Trappe. Really a work of art and of perfect taste, even if a little funny, in the style of the last century. But charming. Spoke of having fought in World War I side by side *"Avec des camarades de vos régions lorsqu'on se battait aux Eparges dans la Meuse* [With comrades from your neck of the woods when we fought at Eparges in the Meuse]." An inexpressibly moving testimony of a world that is perhaps ceasing to exist.

I am moved in somewhat the same way by the things said, with such wholesome simplicity, by John XXIII – a wonderful spirit of Christian and European civilization. How far from what is developing everywhere, here, now.

Answered the beekeeper today, at any rate.

And so, back to the *Dhyana.*[6] "That makes nothing arise."

February 27, 1962

Wrote a poem about the man in space. I forget what day he was in space. He went up a major and came down a colonel. Rah! Rah! Still, it is an exciting and wonderful thing that he was up there weightless and all. And an American. And in full view of the press and everybody.

Seriously: from a human and rational viewpoint there is every chance of a disastrous war in the next three to five years.

Although it is almost unbelievable to imagine this country being laid to waste, yet that is very probably what is going to happen.

Without serious reason, without people "wanting it" and without them being able to prevent it, because of their incapacity to use the power they have acquired. They must be used by it.

Hence the absolute necessity of taking this fact soberly into account and living in the perspectives which it establishes – an almost impossible task.

1. *Preeminence of meditation* and prayer, of self-emptying, cleaning out, getting rid of the self that blocks the view of truth. The self that says it will be here and then that it will not be here . . .

2. *Preeminence of compassion* for every living thing, for life, for the defenseless and simple beings, for the human race in its blindness.

---

[6] The stage of yoga leading to the final state of contemplation.

For Christ, crucified in His image. Eucharistic sacrifice, in humility and silence.

3. *Weariness of words*, except in friendship, and in the simplest and most direct kind of communication, by word of mouth or letter.

4. *Preeminence of the silent and conclusive action* – if any presents itself. And meaningful suffering, accepted in complete silence, without justification.

March 2, 1962. First Friday

Nearing the end of my week as Hebdomadary. Mostly cold, rainy days. There are floods all over Kentucky.

Several from the *Catholic Worker* spent the week here. Jim Forest, Bob Kaye, Nelson Born, Alex Marchant. George Johnson was here but had to leave last Sunday. Very good and very comforting to see the spiritual awareness and aliveness of these kids who have prayed, fasted, in vigil outside the UN, the AEC etc. for Peace. The new generation of the sit-ins. They are the most hopeful of signs and a great consolation. The truth is in them and they are simple and good and have nothing to do with anybody's official nonsense, certainly God is in them and guiding them – they are something of a faithful remnant in this eschatalogical time – friends and associates of the ones who went on the SF [San Francisco]–Morrow Peace March last year. I am happy that they have come here and that I have unceremoniously turned out to be part of all that goes on among them.

And now, at the end of their retreat, news comes that Kennedy will announce the resumption of Atomic Testing. They will go back to fasting and sleeping on sidewalks.

I like Bob Kaye's hot language ("groovy cats," "it's a gas, man!"). Jim Forest is an exceptionally good and gifted person. They all write hundreds of poems, very much influenced by this girl Jean Morton, who also writes hundreds of poems and likes Zen etc. etc. It is a blessed generation.

Geo. Johnson also touched by God in a special way after much suffering. A meek and dour person, afraid of getting arrested, for he was years in a kind of reformatory. Full of surprising and holy insights.

Reading Wright Mills on the *Power Elite*. How can we avoid war? The Pentagon is moving the country and forming everybody's mind for war. The picture that has meaning to most people is basically military. He contends, I believe rightly, that since WWII the military have really taken over from the politicians (or taken the politicians over). The country is on a *permanent* military basis. This I had not realized so clearly, still thinking in terms of 1940 when I entered.

———

Reading a booklet on "Cybernation." Thought of a story, a diary of a machine, lonely and busy, still functioning very actively in a bombed-out world ten years after all the people are extinct – commenting on nothing, but brightly, busily, efficiently, in joyous and mechanical despair.

Question – more or less abstract – whether to write book on Cassian for the Benedictine Studies. Probably not, or not now. Too many people coming around, and what time I have is better spent alone in meditation.

March 4, 1962
"The secret which is hidden in the heart of the Father, has become Man."
– St. Thomas Comm[entary] On Tim[othy]
That Christ is not a human nature conscious of Himself as (human) subject. To say He is *natura humana sui conscia* [human nature with self-consciousness] would be saying He was a Human Person (subject). Hence Nestorianism. So some distinguish two *consciousnesses*, divine and human, but there is only one (divine) subject.
What does Buddhism attempt to do with the *natura humana sui conscia?*
What happens to it in mysticism?
Implications? Difficulties?

March 6, 1962
There is unquestionably a great nobility in Sartre's morality of "authenticity," at least as he expresses it in his book on anti-semitism. And this too throws a different light on the "situation ethic" which is so spat upon – when it is represented as a form of opportunism and an evasion of responsibility. Here on the contrary it is an *acceptation of responsibility* – in the fullest and most direct way.

> "[If] it is agreed that man may be defined as a being having freedom within the limits of a situation, then it is easy to see that the exercise of this freedom may be considered as 'authentic' or 'inauthentic' according to the choices made in the situation. Authenticity, it is almost needless to say, consists in having a true and lucid consciousness of a situation, in answering the responsibilities and risks that it involves, in assuming it in pride and humiliation, sometimes in horror and hate."
>
> Anti-Semitism [New York, 1948], 90

He then goes on to say pointedly and with delight that "most Christians are not authentic."

Follow fifty pages or so about the way a Jew, under pressure of anti-semitism, is "inauthentic" and in trying to escape his condition as Jew simply makes that condition all the more inescapable. There is then no escape, no hiding, in a "universal" human condition that makes one anonymous. There is a point to this. He is not speaking metaphysically (at least here) but as a sociologist.

"The authentic Jew abandons the myth of universal man."

Is perhaps the weakness of pacifism its tendency to take refuge in a myth of universality? Yes, when pacifism is not Christian. Christian pacifism on the other hand, should be existential – "authentic" and start from one's present reality. It seldom does. Perhaps the bellicism of so many moral theologians is in a way more "authentic" – but disastrously so. True to a fatal heritage.

Note that the "repressive social force" of anti-semitism is very active in Russia today. Is Russian communism authentic? By no means.

In any case, S[artre] says, "Anti-semitism is a mythical bourgeois representation of the class struggle and it could not exist in a classless society . . . in a society whose members feel mutual bonds of solidarity because they are all engaged in the same enterprise. There would be no place for it." So his own romanticism now comes to the fore!

But he is right when he says that anti-semitism is not a Jewish problem, it is *our* problem.

(As Richard Wright said: "There is no Negro problem in the U.S. There is only a white problem.")

March 9, 1962. St. Gregory of Nyssa

In the refectory, over the weekend, Fr. V. read with intense seriousness an essay on the Eucharist by Card. Vaughan. The superficial apologetic approach, pseudo-scientism, popular 19th century clichés and half truths, having little or nothing to do with the real mystery of the Eucharist.

This is what passes for Catholic faith.

I reflected that the Buddhist texts I am reading are in reality far closer to the depth of Catholic Truth. If others can beguile themselves with the trivialities of western popular science, certainly I can enter into the Oriental mysticism and ways of meditation, which open the heart much more deeply to the action of God's light. The futilities of the true apologist create and purify the spiritual ignorance which the Orientals remove and dispel.

Reading Hans Küng on *The Council, Reform and Reunion* [New York, 1961].

If I wanted to start copying bits of it I would end by copying page after page, because I am so glad these things are at last said.

Yet they are after all only *obvious* – even trite.

That this Church is stuffy, dusty, narrow, that the hierarchy has been immobile, stupid, passive, repressive, etc. etc. The *closed mind* of the Churchman today!

What I fear is that this will only engender a lot of intense activity and legislation, decrees, "reforms" etc. which will authoritatively impose a lot of new obligations and change all the burdens from one shoulder to the other. Without freeing the heart to receive the H[oly] Spirit in abundance.

They are not easily beguiled. They know and have known for years how to make a lot of fuss and tighten up a lot of bolts in lieu of real reform . . .

He has a very lucid page on *false adaptation* – an external justification with a contemporary trend with no inner understanding of the contemporary need. "Playing" at being adapted with the help of slogans and programs.

And on the other hand – "churchiness" – regarding organization as an end in itself. He opposes the two to each other. They very easily combine.

This he sees. The alliance of the Saducees and the Pharisees ag[ain]st Christ.

March 10, 1962

Whether it is easy to love the Church, the Church as she *is* [underlined twice] and not as she might be . . .

To love the "poor" sinners, yes. For we count ourselves among the poor ones.

But the great, complacent, obtuse, powerful and self-satisfied sinners who are aware only of their righteousness, who close the doors, who do not enter in and help others out, the Grand Inquisitors who build their own structure on top of God's structure and attach more importance to what they themselves have built than to what He builds . . . Yet they are in their own way patient and gentle. They too suffer. They too have a kind of humility. But they are *closed* [underlined twice]. There are human realities to which they absolutely refuse to be sensitive. For they have somehow come to believe that a certain kind of compassion is a weakness they cannot afford.

It is not a question of who or where you are in the Church – at the very top is the most humble and compassionate man, a wonderful father, John XXIII. And near him are many such. But also others, alas!

And so we are already handing out "victory communiqués" in abundance.

"Genuine suffering on account of the Church springs from love of the Church; love for a Church who is too unlike her Lord." *([Küng], p. 39)*

March 12, 1962. St. Gregory

After days of rain there was a little sun this morning. Now it is cloudy and windy again. The Lenten fast seems to be doing me good. But I don't always use my time well. Yet being hungry slows me down, and I use it less badly than I might otherwise.

Paul Sih was here the other day, and we got going on Confucius. I learned from him the rather complex skill of reading the Chinese Dictionary, and I will keep at the classics in the original (with a translation handy of course!). Even if I only learn one or two characters, and look long at them in their context, something worth while has been done.

March 15, 1962

Hungry. Quiet morning. Waiting in the hermitage where I am to give a retreat conference to Frs. Felix and Linus (for Diaconate – this is Ember week).

Ought to come here more often in the morning when I am free (Tuesday and Thursday). What prevents me? Writing letters – which to tell the truth are necessary enough!

"When Ignorance has been got rid of and knowledge has arisen, one does not grasp after sense pleasures, speculative views, rites and customs, the theory of self." *– in* Buddhist Texts, *p. 75*

March 17, 1962

Beautiful early spring day, cold and bright. St. Patrick's.

As though the world still went on the same as ever and as though there were a St. Patrick's day, as in the days of old.

Long morning with ordination Mass (Diaconate Frs. Felix and Linus). The litany seemed long, with the stomach so completely empty! But the fasting is excellent and clarifies the mind.

After the Mass the Auxiliary Bishop (Maloney) stood in the cloister and smiled in his finery and gave forth drolleries about St. Patrick and Leprechauns. Just like in the old days when there was an Ireland.

And another Irish auxiliary bishop, this time in Washington, landed on me hard in an editorial denouncing my peace article in the *Commonweal*.

Heard last night of the death of Fr. Patrick (Finn) who was in theology with me. Went to the Utah monastery and left after ordination to go on the missions in the Pacific – and after left the priesthood, reduced to the lay state and died as a layman, I think without sacraments. Poor, tall, irresponsible man, with his jokes and his angers and his friendships. Flashing eyes and a great grin. And I think desperately sad a lot of the time.

March 18, 1962. II Sun. Lent

Jim Forest and a lot of others from *CW* were jailed some time ago for demonstrating before AEC building in N.Y. Released but will be tried in four days, on the 22nd.

I am not totally happy about the peace movement. There is much that is morally sloppy and irresponsible about it, yet there is generosity and the goodness of kids who are awake and discontent with the utter triviality of a society that, in addition to being futile, is also self-destructive.

"The sin of Judah is written with a pen of iron; with a point of diamond it is engraved upon the tablet of their heart and on the horns of their altars . . .

"The heart is deceitful above all things and desperately corrupt, who can understand it?

"I the Lord search the mind and try the heart and give to every man according to his ways," (Jeremiah 17[:1, 9–10]).

I like this translation from the RSV.

Deeply moved in my heart to think seriously of death, and of untruth, and deception, and the power of Satan, and the light of Christ our Salvation.

"He sent forth His word and healed them" (Ps. 106:20) [see footnote 2].

Karl Rahner's [*On the*] *Theology of Death* [New York, 1961] is a most exciting book. First time I have been completely won over to him.

Basic idea: that death by its nature is meant to be an act of fulfillment.

That by sin it has become a dissolution – suffered and undergone – a final manifestation of sin.

That by grace it becomes once again, though hiddenly, an act of faith and submission, an act *done* [underlined twice] – while also the body and soul suffer separation.

This emphasis on the *act* [underlined twice] of death in fulfillment and self-transcendence is to me startlingly Buddhist in the highest spiritual sense of Buddhism properly understood. Here is a real point of contact between Buddhism and Xtianity.

"Mortal sin is *the will to die autonomously,*" a tremendous intuition.

"Death because of its darkness is faced rightly when it is entered upon by man by an act in which he surrenders himself fully *and with unconditional openness* to the disposal of the incomprehensible decision of God, because in the darkness of death man cannot dispose of himself freely and knowingly." p. 52

On p. 53 he appears to include a kind of Buddhist spiritualization under the "sinful act" of autonomous death. In reality this could not be true Buddhism – it would be the spirit's affirmation of itself as intangible. True Buddhism as I understand it is a perfect spiritual humility and a *total openness*.

Properly understood, Buddhist concept of liberation should open me to Xt. Improperly it would close one inexorably!

I am aware of the foolish sin that has always nested in my nature, and that even grace has not altogether thrown out – a silly, unquestioned supposition that there is in me some innate cleverness that will outwit death when it comes, and, of course always with grace, be saved. It is from this folly that I probably deserve all the bitterness that is in my life. May the Cross of Christ rescue me from such absurd wisdom! May I learn from Him true abandonment and trust, and leave this delusion.

March 20, 1962

Whole day at hermitage – first time I have had permission for this.

Eating lunch here is a great advantage. It makes a very big difference to the peace and recollection of the day – not *having* to go anywhere or do anything – and quickly losing all desire for any useless activity. Such a condition is rare in the monastery or non-existent. Except perhaps in the infirmary.

March 24, 1962

Spring for real. Warm sun. I am in the cool back room of the hermitage.

The *Catholic Worker* has printed a first draft of an article – a text I did not want printed and that contains many statements I wanted to change – on peace. It is clear to me that under cover of being honest, frank and just I have been too eager to speak and too eager to say things that a few people wanted to hear – and most people did not want to hear. Better to have waited and simply tried to say, with utmost care, what is true. Of course when I write anything I write what I think is true. But what is true can also be said so badly that it becomes a misrepresentation of the truth.

Tree planting since Wednesday afternoon (Annunciation) when it was cold and rained. Since then it has gradually cleared.

Much rain this spring, probably full of Strontium 90 from the Russian tests.

Yesterday finished the [John Howard] Griffin book *Black Like Me*, moved and disturbed. As someone said – what there is in the South is not a Negro problem but a white problem. The trouble is pathological.

Finishing the Küng book on *The Council, Reform and Reunion*. Tremendous, clear, outspoken. Will his hopes be realized? He is sane about them, and realistic. A sobering discussion of possibilities which may never be realized. If they are not, it will be a disaster.

We cannot afford *not* to do our best to fulfill great hopes.

March 26, 1962

– F. of the Annunciation today (yesterday III Sun. of Lent – *Oculi [mei semper ad dominum.* My eyes are always open on the Lord]).

Joy before the ikon in the hermitage yesterday afternoon!

Need for discretion. Especially in my writing. I need to check and recheck. Above all my conviction that I am bound in conscience to speak out on such an issue does not guarantee that I know what to say. For instance my readiness to assume that thinking in the U.S. is building up to a preemptive strike may quite conceivably, if too bluntly stated, actually contribute to the formation of that kind of mentality – both here and in Russia!

Again moved by a little bit of information on [Franz] Jägerstädter – the Austrian peasant beheaded by Hitler as a conscientious objector – though advised by priest and bishop to conform and obey. In a child's notebook he wrote a precise essay on "Irresponsibility" which exactly hits the point everybody is missing. Two Germans both perform the same services for the Nazis – one believes in Nazism, the other condemns it – and thinks himself better. Actually he is the more guilty of the two.

March 27, 1962. Tuesday

An utterly lovely bright day. Warm and clear, like May in upper New York, the time John Paul came in his car and we drove about the hills – twenty-one years ago.

This morning the dull shine of the steeple through the trees. Woodpeckers and blue jays in the tall trees. Soft warm carpet of dry leaves on the ground. First faint buds on one of the maples. The ants beginning to come out of their huge hills (they had begun last Thursday when we were planting trees).

Justus Lawler sent a copy of his excellent article on "The Council and the Bishops." It seems this is one of the really vital issues, the restoration of the episcopate to their full as Teachers and Pastors, not just canonists and functionaries. We may need this very badly, very soon!

March 29, 1962. Mid-Lent

Another beautiful day. Abbot has gone to Georgia for installation of some bishop – the Prior got us out of chapter at 6:50 (I was fearing a theological conference that would have kept us in there until 7:15 or longer). Had plenty of time to say "*my*" mid-Lent Mass slowly, in the sunlight; with a happy din of bluejays and cardinals in the great willow outside the chapel window. "The sacrifice from which all martyrdom took its beginning" – "*certa salvatio* [assured salvation]."

I am glad of all the intelligent letters that have come in as a result of the peace articles. "Fellowship" seems to get around! Justus Lawler wrote about the *Commonweal* one some time ago suggesting a book for Herder and Herder. Today a letter from an old mid-European professor somewhere in Maine, a clear-cut historical analysis of our (American) problem.

A great pair of hand-knitted socks from Aunt Kit.

April 1, 1962. Laetare Sunday

Alternating sun, rain and sleet. Chapel smelling sweetly of hyacinths. Fr. Ailred (Smith) from South Africa and Fr. Amedeus (Sylvester), a West Indian Negro, took the habit together and served my Mass.

Reading the Van der Meer book on Augustine, monumental (also expensive) and vastly interesting. Yet I am no longer able to be enthusiastic about Augustine.

April 14, 1962

Tomorrow is Palm Sunday.

[W. H.] Ping Ferry was here this week, and one of the best things we did was take pictures of the old ruined distillery at the Dant Station. The long red warehouses, and the wonderful proportion of spaces in the well, broken up with an interesting low line of narrow windows. Other side, down the road to the creek, windows and doors broken open and Dant labels lying all over the ground in hundreds.

Annoyed, gratified and perplexed by the sudden growth of the Peace Movement. It is good. I do not fully know where it is going, but it is a good movement. Jim Forest is in Nashville on a Peace Walk, after 2 weeks in Hartz Island for the sitdown at the AEC.

Activity of the American Nazi Party also – always in support of General Walker.

Good Sermon of St. Leo in the refectory today. And spring weather. Red leaves beginning to break out on the maples. This week, Holy Week, everything will start to bud.

The need for meditation.

April 26, 1962

Nuclear testing was resumed by the U.S. yesterday. We had the Procession of St. Mark, and before that I read to the novices in a conference a bit of the Peace ms. – on Machiavelli – and Teller.

Beautiful Easter day, much sun, hot, but dry. There have been fires in the woods and brush everywhere, including one started by Andy Boone's son Good Friday evening. With seven novices I came and helped put it out, and I stayed up at the hermitage until 7:45. Planning some kind of a fieldstone wall along that side.

Wednesday in Holy Week my prayer for peace was read in Congress. Congressman Kowalski had asked for it.

Reading Origen, *Contra Celsum*.

April 27, 1962

In difficulties about the articles etc. concerning war.

It seems finally that the opposition of censors and of the Abbot General (not to mention the Abbot General's secretary) has become intransigent. Yesterday Rev. Father gave me a bunch of letters and reports, the main item being a letter of the General dated Jan. 20th which Rev. Father for some unaccountable reason had been saving up. (The letter was addressed to him, of course, but concerned me and was in fact for my benefit.)

The decision seems to be (it is not absolutely definite) that I am to stop all publication of anything on war. In other words I am to be in effect silenced on this subject for the main reason that it is not appropriate for a monk, and that it "falsifies the message of monasticism." Certainly there is a lot of truth in this, from a certain point of view, but that is not a matter to be debated one way or the other.

I still do not know quite where I stand in regard to the book that is practically finished for Macmillan.

1. It is basically made up of articles already censored and published. Yet these articles have been greatly expanded and developed – hence I suppose it is *new* material. It would have to be recensored.

2. Censor finally suggests no more material to be submitted for censorship.

3. General does not order compliance but indicates a strong preference "personally" to drop all writing on this subject.

4. *Abbot* seems inclined to let the book go through and be censored at least, then published if passed.

At the moment I would be inclined to drop the whole matter and let the publication go. It certainly is the simplest and most direct response. Yet I am not absolutely clear that this is God's will. Will see in confession today.

If this is indeed a valid "sacrifice" and not just an evasion, I will gladly make it.

May 1, 1962

Early morning. Blessed rain, cooling the air, making the woods wet, where there was fire and danger of burning for weeks, since before Easter. Fire on the lake side, fire over across the creek in a hollow, fires down the valley. Now all is wet. God be praised for the rain.

Contra Celsum is fascinating though I am tempted to renounce it as "getting nowhere." And yet if one follows allusions (for instance into the city at the end of Ezekiel) and sees it in the light of Mircea Eliade, it is awfully rich.

Fresh green of the valley. Lovely yellow tulips surprised me outside the hermitage. I thought the rabbits had eaten them all but the rain brought them out. A pure and lovely yellow, purer than that of buttercups.

I regret the time I have wasted here this winter working at books. What moments have been lost – moments of realization, lost in the flux of obsession and work. Statements to show, for what?

A train in the valley – that old song.

"Those who have the *dharma* should devote themselves only to its practice. Disputes arise from the desire for conquest and are not in accordance with the Way."
– from the T'an Ching *of Hui Neng*

May 4, 1962

Unrest, action, protests here and there since atomic testing was renewed. Note the *symbolic* part taken by *milk* in the protest. Other foods (wheat = bread) get as much or more Strontium 90 in them. Milk is the American symbol. Mother is full of Strontium 90. Mothers protest. Motherhood undermined by the bomb. Sex symbolism of the bomb, and question of genetic effects. The sex life of America, Kinsey Report, and H bomb were contemporary.

On May 8 Jacqueline Kennedy is to launch a New Polaris Submarine at Electric Boat in New London.

There is a plan to launch a Polaris submarine called The *William Penn!!*

May 7, 1962

"If India were to hear the word of Christ and be converted, it is possible that she would be hardly capable of considering the divine mystery in the ways traditional to the Christian East and West, full of living inspiration though they are. Young in the faith and proud of her own cultural heritage, she might give us instead a Hindu theology of the Trinity."
– Bernard Piault in What Is the Trinity? *[New York, 1959], p. 118*

Especially in getting away from the Augustinian *psychological* treatment of the mystery.

In the theology of the Trinity as we have it in the West we are under the domination of Augustine's introspective and generally *non-mystical* contemplation that is centered on the self as medium to that which is above the self. Meeting of the logos and the soul in the soul's concept of itself, experience of itself?? Surely not mere *reflection* on our own experience of ourself and hence to the Trinity by inference. It must be more than that.

May 10, 1962

Fascinating books by Mircea Eliade.

Finished (two days ago) *Image and Symbol* and began today the new one, *Forge and Crucible*, about alchemists. Opening up the meaning of myth in primitive technology which is always mystical. Why engineers are happy without religion?

Finishing at the same time the [Edward] Teller book. *Legacy of Hiroshima.* His convincing myth of the tactical nuclear weapon. And there may be something to this. As opposed to the awful and deadly myth of the megatomic weapon.

Missiles: note the war between the God of heaven and the God of the hurricane – the storm god, who hurls thunderbolts.

May 11, 1962

Laxity and lack of direction in my interior life. I am aware that my thoughts are undisciplined and irresponsible. Need for more serious meditation. A need of which I *cannot* be or remain aware as long as I only meditate for the ½ hour in the morning and ¼ hour in the evening. We do not normally have sufficient time or silence for meditation here. But I have a special opportunity at the hermitage and I must take it seriously, for my own soul's sake, for the novices, for the entire world.

Today I have become aware of the importance of this work and this vocation.

May 12, 1962

Glorious 4th Chapter of Tertullian's *De Oratione* [*On Prayer*].

The Latin, sharp, austere, brilliant and torrid.

Underneath the words, the history, the situation: to martyrs. *Ut . . . sustineamus ad mortem usque.* [That . . . we may endure even unto death.]

The *reality* of God's will as an immense power. And suffering. Saying *Fiat voluntas tua, ad sufferentiam nos metipsos praemonemus* [Thy will be done, we warn ourselves ahead of time that we will have to suffer].

May 18, 1962

Saturday a letter arrived, most moving, from Hal Stallings, the Quaker who, with two others as his crew, is sailing the 25 foot "Everyman" from San Francisco to Christmas Island to protest against the H bomb tests. I sent a wire, but apparently they did not sail Sunday after all.

Today a letter from one of the women who went on a Peace Pilgrimage to the Disarmament Conference at Geneva.

On the one hand – the good will, the sincerity, the meekness of all these people with enough sense to see what nuclear war means, and on the other hand the stupidity, the solemn and rigid absurdity of the officials and their double talk. The madness goes on. Now they will test an H bomb 500 miles up in some magnetic field, having announced that they *think* there is no special danger.

And the prayer card for the late Countess Christine Von Metternich, who was English, and had a face utterly good and charming. She apparently read and loved my books. I pray for her and think of her with fondness, all the more so because she does after all represent the civilization to which I am attached and which is being destroyed by the barbarism that has arisen within its own bosom. I do not refer to Russia, but to our own stupid world of robots and managers.

The weather is getting hot.

This is a year of kingbirds and other ones I do not identify, whistling in the echoing heat of the clearing between pine groves.

Yesterday, translated some poems of Alfonso Cortes.

May 19, 1962

Weather hot as midsummer.

Rereading *The Cloud* – working over the essay on the *English Mystics*. Why? I hardly know. At first I thought it was for the *Reader*.

(Much trouble with the *Reader*.)

"Instead you should sit completely still as though you had fallen asleep, worn out by crying and sunken in your sorrow. This is true sorrow. This is perfect sorrow. To achieve this sorrow is a very great thing."

p. 161, Cloud of Unknowing

———

Heartbreaking picture of a Chinese refugee girl collapsed in sorrow at the borders of Hong Kong, where hundreds of thousands are now refused and turned back into Red China by the British. Mass for the refugees this morning.[7]

Terrible news from Algeria. Murder upon murder, though there is supposed to be peace. Is the world going to be taken over by werewolves? The OAS [*L' Organisation de l'Armée Secrète*, Secret Army Organization] and its secret officers, fomenting trouble in the garrisons of French soldiers in Germany, where fanaticism is also generated among Americans. Where will we be ten years from now?

What they are doing now?

Emphasis on Chemical and Biological weapons of mass destruction "a major U.S. military effort." "Top-secret seminars" – "breakthroughs" – toward a "1965 climax"!

46 million for CBW [Continental Ballistic Weapons] research in 1960. *150 million allotted for 1963.*

Especially efforts in genetics – developing new bugs. 40 biochemists, biophysicists, bacterial geneticists working full time on this "problem" at Fort Detrick . . . Developing not only mutant bacterial populations, new viruses, new "deadly and resistant" strains and even new mutants of disease-carrying insects with increased resistance to insecticides . . . etc.

The commanding officer expects "major contributions to biological weaponry." When it is said this is as a *deterrent*, there is no really serious indication of any inhibitions about using the CBW weapons *very* freely in case of war.

May 24, 1962

During the morning meditation there was a fine thundershower, shaking the whole monastery, floods of rain. All clear by the end of Lauds, and the day has been bright and hot, but more like May. Away in the south a huge solid cool mountain of cloud over Tennessee.

Fr. Prior got us out of chapter at 6:45 – a great wonder. Had time to read a letter of Tertullian on *Patience* after my Mass and thanksgiving and I

———

7 Merton's poem "A Picture of Lee Ying," inspired by this event, appeared in *Emblems of a Season of Fury* (1963) and in the *Collected Poems*.

guess I need to. Have nearly finished Milarepa. Wrote to Dezhung Trulka about it (Tibetan Buddhist scholar at U. of Washington who has meditated in various caves once frequented by Milarepa).

In the refectory – two chapters from the Moral Theology of Ford and Kelly on Situation Ethics. There is always some zealot who thinks that if one of the monks starts getting late to office, the whole house is crumbling with situation ethics. Anyway the chapters are interesting because in point of fact the chief thing about the Nuclear war boys and the theologians who support them is that in fact they are practicing situation ethics – the end justifies the means. But they are less honest than the existentialists in that they manipulate and twist the objective standard to make it seem to come out in their favor.

May 26, 1962

Letter from the [Abbot] General asking me to publish nothing more on war and peace – i.e. vetoing the book *Peace in the Post-Xtian Era*, the typing of which was finished today! Well, a few people can read it in ms. I have no difficulty accepting his clear decision and in a way it is a relief not to go on with this thankless struggle which few or none will appreciate.

Someone told our Abbot of one of our houses that the *Catholic Worker* was "Communist controlled" and he told the Abt. General. That evidently had a lot to do with the decision.

A Frenchman, professor at the School of Political Science in Paris, Roger Robin, stopped here and I had a short talk with him after dinner. He said that Buddhists he knew in Viet Nam were not in contact with sources, learned Buddhism from studies by English and French scholars. That there is no real Moslem revival except on a political level, not spiritual. He knows Dom Denis Martin at Toumliline.

May 29, 1962

Hot, stuffy, misty, summer weather.

Now I have got to get my life in order at last without desperation and without compromise. A long succession of wasted opportunities. The need for serious spiritual discipline, especially long periods of meditation. Going on my own, not being held within the limits of accepted practice and custom in the community. I owe it to the community, which has allowed me opportunities for it, more or less, to forge ahead where they do not go. This is certainly implied by the situation in which I have been placed.

I have misused this to a great extent, thinking I was obliged to form a judgement concerning world affairs. That obligation is by no means certain, whereas my obligation to explore "the interior space" is absolutely clear.

May 30, 1962

Malim nullum bonum quam vanum. [I'd rather have nothing than vanity.]

Tertullian

When we face the vanity of our best efforts, their triviality, their involvement in illusion, we become desperate. And then we are tempted to do *anything* as long as it seems to be good. We may abandon a better good with which we have become disillusioned, and embrace a lesser one with a frenzy that prevents us from seeing the greater illusion.

So, through efforts that may seem wasted, we must patiently go towards a good that is to be given to the patient and the disillusioned.

May 31, 1962. *Ascension Day*

A bright, clear, blue day, warm, but with a cool wind. Doves and woodpeckers echoing in the trees, and distant crows, and near flycatchers.

This morning served as assistant priest while old Dom Vital officiated in an Abbatial Mass. It was touching and salutary to be there with him, in his simplicity and goodness. A beautiful Mass, one felt a great charity in the sanctuary and a peace not usual in the tension of the big functions.

Dom James is still away on his visitations and a letter from Mepkin (of his) was read today in the refectory.

Tom McDonnell is finishing up work on the *Reader*. Sent a clipping about the Fallout shelter the Trappists at O. L. of the Genesee have built for themselves. It is sickening to think that my writing *against* nuclear war is regarded as scandalous, and this folly of building a shelter *for monks* is accepted without question as quite fitting. We no longer know what a monk is. Putting two and two together = the shelter is the logical consequence of those nauseating "monks' bread" ads in the New York papers. It all goes together.

June 2, 1962

Cum ergo Christum videre gaudium sit, nec possit esse gaudium nostrum nisi cum viderimus Christum, quae caecitas animi quaeve dementia est amare premuras et poenas et lacrymas mundi et non festinare potius ad gaudium quod numquam possit auferri. [Therefore, since to see Christ is joy, and this joy can't be ours unless we see Christ, what blindness and madness of the spirit it is to love the burdens and pains and tears of the world and not rather to hasten toward the joy which no one can ever take away.]

Mundus sui mutat et labitur et ruinam sui non senectute rerum sed fine testatur; et tu non Deo gratias agis, non tibi gratularis quod exites maturiore subtractus, ruinis et naufragiis et plagis imminentibus exuaris? [The world changes of itself and tatters and testifies to its ruin, not by the age of things but by its end; and you don't thank God, you don't rejoice that you will be leaving this world, spared of all the ruin, shipwreck and plague that is about to happen?]   *[St. Cyprian,* De Mortalitate*] ch. XXV*

June 3, 1962

A fine visit with the Hammers who came yesterday. Victor brought the portrait which was impressive – maybe somewhat idealized. The drawing, however, is not, or I do not think it is. We sat by the shallow lake, which got greener and greener as the skies darkened, and then a great storm began. We drove back to the monastery in the Volkswagen and sat outside the gate as though in a submarine, ready at any moment to be swept away by the flood.

Now (Sunday evening) it begins quietly to rain again. Distant thunder.

Animal Farm is being read in refectory.

An article on Dom Lambert Baudouin was finished there today. Once again his life is very instructive. How many years he had to spend far from the monastery he founded and having little or nothing to do with ecumenism!

June 4, 1962

Comparing the tracts on patience by Tertullian and St. Cyprian, I think I prefer Tertullian – whom Cyprian in any case irritated. There is a great vigor in T.'s thought, and a greater, more austere genius in his style. The struggle for him was far greater and his understanding was deeper. Here was a violent man who realized he had to take with complete seriousness the command of Christ to abandon violence. And who saw that it was naturally impossible. When Tertullian reduces all sin to a root of impatience with God he is not being arbitrary. What he says is very deep. We need to recover these perspectives.

224

June 5, 1962

Wonderful insights in the *Apologetic* of Tertullian, more subtle than Hannah Arendt, and of the same kind: on the irony and inner contradiction of the forced confessions extorted from the martyrs.

Lanza del Vasto has seen a deep connection between *play* and *war*. Our society totally devoted to one (everything is a game) necessarily ends in the other. Play – is aimless, and multiplies obstacles so that the "aim," which does not exist, may not be obtained by the other player. Getting a ball in a hole.

"*La guerre c'est le grand vice public qui insiste à jouer avec le sang des hommes.*" ["War is the great public vice that insists on playing with the blood of men."]

War is not caused by hunger or by need. It is the powerful and the rich who make war. The beauty of the grave: it demands a *suppression of conscience*, and this is done as a matter of "sacrifice" and "duty." To sacrifice conscience, and then "let go" and kill, for the exaltation of one's nation, mad with the need for systematic irresponsibility. Reproach them for this, refuse them their outlet, and they will slaughter you.

June 6, 1962

Evora Arca de Sardiña writes that her husband (whose price according to Castro is $100,000) has been moved by night from prison in Havana to the Isle of Pines. And she speaks as if there would soon be military action by the United States. I do not like to think what madness is about to begin, what fury, what horror. One simply ceases to think of it. And on it comes, inexorably. Nobody claims to want it. Perhaps everybody, in some strange way, wants it. But we are beyond merely doing and getting what we want. We are involved in all the accumulated consequences of all that we have all wanted for centuries.

At such a time I cannot even attempt to think in purely political categories. Politics is the mask for eschatology – and for the terrible relentless actions of principalities. These one must sense in horror, and then one must fall down before God in supplication. The supplication will avert nothing but only save a few olives on top of the tree.

June 7, 1962

The serene, pure music of Cassiodorus's prayer at the end of his *De Anima* [*On the Soul*]! What nobility of mind. Christian and classic nobility, simplicity, harmony. And what depth of religion.

June 8, 1962

A particularly fine gardenia, like a mandala, like a wheel. Picked yesterday, the petals are fluttering back now, and tiring. But it was full. Gardenias now for La Soledad since May 26th – ordination anniversary.

O Cassiodorus, reading you is like coming home to everything germane to my spirit! The existential acuteness of the *De Anima*, which, considered superficially, might seem to be only an exercise in fantasy.

June 9, 1962. Vigil of Pentecost

I never thought I would discover in myself a hunger for something like Cassiodorus' Chapters on Rhetoric, or even Grammar. And even for Donatus, to whom he refers. But everything in Cassiodorus is attractive because it is clean and clear. One can appreciate his clarity without attaching an indiscreet importance to the subjects on which he speaks clearly. But perhaps we have forgotten that grammar, rhetoric and the other liberal arts *do* have an importance.

The awful, crucial significance of martyrdom: that in some sense it is the *only* way of being a fully perfect Christian, and that other ways of perfection are valid and genuine in so far as they can be said to substitute for martyrdom.

But can anything substitute for martyrdom?

Is it not terribly dangerous to claim that, when nobody is a martyr, *everyone* is a Christian by virtue of some substitution?

Some petty virtue? Some gift of pennies? Some sacrifice of dessert?

The necessity for the acceptance of destruction of all that one is, as a social and "worldly" being, the total renunciation of one's profane self: this is in fact, if it is true and complete, a martyrdom – provided God accepts it as martyrdom, and there is no way of forcing Him to accept it!

The falsification, corruption of martyrdom today.

In a sense those who suffer and die political deaths at the hands of Communists, because their religion identifies them with a totally profane and secular economic and political system – are hardly martyrs! They are, if you will, victims, victims for this sinful identification of the sacred and the profane. Victims of expiation – in so far as they are themselves in good faith.

To be cleansed of personalism, the myth of autonomy. This was provisional and not totally helpful as a *point d'appui* [fulcrum], steadying myself against the demands for surrender made on essentially *profane* grounds and with secular motions and justifications, though invoking God.

Surrender demanded as an unqualified approval of policies and attitudes rooted in the transient and in the corrupt.

There is a higher "No" than the No of autonomy and self-affirmation which ends in the same error or worse.

The "no" of love standing at the borders of death and eschatological liberation.

The No of solitude in non-being and non-affirmation.

Not the no of the self to the other, the subject denying its object on which itself depends – but the pure and simple "No" in which subject vanishes and object with it!!

June 10, 1962. Pentecost
What more beautiful or more appropriate than these lines of Cassiodorus where he speaks of the soul as a light, in the likeness of the divine light? Then of God:

> *Illud autem quod ineffabile veneramur arcanum*
> *Quod ubique totum et invisibiliter praesens est*
> *Pater et Filius et Spiritus Sanctus*
> *Una essentia et indiscreta majestas*
> *Splendor supra omnes fulgores, gloria supra omne praeconium*
> *Quod mundissima anima et Deo dedita potest quidum ex aliqua parte*
> *   sentire sed non idonee explicare.*
> *Nam quemadmodum fas est de illo sufficienter dici qui creaturae sensu*
> *   non potest comprehendi?*
> [But that which we reverence as unspeakable secret
> which is everywhere totally and invisibly present
> Father, Son and Holy Spirit
> One essence and undivided majesty

Splendor above all light, glory above all honor
Which the purest soul dedicated to God can experience
everywhere but not explain.
For what can ever be said of this being who cannot be understood
by his creatures?][8]

June 12, 1962

Gloom and murk of drizzling rain across the valley, more like a cloud than falling rain. What is it full of? But in the twilight day lilies flare discreetly, and poplar leaves turn up in the wind that does not blow this cloud away. It keeps hanging over the valley.

It rained all yesterday afternoon, and rained hard. Had long talks with two novices who will soon, or eventually, leave (Bros. Urban and Columban). Read a little of the new *Théologie Monastique* [*Monastic Theology*], which is perhaps in some ways slighter than I expected, but informative. It does not seem very often to reach the level of theology: a series of historical background notes for monastic theology perhaps.

The *Merton Reader* is finished and with the publisher. I am content with Tom McDonnell's final job, and with him. He is a good editor, amiable too, simple, ingenuous and sensible. The details of the war between the publishers are still not clear. F. S. and C. [Farrar, Straus & Cudahy] wanted to trade me for Lowell and Eliot, which is exorbitant all right! Not flattering, just a little sickening.

Then Sister Thérèse[9] has come up with a remarkably interesting (to me) list of the items in her "collection."

But for me, can all this have any serious meaning? I suppose I would earnestly like it to, and secretly believe it does: as if the image were real. As if there were a genuine mosaic of achievement and as if all the little pieces added up to form the face of a real person. That is the illusion. Not that I must repudiate it all, but still, it is not significant. And the irony of total destruction hangs over it, to keep me wise.

---

[8] Merton will later publish a more refined translation of these lines in *Conjectures of a Guilty Bystander* (New York, 1966), pp. 208–9.

[9] Sister Thérèse Lentfoehr was the recipient of various manuscripts, letters, page proofs, etc., over a period of over two decades. That large collection was donated to the Columbia University Libraries, where it is now housed.

June 15, 1962

An indigo bunting flies down and grasps the long, swinging stem of a tiger lily and reaches out, from them, to eat the dry seed on top of a stalk of grass. A Chinese painting!

The king of death, says a Buddhist poem, does not see you if you do not see any self in yourself.

"Where is no thing, where naught is grasped, this is the isle of No-Beyond."

June 16, 1962. Pentecost Saturday

Brilliant days and cold nights this week. Fast day. Cannot get caught up with mail. Frs. Felix and Linus were ordained today and dinner was a half hour late.

New tractors each year and each one makes more noise than the last. The one in the valley now sounds like a big bulldozer. Round and round the alfalfa field, in fury. What thoughts it represents, what fury of man, what restlessness, what avidity, what despair.

Around and around it goes, clacking its despair.

June 19, 1962

"When the Chilean earthquake was reported in San Francisco, about the time de Gaulle went ahead with testing in the Sahara, it was right after an epidemic of sharks at the beach, and a report that a whale had been washed ashore with ulcers . . ."   – *H. Blau in* Second Coming

June 26, 1962

On St. John Baptist's Day Fr. Matthew (Kelty) made his solemn profession and John Wu arrived for a visit. He was kneeling near the sanctuary with the three SVDs [Society of the Divine Word] who came down for the profession.

The great simple spirituality of John Wu – who knows Tao and the logos and the Spirit. Flashes of wit and depth in the things he said, with much searching for words and matter and complaints that the Holy Ghost had gone to sleep.

For instance – that suffering is the core of existence.

That we monks can laugh in this monastery as men who know nothing worse can befall them.

Stories of Bodhidharma – familiar, but well told, with his own viewpoint.

He told Pauline (Sister of St. Thérèse, Prioress of Lisieux) that she was "not Theresian" when she wanted him to intervene in Rome to make trouble for Van der Meersch and his book "against our little saint and our Carmel."

His friend, who was a close friend of Céline, and complained to him bitterly of the new pictures now being published, of how Thérèse "really looked," discrediting Céline at least implicitly. He replied, "Céline is in heaven in spite of her paintings!"

He agreed with Pius XII when the Pope told him it was because of "his merits" that he had such a lovely family.

He made some astute remarks about pragmatism in the "contemplative life" when questioned about what was "dangerous" to monks in America (the questioner wanted him to say something else, perhaps about love of comfort).

He spoke to me, with enthusiasm, of [Thomas] Traherne's *Meditations*.

July 3, 1962

Hot, murky afternoon.

This morning fasting, translated Cassiodorus' prayer.

What is with Fr. Raymond? He eats in infirmary refectory and says it is because he had sunstroke. I see him at no other exercise.

Still reading Van der Meer's great Dutch (thorough) book on Augustine in refectory. Abbot away for the western visitations after moving his office into the new hotel [guest house].

Saturday (Sts. Peter and Paul), Fr. Matthew and I hauled rock up the hill, and took some wood from the wrecked first floor of the old hotel to use as firewood, wood from the soundproof ceiling of the Abbot's old room, that heard my despairs and misplaced confidences.

Harcourt Brace announces the *Reader* for October.

A second CNVA [Citizens for Non-Violent Alternative] sailboat, Everyman II, has sailed, I hear, from Hawaii and is in the test area.

Etta Gullick writes of all the ban the bomb people at Oxford parties.

Dr. Good, barefeet, from the Punjab, asks about my "experiences." What experiences?

Discovery of Lactantius, particularly *De Opificis Dei*. Because I read and like St. Augustine and St. Gregory in the novitiate, I thought of myself as one who was somewhat familiar with the Fathers. An illusion. I have not even begun.

Reading [Wm. of] Conches [?] superb selections on Perfect Wisdom. *Prajnaparamita* [perfection of wisdom] – My way. What way?

July 8, 1962. IV Sunday after Pentecost

Hot stuffy night, with mosquitoes. Lost several hours of sleep and thought the Night Office w[oul]d be grim, but actually it was clear and pleasant. I was alert and not tired. Reason was probably that I had eaten no supper, and was empty and free.

The Hammers were here yesterday. Brought Notker Balbulus and the little paper of *Hagia Sophia* including the finished copy. It is pretty, but my theology is strange in it. It needs revision and reformulation.

I gave them the translations of the Cassiodorus prayer. It was hot, hot, hot.

July 9, 1962

Businesses are sects. They are little religions – at least in America.

One believes in the product, and preaches it. Your belief is an essential constituent in its goodness.

"The new evangelism, whether expressed in soft or hard selling, is a quasi-religious approach to business wrapped in a hoax – a hoax voluntarily entered into by producers and consumers together. Its credo is that of *belief-to-order*. It is the truth-to-order as delivered by advertising and public relations men, believed by them and voluntarily believed in by the public."

– *Alan Harrington*, Life in the Crystal Palace *[New York, 1959], p. 194*

July 14, 1962

Very hot.

Two Episcopal ministers who were here the other day (or rather Anglican priests, they would prefer) were talking about Alan Watts, who had been a minister and chaplain at Northwestern U. and took off to write books on Zen.

They had in their breviary the Solemnity of St. Benedict, which *we* have not.

Lately discovered the *Regula Magistri* [Rule of the Master][10] and began to take an interest in the whole question about it. Article of Fr. Eugene [Man-

---

[10] Monastic rule that predates "The Rule of St. Benedict," the standard guide for living in Benedictine and Cistercian monasteries.

ning] of Rochefort in the *Collectanea* got me started. Have read a little of the *Regula* and it is wonderful.

Bro. Ailred, the South African, wants to leave and go to the Paulists. Bro. Cyprian doesn't want to leave but now, I think, should. Bro. Columban will leave eventually, but can't make up his mind when.

Reading Rose MacCauley's *Personal Pleasures* – published 1935. Therefore her swim in the Cam [river in Cambridge] might well have been the same year as mine, though probably earlier. An entrancing book, and baffling, for that world has ceased to exist so completely: yet thirty years ago it was the only world I dreamed of as possible. The world of civilization and books and ease, and humor and perhaps a lot of nonsense and falsity that did not have to be taken too seriously. Since that day, absurdity has won.

Her lovely piece on the "Bird in the Box," and on "Book Auctions" too. But the bird has become a symbol of that whole world, and I suppose without fully realizing it, she knew this!

Buddhist concept of *pratigha* (repugnance) important. The will with regard to suffering and things pertaining to suffering – and toward people who seem to be somehow partly responsible for suffering. All this is the center of my own illusion. It must go.

July 17, 1962. F. of Our Lady of Carmel
Dazzled with something.
Stillness. Who?
Repugnance for letters. Useless scratching, gestures, desperate too.
Today again the Red Cross here for blood.
Bro. Cuthbert said he gave the first bottle and was pleased, and I was pleased. So simple are the joys of life. I don't know what pint I gave but I was lighter after it, yet drank more of the good coffee than I needed and joked with the ladies.
Today for the first time I was told that my blood pressure was a "little high." The ladies called Fr. Eudes, but it was only 130/50, whatever that is, so it is not very high. I forget the adverb he used for how high it wasn't. And my pulse was 96. Not fast. Not *too* fast.
Better than to know the number is to be mindful, as the Buddhists are. And now the difficulty about ants, killing them I mean. It is the one law I

break. That and drinking a cocktail when Jim Wygal buys me lunch in Louisville. The ants and the cocktail spoil everything. I have no excuses.

Stillness. Henry Miller has Carmelite friar friends in England and with them is putting out an issue of their magazine in honor of his friend [Joseph] Delteil.

But now looking into the Spring number which Fr. Bernard Swell has sent me, I am moved by a bit of verse by Carron Gray, of whom I had never heard before.

> Enough of the world is mine
> more than the envious know
> I have dug in a deeper mine
> than depths where rubies glow:
> I have sailed in a fairer ship
> The ruin of a vaster sea
> than sleep or companionship
> ever were sweet to me.

July 21, 1962

A brilliant Saturday. Bright sky and clouds. Not too hot.

Everything I see and experience in Kentucky is to some extent colored and determined by the thoughts and emotions I had when I first came. It cannot be otherwise. So this day too. It is another day of the time and another link in the chain that began then, and began long before then.

The war people have not slept and now it appears that the country, as I vaguely expected, is more or less officially adopting the air force "counterforces" strategy.

Curious thing about this strategy which probably leads more surely and inevitably to nuclear war than any other, it is the one which, if occasion demands, can be made on paper to look *more moral*. It theoretically excludes cities (though everyone knows such a thing is not possible).

And the "minimum deterrent," which curiously *might* temporarily work and leave the way open to disarmament, concentrates on the "second strikes" against cities – more as a threat than as a planned policy. That is to say it is more genuinely "deterrent" and more of a "defense," though not much better than the first, and as far as I can see completely immoral.

But the other one – "counterforce" – implies an enormous, unlimited arms race to attain "absolute superiority."

Incidentally, the neurotic fears on which it rests go back to the "missile gap" business, where Russia was supposed to have scores of new weapons. Intelligence discovered that little was going on and they had only a few – far less than theorists had calculated.

July 23, 1962

Strange visitor, an Orthodox Russian, but with a weird background. Born in Java, originally Jewish, studied at Lausanne. Story of escaping from the Russian soccer squad at the Helsinki Olympics. Ivan Englesicvich – did not catch the "familya" – maybe it was Fugate, which is not a Russian name as far as I can see.

Speaks of attending the Council with "Bishop John" [Gran] as an observer.

I have a curious feeling that he might be more than the ordinary ecumenical visitor. He spoke of one of my books (*Waters of Siloe*) having been reviewed in the "Literaturnaya Gazeta" and of Pasternak quoting me in an article there . . .

I gave him *Original Child Bomb* and have a kind of a hunch it may turn up in Russian one of these days; let it.

Very curious.

He spoke to the novices in such a way that the least possible amount of sound would be caught by Bro. Killian's microphone. Did not seem too well up on religious affairs, did not know about St. Procopius Abbey . . .

Hawk. First the shadow flying down the sunlit trees. Then the bird overhead, barred tail, spotted wings with sun shining through them. A half circle above the elm, then he seemed to put his wings in his pocket and fly like a bullet into the grove across the field.

July 24, 1962

In Louisville some weeks ago I found the new Suzuki anthology (*Essentials of Zen B[uddhism*, New York, 1962]) – really a thorough "Reader" and since reading it I am almost irresistibly tempted to write him another letter. Poor good old man.

I know he must be flooded with mail as I am, and that he does what I do: puts the letters in a big box and forgets them.

Asked to speak in a "scientific" symposium on "New Knowledge in Human Values," he handled it with consummate wisdom and latent humor, the serious, humble, matter-of-fact humor of emptiness.

"If anything new can come out of human values it is from the cup of tea taken by two monks."

July 28, 1962

Antigone and stoical tropes of St. Eucherius in his *contemptus mundi* [rejection of the world]: the beauty of his prose. How the heavens observe the laws of God when they have been once commanded and we, with volumes of laws, do not obey Him.

This morning, the indescribable magnificence of the dawn. Cirrus clouds on the horizon, first glowing with an angry and subtle purple fire, then growing into a great mottled curtain of iridescent flame, of what color I don't know. But off to the south, a pile of mottled grey with all kinds of delicate pink highlights on it, like some Oriental porcelain.

Drinking coffee and getting distracted about getting M.L.W. Laistner down here to give talks on people like Bede, Alcuin, Cassiodorus.

I must get Justus Lawler's tape recording of his English class, for some of the students – and Bros. Cuthbert and Placid go on retreat today for their simple profession. I am very fond of them both, as if they were really my own children, and Bro. Cuthbert is perhaps one of the best we have had in the novitiate, even though so many are excellent.

Bro. Gerard, on the other hand, celebrated his jubilee in absurd and unwilling splendor. The silly pomp we impose on the old must embarrass them to death. The cane and the chrysanthemum! But he gave a very good talk in Chapter, about how before entering the monastery in 1900 he had herded sheep in North Dakota (came originally from Flanders).

Eucher[ius]. On that sunrise!

> *Aut si cogitemus quantus in posterum splendor lucis possit hominibus occurrere, cum nunc tantus institisset:* quam magnifica fulgebit perpetuis forma rebus cum nunc tam speciosa perituris. [Or if we think how much more in the future the splendor of light will be to us, if it strikes us so brilliantly now: *in what a magnificent form it will shine on eternal things, when it is so beautiful for things that are passing away.*]

August 4, 1962

Dan Walsh, back from California, Mexico et al. – speaking of the Institute of Medieval Studies in Toronto. It is considered a "failure" and "not fulfilling its function" and will be changed into an "Institute of Ecumenism." This seems to me a tragic levity!

I understand the same drags and temptations in my own study – the sudden almost intolerable urge to leave what I know to be good for me and to embrace what is popular, what everyone is mad about.

If I have the sense to keep to the writers of Christian antiquity, for the moment, for the next few months at least, I think it will mean a great deal. Perhaps, though I have no real obligation to specialize, I ought to specialize in them: not neglecting the Medieval writers.

For instance, today, had to resist a real madness, and stick to Vol. 50 of the *PL* [*Patrologia Latina*] and found much light and interest in the *Vita S. Honorati* by St. Hilary of Arles. His style, his manner of approaching his subject, his classical *topoi*, all might seem corny; actually it represents a real culture and a very *different* one from that of, say, Peter of Celle, whom I was also reading, but for work's sake, the other day.

August 8, 1962
Aversion for slogans, for the pressure boys, for eagerness.

Why? Perhaps because I fear being reduced to servitude under somebody else's idea? To serve somebody else's project? But isn't this a weakness, an unpardonable one? The key word is "unpardonable." I suppose all it amounts to is that I would like to be dispensed from participation in somebody's big project, but with a guarantee of *pardon*.

Is this a deception, or is there an underlying truth?

Isn't the Church really big enough to pardon me for not loving all the latest movements?

Erasmus: "True piety, which flourishes only when the spirit spontaneously strives to grow in charity, withers when the spirit sluggishly reposes in external ceremonies chosen for it by others."

Emerson: of Thoreau: "His senses were acute and he remarked that by night every dwelling house gave out bad air like a slaughter house. He liked the pure fragrance of melilot."

Thoreau's idleness was an incomparable gift and its fruits were blessings that America has unfortunately never learned to appreciate. Yet he made his gift, even though it was not asked for. And he went his way. If he had followed the advice of his neighbors in Concord, America would have been much poorer, even though he might have sweated a great deal. He took the fork in the road.

August 9, 1962

Dark dawn. Streaks of pale red under a few high clouds. A pattern of clothes lines and clothes pins and shadowy trees.

I think I am tempted about the Church. Perhaps more tempted than I realize, though it is not surprising. And because I am not surprised I am not that much tempted, or think I am not. For I find in myself not the slightest inclination to be anything other than a Catholic, simply because any further question of organizations and categories is ludicrous and I believe in the Body of Christ. I wish I had more charity, and I wish I felt less resentment towards some of the dead aspects of Church authority, the immobilism – or is that it? – the dead weight, the pressure of power. There is no question that they love their power, many of them, and are jealous of it. There is no question that they stifle the spirit by using people and energies of people for projects in which they themselves are glorified. But I myself have also been hungry for glory, and I must stop complaining. Until I do, I won't see all I need to see, but only what I have to see, under some compulsion or other.

The fact that what I am compelled to see may be true does not justify my complaints.

What is the Church becoming? When someone like Fr. [Thomas] Stransky is here, I think she is waking up. Yet all those who are enthusiastic for the good new things, the Küng book etc. are not free from reemersion in the peripheral. I cannot help thinking that a lot of the liturgical stuff is peripheral, though the central principle is fine.

The "social gospel" makes more sense, but does it go far enough? About these things I am ignorant.

For instance Don Giovanni Rossi and his Pro Civitate Christiana – it seems to me a good, worthy game for grown up children in soutanes, a day dream.

I don't believe in the optimism of contemporary Christians. I am more and more convinced they are kidding themselves. It does not have the dimensions of hope, it is only optimism.

A very good priest, young priest from Oklahoma, Fr. [Robert] McDole, was here. He has been active in the sit-ins. This we can and must regard as phenomenal. And yet *every* priest should have been and should be active in that!! Every priest should be active in the peace movement. The majority in the country are interested more in the extermination of Russia.

Fr. Peres' work is tremendous. Bert Sisson did a moving article on him. The rest of us sit on our cans and applaud. (Bert is a Quaker!)

I have got to say things like this, but I suppose better to say them to dear diary than to people in letters.

August 11, 1962

Henry Miller's tremendous essay on Raimu deeply significant, touches the real nerve of our time, the American nihilist, the movie dreamer, who commits crime in his sleep, a bomb wrapped in ideals, as against Raimu the *human* European, caught in the mess of real politics.

The thought of going somewhere, anywhere, especially of course to some fabulous mountain monastery and to be a dreamer, a distraction avidly loved without too much guilt, almost a prayer.

Now the thought of going anywhere is all exhausted, hopeless spasm of the heart, without life, without energy, without tone, without sense. There is no longer even any real conflict, it is beyond guilt, the nauseated turning away, the sufferance, the incomprehension that is beyond yes and no.

India, no. Himalayas (a faint flicker, but really no). Greece – a Greek island? Athos? No. Rome: if I were called to Rome by the Pope himself I would want to refuse. *Anywhere* but Rome! Paris – no. A faint flicker for Devon and Cornwall, and almost a leap, still, for Ecuador (Quito, Cuenca). The Hebrides – yes, maybe the Hebrides. But one would have to go perhaps to Liverpool on the way. Rather die. Dublin? Rather die. Russia? Better dead. Better dead. The Grande Chartreuse? No, bud, leave me alone; No!

"People will do anything, no matter how absurd, to avoid facing their own psyches. They will practice Indian Yoga and all its exercises, observe a strict regimen of diet, learn theosophy by heart, or mechanically repeat mystic texts from the literature of the whole world – all because they cannot get on with themselves and *have not the slightest faith that anything useful could ever come out of the psyche.*" [Merton's emphasis]
– C. G. *Jung in* Spiritual Disciplines, Papers from the Eranos Yearbooks *4. BS. XXX. p. 366*

August 21, 1962

Hot. Yesterday, the dip in the path to the woods beyond the sheep barn was like an oven. The breeze like the breath of a furnace. Cooler in the woods where I read [Jakob] Boehme's *Confessions* and a bit of Miller's *Wisdom of the Heart* (a fine book). The *Confessions* are the only book of Boehme so far I have been able to understand.

Last week was tremendous, busy, exciting. First Zalman Schacter came with Rabbi L. Silverman from Vanderbilt, who talked about the Dead Sea scrolls. Then Fr. Dan Berrigan, an altogether convincing and warm intelligence, with a perfect zeal, compassion and understanding. This, certainly, is the spirit of the Church. This is a hope I can believe in, at least in its validity and its spirit.

The dimensions of living charity come clear in talks such as he gave and that does much to exorcise the negativism in me. Yet it is deep. I do not mean resistance to *this* spirit, on the contrary! Yet hopelessness and weariness and resentment from having been so long suppressed and made to look (unwillingly) only to the rigid existing structures.

Tony Walsh from the Labre house at Montreal – another utterly fine and good person.

Sense that the Abbot mistrusted them and did not really like having them here. Most of the community were delighted with them.

Proofs of the *Merton Reader*. This book is a good one. It lacks some of the best materials that should have gone into it. Farrar Straus and Cudahy refused to let Harcourt Brace have anything from their books. Hence three of the most important sources were excluded. *Thoughts in Solitude, Disputed Questions* and *The New Man.*

Up to mid-August – There have been *106 nuclear tests in the last year.* 31 *by the USSR,* 74 *by the U.S.A. and 1* by Britain (in Nevada).

The U.S. tests have been 29 in the atmosphere (the South Pacific) (three in Nevada), 1 high altitude and 44 underground (New Mexico).

Total tests since the beginning. U.S.A. 229, USSR 86, UK 22, France 5. Grand Total 342 of which 282 in the atmosphere.

Nice going, boys!

[No date.] Private Day of Recollection

Today I realize with urgency the absolute seriousness of my need to study and practice non-violence.

Hitherto I have "liked" non-violence as an idea. I have "approved" it, looked with benignity upon it, praised it even earnestly.

But I have not practiced it fully. My thoughts and words retaliate. I condemn and resist adversaries when I think I am unjustly treated. I revile them, even treat them with open (but *polite*) contempt to their face.

It is necessary to realize that I am a monk consecrated to God and this restricting non-retaliation merely to *physical* non-retaliation is not enough – on the contrary it is in some sense a greater evil.

At the same time the energy wasted in contempt, criticism and resentment is thus diverted from its true function, *insistence on truth*. Hence loss of clarity, loss of focus, confusion and finally frustration. So that half the time I "don't know what I am doing" (or thinking).

I need to set myself to the *study* of non-violence, with thoroughness.

The complete, integral *practice* of it in community life.

Eventually teaching it to others by word and example.

Short of this, the monastic life will remain a mockery in my life.

It will extend to civil disobedience where necessary. Certainly to non-cooperation in evil, even in monastic policies. But polite, charitable, restrained. I need grace to see how to do this, etc. I normally tend to express non-agreement in an insecure, therefore forced manner.

August 27, 1962

Bright day, after a stuffy, wearying week.

Finished an article (Saturday) on Virginity and Humanism in the Fathers, went over it today. Tired of the intensity of the work involved in writing. Feast day on Saturday was tiring. Victor Hammer and Wayne Williams came over. Really there have been too many visitors and retreats. Better to cut down on those if I can.

Yet it is most important to come to see these visits and contacts correctly. If I did, I suppose they would exhaust me less. Under everything I doubt the seriousness and the meaning of these conversations, and v.g. the big week with the Rabbis, Dan Berrigan etc. Yet it all has meaning, and they seem to get something out of it. They assure me it is a way of sharing something we alone have here.

Returned, after a long time, to the unfinished book by Vinoba Bhave on the *Gita*. Great nobility and seriousness. A most practical and meaningful book about the conduct of life. Thirst for wisdom!

The book *Breakthrough to Peace* has finally come from the printer. I am glad of it and proud of it. What I wanted to do last August, I have done. I have taken my position, and it is known. I hear also that I am quoted. So anyway, it is no secret what I think about nuclear war.

August 28, 1962

There has been a death from bubonic plague in its gravest and in an incurable form.

The death was that of Dr. George Bacon, an expert in microbiological warfare.

There had been no cases of plague in Britain since 1910.

There were barely 300 cases in the world in 1960.

But at Parton Downs, Wiltshire, where, it appears, they have discovered a virus that resists all known cures.

Dr. George Bacon died of the Bubonic plague.

It was announced that he was trying to find a defense against it.

Having found an incurable form of plague, he did not find any defense against it.

The death of Marilyn Monroe at the beginning of this month was considered far more important in the press than the resumption of nuclear testing in Novaya Zemblya, by the USSR. Yet the death was as much a symbol as the bomb – symbol of uselessness and of tragedy, of misused humanity.

"To pursue at the same time policies of armament and disarmament is not contradictory."   *Roswell L. Gilpatrick, U.S. Deputy Sec. of Defense*

August 30, 1962

Interesting hypothesis of Joseph Campbell in *Eranos Jahrbuch* XXVI, p. 430 ff. That the *mandala* appears at end of hunting societies. Because in the primitive bushman type society the individual has in himself *all he needs*, he knows the whole culture, and is not a *fraction* of his society.

Where agricultural society comes into being, the individual has a specialized function, is a *fragment*, and is under stress until he can "realize" his relationship to the whole. He does this by means of symbols.

This agricultural society goes back 8,000 years, while man has been on earth for 600,000 years.

And we are now entering an industrial age (since 200 years!!) in which symbols of agricultural society break down.

The highest concern of all mythologies and ceremonials, ethical systems etc. has been to suppress manifestations of individualism, "by compelling or persuading people to identify themselves not with their own interests, intuitions or modes of experience but with archetypes of behavior and systems of sentiment developed and maintained in the public domain."

p. 448

"The rhythm of the shaman's drum is the syllable AUM; his trance is the bird-flight of the feathered arrow. His mind, disengaged from the protection of the symbol, is to meet directly the *mysterium tremendum* [a mystery before which one ought to tremble] of the unknown." *p. 454*

And this – from *"sickness that forced me to become a shaman."* [Merton's emphasis] *p. 456*

Important that the symbol should not draw energies to itself by assuming a definitive meaning, but that it should serve as an agent of release – into *nada* [nothingness]. Paradox "There is nothing to be done . . . in our very bondage we are free, and in our very striving for release we are linking ourselves the more to bondage. . . ." *p. 466*

A good conclusion: ". . . there is precise relationship between the format or stature of the psyche and the quantum of immediate experience that one is capable of sustaining and absorbing, and that the training *and shaping of the mandala-conditioned psyche of the part man . . . has simply unfitted him for the reception of the full impact of any mysterium whatever.*" [Merton's emphasis] *p. 472*

The goal of the process of individuation is that of dissolving – not reenforcing – the individual's identification with the collective archetypes.

September 2, 1962. XV Sun Pent[ecost]

Am in hospital for examination.

I learn from the newspaper that the high-altitude H bomb explosion set off by U.S. July 9 has permanently knocked out the communication of several satellites sent up by the U.S. and created a whole new radiation belt which "phenomenon is not fully understood." In other words it was a completely absurd and irresponsible experiment, fruit of the military mind, and a promise of more stupidities to come!

Read an excellent short manuscript of translated excerpts from Rabbi Aaron Samuel Tamaret, a "passionately concerned Rabbi" about the time of World War I (sent by Ferry, done by a Rabbi friend of his) – very powerful, clearsighted stuff on nationalism as idolatry, on the hypocrisy of politics, on the spiritual root of war, on the spiritual duty of the Jew to be alert and understand these implications.

Nothing has showed up in tests. Dr. Ryan suggested I go out a little. There is nothing whatever downtown on a Sunday – did not feel it was even worthwhile to wait for the library to open. Interesting old desolate two-story houses bought up by the city and left empty along first street – would have liked to take pictures of them. That is all! Otherwise I felt much better off in a silent (and air conditioned!!) room, reading and thinking.

Especially Sqam Po Pi, sent by a Tibetan master who is at the University of Washington.

This morning finished correcting ms. of *Prayer as Worship and Experience.* Wanted to send it to Macmillan today but could not register it at the P.O.

I hear censors have now stopped my article on the *Jesuit Missions in China!* What next? I suppose if I just wrote out the Our Father and appended the comment "everyone ought to say this prayer," one of the censors of the order would find fault with my work.

Beautiful lines of the Japanese poetess Komachi, quoted by L[awrence] Binyon in *The Flight of the Dragon* [London, 1911].

"It is because we are in Paradise that all things in this world wrong us; when we go out from Paradise nothing hurts for nothing matters."

September 3, 1962

In a resort town in Oregon some thousand youths with nothing better to do started rioting and pulling the place apart. That was yesterday's boredom. They were great jumpers, for the papers (I am still in hospital) says, "Some persons jumped atop buildings and began pelting police with beer bottles and rocks." A riot of large human grasshoppers, hitting firemen with beer bottles!

And in Iran – a frightful earthquake.

And in Cuba, Russians.

And in (independent) Algeria – civil war.

English leaving Kenya have left their pets and given money to houseboys to exterminate the pets. But this has not been done. The existence of the pets now, for some unknown reason, says the paper, constitutes a problem. For whom? For the Royal Society for the Prevention of Cruelty to Animals. This is an ambiguity beyond bearing.

The KKK burns crosses all over Louisiana, as schools reopen.

[Norman] Birnbaum in an interesting article in *PR* [*Partisan Review*] (Summer 1962).

"The growing conviction amongst American social critics that acceptance of [the prospect of] thermonuclear warfare is an expression of disdain for life itself is an insight of considerable profundity. It is not, however, one with which it is easy to live – and *the labor of developing a politics which would cure this pathology* seems Sysiphean." [Merton's emphasis]

("*The [Coming] End of Anti-Communism,*" p. 394)

This is the precise point: the survival of western civilization depends on the capacity of America to develop at last a mature and sane form of politics – instead of the absurd game that now goes by that name.

As opposed to the nonsense and chaos of the society, that appears to be around us: [Merton circles the numbers that follow.]

1. Conviction of the possibility of order, morality, sanity.

2. Conviction of the basic good potentialities in man – now cruelly deviated, wasted, misused.

3. Importance of rational and spiritual goals, conviction of a relative perfectibility of this conduct – development of spiritual freedom and insight, with which to help others find themselves.

4. Importance of *independent effort* to break through the inertia and state of permanent delusion fostered by a sick society, even by the monastic society.

In the hospital – under a coat of ugliness and irrationality for which no one is responsible, a great human goodness and beauty, an extraordinary fund of richness in the people, the nurses, the sisters, doctors etc. The nurses are in many ways the best. The great beauty of their gift of themselves.

In many ways perhaps the old western outlook is bankrupt, at least morally. After centuries of "observation," "objectivity," "comment," "civilization," we have lost ourselves in a world of meaningless facts and finally of fictitious events, fake "objects" of inspection, artificial experiences, and nothing is real, least of all life. Life poisoned with falsity and unreality. We must recapture this reality of our own existence and our own meaning, not as objects but as subjects.

September 6, 1962

Coming back to the monastery (last evening) was never better. Sense of recovery, of returning to something good and sane, principally the quiet here.

But the novices also. Yet the student nurses in the hospital – same generation as the novices, also impressed me as sharp and alive – very good kids, interested and seeking truth. (This I suppose I say because they consulted me about it often, wide-eyed.) (Behind this – the sisters who taught them in High School and told them I existed, I imagine.)

Coming home – cool evening, grey sky, dark hills. I felt again, once more, a renewal of the first intuition, the awareness of belonging where these rocky hills are, that I belong to this parcel of land with pine trees and woods and fields, and that this is my place.

Louisville left me with a sense of total placelessness and futility. The immense movement, spread over everything, of hot traffic and irritated people, in a complex swirl of meaninglessness. They could have everything within reach. Why all this senseless movement? And the noise and the stink. The utter dilapidation of whole sections of the city, empty brokendown houses where the winos howl in the night and the bums come to sleep. Yet I love the city too and the people in it, though not their foolishness (which of course is not their fault).

Meditation on Aristotle in the university library where the air-conditioner broke down. For this they closed two hours early and everybody went home!

Home to letters, a note from Msgr. [Ivan] Illich and maps of South America. Another indignant, impassioned, illegible letter from E. I. Watkin, about the Peace Book. He asserts he would listen to *no* authority against conscience on this issue. But my position loses its meaning unless I can continue to speak from the center of the Church. Yet that is exactly the point: where is that true center? From the bosom of complacent approbation by Monsignors?

Finally a note from Fr. Gerald at my place in the refectory hidden in the napkin, saying he had got out to be a hermit – in Martinique like Fr. Sylvanus – and he wanted me to write: which Dom J[ames] will never permit. I cannot write to Sylvanus either. I am happy for them – but will they make it?

Fr. Bruno James is on his way to America (in fact he is now in N.Y.), wants to come here: writes that he has heard at Downside that I have joined the Carthusians and wants to make sure I am here before he comes down.

Bright, cool afternoon. Lavender flowers on the soybeans in the field below the novitiate. As I came into the woods a covey of young quail started up out of the long grass and I was very happy – for I had worried about them. I hope the hunters keep away from there this fall.

A very fine, penetrating essay by Mgr. Illich on missionary poverty, not clinging to one's own culture and background. I must rethink all this in the light of my own vocation, for I have not been good at that kind of poverty. On the other hand my studies etc. are useful for the community and for what I write. But I must be careful to distinguish where I am "not poor." My greatest failures are perhaps in poverty.

A cool wind moves all the leaves in the forest and blows joyously and freely all through the house.

September 7, 1962. Vigil of Our Lady's Nativity
A dream.

I am in a village "near Bardstown," out of the monastery, it is late, the monks are going to bed – will I get back by bedtime or be out after dark. It is dusk, still daylight.

With another man (Tony Walsh?) we meet two lovely young women dressed in white, in the almost deserted village. I say delightedly, "With you, we will easily get a ride!" We plan to hitchhike, so as to get back to the monastery before it is too late.

They smile and do not object. I pair off with the less nunlike of the two (the other has a suggestion of a hood or veil) and with my arm around her waist, we walk off down the road. All through the dream I walk with my arm around her. She is fresh and firm and pure, a beautiful sweet person, a stranger yet freely intimate and loving. However, at one point she tells me seriously I must never need try to kiss her or to seduce her, and I assure her earnestly and sincerely I have absolutely no such intention. This does nothing to alter the intimacy of our relationship and friendship.

(Hereafter the other two vanish out of the dream. I am with A. (Let us call her that, the question of knowing her *name* never really arises at all. It is totally irrelevant.)

Though the village has been dark and empty, now we are outside on the highway, at a crossroads. It is light. We decide that if possible we will take a bus to Bardstown and get from there to Gethsemani. Now there are half a dozen people waiting for the bus. They all know A. because she has preached in their village a new doctrine – (sort of Shaker theology) – and they twit her about it. One who kids her is an American Indian. Another says something with lewd implications and I solemnly and hotly defend her – she lets me know it is hardly necessary.

The bus comes, I get in the front, there is nobody there. A. comes in through another door. We meet in the bus.

We are out of the bus, again in the midst of the country.

I see a chapel. It is the chapel of a novitiate of a foundation of Gethsemani, Genesee (*Je ne sais [pas]!*) [I do not know!]. We will go to the monastery and wake them up. They will understand, someone will give us a ride.

Outside the monastery, a young secular and two or three girls. They are in bathing suits, have been swimming in a pond in the farmyard. We will not wake up the monks. This boy will drive us. But we must get to his car without awakening anyone.

Complication in the build-up. We do not find the car.

On the road. High columns of silver grey smoke go up from the direction of Bardstown. "Tactical atomic weapons." Beautiful, though. Some kind of test. It is here I think A. told me not to kiss her.

We turn back. Now *all the monks* led by their abbot, Dom Eusebius, are out on the road, dressed as soldiers! He leads them with determination, surely I will be caught. As we pass through the midst of them A. conceals my monastic crown with her hand. But is this going to be enough?

Are they after us?

I am in a barn (without A.). I set fire to straw – if the barn burns it will divert any pursuit. But can I myself get out? After seeming to be trapped, I am now completely out, on the "other side" in open country, see a vast landscape, most moving with a church in the middle, Dutch with a thin spire – and sacred objects in the sky or country around, for instance a cross.

I am going past the church with the open country when I wake up.

September 15, 1962. F. of Holy Name of Mary

Relaxed, relieved, slouching out after a week of tension – more than that, – tension and fun since I went to the hospital. Then this week singing the conventual Mass – and going to see Wygal who advised me to give up singing, if it churns my stomach up too much. I am afraid it does. That is, appearing in the sanctuary, standing at the altar, singing. I suppose I am morbidly afraid of making a mistake, and I know this is lack of humility, but I get myself so worked up that I find myself making a complete botch of it, in an agony of tension – though most of the time I manage to be re-laxed and to sing well.

Anyway perhaps today is my last Mass as hebdomadary for a time at least (until the situation changes – maybe a couple of years). Yet I was very free and enjoyed it. But there is no way of getting out of the extreme tenseness and self-awareness: thoughts of God etc. only make it more extreme.

Finished [J. F.] Powers' new novel [*Morte d' Urban*, New York, 1962] yes-terday – will perhaps review it for *Worship*. It is very competent and deserves an article. Complete change in the hero who suddenly becomes human, in-stead of an obsessed clerical zombie, around the middle of the book.

I keep thinking: haven't got much more time! Wind up your affairs! And I relax and listen to the wind in the trees and the diesel train in the valley and realize I perhaps *have* no affairs to wind up. The writing to be done – which does not need to be done – does not perhaps count.

Certainly the Cassian book – I will write it soon to please the Bene-dictines. The article on Cassiodorus because he is a pleasant figure (though perhaps not the man Boethius was!). And a preface in the book of Fr. [Al-fred] Delp, the ms. of which came to me today. All this can be done or not done, it doesn't matter.

No other affairs, certainly.

It is really getting possible to do all these things as if somebody else were doing them, and not to attach importance to them.

September 18, 1962

How long can the menace of war grow and grow, and still not end in war? Not indefinitely. We are close. Closer than last year – very much so.

And yet there is no telling what is to happen, or when, or how.

We are victims of our own monstrous irrationality, our intellectual dishonesty (which reduces everything to vague gibberish and pointless rhetoric, in order to avoid real issues). There is no clarity, no perspective – no truth.

September 20, 1962

This morning Fr. Timothy [Vander Vennet], of Vina, showed up suddenly in choir for Lauds of all things! The characteristic concerned throat-clearing. He is on his way to Rome.

In a paper by Lou Silberman on problems of prayer – he draws analogy from architecture, in which form must follow function. If our prayer presents difficulties, there is no use fiddling with nonessentials, but we must examine whether our form of prayer really expresses our attitude, our ideas and our faith.

He quotes someone – Ahad ah-am, "We raise the skill to the dignity of the kernel and do not rob it of that dignity even if the kernel withers, but make a new kernel for it."

September 21, 1962

The General Chapter has taken steps to unite the brothers and the choir monks in one canonically homogeneous group – though the brothers will continue to have a different schedule and a somewhat different life. But there is to be one novitiate, and one formation. I do not know what this will involve. The discussion of this move seems to have been centered almost entirely on canonical *status*, so that in order to get the brothers qualified as *monachi* [monks] and therefore with a right to vote, the risk was run of getting them obligated to the choir, which is foreign more or less to their vocation (but Dom James likes a big choir!). I think the danger was avoided – but it is and has been real. Danger of an abstract concept becoming more important than the real lives of real people.

Fr. [Godfrey] Diekmann definitely wants me to review the Powers book for *Worship* and it will be a pleasure. Still more moving and important a task, one that stirs me deeply, is the introduction to Fr. Delp's meditations

[*The Prison Meditations of Father Alfred Delp*, New York, 1963] in prison. It is perhaps the most clear-sighted book of Christian meditations of our time. A strange contrast and comparison with Boethius. Not "consoling" except in the profound sense in which the truth consoles one who has been stripped of illusions. How honest he is about the Church and about modern man!

Long, interesting letter from Leslie Dewart and a copy of the article he sent to *Commonweal* as a follow up on mine. Clear and excellent. Shows the immorality of *total* war in which victory (not "defense") becomes an absolute end in itself, and the destruction of the adversary is an end toward which the whole society is geared, even in "peace."

September 23, 1962

A letter came from a woman in France, asking me to ask the prayers of the community that America may at last start a nuclear crusade against Soviet Russia and draw all the lazy and fearful western European nations with her! This a serious proposition, on religious grounds! "We cannot stand any more!" she said.

Meanwhile, though I knew there were fanatics in this country who were proposing a nuclear first strike against Russia, I had no idea how numerous or how powerful they really are. The situation seems to be most serious – incredibly dangerous in fact. Perhaps a little more time – but it seems only a matter of months, perhaps two or three years, at most, before these people finally bring on a cataclysm. And one scarcely knows what to do! All that is possible to me seems pitifully small and useless. To speak out (and I cannot do this in print!). To join with and encourage those who are against war, to pray – and what else? It seems absurd. Is there no meaningful form of political action other than picketing the Pentagon (and this does not seem to have much meaning).

The fact is that anything that does not strike at the very roots of the situation is nothing but a meaningless gesture.

September 26, 1962

A fourth letter from Fr. Abbot from Rome, triumphant conclusion to the General Chapter, with the fabulous mixture of changes in the lit[urgical] calendar, which I no longer try to explain to myself, except that some are evidently subtle expressions of some kind of policy attitude (St. Francis Xavier substituted for St. Gregory, hermit long venerated in the Order!).

The general impression is one of aroused and concentrated conservatism, very fearful of certain new trends, not of others – willing to amalgamate the brothers and the choir – in the long run this may reinforce the *activist* tendencies. In the main, resolute opposition to any kind of pastoral work, on the one hand, and to solitary tendencies on the other. One feels that with a certain amount of confused, but dogged concern, the standard image of the active Cistercian, with an "active" prayer life, plenty of observances and rites, and not an overwhelming amount of time or need for thought, is being reinforced. And that there is a fundamental lack of understanding between the older and younger generations.

The basic issue is, it appears, the conservation of the large, prosperous, active, business-like abbey-corporation in which the individual monk is a contented functionary, more and more tendency toward a monastic bureaucracy, and centralized organization – a population content with the externals which are "satisfactory," and not desiring a "more contemplative life" or any "new formula" – in fact an assertion of the Trappist Corporation against the new primitive Benedictine monasteries which have a young and exploratory outlook, and are willing to experiment.

The general spirit of our superiors seems to be one of fear of trends toward solitude and of attachment to the collective prestige which the Order presently enjoys. They now have what they want, and they are very anxious for its value to be accepted completely, without thought of anything further, by the subjects. In this monastery one feels that the atmosphere is one of people who cheerfully refuse to take the whole thing seriously (except perhaps the business brothers).

A short visit by Dom Leclercq last evening to this morning. This time I felt there was a very complete understanding between us, and that he is a man to stay with and work with, as far as possible. The future of monasticism has a great deal to do with efforts like his and he has a considerable influence in many monasteries. Also on Fr. André [Louf] of the *Collectanea*, Fr. Placide [Deseille] of Bellefontaine, who is rewriting the Directory etc. These are hopeful signs.

Reading the magnificent *Prison Meditations* of Fr. Delp. In ms. I am to write the preface for Herder and Herder. Superb, powerful material. Totally different from the rather depressing false optimism of our establishment. Here a true optimism of one who really sees through the evil and irreligion of our condition and finds himself in Christ – through poverty, crying out from the abyss, answered and rescued by the Spirit.

And I realize how all around me are answers to prayer, as though I were living in the midst of a world that had been all made out of my prayers and needs, *in spite* of everything that went contrary to them.

Yet I can live as if God were not living and praying in me! What a fool, what lack of faith!

Delp says: "Of course the Church still has skillful apologists, clever and compelling preachers, wise leaders; but the simple confidence that senses the right course and proceeds to act on it *is just not there.*"

September 27, 1962

Fr. Roger de Ganck, of Westwalle, on his way to the new foundation of Belgian Cistercian Nuns in California, has been here two or three days – leaves this afternoon. A sensible, jolly, balanced person. I like him and am impressed by him. A solid type, who does not wholly like the trend in the Order either, interprets it as "solutions to the problems of French monastics being imposed on the Order as a whole." I do not know how true this may be.

September 29, 1962

This morning, in John of Salisbury, ran across a quote from the *Georgics* which has entered into the deepest part of my being since I learned it thirty years ago at Oakham – and was moved by it then, studying I think one June morning before the Higher Cert[ificate Examination], by a brook behind Catmose House.

> *Felix qui potuit rerum cognoscere causas*
> *Atque metus omnes, et inexorabile fatum*
> *Subjecit pedibus, strepitumque Acherontis avari.*
> [Happy is he who can have known the causes of things,
> and has placed under his feet
> all fears and inexorable fate and the rumbling of greedy
> Acheron.]

Inexhaustible literary, spiritual, moral beauty of these lines: the classic ideal of wisdom. What a gift to have lived and to have received this, as though a sacrament, and to be in communion of light and joy with the whole of my civilization – and my Church. This is indestructible. Acheron (whose *strepitus* [rumbling] was never so full of ominous rumblings) has nothing to say about it.

And John of S[alisbury] – glossing this with words about faith as a way to the highest truth, adds:

Impossibile est ut diligat et colat vanitatem quisquis et toto corde quaerit et amplectionem veritatis. [Merton's emphasis] *[It is quite impossible for someone to seek and foster vanity and wholeheartedly at the same time seek also for the embrace of truth.]*

October 1, 1962

Yesterday, Sunday, a little comedy and exaltation in Vespers, thinking of the School of Chartres, and the cathedral, and the Sunday antiphon "*Amice, ascende superius* [Friend, take a higher place]" – come into the banquet and they will rejoice with you.

And today the wind swinging the long branches of the weeping willow, opening curtains upon the fall woods and on the sheep barn – everything rusty.

Turning point. Getting ready to come up out of Egypt into my own country. More and more the risk of it. To work free, inside myself, to loosen the garments of flesh (as if I could do that!). Begin! Anyway, you can want to begin. Even if it is nonsense, partly comedy, partly imagination.

October 2, 1962

Today, the community begins the novena for the II Vatican Council. Pouring rain all morning. (Half holiday for the F. of the Guardian Angels.) The Council is certainly a most momentous event. Much more than we realize, although we keep telling ourselves how important it is. Important not at all as window dressing or public relations, but as a supernatural event. I have no patience with the thesis that the main purpose of the Council is to show the rest of the world that the Catholic Church is united, coherent; articulate (indeed, there is talk of struggle and conflict). It should by no means be simply a meeting of a monolithic party and it will not be.

There is no particular point in guessing what will come of it, or whether "enough will be done," or whether it will be broken up, as the last one was, by a major war. It is quite likely that there will be some major liturgical reforms. Already the most important thing – the mere calling of the Council – has drawn attention to the importance of the *bishops*. This seems to be on everybody's mind.

True, those who fulminate about "discipline" will probably want the Council to tighten the screws on the laity and lower clergy and religious rather than make reforms on administration, liturgy, etc. But if that is what happens, the foregone conclusion is that it will not be very effective (cf. Roman Synod).

Our hopes for the Council have got to be supernatural. What matters now is prayer.

Though I am nearly 48, and it is doubtless time to feel a change of climate in my physical being, which begins to dispose itself for its end some one of these years, it is useless to interpret every little sign or suggestion of change as something of great significance. This is a temptation I yield to. I am still too young mentally to be in the least patient of any sign of age. My impatience is felt as an upheaval of resentment, disgust, depression. And yet I am joyful. I like life, I am happy with it, I have really nothing to complain of. But a little of the chill, a little of the darkness, the sense of void in the midst of myself, and I say to my body: "OK, all right then, *die* [double underlined], you idiot!" But it is not really trying to die, it just wants to slow down.

But this war scare aggravates it, and the sense of death and desperation running through my whole society, with all its bombs and its money and its death wish. The colossal sense of failure in the midst of success, that is characteristic of America (but which America cannot really face). I have a comfortable sense of success, which I know to be more or less meaningless, yet I want to make my will, now – as a writer. Go on, fool! Forget it! You may write another twenty books, who knows? And in any case, does it matter? Is this relevant? On the contrary, now is the time I must learn to stop taking satisfaction in what I have done, or being depressed because the night will come and my work will come to an end. Now is the time to give what I have to others, and not reflect on it. I wish I had learned the knack of it, of giving without question or care. I have not, but perhaps I still have time to try.

October 7, 1962

Bro. Basil McMurray made his vows today and a postulant entered. And some of the many changes made by the General Chapter went into effect. They are not important changes. The really big change, the merger of the brothers and the choir, will probably not be for another six or eight months.

Everyone thinks about it, wonders about it. Perhaps those of the Brothers who are really Brothers, are not too anxious for it to come about. There are all kinds of guesses as to how many brothers may want to become choir monks. Some think almost ¾ of them, in which case the whole economy of the monastery will be disorganized. My guess is – not more than 12 or 15 of them will come over to the choir. Why should they? They have a more flexible schedule, an English office, fewer of our particular burdens, and perhaps many opportunities to be better monks than we are.

One novitiate for choir and brothers may be a difficult thing to handle. There is no indication I will necessarily be the one to handle it.

A book has come (from the U. of Minnesota library, borrowed for me by Ray Livingston) *La Doctrine de la Création dans l'École de Chartres.* I am really fascinated by these people. I have been trying to read the *Timaeus* and find it sometimes impossible. Yet what they have made of Plato, these men of Chartres! Also reading the II Book of the *Summa Contra Gentiles* [St. Thomas Aquinas].

And the *Mirror of Simple Souls* which Etta Gullick sent. What a charming and wise book! Yet I think it is Marguerite Porete who wrote it, and she was burned. What sad, impossible things have happened in this holy Church!

I suppose I ought to be afraid for my own skin. Fury of a Japanese monk at Cîteaux who thought *Original Child Bomb* was a glorification of atomic war and denounced me to the [Abbot] General! I have now been denounced by both sides, and am on everybody's blacklist. I have not written as I have merely in order to please people. But it would be nice at least to be understood.

In the last two or three days – appalling, sinister fogs, rain, mists hanging over the hills, weird clouds, one thinks of the fallout, for levels are very high in some cities, since all the tests (particularly those in Nevada). Last week I finished the Introduction to the Delp book.

October 8, 1962

The *Moralium Dogma Philosophorum* of Wm. of Conches is an utterly delightful book. Clear, full of wisdom, full of strength. Magnificent structure of moral virtues in a unity built on justice. I think he is a great man, too long unknown.

Letter from Rabbi Gendler at Princeton wanting to interest me in "Hostages for Peace." Letter from a Prof. at Duke wanting to "take initiatives" in formulating international law for outer space. Someone has said the latest big Russian bomb will, by its fallout, affect some 300,000 unborn children. Some to be born dead, some deformed, some mentally deficient etc. 300,000. But an illusory "political advantage" is preferred to them.

About "Hostages for Peace," in itself it is a good idea. But like all such ideas it is more of a prank than an idea. It goes nowhere. Yet it might mean something, nevertheless. I would certainly sign up for it if I thought there were the remotest chance of getting an intelligent hearing from Dom James. His mind is totally *closed* to all really constructive or daring moves for anything in the way of peace. Or anything important. He thinks in terms of white habits for the laybrothers, and whether one should have one's hood up or down when reading is going on in the refectory.

I have to face the fact that my life here may in some sense have reached a stage where the "better," the creative, original course is automatically *blocked*. (Only possibility – the hermitage. *Must* grow in meditation, it is the only way left.)

We sang a high Mass *ad tollendum schisma* [for the removal of a schism] and the Gradual – (*Fiat Pax in virtute tua* [Let there be Peace in your strength]) – like indeed all the rest of the Mass, was sung against a background of artillery fire at Fort Knox.

October 10, 1962

Refectory reading: the rebellion of Luther. Fr. Abbot cuts it off at a key phrase about the die being cast and "I shall no longer be reconciled with Rome!" Actually there was still lots of time left. But he likes to give the *Tu Autem* [But you, Lord] . . . as a way of underlining the last sentence or phrase.[11] (Third ear: as a way of reminding everyone who is the boss, who chooses the reading and for what purpose!)

I wish religious life were less of a cold war between superiors and subjects – and usually over nothing except niceties and proprieties and nuances of "who is boss." That is partly the kind of thing that produced Lutherans.

[11] *Tu autem* is an abbreviation of "*Tu autem, Domine, miserere nobis* [But you Lord, have mercy on us]," a phrase that by tradition follows the last selection of a reading during Nocturns at Vigils in the monastic Divine Office.

After dinner – reading about Abelard, in R. L. Poole. I have an enormous amount of sympathy and pity for Abelard. And a profound admiration for the human greatness of Heloise (not brought out in Poole, but evident in Gilson). Abelard suffered far more than Bernard ever did (if one can estimate such things!). If suffering makes the greater saints then, perhaps . . . oh, what have I nearly said!

But it is true, dear diary. After all these years I have a greater liking for Abelard than for St. Bernard. I understand him better, am closer to him. His weaknesses were great, his character had terrible flaws, he was vain and impressive. He did not control his vanity as Bernard did. It ruined him.

It is a hot fall day and I am sure everybody in all the world is very kind. Kind, concerned people with big bombs. The Bernards and Abelards of the 20th century will not confine themselves to words and excommunications.

October 11, 1962

"Counterforce." Sounds moral – it involves a strategy in which U.S. – with far more numerous weapons – might in a first strike annihilate Russian missile sites – retaliation against cities being "renounced" by the Russians. (Who are counting on one or two weapons to deter us by threatening cities from secret bases.) Morality really irrelevant to the proponents of the strategy. It is a cold war strategy. What can it lead to?

October 13, 1962

The very disturbing case of Fr. John of the Cross, who is probably going to leave. I hope there is some chance of his finding something good and landing on his feet. But this is a symptom of the deficiencies of this monastery – for he has been, since the beginning, one of the most unusual and gifted people in it. And one who has the most profound effect on the people he advises. I wish there were something I could do, and am disturbed to think that his decision may in the long run be traced partly to my influence, and his independence to an extreme interpretation of some of my own teaching. And yet it is so hard to understand this case. He is a complete mystery, and you never are sure whether you are dealing with a saint or a heretic. He can still be a saint.

It is possible that the two novitiates may merge in January, then. This is going to be very difficult. The whole affair is sad. It is easy enough to say,

"If the Abbot had more understanding . . ." But we *all* need more understanding, and we all sin and err constantly. When will we ever see straight?

What has been the use of all the things I have said, all the spiritual conferences I have given in the last eleven years? All the "monastic spirituality"? The books have been less bad. Perhaps the only thing that can be said for all my "teaching" is that it has been more interesting and has taken a broader view, covered more ground, perhaps gone a little deeper than was usual. But what does *that* amount to? Fortunately I have also, to some extent, tried to live, and pray, and read, and listen to the silence of the woods.

October 16, 1962

Hot, stuffy October weather, tense weather.

Bluejays scream in the pines. A big flicker with a smart black bib was rooting around in the grass outside the window.

Machines in the valley.

Wars in the weather. The machines will make war, when the days are tense like this. (I hear one making war on the soybeans.)

We have an instrument flying to Venus, and as it goes past, for thirty seconds it will have a view of the clouds. This will be in December. Then it will go on out nowhere, it will be an eye nowhere.

People who believe they exist have attacked Gordon Zahn because he defended Ferry, who attacked J. Edgar Hoover, who is a dirty mingling of red ink ferocity and attempts at being reasonable, in letters to or about Zahn, with promises that they will all be sure to see he is fired from Loyola, "an institution conducted by men of God."

When John XXIII was first Pope, he would sleep his short sleep and wake up saying, "I must consult the Pope about this." And then, as his mind cleared, he would say, "But I am the Pope."

Now he is Pope and he has his Council. It has been a great opening. He received the diplomats in the Sistine Chapel, pointed to the Michelangelo Jesus of the Last Judgment, and said "Gentlemen: what will it be?"

He said what needed to be said. What has been said before, but never so forcefully or directly. He is a great Pope.

He said the people of the world want peace. That God will judge severely the rulers who fail in their responsibility to the people.

But in America, what is the situation? The President, certainly, wants peace. And most of the people, if they know what they think, think they want peace: at least they will go along with the idea of peace provided it is not definitely clear that *Time* and *Life* regard peace as something utterly disgraceful.

And yet there are a lot of Americans who want war. They are already convinced of the necessity of war. They believe that they are at all times and on all sides threatened by communists – which in a way they are, but not in the way they think. And they want to annihilate Russia.

Among them are Catholics – and not a few priests. Perhaps *most* of the Catholics in the country.

These people are, by their belligerency and fear, able to plunge the whole world into a disastrous war that will ruin what they think they are trying to defend and perhaps make things impossible for the survivors.

After a 4-year study the UN radiation committee, last month, warned that continued nuclear testing could seriously endanger the human race for the next 20,000 years.

How seriously? Why 20,000? What do you mean endanger?

And up goes another bomb. Two big Russian bombs *at least* since then – and how many of "ours"?

"Also the East-West committee of scientists dropped its previous position that genetic harm would occur only through excessive radiation doses and warned that 'any doses of radiation however small' would cause inherited abnormalities."

History of Disarmament

1954. British and French propose reduction of arms and armed forces, prohibition of all weapons of mass destruction, under adequate (international) control. Russia refused, U.S. accepted.

1955. Under pressure of world opinion, Russia accepted. U.S. said "our ideas have been accepted in large measure . . ." then backed out. Russia had spied over an inspection.

1959. Khrushchev proposed "general and complete disarmament."

UN general assembly votes unanimously for this "under effective international control." Ten-nation committee begins work on this in 1960. U.S. supporting gradual disarmament with inspection. Russian disarmament first and inspection afterwards. Ended in failure June 1960. Since then – stalemate.

October 20, 1962

A clear day (though it was cloudy for a while after dinner).

Clarity in the early morning studying the gloss of Wm. of Conches on the *Timaeus*.

The dark, the silence.

Then, clarity at Mass, exactly at dawn. The sun is now rising at seven and I am clothed in dawn light as I stand at the altar (the first rays of the sun add the only warmth in the chapel).

Then after that the day is warm.

The U.S. is now spending more each year on armament than was spent in any year before 1942 for the *entire national budget*.

The people who demand that the government "interfere" in nothing – just pour money into the armament industry and provide a strong police for "security." But stay out of everything else! No interference in medicine, mental health, education, etc. etc.

But these are the ones who have their way.

Never was a country at once shrewder and less wise – shrewd in non-essentials and lunatic in essentials.

I have no doubt the world feels toward America the way many monks feel toward an abbot who wants to exercise total power, to receive unquestioning obedience on the basis of slogans about which he himself ceased thinking 25 years ago, and who above all wants to be loved, so that he may never, at any time, to himself, seem to be exercising power, or loving it. Nobody denies him the power he has: few give him the love that he needs in order to feel safe and content. And therefore he uses his power, from time to time, in unpredictable, arbitrary and absurd ways in which he defeats his own ends and makes everybody miserable.

October 22, 1962

More than half the population of the U.S. is watching TV every evening.

Sets in 90% of households. Average viewing: 6 hours a day.

Policy of TV industry – standardization – give what offends no one of the accepted groups – business, military.

Aim – to keep everybody loyally and happily *consuming*.

"Consumership" and the techniques of manipulating people and order them [to] consume as much as possible.

Games theory. Box-score approach to Cold War.

The "American way of life" is the American religion.

"Religion is America's most powerful weapon" (vicious circle).

Minister – businessman mixed up in paper work, unable to face nuclear crisis (from a paper by Dallas Smythe).

October 23, 1962

The "pessimists" whom the Pope criticized in his opening address at the Vatican are the integrists, the conservatives, who think the Church has to condemn everything modern. This is the great struggle at the Council.

Struggle among the bishops, also, in electing members of various committees. French and Germans not willing to accept proposed lists. I am not sure what the issue is, but it is French and Germans vs. Italians. A little Worlds Series touch that makes one think he understands. But it is *most* important! Card. Liénart rallied a group together for action rather than passive and automatic acceptance, and apparently it worked. The stories are not, and cannot be, clear. This is already "old," but new for us.

Brilliant, windy day – cold. It is fall. It is the kind of day in October Pop used to talk about. I thought about him as I came up through the hollow, with the sun on the bare persimmon trees, and a song in my mouth. All songs are, as it were, one's last. I have been grateful for life.

Many strange things I remember: for instance, if I had only stayed with the cross country team, at Columbia, until the end of the season, I would have had my "letter." Why think of that?

Great clouds of seeds fly in the wind from the poplar tree.

The new magazine, *Ramparts*, with two impressive pictures of Bro. Antoninus are in a black and white Dominican habit, among birch trees. I know he often feels as I do. I must write to him and say, "Courage! We are honest men!"

Deep pessimism in a letter from E. I. Watkin. I cannot say there is much hope to be seen among politicians and military men.

October 24, 1962

Brilliant cold night. All the stars! And a very thin rind of moon.

After the Night Office, in the doorway of the novitiate, Br. Basil whispered something about a speech of Kennedy (Rev. Father must have announced this yesterday evening) – there are missile sites in Cuba. There is a naval blockade. If any missiles come from Cuba, the U.S. will bomb Russia. And so on. How, in a situation like this, a nuclear war can be avoided is difficult to see: doubtless it *can*, but taking into account the past patterns of behavior and the accumulated commitments of each side, I would say the folly is inevitable, unless all the politicians and military men suddenly drop dead – and the business leaders with them, along with the Communist Party and about five million other people.

This event will surely do more still to paralyze thought at the Council on nuclear weapons. Nothing is up for discussion on this *yet*.

October 27, 1962

Life is a series of jolts that are soon forgotten. Already in the monastery it is as if there had never been any trouble over Cuba. All is forgotten. I happened to go to Louisville on Thursday (Kennedy's speech was Monday night and I heard of it Wednesday morning). I got a good picture of the situation. Yes. There is a blockade. But already they had apparently let a tanker through with only perfunctory inspection. Other Russian vessels had, however, turned back. The search is for atomic explosives. The move seems to be reasonable in the context of power politics. After all, if Cuba is full of missiles, a nuclear war is all the more likely. If a blockade is safer . . .

Needless to write about the nuns from Nazareth (Belgian) who came through here and whom I saw Wednesday. Very bright and human. Best nuns I ever saw. They made me happy about the Order – that there should be such people in it. Mother Myriam [Dardenne], the Superior, is very much on the ball.

Fr. Godfrey Diekmann writes of the Council (where they are now discussing liturgy). And a joke: "Where are Cardinals Ottoviani and Ruffini these days? – Oh, they are on their way to the Council of Trent!"

October 30, 1962

The complete capitulation of Khrushchev on Cuba, and his promise to disassemble the missile sites, a practical repudiation of Castro (?) – all this was a surprise and a great relief to everyone. I heard it Sunday evening from Fr. John of the Cross, who is trying to leave and wants my support. While Fr. Eudes and Fr. Abbot want him to stay and want my support. The situation is curious and I hardly know what to think of it, except that Fr. J. is determined to leave and there is no real point in forcing him to stay, even if he has a vow. I am in the middle, dubious, trying to advise him to go slower than he is going and take a little more care. All he hears is that

I do not tell him absolutely not to go. Then he quotes me as saying "go!" Actually in the last two or three years he has gone through a queer evolution and has apparently done strange things, though nobody knows quite what he has done.

A very clear, concise speech by Fr. Brown, S.J. (began it in Washington last Thursday and sent me a copy): on the fact that should be obvious that Communism is striving to attain its ends by political and revolutionary means, not directly by military force – except when that is very easy and so to speak works all by itself. It would be much safer if everyone had a much clearer idea of what is going on, instead of this confused, agitated and fevered perspective produced by the cold war.

This country has been very much stirred and is almost on a mobilization basis since Kennedy's speech.

News coming – smuggled – out of Angola, shows that in the last year or two the repression has been utterly savage and barbarous: a greater barbarity and ferocity than anywhere, including Red China or Stalinist Russia (except quantitatively) and practiced by *Christian* colonialists!!

China is economically shattered, practically abandoned by Russia. The big drive to industrialize has collapsed and now the armies are moving over the mountains to India – presumably for a diversion of attention from unbearable problems. The most orthodox Marxist society proves, in practice, the futility of doctrinaire Marxism applied rigidly and dogmatically – and "scientifically"!

I have been having good discussions in the evening, once a week with Dan Walsh, on the School of Chartres, using such texts as are available. And quite a few are. Wm. of Conches on the *Timaeus* and Boethius, Thierry of Chartres on the *Hexameron*, and so on. I think Wm. of Conches is a real discovery: his tremendous philosophy of nature and emphasis on secondary causes, an anticipation of Thomism. Or perhaps an inspiration of it. But more than that, his contemplative sense of *esse* in his doctrine on formal causality and "wisdom."

November 2, 1962
"It is impossible to get rid of violence when one is oneself full of violence. On the contrary, one only adds to the number of the violent."
Vinoba Bhave

November 5, 1962

Foul cold grey weather – today, however, with a few bursts of sun.

I feel the need of greater austerity – or *some* austerity – in the refectory. Everything is better when I eat less.

Cannot cope with mail. Trying to correct [Sergei] Bolshakoff's manuscript on the Russian mystics. I don't know what to make of him. He claims he played a decisive part in bringing Card. [Eugene] Tisserant and Archbishop Nikodim together and others bringing Russian observers to the Council. Doubtless. That is not my area.

Saturday I finished a preface to Dom Denys Rutledge's book *In Search of a Yogi* [New York, 1963]. It rambles too much, and he is too sarcastic in places – though I can understand the temptation. There is an aura of pretentiousness that gets into Indian religiosity sometimes – perhaps as a reaction to Christian claims to be absolutely the only true religion.

I hope to finish conferences on Cistercian history (the Sunday ones) by the end of November. And end the year with one or two on the *Regula Magistri* and Lérins.

November 6, 1962

Only just beginning to realize what a grave shock the Cuba crisis was to the whole world, and how near it really came to nuclear war. One thing it seems to show is that the U.S. is more single-mindedly militaristic than the USSR – (but not more than China!).

What a shock it must have been to the *people* of Russia!! They are probably not angry with Khrushchev for backing down.

Of course it shows the immense strength of U.S. bases all around Russia, in Turkey especially. They knew they were destroyed already, if a war started. But is this something for us to be glad about? I am afraid the country at large is glad. It is a "cold war victory" (almost hot).

Unfortunately this will encourage the extremists to go on further. Now *we* know what it is like to have been "appeased." It is very dangerous. This may in fact lead the country on to a more adventurous and aggressive policy, and perhaps, who knows, to the hegemony it has been accused of wanting. It will learn from the accusers, and will perhaps fulfill prophecies.

In a letter from Dallas Smythe (U. of Illinois) (dated Oct. 29, a week ago).

"Three of our graduate students came to me during the week and in various sly ways contrived to say that they were about to remove their wives and kids to Mexico. . . . Another added that day he had gone out and bought an Enfield 703 rifle to protect his wife and kids. Two faculty men were on the point of decamping to Mexico Friday. . . . Eavesdropping on the CD [Civil Defense] rehearsals disclosed what the press is censoring, namely that there were heavy runs on gasoline and food supplies all over the country last week as people bought and hoarded these commodities."

November 13, 1962

Finishing Wm. of Conches' *Philosophia Mundi* [*Philosophy of the World*] – the plan is interesting, and having discussed the world, then man's body, then the soul, he ends with man's education. Beautiful little chapter on the Teacher. I was very moved by it. I usually ignore this element in my own vocation, but obviously I am a writer, a student and a teacher as well as a contemplative of sorts, and my solitude etc. is that of a writer and teacher, not of a pure hermit. And the great thing in my life is, or should be, love of truth. I know there is nothing more precious than the bond of charity created by communicating and sharing the truth. This is really my whole life.

". . . *Nec si deficiet multitudo sociorum desinet,* sed ad instructionem sui et aliorum vigil et diligens erit." [Merton's emphasis] ["Nor would he cease if many fellow workers fail *but would be watchful and diligent in the instruction of himself and others.*"]

It is the feast of All Saints of the Order. Wrote to Fr. Ronald, at St. John's, about the monastic formation project here. I must get notes together on the project itself. Censors approval came for the Preface to Fr. Delp's *Meditations* (I got the *English* censors to do it). Must write to George Lawler about it now. He will be pleased. Paul Peachey, the Mennonite, of FOR, who translated a German Jesuit's book on Zen [Heinrich Demoulin, *A History of Zen Buddhism*], was supposed to be here today, but a telegram says he has had a "slight auto accident" and must wait to come some other time. I am sorry.

After several days of rain and fog it has cleared. Came up to the house and recited "*Quam dilecta tabernacula tua* [How lovely are your dwelling places]" and felt v[ery] happy; probably the 70 Baptists who were here from the seminary yesterday have prayed for me. I enjoyed talking to them.

Yesterday Aidan Nally came up to me by the woodshed and said, "Father, it seems the wars have ceased."

Later I conjectured he was referring to the cessation of atmospheric nuclear testing announced by Kennedy.

November 16, 1962

24th anniversary of my Baptism. Am reading Ignace Lepp's *The Christian Future*, which concerns me deeply. I have never had any doubts about my Christian faith or about the Church as the Body of Christ. But the more I see of a certain organizational and social aspect of Christianity, the more I agree with Fr. Lepp. In a certain sense I am scandalized by my own Catholicism.

To belong to an organization – well, a "visible society" (and I believe the Church certainly is and must be visible) – in which one is obliged constantly to yield to officialdom and follow the decisions and regulations of bureaucrats. That is bad enough. But to find oneself doing so more and more in cases where there seems to be a clear conflict between the dead regulation on one hand and living, spontaneous moral action on the other . . . Of course the conflict is never *quite* [underlined twice] clear. And there is always the danger of deceiving oneself. The angel of light, you know! And "true charity" always means "first of all obedience" . . . etc. And yet! Fortunately it is not a clear-cut case always: there is always enough charity left among bureaucrats, there are always clergy who are deeply comprehending and human, and in this monastery there are the people themselves and one's duty to them.

In short the only things that really keep me where I am (at Gethsemani) are first of all the community (least of all the Abbot; though he is the one who exerts the most pressure) and secondly my responsibility toward those who have read my books, though this also is ambiguous.

Especially love for and appreciation for the novices, realization of Christ's love for them: these are very important to me, sometimes makes all the difference.

In them the Church is easily visible to me. More visible, I fear, than in Rome. I don't refer to the Council, for that too has had its charismatic visibility, at least in the beginning.

I wonder how long I am going to be able to talk as I did the other day to the Baptists from the seminary in Louisville – with such uninhibited frankness. And they too, I think, are wondering.

Lax is in Greece. I got a letter today from Athens. Jim Forest wrote of the way Communists tried to take over a strike meeting for peace and occupy the speaker's platform. The CNVA [Citizens for a Non-Violent Alternative] and people like that are going to have their hands full if the Commies have suddenly decided to take over the Peace Movement. That is a sign that there must be a real vitality in the Peace Movement.

November 17, 1962

Today (a blacker day than usual, and there have been many) Aidan Nally met me out by the greenhouse just before dinner and uttered some prophesies of doom according to something he had seen on TV. None of it was clear. Probably the Russians trying to make up for their loss of face over Cuba. Something in Germany? Berlin?

The problem is not to lose one's sense of perspective and of seriousness. It is always "the end" and each time it gets closer. The students at the Oxford Union drank up their best wine in the Cuba crisis. They will not have any for this one, whatever it is – if it is a crisis, and not something imagined by Aidan. But Aidan's imagination is as good as any paper – only a little foggy.

The [Jules A.] Clerval book on Chartres [*Les Écoles de Chartres au Moyen-âge*, Paris, 1895] came from the Institute of Med[ieval] Studies at Toronto, and a lot of poems and articles which Cardenal has been publishing in Colombia.

November 18, 1962

"It is truth, not ignorance, which makes us humble and gives us the sense of what remains unknown in our very knowledge."   *Maritain*

November 20, 1962

The dismal black curtain of drizzle (and fallout!) has cleared a little, after five or six uninterrupted days of it, and there have even been moments of pale sunshine this afternoon. No one knows whether or not really to expect an invasion of Cuba, which could and probably would be a disastrous mistake. No real news of the Council, no real news of the Chinese fighting in India – in a word, no real news of anything.

This is apparently going to be a busy week – with the Novice Master from Genesee coming to gather information, Episcopalian seminarians from Nashoda, to whom I am to speak, and a Building Committee meeting Thursday, probably in view of the changes that will be involved with the merging of novitiates.

Tomorrow, F. of the Presentation, I will offer Mass for Louis Massignon who died at the end of October. A great man! Mrs. Roosevelt (Eleanor) also died recently – a woman who accepted a lot of falsification and malice from others with patience and courage.

"The trouble is that communism long ago ceased to be a truly progressive force and has formed the worst type of orthodox ranks. Although the progressive Christians are aware of this they dare not openly proclaim it for fear of appearing reactionary."

Ignace Lepp [From Karl Marx to Jesus Christ (New York, 1958)]

This is a very significant observation. It ought to be obvious, but is not, because there are so few Christians who are really able to stand on their own feet, and not propped up by reactionaries of the right on one side or those of the left on the other. In this correctly they are almost all on the right. In Europe there is a clearer division. But who is there who can stand in the middle and go his own way as a Christian? Probably there are some, but not as many as claim to be.

Lepp also says what many of us feel – and have tried to say – about Pope Pius XII's vision and the way it was exploited. The whole thing is unpleasant – at least as regards the neutrality of those who exploited the event – deeply suspect.

November 24, 1962

From Chartres back to Boethius: *De Hebdomadibus.* Magnificent meditation on being and existence!

Thanksgiving day was bright, for a change. Long building committee meeting in the afternoon. Changes in the house inevitably bring up the question of the changes of policy which make them necessary. Strong feelings of some of the more mature and older laybrothers (Giles, etc.) who feel their life is being unduly complicated and tampered with, that a "sung office" is being forced on them etc., and that they are being inveigled into a too organized piety. It is true that their Master may be tempted to go in this direction a little, helped by some of the younger brothers and approved by the abbot. It is a more active and busy spirituality which does not recognize the value of the old simplicity, and its potential depth for contemplation. Perhaps this is getting to be rather more general.

Anglican seminarians from Nashoda here on retreat came up for a talk yesterday afternoon. It was lively and I liked them. Yet perhaps we tend to make too much of these meetings. They are still new, and seem to be events. And I suppose they are events, but ordinary ones. It is good that they are.

Woke up very tired this morning, could hardly get out of bed and down to choir, and was hardly able to keep awake during night office. Exhausted, I suppose, by the unusual strain of so much talking (for there was also a moral conference and then in the evening a seminar with Dan Walsh).

At Mass, which was all before sunrise and without lights, the quality, the "spirituality" of the pre-dawn light on the altar was extraordinary. Silence in the chapel and that pure, pearl light! What could be a more beautiful liturgical sign than to have such light as witness of the Mystery?

Only after Mass, when the sun rose (at about 7:35) was I able to feel any real strength, and shook off the torpor and weariness.

Things I should probably *not* write.
A prayer for the FOR (not yet) (for "Fellowship").
Certainly not the teen-agers' book of saints requested by Burton!!
But perhaps a preface for Dan and Phil Berrigan's new book – and the one I have promised for Fr. Perrin's *Catherine of Siena*.
There are too many books and too many prefaces and too many blurbs. Good books get lost in the tide of bad ones. Yet there are many good ones!

November 26, 1962
Lament of Ezechiel over Tyre (Ezech. 27):

Quae est ut Tyrus quae obmutuit in medio maris? Nunc contrita es a mari, in profundis aquarum opes tuae. Vae quoque bellatores tui cadent in corde maris in die ruinae tuae. [Who is like Tyre, which is silenced in the midst of the sea? Now you are broken from the sea, in the depth of the ocean lies your wealth; woe also, for your warriors have fallen into the heart of the sea, in the day of your downfall.]

Wild grey kitten among the dead leaves in the garden, fleeing to the hole in the wall. Sun on the building work, the waterhouse. Dead leaves. Man in a car on the road undoubtedly dislikes Cuba, roaring by very fast, for all dislike Cuba. It is sad there will be no war – only what is necessary to punish Cuba. But according to Dorothy Day, things are peaceful in Cuba (or were at the beginning of October) and one can still exist as a Catholic and on the whole her article rings a bell. It makes sense. That it is about time for Catholics to go along with the movements that will improve the lot of the people in Latin America, refraining from any ethical or religious compromises, however.

November 27, 1962

Hawk on the way up here, over the cedars in the low bushy place where the quails were: (*were*!!). He circled four or five times, spreading his tail which shone rusty in the light, and he flashed silver like the dove in the psalm, when sun caught him under the wings.

Am impressed with the great monastic revival of 19th-century Russia, prepared by Poussius Velichkovsky at Athos and in Rumania. The *Staretzke*. A very significant phenomenon – the great center of mysticism a hundred years ago was *Russia!* Work on the Bolshakoff ms. is not boring.

November 30, 1962

Long talk with Fr. Abbot yesterday about the "case" of Fr. John of the Cross. And this morning I had many, in fact too many, insights into the problem. So many I think they were too true to be good. And so I will stay far away from putting them down. When you know people too well –
. . . Yet for the first time I think I had a little restraint and compassion for the Abbot even when seeing the depth and complexity and unconscious deceit with which he so innocently and terribly persecutes those he claims to love! Here is a man who in some sense is a saint, and is certainly revered as a saint by many who know him – know him a little, or only enough to accept the image he wants to project; the image he himself believes in! – who is doubtless in the sight of God a well-meaning, somehow patient, in many ways self-sacrificing and generous man. Who can be kind, longsuffering, and is by all means devout. And he has a certain simplicity, a certain humility, and intention to love.

Underneath which one gets sudden glimpses of cowardice, ignobility, hypocrisy, vengefulness, of which he is *entirely unconscious*, and which therefore he can exercise quite ruthlessly against people, thinking it is "for their good," and with what self-righteousness! And it never dawns on him. If anyone tries to tell him – as Fr. John of the Cross barely began to try – what a process is mobilized to bury all the suggestions that point toward what must remain hidden!

How yesterday his mind operated on John of the Cross, "I thought so highly of him! . . . I placed such hopes in him. . . . I would have made him prior. . . . You never can tell what lies below the surface. . . . Dom Edmund always said, 'I don't like those *deep* ones, you never know what they are thinking. . . .' and then this morning in chapter, a homily for Fr. J. who was not there – 'the barren fig tree – beautiful in appearance but *no fruit . . .*'" etc. The theme of deception. Judas. Betrayal. Rejection of Christ's love . . . All because Fr. J. very reservedly pointed to two unjust and irregular actions by which the abbot had, in a seeming abuse of his powers, interfered with Fr. J's relations with penitents in matters of conscience. And how the abbot manipulates facts to favor himself, habitually and without batting an eye!

The thing that is so terrible is the clarity with which I realize that such things seem to have been true of canonized saints, saints of the Order, even Bernard! There is an awful wilfullness and unconscious fury in manipulation apparent in some of the stories, some of the partisan accounts of struggles . . .

All this is a shocking temptation against faith in the Church – and yet not. Because all such things are equally in myself and in all men. And in the abbot himself I must accept them and understand them, and not try to punish him for them, but patiently work for the good of others, for healing, to see that too many are not hurt too much, and that *this clarity is no privilege*, it does not justify me in anything, it does not entitle me to condemn, to criticize, it is only a burden, an affliction for me, about which I must now learn to be silent.

There is no use in a reforming frenzy! These are things so deep and so unconscious they *cannot* be reformed and in human nature there is no end to them. Only the grace and the mercy of God eventually changes them. There is no use in recriminations, tirades, accusations, homilies. Here is where I must really begin to love people whose sins are utterly distasteful to me perhaps because they are also my own sins and I am not able to realize it.

Perhaps it is better to learn simply to overlook these things. And to remember that after all, as men go, this is a "good man" and he remains good in spite of the awful clarity with which I seem to see things that are less good. He loves God, and God loves him. But that is the terrible thing: that in good people there is the same cruelty as in others, but it is made *unassailable by their goodness*. This is the principal scandal! For the abbot is in some ways the best man in the house, and one who, in doing much good, hurts people incessantly and does tremendous harm – for which he will perhaps never be blamed, and for which they also will receive merit and reward, for their suffering. Yet to say that is the monastic life would be unutterable blasphemy!

And the ultimate justification he creates for himself is precisely this, that his sweet unconscious inhumanity is elevated to the level of a "supernatural" ideal!

December 4, 1962

There was a fire up the road on neighbors' land and we got in the truck to go there, but no one was fighting it and it eventually burned out, among the pines and scrub, doing good or evil to nothing.

In the volume of *Testimonios* [*Testimonials*] for Victoria Ocampo, I appear as Thomas Merton *S.J.* Ever closer to the Rothschild ideal!

And now everyone analyzes the Cuba crisis – there are curious aspects of it (nothing was really hidden and it seems, as I myself had guessed, that Khrushchev *provoked* it, though he got perhaps more than he expected). The fact remains that it was very close to nuclear war.

December 6, 1962

Cold wind and a little snow, the wind making one feel the silence after noon. Steps on the concrete floor of the novitiate. A good day to read about Copernicus. And perhaps later the new book on bombs, *Kill and Overkill*. And later to cut wood, and see the Abbot, and sign books for Dan and see Fr. John of the +'s [Cross's] mother, and give direction to Bro. Boris, all that, and all that. Nice winter day.

December 8, 1962. Immaculate Conception

I had the sermon today. Then in the morning the cloister began to smell of liquorice (that was being put out in refectory). And stank of it all day. Liquorice and Origen at dinner – and coconut cake which I could hardly eat.

Grey silent afternoon in the woods. In the evening finished the Cistercian History conferences.

December 9, 1962. II Sun Adv[ent]

Hurt my hand falling on a sharp stone in the garden (in the dark) on the way to Prime. Moral: don't be looking at the stars on the way to Prime.

It is beautiful Advent weather, greyish and cold, with clouds of light snow howling across the valley and I see it is really winter. I put some bread out for the birds.

Twenty-one years tomorrow since I landed here! I feel closer to my beginning than ever, and perhaps I am near my end. The Advent hymns sound as they first did, as if they were the nearest things to me that ever were, as if they had been decisive in shaping my heart and my life, as if I had received this form, as if there could never be any other melodies so deeply connatural to me. They are myself, words and melody and everything. So also the *Rorate Coeli* [Drop Down Dew] that brought me here to pray for peace. I have not prayed for it well enough, or been pure enough in heart, or wise enough. And today before the Bl. Sacrament I was ashamed of the impertinences and the deep infidelities of my life, rooted in weakness and confusion.

The new book of Harrison Salisbury [*A New Russia*, New York, 1962] shows there is a surprisingly deep rift between Soviet Russia and Communist China. And other things important perhaps. In a pragmatic way for peace – for the time being. The young writers in Russia who are speaking out – they are perhaps very important people, though perhaps also the Luce press makes too much of them. There is a tendency to think of them as Americans in Russia, which is fortunately not true and I have no reverence for such Russians as merely want to have their own cars and be "Americans." To put any hope in *that* is a real folly. Some do.

But then there are the Seurichastny's! . . .[12]

[D. M.] Chenu's article on Theology and History in the 12th century is, like everything else of his, instructive and important.

How much we have done to lead ourselves astray with theories about ages of the world, and extrapolations from prophecies of Daniel about the Roman Empire – to Charlemagne – to Barbarism and what not. This was the contribution of a Cistercian, Otto of Freising. We have never given up thinking in such terms. No one, however, has yet formulated anything

---

[12] Merton refers to individuals who accommodate themselves to the needs of the party, and specifically to Vladimir V. Seurichastny, who carried out an assault on Boris Pasternak.

about the "Western" realm of America being the heir of the Holy Roman Empire – or perhaps some Spaniard did. Yet that is how we think, still, and it is built in to our Christianity as a permanent delusion.

So also the delusion of Holy Russia.

There are too damn many holy empires with archimandrites to shower them in holy water.

I want to do more translations, and if I do, won't have time to write much next year; still I hope to translate: for instance the Cuban poet Centio Vitier, who sent me five fine little white books printed, as they say, by Orizen. But a good poet. I have written him and hope the letter gets through all the hostilities, at this end and that.

Yesterday my Mass was for the new generation, the new poets, the fighters for peace, and my novices. There is in many of them a peculiar quality of truth that older squares have driven out of themselves in days of rigidity and secure right thinking. May God keep us from being "right thinking" men, who think, that is, with their own police (and since the police don't think, neither do these others).

Girri too, I might translate, and some more of the young Nicaraguans above all.

December 10, 1962

Conclusion of the Salisbury book – what it seems anyone with any sense must realize: that the only real hope for peace is in the continued liberalizing of Russia under Khrushchev and that if the extremists take over after his death – or even before it, and join forces with China again, then there will surely be very much trouble.

December 11, 1962

Otto of Friesing was so convinced that Constantine had finally inaugurated the Kingdom of God, that he spoke at last only of *one city* in his history of the "Two Cities." When the Emperor became Catholic, then Christendom = the Kingdom of God, i.e. the Christian politico-religious world is the kingdom of God.

Hence there is no more to be done, but to preserve the status quo of the kingdom, if necessary by violent repression, coercion rather than apostolate. The apostolate of united coercion!!

And as the genuine Christian spirit must *necessarily* resist the identification of the Kingdom of God with a limited human society, then the focus of "Christendom" did in fact tend to repress those movements which tended to genuine development, thrusting them outside the "city" where their evolution became distorted and unhealthy.

Hence another Cistercian, Joachim of Fiore, rises up against Otto of Friesing's Constantinian theory with an apocalypse of the "Spirit." He was in fact expressing the stirrings that were to bring about the birth of a new age and break down medieval society.

Two temptations, then: to evade the responsibilities of a Christian in history by saying that the kingdom has arrived and medieval Christendom is/was the kingdom, or to do the same by saying the kingdom will arrive only at the end of, or outside of time.

The true responsibility – to receive the Holy Spirit and cooperate with His transforming work in time now.

(I have a doubtless rather good little publication on/for Catholic intellectual and social movements. It is called what? *Pax Romana!* And the uneasiness with which I cannot help viewing Don Giovanni Rossi's Pro Civitate Xtiana and all other such movements, comes to the same thing!)

Already Catholics with this mentality but tired of western capitalism, are beginning secretly to dream of a Constantine in Moscow and a new Muscovite Christian Kingdom of God! As if this were a *new* dream!

Afternoon – the primary duty, to seek coherence, clarity, awareness, in so far as these are possible. Not only human coherence and clarity but those which are born of silence, emptiness and grace. Which means always seeking also the right balance between study, work, meditation, responsibility to others, and solitude.

Very cold. Some snow. Bright, silent afternoon.

I have been shocked at a notice of a new book, by Rachel Carson [*Silent Spring*], on what is happening to birds as a result of the indiscriminate use of poisons (which do not manage to kill all the insects they intend to kill).

Someone will say: you worry about birds: why not worry about people? I worry about *both* birds and people. We are in the world and part of it and we are destroying everything because we are destroying ourselves, spiritually, morally and in every way. It is all part of the same sickness, and it all hangs together.

I want to get this book. Why? Because this is a truth I regard as very significant and I want to know more of it.

Affairs: Perhaps a review for the *Monastic Studies* they are starting at Berryville. In this I must certainly try to help.

Perhaps finally I will do that article on Cassiodorus and give it to them.

First I have one more chapter to do in the book for Macmillan (*Prayer as Worship and as Experience*).

Arrange with Farrar Straus, finally, about the book they want on the liturgical year, or on parts of it.

Draw up some notes on this "monastic formation" project we are supposed to be starting – at least to help keep the thing from getting too muddled.

What I am more interested in perhaps: translations of Latin American poets. And a letter to one of them – a student in Nicaragua – Napoleon Chow. A translation by me of a poem of Alfonso Cortes appeared, with the original and some comment, in *La Prensa* of Managua.

December 13, 1962

Profound remark of Gunther Auders that while in the past it was always assumed that our imagination far exceeded anything we could do, now in the nuclear age there are many decisive things we can do, whose power and scope is beyond our imagination.

And the chief of them, is of course that we can now destroy our world, and that the effect of this discovery is already irreversible. We live in a different kind of world: one potentially destroyed.

Yet all the Apocalypses knew this before.

What we have come upon has long been awaited, unfortunately.

December 15, 1962

In the presence of the bomb and of the new outlook which it commands, the Church is by and large doing what she did when faced by Galileo's revolution in astronomy: she is refusing to change her focus because she partly fears the implied consequences and partly is unable to see any *need* to change.

Charming letter from Eleanor Shipley Duckett who, on returning to Smith from England (Cambridge), found some notes I had sent and is making them her "Advent reading." I am very attracted to her, she is a sweet person. She wrote part of her letter in Latin. Though I have so far not had much contact with her (it began when the U. of Michigan press sent the proofs of her *Carolingian Portraits*). I feel we can be very good friends, and that this friendship can be really precious to us both – with the autumn quality of detachment that comes from the sense that we are coming to the end of our lives (she must be quite a bit older than I, in her sixties, I presume). But this sense of being suspended over nothingness and yet in life, of being a fragile thing, a flame that may blow out, and yet burns brightly, adds an inexpressible sweetness to the gift of life, for one sees it entirely and purely as a gift. And one which one must treasure in great fidelity, with a truly pure heart.

It has been said that, even in its first session, the II Vatican Council has *ended the era of the Counter-Reformation*. Solemn and tremendous words! I hope they are true and see every reason to believe that they are. A note came today from Fr. Daniélou, who has been working on the new schema for the founts of revelation and seems happy about it.

It is warmer this afternoon.

Unexpectedly today I undertook and finished a short chapter that was left over, for insertion in *Prayer as Worship and Experience*. It is perhaps not yet adequate, but the hardest work is done. This will perhaps be a slightly better book than the rather trifling one called *Life and Holiness*, of which I sent in the page proofs yesterday.

December 17, 1962

Today, sent off three envelopes full of articles etc. on peace to the Goss-Mayrs in Vienna. They have seen the Abbot General and have his permission now to collect a "dossier" of my material and present it for consideration by the Council Fathers and theologians who are perhaps to prepare a schema on nuclear war for the Council. In any case I am grateful to have some paper to offer, even though it may not be very clear theologically.

Generally the feeling is that the "strong stand" on Cuba paid off very well and that America is now in control of things. Hence we can ride along happily and not feel threatened since, for the time being, we are not. But no one reflects that all this has been bought at a price: *real politik*. Because our cause was "just," we threw law and justice out the window, and everyone applauded us for it, even Khrushchev! As if everyone were expecting us at last to become "practical."

What does this prove? Most of all that the deterrent does not deter. You will say: Russia gave in to the threat of our weapons. Yes – *we were not deterred* by *their* weapons! This time, of course, there was a considerable gap between the two sides. Next time, when both are even, will one risk a first strike?

Who knows? Who cares! At present we are in control, and since everybody respects us, we respect ourselves.

December 18, 1962

On Pearl Harbor – in retrospect:

Following statements from an article by Harry E. Barnes.

1. One of the decisive battles of history – since it led remotely to atomic war, it "may well have determined the fate of mankind."

2. The same pattern today – given the same national habitual ruts of thinking and action would almost surely destroy civilization.

3. Roosevelt knew the attack was coming (Jap codes broken) and kept the information from those in command at Pearl Harbor.

4. The need for a Japanese "incident" to get U.S. into war ("attacked" – was to be "defended") was due to fact that no such incident had been provided in Atlantic. Provocation: July six 1941 – restrictions imposed on Jap trade. Ultimatum on Nov. 26. (This unknown to those in command at P.H.) rejects all negotiation on trade. War *certain*.

5. From Dec. 4 on no one would send any warnings to Pacific without Gen. Marshall's consent. He was not able to be found on Dec. 6 or 7 until too late.

6. Most noxious was the moral depravity of the campaign to cover up responsibility after the attack. Officials were intimidated or smeared, documents destroyed etc.

However, it is disputed that R. *deliberately blocked* all warning to P.H., and that there was a deliberate conspiracy bet[ween] Roosevelt and Marshall.

A great full-throated frightful baying of hounds in the wood, echoing hell-cries awful, like a movie – bloodcurdling stuff – one pitied any poor animal they might be after! The sound came nearer and nearer . . .

Then I saw them in the bushes: a bunch of motley, idiot, nondescript mutts, fussing and fiddling around with utter futility, obviously after something that had vanished three hours ago: yet all this dramatic bloodfreezing noise! A real parliament of mutts in action!

Jacques Maritain has sent Raïssa's journal, a most moving and lucid and soul-cleansing book. It is wonderful to read and to share so perfectly such things, on which one's own whole life is centered. Especially the trials and their meaning.

December 22, 1962

Joost Meerloo sent one of his offprints, in French, on the ritual of giving and receiving Christmas presents. It is really very amusing and interesting, and in the middle of it I saw the connection with my own life, and my failure to really trust another person enough to give myself completely to her. My sexual adventures were always seductions – I wanted them to be conquests, in which in reality I gave nothing, only "took." But I believe my need, and perhaps my latent capacity to give myself was once very deep. Now – well, I get depressed. I remember the frequency of Christmas depressions in the past few years, and have come to expect them as a matter of course. Yet my first Christmas here, which was certainly an unreserved gift of myself to my vocation, was fantastically pure and happy. Nor has that happiness ever really left me, in the depths of my soul at least.

"*Pour certains enfants, donner activement suscite la crainte de ne plus rien recevoir ensuite.*" ["For some children, giving actively raises the fear of not getting anything more later."]

December 24, 1962

I keep expecting this to be a difficult Christmas and New Year – with Fr. John of the Cross going off on a leave of absence, no one knows quite what his ultimate goal will be – and with the merging of the two novitiates, in which I will have to try to combine two kinds of formation in one effort.

What shakes me about the departure of Fr. J. is that it awakens all my own latent desire to be "free" of the confinements and eccentricities of this place, and my own realization that there is absolutely nothing awaiting one here except death.

It is like standing on the deck of a sinking ship and watching everyone else go off in a lifeboat: that is, for my human nature it looks so. For what I am now facing is the slow and inexorable sacrifice of my will and my life.

For it is not only that I must physically die sooner or later, probably within a few years, say five or ten – if not much sooner. But also my will is going to be finally ground to death and I am going to hate the process and be in rebellion against it, without hope, without sense. Only in the depths of my heart is a repeated, "forced" acceptance, without taste, without joy, without light. One thing I am determined to keep – a certain spiritual integrity in which I do not submit to the indignity of perverse thought behind the human power that sweetly grinds me to death.

Yet it is not that anyone wants to be cruel, or that there is any deliberate unkindness: on the contrary, there is much consideration and kindness, but it is all of a type that savors of bribes, and which buys submission. I am caught in a state of allegiance to ideas and policies which are to me in many ways utterly absurd, and yet in serving under those who propound them I can perhaps save others from the effect of their kind of thinking, and lead them in a right direction.

December 25, 1962. Christmas Day

First of all it is useless and profoundly stupid to judge those with whom I live, I mean of course those whose anguish and insecurity impose on all the rest absurd and futile burdens, ways of conduct and of worship. I *must* learn compassion for these also, and above all, speak a truth they and I can both understand.

Yet last night after Midnight Mass and Lauds, I was tired and deeply impressed by the superficiality and shallowness of all our three hours – or rather 4½ hours of chanting and ceremonies. In the heart of all was buried and hidden the word of Truth and the sanctifying presence of the Redeemer. But we are so concentrated on the externals and accidentals (even though we think we are not) that we exhaust ourselves in fruitless gestures and play. This has a certain necessity and validity, and the closer to the essence the more valid it is. *But* – what is gained by singing over and over the Communion antiphon *usque ad nauseam* [to the point of nausea] – is there any real difference between doing this and listening to a lot of silly carols? Last night we had both: the carols first and the repetitious chant of the antiphon afterwards.

After Vigils, for a half moment that made sense, I stood outside in the darkness with snow falling on my cheeks and listened to the deep silence of the woods at midnight! If we are thinking of Cuba and shepherds, let us then remember that it was in such silence as this that the shepherds watched their flocks! And heard the message of God!

Nevertheless, all this nonsense cannot get in the way if one does not let it. To use the best in it and forget the trash, to be patient in one's own poverty and anguish, to pray with the Church which, no matter what the rest of us do, remains the Church of the poor and the disinherited, to stand before God as a desolate sinner who finds no comfort and little warning in what consoles others – and not to consider what the others are doing, for that is *their* business – this also is grace and there is truth in it. Above all true hope is comfort and of the wreckage of what is essentially hopeless.

Hence: not to impose any of my own hopelessness on others in the form of expedients and comforts which are bound to fail, but to give them as best I can only truth – or only what I am morally certain is really valid, and not just something dreamed up in a collective delusion.

I think more and more in terms of self-emptying and self-forgetfulness – but *not* in order merely to drown in a communal superstition and hopelessness. To renounce myself to serve truth and to patiently minister to individuals who, one by one, come needing help. To see their need, and try to minister to it, and not worry about results, or rewards. *Ecce!* [Behold!]

Evening: rain, silence, joy.

I am certain that where the Lord sees the small point of poverty and extenuation and helplessness to which the monk is reduced, the solitary and the man of tears, then He *must* come down and be born there in this anguish, and make it constantly a point of infinite joy, a seed of peace in the world. And this is, and always has been, my mission. There is for me no truth and no sense in anything that conceals from me this precious poverty, this seed of tears and true joy. Hence the demonstrations and distractions that take me away from this are foolish and useless and can even constitute infidelities if they are evasions from it. I have a right to speak to others in so far as I speak to the same truth in them, and assuage their doubts, and make them strong in this small spark of exhaustion in which the Lord becomes their wisdom and their life everlasting. What do the Psalms say but this?

Constantes estote, videbitis auxilium Domini super vos! [Be firm, you will see the help of the Lord upon you!]

How deep is this truth, how tremendously important.

We do not *wait* for this *auxilium Domini!* Others announce it has arrived, and we feel that it has *not*. *Constantes estote*. It will arrive for me also at the proper time, and in secret, and in God's own freedom beyond all control of timetables, even ecclesiastical! This is a deeper and truer aspect of the Church's mystery: the freedom of her inner life which may or may not correspond to the exterior indications of the ritual moment.

December 27, 1962

Jacques Maritain sent Raïssa's *Journal*, a most remarkable book full of clarity and simplicity. She had an unusual life of prayer, a very *intelligent* life of contemplation, very pure, great virginity of spirit and of intelligence. Surely she was a saint and I am most happy for this privileged look into material which may never be given to the general public (and I have urged Jacques *not* to publish it).

I am sure this book has come to me providentially. It helps set so many things in order. One sees the emphasis on "contemplation" that was more accepted and popular in those days, in a new perspective. The language and outlook have changed, but not this substance, of a life totally surrendered to the will of God. What else can any form of prayer do but that?

This is what comes clear: not this or that approach to prayer, but the complete surrender to God. And I see too that I have never really so far come close to meeting this surrender . . . I have, I think, obeyed God. And I have obeyed Him in difficult things even to the point where I ask myself if I have surrendered rights He did not want me to surrender . . . But I think my obedience has been valid. Though in my heart there has been resistance and criticism and disgust, even a certain unwillingness, in any case great repugnance. And much doubt, much hesitation.

Perhaps now I will begin to get rid of these, by His grace, if I stop complaining and see at last that *everything* now leads in one direction: all the water is heading for the falls, and for my death, so that I must want all, eagerly, to be part of my ultimate and complete offering of my whole life in His beloved will, beloved because it is life giving and perfect. The will that raised Christ from the dead (and not at all because it is clothed in the absurd and negative philosophy, the death language of those who happen to be ministers of His will).

PART IV

Gifts of Quiet and Nature

January 1963–July 1963

For all around is the sea of paradise.

May 21, 1963

The New Year has begun well, though I have had a filthy cold.

The merger of the two novitiates is proceeding well, mainly because all the novices are so good. I am happy with the Brother novices, one loves them immediately. They really have something, a special grace of simplicity and honesty and goodness. It is a great grace to have them there: choir and brothers seem happy with each other and everyone seems agreed that the plan is working well – in fact there seem to be all sorts of good things about it that one had not anticipated.

The unifying of the novitiate is certainly important and salutary. I think it will mean a great deal – and further I have to admit that though I am carrying it out, it is not originally my idea but the Abbot's. However, I did take a certain initiative and he was pleased to let me do so.

I think the grace the brothers have comes from their work, which keeps them perhaps (when properly done) from getting too obsessed with themselves and with their spirituality. It is wonderful how they will go into anything and get it done, not standing around scratching their heads with the dubiousness of the choir, or wanting to be told each next move.

This afternoon, working on the Bolshakoff ms., have come finally to Theophane the Recluse. A magnificent and saintly figure. He makes a tremendous impression. After dealing with admirable people (the beloved Staretz of Optima) one feels here that one is in the presence of real greatness, nobility, wholeness, and perfectly integrated sanctity. Here is a life that is truly balanced, and really makes sense! A man who was *above* the vicissitudes of life, who lived on a really high plane, and yet was fully human – a figure like Isaiah among the prophets! How he stands out above them all!

And in his presence I see the disorder, the confusion, the lamentable weakness and shoddiness of my own life!

Of course, he was able to see what to do and able to do it. His way was clear. Mine is not. I am caught in an absurd corner, hemmed in by the arbitrary fantasies of a system in which, to do some of the right things, one has to proceed backwards as if he were doing something else.

He could walk straight forward and follow God. If I had more of his clarity and courage perhaps I would be a little less trapped!

January 5, 1963

Large group of brothers at my class on St. Bernard today – more than I thought – not only all the simple professed but perhaps also solemn professed (I am not sure!). Somebody is probably making them come, and some surely looked as if they had no reason of their own to be there. This is embarrassing, and also quite foolish. I have suddenly, and for no real reason, become part of a magic and desperate answer someone has dreamed up for the Brothers. I have to take the assignment as it comes, from God, and treat them with sincerity and concern for their *real* needs. They do not need a "course on St. Bernard"!!

I would much prefer simply to have small and quiet classes with my novices – after all, that is supposed to be my job!

On the other hand this will require prayer, more prayer, and perhaps more study and even more care, and honesty, because novices are ready for anything, but these men have been fooled and disappointed before and some are perhaps on the verge of leaving.

Began reading Heschel's new book, which he sent, on the *Prophets* [New York, 1962]. Exactly the kind of approach with which I am in sympathy and which makes sense to me. The kind of deep reflection leading to insights which enable us to "be" the prophet we are reading – while yet remaining in all our proper distribution.

January 6, 1963. Epiphany

I think Trevor Smith, instead of returning to the seminary in South Africa, will reenter the novitiate (he was only in the guesthouse with his red hair uncut, and did not break his novitiate). I am glad of this.

With the Brothers now in one novitiate with the choir, I certainly have a whole new view of life. There is no question they are "poorer," simpler, more vulnerable.

For instance Bro. B. – a Mexican from Texas: what he thinks might be "faults" are in reality the wounds that come from being *poor*. The poor man is and remains vulnerable. How can the really poor, the really "hurt" survive in a place like this? We are not so vulnerable and we wound others even when we are being "good," perhaps especially then.

Then I saw suddenly at High Mass the value of my own "cross" and "problem" –

– That I have to defer to an uncomprehending, self-complacent figure, who is totally "American" in all his prejudices and limitations in his mental clichés.

– That I have to see through all this and have no hope of coming to grips with it, explaining it, clarifying it.

– And that he despises me, uses me (outwardly respects me), and fears me because I am different from him, and have no part in his kind of image!

What does all this do but put me in the position of being like a talented negro accepted in white society . . . ? That is exactly my position with my superior – though not with the community, for also I am a man with many privileges and an enormous reputation and hardly, in that respect, a negro!

Yet I think I can dare to accept what vulnerability I have (largely my own fault perhaps) as that of an exile, an alien, and feel it also as that which is *normal* for all the poor. Should it not be normal for me? Then why do I resent it? Because that is part of the wound!

January 8, 1963

I understand this last was considered a very peaceful Christmas with very little actual *war* going on anywhere, with Russia smiling at the West and frowning at China.

But Kennedy and Macmillan had a meeting, and Kennedy said that though he would unfortunately not be giving England any skybolt missiles, wouldn't they perhaps like Polaris missiles instead? Much, much better!

And now in Montana eleven minute men stand in their holes loaded with good old solid fuel, ready to take off in fifteen seconds and do what they are told. Happy New Year!

Deeply touched by Raïssa Maritain's poetry, *Au Coeur du Rocher* [*In the Heart of the Rock*], which Jacques has sent. I will translate some of it.

> *Et il n'y aura pas d'acquittement pour les nations,*
> *mais seulement pour les âmes, une à une.*
> [And there will not be acquittal for nations,
> but only for souls, one by one.]
>
> *(Raïssa M.)*

January 9, 1963

A most moving letter from Jacques Maritain came this morning. I don't think I have ever received such a beautiful letter in my life – a response to my own love for the clarity and suffering of Raïssa in her journal. I found P. Van der Meer de Walcheren's book in the afternoon and translated Raïssa's poem on Chagall. Also in the morning came a letter from Christine de Walcheren, about the nonsense in Christian's book on Satan – repeating the old, absurd accusations that Bloy was a Satanist. Christian apparently retracted, in a letter.

January 15, 1963

The noise and concern about the novitiate and all those who come to the classes, are having a deep effect on me. The work is hard, though I am doing more than I probably should, in my concern to be well prepared. But also realize the limitations of anything short of prayer and abandonment, as preparation. The limitations of my own capacity. Hence in everything I have come to feel more than ever my need for grace, my total dependence on God, my helplessness without His special intervention, which I may need at any moment. Never has this been so clear to me. Perhaps it was never before as true as now.

In consequence my attitude toward the monastery changes. They have need of me and I have need of them. As if without this obedience, and charity, my life would lack sense. It is an existential situation which God has willed for me, and it is part of His Providence – it is not to be questioned, no matter how difficult it may be. I must simply obey God, and this reaches out into everything. Even at the hermitage it is less a question of seeking Him than of total submission and obedience to Him to whom I belong in love. And when I do something neutral, that for some reason does not involve a direct submission to His will (even though it is not theoretically *against* it), I feel the futility and meaninglessness of it with real anguish, so that it appears to be *intolerably* stupid. For instance – an apparently legitimate concern with a critical article on a book. Something I did not need to know (yet *might* have needed to know).

In this new condition my attitude toward the abbot is changing. Of course it is obvious that my complaints and discontent have been absurd. Though I can perhaps back them up with plausible arguments, they have no real meaning, they don't make sense. He is what he is, and he means well, and in fact does well. He is the superior destined for me in God's

Providence, and it is absurd for me to complain. No harm will ever come to me through him – it *cannot*. How could I have thought otherwise?

Hildegard Goss-Mayr wrote, wanting to publish several chapters of *Peace in the Post-Christian Era* in her magazine in Vienna, and insisting that the book should come out in America.[1] Also wisely saying there is great need for a positive theology of love and non-violent action.

Optimism or Pessimism? In this peaceful new year (many heavy salvos today from the guns at Knox) – the only human basis for optimism is that there is a general feeling that nuclear war has been avoided and will not be a danger again soon. There is a mood of confidence in this country and a lot of peaceful gestures on the part of Russia, so that it seems unlikely that in 1963 American or Russian instincts of belligerency would be exasperated to the point of danger. Is this optimism? I don't think so. The mere conviction that "everything will come out all right" seems to rest on nothing more solid than our incapacity to imagine or to face the possibility of anything else. To collaborate in fostering this kind of optimism is not, to my mind, a good Christian work.

I think we have to "be sober and watch" because there are grave dangers against which we must guard, and we must seriously begin to work for a peaceful world. The hope of permanent peace in our present condition is pure delusion.

Optimism in the sense of trusting God to help us if we ourselves also make serious efforts: this, yes. But not in the sense that we can go on doing what we have done and are doing without inviting disaster. It is true, we might muddle through somehow: but should we simply trust in our luck not failing? What reason have we to do so?

January 17, 1963

The great trial of fidelity in Christian life – a trial which springs from the fact that we too closely identify *fidelity to God* and *fidelity to external organization* in the Catholic Church. Hence there is invariably a great trial when an apparent conflict is precipitated (and it is easily precipitated). There are times when it seems that fidelity to God is *not* compatible with mere obedience to an external norm, where fidelity to God requires something else:

---

[1] See Merton's extensive correspondence with Hildegard and Jean Goss-Mayr in *The Hidden Ground of Love* (New York, 1985).

certainly not revolt or disobedience, but a presentation of alternatives and deeper views.

A "fidelity" which *always* demands the sacrifice of the interior and the more perfect in order to conform to an external norm that is mediocre, and requires of us only passivity and inertia, is an infidelity to God and to His Church. Yet at the same time we must not make a fetish out of autonomy and be "faithful" only to our own will, for this is the other way to infidelity.

The answer is in the Church considered less as an organization than as a living body of interrelated freedoms. Fidelity belongs not so much to the realm of Law as to the realm of love. But it presupposes obedience and self-sacrifice.

January 18, 1963

Problems and sufferings of the spiritual life today come from the fact that the mentality of our times blocks the total response that is necessary for a completely healthy and fruitful spirituality. We "believe" in our head, but the heart and the whole body do not follow. Or else the body and emotions follow a certain line, but the mind remains confused and unenlightened.

The peculiar suffering of deeply spiritual people like E.G. [Etta Gullick] is due to the fact that their mind and heart go to God, but their whole being does not obey and they have *no way* of obeying because they are not told. Hence they remain paralyzed, inarticulate, in confusion and suffering.

Retreat began last night.

Cleaned out the room yesterday. What a relief!

That even the order of my room – is pleasing to God (as well as to myself and to those others who benefit by it). I am encouraged to believe by St. Thomas' *De Divinis Moribus* [*On the Divine Customs*]. What a perfect little treatise! What moral beauty!

It is short and easy and needs to be translated, and really I think I must do it.

How far it is from the compassion and moral squalor of our time, and from our peculiar problem of truth. Such an agonizing problem because potentially good and really gifted people, revolting against the standardized lies of our society, seek truth in evil and perversion, and thus defeat themselves, confirming all in evil and in lies. This because God has entirely disappeared from all our mental vision. And of course He is not visible anyway: but His invisible light is gone.

January 20, 1963

Again the great problem is the gap between thought and action.

On one hand, especially here – an abstract spirituality, supported by an *abstract activity* which symbolizes and "supports" it.

On the other – outside – an activity more and more irrational and without thought, based on the projection of favorable or unfavorable images which justify it.

My interior anguish and sense of failure and dishonesty come from the fact that my thought is not incarnated in an activity which supports and expresses it in a fully valid way.

The best I can do is now an effort at a deeply and honestly human concern with my brothers and their life, and this is not sufficiently taken care of by talking at them or advising them.

It means a concerted effort to get at *all* our *real* problems and work at them effectively together.

Later – what is said above is substantially solid, but the way in which I arrived at it was wrong, and the result is a statement completely out of perspective. As if there were some secret "activity" which we all had to discuss and engage in, and then our thoughts would fall into place! Above all as if I had to wait for others to do this before my own anguish would cease. Most of all, that something in my life depends on a new discovery.

Actually no discovery of that kind is needed.

Fidelity to grace in my life is fidelity to simplicity, rejecting ambition and analysis and elaborate thought, or even elaborate concern.

A breath of Zen blows all these cobwebs out the window.

It is certainly true that what is needed is to get back to the "original face" and drop off all the piled-up garments of thought that do not fit me and are not "mine" – but to take only what is nameless.

I have been absurdly burdened since the beginning of the year with the illusions of "great responsibility" and of a task to be done. Actually whatever work is to be done is God's work and not mine and I will not help matters, only hinder them, by too much care.

January 21, 1963. St. Agnes

Very cold morning, about 8 above zero. Left for the hermitage before dawn, after retreat conference on sin. Pure dark sky with only moon and planets in it, stars already gone. The moon and Venus over the barns, and Mars far over in the west over the road and the fire tower.

Sunrise – an event that calls forth solemn music in the very depths of one's being, as if one's whole being had to attune itself to the cosmos, and praise God for a new day, praise Him in the name of all the beings that ever were or ever will be – as though *now* upon me falls the responsibility of seeing what all my ancestors have seen, and acknowledging it, and praising God so that whether or not *they* praised God then, themselves, they now do so in me.

Sunrise demands this rightness, this order, this true disposition of one's whole being.

January 22, 1963
From *"L'Abandon Intérieur"* ["Inner Abandonment"], poem of J. J. Surin.

> *J'aime bien mieux souffrir l'injuste blâme*
> *de ces prudents qui craignent de périr*
> *qu'en conservant trop chèrement mon âme*
> *ne rien risquer, et ne rien conquérir . . .*

> *allons amour au plus fort de l'orage*
> *que l'océan renverse tout sur moi*
> *J'aime bien mieux me perdre avec courage*
> *en te suivant que me sauver sans toi . . .*

> *Heureuse mort, heureuse sépulture*
> *de cet amant dans l'amour absorbé*
> *qui ne voit plus ni grâce ni nature*
> *mais le seul gouffre auquel il est tombé, etc.*

[I much prefer to endure an undeserved accusation
from those careful ones afraid to perish
than to guard my soul so dearly
and risk nothing, and gain nothing . . .

Let us go, love, to the heart of the storm
that the ocean pours over me
I prefer to perish with courage
Following you, than to save myself without you . . .

Happy death, happy burial
Of this lover by love absorbed

Who no longer sees either grace or nature
But only the gulf into which he has fallen, etc.]

A magnificent poem, and great spirituality. In its basis it is solid truth. However, it can happen that one may have a completely illusory idea of what this annihilation is and what it involves, because one gives reality both to that which is annihilated and to the things which menace it. This may result in an imaginary process of annihilation in which a figment is annihilated by a figment, and all the while we guard our "self" against destruction.

"Humility" as the last refuge in which the self becomes impregnable!
This is what we are looking for.

Yesterday's retreat conference on humility was central for me – I had heard all those things before and will hear them again. Of course – Card. Merry del Val's Litany of Humility. Yet I got the point of it and responded in my heart, not just intellectually or "appreciative[ly]." Those are all things to which I must tend with all my being.

This means first of all letting go of any reputation as a writer and a spiritual man – not that I will not write, but there is no need to go on publishing at the present rate, which is entirely compulsive. I mean, the books on "the spiritual life" especially.

With things about peace, etc. it is different, for this is an emergency, yet precisely here I am supposed not to publish. But I should still write certain things at least for private circulation.

January 24, 1963
Very cold. 15 below zero this morning.
Wonderful afternoon yesterday walking in the snow to the pig barn to clean out the pens and coming back: the lonely road down to the new bridge, with the sun in the haze and the winter trees all grey and wind blowing the snow all over the road.

This morning the morning star above in the sky. Read Ruysbroeck's *Livre de la plus haute vérité* [*Book of the Highest Truth*].

January 25, 1963
Still very cold and bright.
The best thing about the retreat has been working in the pig barn and then walking back alone, a mile and a half, through the snow.

I think I have come to see more clearly and more seriously the meaning, or lack of meaning, in my life. How much I am still the same self-willed and volatile person who made such a mess of Cambridge. That I have not changed yet, down in the depths or perhaps, yes, I have changed radically somewhere, yet I have still kept some of the old, vain, inconstant, self-centered ways of looking at things. And that the situation I am in now has been given me to change me, if I will only surrender completely to reality as it is given me by God and no longer seek in any way to evade it, even by interior reservations.

Hitherto my interior reservation has been always "Of course there must be something better – and who knows if that is not for me!"

Well, there *is* something better: but it must come out of an inner transformation of my own self, in Christ. What is better is Christ, that is to say, for me to live completely in and by Him; I already do live in Him of course, but there remains much to be surrendered that still remains "my own."

January 26, 1963

Last day of retreat. Reading Rufinus *Historia Monachorum* and also *Dialogues* of Sulpicius Severus. Utterly ashamed and annoyed that I have never read the *Hist. Monachorum* before. What have I been doing? I have been under a kind of delusion that I was living as a monk all these years – and that I knew what the monastic life was and had read a great deal of the traditional source material. I haven't even scratched the surface, and my heart has not been that of a monk. The story of John of Lycopotis, the urgency of his lessons, the sweetness and simplicity of the style move me very deeply.

January 28, 1963

Here at the hermitage, in deep snow, everything is ordinary and silent.

Return to reality and to the ordinary, in silence. It is always there if you know enough to return to it.

What is *not* ordinary – the tension of meeting people, discussion, ideas. This too is good and real, but illusion gets into it. The unimportant becomes important, words and images become more important than life.

One travels all over vast areas, sitting still in a room, and one is soon tired of so much travelling.

Wm. Miller, of the FOR [Fellowship of Reconciliation] and Paul Peachey of the Church Peace Mission were here – and I was eventually strained and tense from all the talk. It was quieter this morning with Peachey alone. We discussed my peace book which is not being published, and his translation of Demoulin's *History of Zen* which has just appeared. It was a fruitful morning.

Yet I need very much this silence and this snow. Here alone can I find my way because here alone the way is right in front of my face and it is God's way for me – there is really no other.

One thing that has contributed to my sense of anguish and tension has perhaps been too great a readiness to open and give myself where I should not have – for instance the publication of my letter which I have permitted in *El Corno Emplumado*. It is true I am to some extent in sympathy with them and some of their poets are fine – but much of it is crass and gross, and nothing whatever to do with me. So that though I can let them have poems, I should not more or less openly become identified with them. This was a mistake and my motives were not sufficiently rational.

This kind of thing must stop, and I must return to a silence more compatible with my vocation.

January 30, 1963

Fog and rain – close to freezing but not quite.

Pale snow, lavender woods, you cannot see across the valley.

Cleaned up today. Tomorrow is my forty-eighth birthday.

February 4, 1963

There is no *need* for me to write or teach.

I do not know if I *want* to write or teach. The very questions themselves are irrelevant. I am really beginning to see this and also to see that the "seeing" is no achievement! What a fool I am to be less simple than the trees, in my own way! It is enough to swing your branches when the wind blows and no one needs to be told about it.

February 5, 1963

Moneo . . . ut cum sis providus, prudens, doctus, et ingeniosissimus, illud pauxillum aetatis tuae quod nondum est consumptum, mundo subtrahias et ipsum Deo sacrificium vespertinum igne caritatis supposito addere non differeas. . . ." [I advise . . . that you, since you are provident, prudent, learned, and very talented, withdraw from the world that little bit of your life that is not yet used up, and when you have put in its place the fire of charity, do not delay that evening sacrifice to God. . . .]

Today (a good warm day, almost spring like after all the cold) I translated this beautiful letter of Guido [the Carthusian] on solitude.

February 10, 1963

Discovery in Manes Sperber's essay on hatred (very challenging).

That there is now in the world an anti-americanism which is a hatred comparable to anti-semitism. This is to me something of great significance and it has a great importance in my own life, because it means that from now on there can be no hedging and I must identify myself with this country and *be* one of its people (as if I were accepting an inevitable Jewish ancestry) and be clearly recognized as one and not put forward my European protective coloring (as if I were a Jew with blond hair and blue eyes).

February 23, 1963

It was warm and then cold again. Zero for the last few days, as if that mattered. The Abbot is hoarse, the postulant has a cold. I sent him to bed after dinner and he hasn't been seen since.

Yesterday evening, Josef Smolik, from the Comenicus Seminary in Prague, visited here. I did not have much time to talk to him and, as it was, George Edwards and I did most of the talking. Then when Fr. Eudes came *he* did most of the talking – about Bultmann and Barth. Apparently in Czechoslovakia they prefer Barth. Not for political reasons but because he believes in the Resurrection.

Smolick said he was surprised and glad that there was more concern in the U.S. now, among students, about peace, than there was when he was last here 14 years ago. Yet he said that even then in this country there was a more or less general acceptance of the cold war and deterrence as "normal." That it seems to us quite normal and acceptable to live under the bomb – while in the East it is not regarded as normal at all. If that is true, then they are a little wiser than we are (and have no reason to doubt Smolick's word at all!).

The main thing that came out of the political side of the talk was the fear of Germany and the stupidity of French nationalism. Surprising how the same old forces are at work, the same that produced the last two world wars. De Gaulle and the myth of Charlemagne and "Christian Europe." This is dangerous, all right. The idea of "Christian civilization" is one of the most explosive myths we have. And of course its danger lies in its rightness, its attractiveness. But I wonder if we have not after all had our chance and missed it. There have been 1600 years of "Christian civilization" and not all of it has been very Christian. Certainly we should keep trying: but the return to Charlemagne seems to me, to put it mildly, a regression.

I think the time has come when we must realize that Christians are not the ones who are running the world, and some of the least Christian people in the world are among the policy-makers of formerly Christian nations. Hence, though there must be a Christian witness in politics, the idea of a "Christian policy" tied up with the decadent structures of warfare states is another matter.

Have read James Baldwin's *The Fire Next Time* and now *Nobody Knows My Name*. He seems to know exactly what he is talking about, and his statements are terribly urgent. One of the things that makes most sense – an application of the ideas behind non-violence, but I think it is absolutely true: that the sit-in movement is not just to get the negroes a few hamburgers, it is for the sake of the white people, and for the country. He is one of the few genuinely concerned Americans, one whose concern I can really believe. The liberation of the Negroes is necessary for the liberation of the whites and for their recovery of a minimum of self-respect, and reality.

Above all he makes very shrewd and pointed statements about the futility and helplessness of white liberals, who sympathize but never do anything. Well, a few have got beat up on freedom rides, this is true. But really the whole picture is pitiful. A scene of helplessness, inertia, stupidity, erosion.

He keeps alluding to the sexual impotency of the whites, and works this also into the symbolic moral love of the liberal white for the Negro in the abstract. The impotency is in our love of abstraction, our inability to connect with a valid image of reality. In a word, total alienation.

Alienation is the real tragedy, the real root of our helplessness. And our lotus-eating economy is responsible for that.

I wonder if the situation is not almost totally hopeless. Yet we do "see" to some extent. Not enough. The fact that we can let ourselves be moved by a book by J. Baldwin seems to be enough to convince us that we are honest and we are apparently satisfied to see ourselves "being honest." That is enough.

That is why I think I will not write an article about Baldwin.

———

Another approach to our dishonesty: the illusion that we can and should solve many problems, all problems (i.e. the desire to see ourselves honestly attempting to do this), and then the pitiful infantilism with which we play at doing this. A few gestures, a few words. And we pretend to be thinking, seeking answers, dialoguing, negotiating.

If we began by abandoning the *whole game*, and started over on a humbler level, attempting to deal with what is *possible*. And went on from there to the next thing!

February 25, 1963

Last night, the novices were two hours in church for night adoration, for the 40 hours. It was wonderfully, idylically peaceful. A delight. They were so good, and so evidently happy and fervent in a very real, simple, unselfconscious way – not the tense way of my own novitiate days. One felt there was really some prayer going on, too – but very simple. I was glad and happy, and the happiness flowed over into today.

Someone mentioned that Bro. B., who is very pious and in fact almost everyone's image of the pious child (though he is no longer a child), knows how to get his own way by manipulation, and this is true. From a certain point of view he is a selfish and narcissistic person, but with a quiet and modest efficiency that startles and disturbs you when you suddenly discover it. Yet I hope he will not settle into that – he is developing – and maybe he will develop real strength instead of accursed adeptness in using the people and the situation to obtain trivial ends.

I suppose, though, what disturbs me is that I have to reflect whether or not I am not selfish in the same way. For though I generally manage to feel deprived, cheated of legitimate ends, still I have attained a lot of "ends" without half trying. They almost attain themselves, and so I say they are sent by God, and then go back to brooding over the fact that I am deprived of something I thought I was fighting for.

The trouble is not so much that I have these petty "ends" to achieve, but that they are perhaps ends which I affect to despise, and in a context which I do in fact despise – acting as if I did not have them, and still anxious to ally every act [with my own intentions].

This is precisely what seems to annoy me in the Abbot, too.

I suppose all the "ends" for which I fight are concerned with some kind of security, some sense of identity. And I know that I do attach importance to the sense of reality and identity that are mine when I am alone in the woods, or in the presence of nature, or working at various things – especially, of course, writing.

Is this something one should not desire? Certainly it is not "wrong" in itself. But I suppose there can be a lot wrong with it.

February 26, 1963

This year appropriation in the U.S. for chemical warfare preparations – (and biological?) $108 million – 50% increase over 1962.

What was written yesterday is absurd, inadequate, in fact wrong. Because if I come into solitude merely to get free from all that is "not I," then it is certainly a regression – and is vain. But one must distinguish.

1. With others, besides the love which transcends itself in giving to them, there is also a wasting and a pouring out of spirit in illusion – collaborating in the collective illusions.

2. And with others there is also the wasted effort of maintaining an exterior self, which to some extent meets expectations, and also jealously defends itself, with its own doubts and misgivings, which are created by the collective illusion. So there is a double effort of defense, and consequently the danger of setting up a private illusion opposite the collective one. Obviously, to come into solitude to reinforce the private illusions is fatal.

3. To come into solitude to discard both illusions, public and private, and to seek God, and to have no (exterior) self and no aims or claims, or pretensions, this is "right" (if the word means anything here) – it is what solitude means. But the problem is precisely that I still tend to come into solitude with an impure love, that is to say with "aims." And with the "I" that can have aims. Time and quiet do much to dispel all this nonsense.

Found fine things in the *Mirror of Simple Souls* [Marguerite Porete] (Dia. IX) today, and am reading the *Living Flame* [St. John of the Cross] in Spanish.

February 27, 1963. Ash Wednesday

The ashes smelled of kerosene. Headache. Good to be empty in the morning, but had too much appetite and ate everything in sight at dinner, so felt stupid afterwards.

Our mentioning of the weather – our perfunctory observations on what kind of day it is, are perhaps not idle. Perhaps we have a deep and legitimate need to know in our entire being what the day is like, to *see* it and *feel* it, to know how the sky is grey, paler in the south, with patches of blue in the southwest, with snow on the ground, the thermometer at 18, and cold wind making your ears ache. I have a real need to know these things because I myself am part of the weather and part of the climate and part of the place, and a day in which I have not shared truly in all this is no day at all. It is certainly part of my life of prayer.

Bored with counter-reformation Italian saints, in the refectory (Daniel Rops).

March 4, 1963

Warm – first thundershowers of the year, after low clouds moved fast and evenly all across the sky. Now rain chasing itself across the valley like smoke. And a quiet, peaceful roaring in the woods. Rain drops busily in the buckets. Yesterday, first Sunday of Lent, was a real spring day, the first. Warm sun, and a chipmunk sitting on a rock in the woods.

John Howard Griffin was here at the end of last week. Spoke of Clyde Kennard, the Negro who suffered unbelievable cruelties and injustices for trying quietly to register at Mississippi State University. (Not the U. of Miss, where the case is very public.) Framed by the police, put in forced labor gang, although he was supposed to be hospitalized with stomach cancer. Somehow they got him out of Miss. He is dying in a Chicago hospital. It is a dreadful story, and bodes evil.

Griffin also spoke of his experiences among the Tarascan Indians, and their contacts with some not too bright American Benedictines who have come to help them catch up with the twentieth century.

We spoke a lot about Maritain (from whom another fine letter came today). M., with a sense that every minute of his life is now numbered, is putting all his free time into editing Raïssa's journal, for publication (it is already privately printed). The nuns of Stanbrook are printing a limited edition of the poems, and my own translations of her are supposed to come out in *Jubilee*. Also in *Emblems of a Season of Fury* which ND [New Directions] is now getting ready to publish.

Griffin says he will try to get me a tape of some of the music of Stephane Lourié, who is living in Maritain's house at Princeton and who never publishes anything, is never played. He lived for a long time in a N.Y. tenement – was stranded in U.S. by the war and never went back to France.

March 5, 1963

Low dark sky. Novices got up late because, with the rain falling and windows closed, our bellringer did not hear the bell in the professed dormitory. We got to choir at the hymn for Vigils.

Vanderbilt seminarians here yesterday. I did not plan to see them but was urged over there for a "few minutes" after collation.

But I think there is not much point in these "appearances," though I like them – especially the Vanderbilt students. And their faculty members. Really, though, what have I to say? Perhaps I could do more for them and for everyone by shutting up.

The hills are almost black, with a thin transparent line of woods along the hogback ridge, like bristles on an animal. Down there, somewhere, is Oak Ridge, Tennessee. And if this were hit by an H bomb the flash would burn my eyes out, though Oak Ridge must be a couple of hundred miles away. Cuban emigrés in Miami, in a fury of frustration, frankly want to do something that will start a world war over Cuba and "end Communism" – together with everything else no doubt. People go on mumbling about these things – nothing new is said, nothing new is done. I hear the New York papers are still out on strike: three months now, since December 8th.

For my Lenten book I have [Gregorio] Penco's competent *History of Italian Monasticism* (in Italian, pleasantly illustrated). The *Sewanee Review* wants my translations of Alfonso Cortes, of which I am glad. Ernesto Cardenal is writing fine poems about Bartolomé de las Casas. I began translating the *De Divinis Moribus* by St. Thomas today.

March 10, 1963. II Sunday of Lent

Day of Recollection. Read a little of Fénelon, who is often very dull. Who ever had the illusion that he was *dangerous?* Yet he is an attractive person, and one loves him for the injustices he suffered with great patience, and for his loyalty to that unoriginal Guyon, who was so discredited and a bit sick into the bargain. Everyone is still afraid of him, and the abbot (though he does not say so) is perhaps disturbed that I should now be working on a preface to Fénelon's letters. The man is not *approved.* The great loud bull Bossuet, he is a great man, now, friend of the king. He was powerful, Fénelon wasn't. There is a lot of pragmatism in our popular evaluation of figures in the history of spirituality! How gladly we all fall into step behind Bossuet and Louis XIV and march with the bands, even if they turn out to be Gallican ones (and of course *that* is not approved. But *still*, Bossuet *did* make a lot of noise, and Fénelon, especially at Cambrai, made very little).

I thought today at adoration what a blessing it was that I did not go in 1956 to be analyzed by Zilboorg! What a tragedy and mess that would have been – and I must give Z. the credit for having sensed it himself in his own way. It would have been utterly impossible and absurd. And yet I think in great measure his judgment was that I could simply not be fitted into his kind of theater. There was no conceivable part for me to play in his life, on the contrary! And certainly it is true that the whole thing would have been unimaginably absurd. He had quite enough intelligence (more than enough, he was no fool at all!) to see that it would be a very poor production for him, for the abbot (who was most willing) and for me. I am afraid that I was willing, at the time, to go, which shows what a fool I was.

In any case all manner of better things were reserved for me. But I have not understood them.

In a Zen koan someone said that an enlightened man is not one who seeks Buddha, or finds Buddha, but just an ordinary man who has *nothing left to do*. And yet mere stopping is not to arrive. To stop is to stay a million miles from it, and to do nothing is to miss it by the whole width of the universe. Yet how close it is, how simple it would be to have nothing more to do – if I had only done it. Meanwhile I am more content than I have ever been here with this unripeness, and thus I know that one day it will ripen and one will see there had been nothing there at all, except an ordinary person with nothing to do in the first place.

The evening light. Purple coves and holes of shadow in the breasts of the hills and the white gable of Newton's house smiling so peacefully amid the trees in the middle of the valley. This is the peace and luminosity Blake loved. Today after dinner, a hawk circling the novitiate and the church steeple, designed a free flight unutterably more pure than skating or music. How he flung himself down from high and swooped up to touch lightly on the pinnacle of the steeple and sit there, then fell off, to cut lovely curves all around the cedars then off like an arrow into the south.

March 15, 1963

Tuesday, Feast of St. Gregory, warm sunny day, finished first draft of a long article on Zen, but going over the mss. of the Platform sutra today I see there is much more to be done.

Novices are planting trees all over the hillside east of the old sheep barn (which is now used for nothing but has some hay in it). The cold killed many of the loblolly pines we had planted in previous years, and still we are planting loblollies. I tried to get the Cellarer to change the order, but nothing doing.

March 16, 1963

Today I have finally realized what a mess my publishing affairs are in! Two books coming out under different imprints, not counting the small ones with New Directions – and neither of the two properly cleared with the publisher with whom I have a contract! How could I be so absurdly stupid! Nobody has been telling me anything, or advising me, or stopping me. This is where I get without an agent. No sense in going back to Curtis Brown. Naomi Burton[2] is one of those who can help me best I suppose. I have got to get some sense, and restraint – and *advice*.

The existential analysts talk a lot about man as developing his existence towards a future. His present is meaningful in relation to a meaningful future. This is very revealing in regard to the problem of the monastic life here. Hope of a terrestrial future is more or less systematically frustrated in theory, and this frustration is promoted by officers who themselves have enough projects and interests to keep them entertained and stimulated. But the subject is not to have a future (other than heaven) and if he has one he has to be guilty about it.

Doubtless there are small futures to live for. Daily dinner after the long morning of Lent. Easter and sunrise.

But when I think of the desperation of such a good kid as Bro. Denis (Phillips) I see that what is wrong is the lack of any real future, in a normal temporal sense for him. One has to learn to love in a spiritual present that is sometimes very luminous and intense, but this supposes also activities that move in time towards their fulfillments. Why is there so much insistence on life remaining unfulfilled – except for razzle dazzle in the choir? The feast-day circus for the monastic plebs.

For myself, it is certain my sense of "future" is sadly diminished. I have of course, whether I like it or not, expected much from books. They have given a livelier dimension to my life in time. Too lively.

I almost hope for the heart attack that may finish me. This is silly.

---

[2] Naomi Burton Stone was Merton's friend and his literary agent at Curtis Brown Ltd.

But how is it possible to be sanguine about a future in this age of the H bomb when this country is by and large so determined to be led by its fears into absurd and catastrophic situations?

"What keeps the patient from accepting in freedom his potentialities?" Repression considered as a rejection of freedom in the use of one's potentialities.

March 19, 1963. St. Joseph
Fr. Philip (great devotion to St. Jos.) came to choir looking tense but determined to be consoled.

> *Quare errare nos fecisti Domine de viis tuis?*
> *Indurasti cor nostrum ne timeremus te?*
> *Facti sumus quasi in principiis cum non dominaveris nostri*
> *Neque invocaretur nomen tuum super nos.*
> [Why have you made us to depart from your ways, Lord?
> Why have you hardened our heart so that we no longer fear
> you?
> We have become as we were in the days when you didn't rule
> over us
> And your name was not invoked over us.]
>
> *Isa[iah] 63.[17, 19]*

Warm, damp weather. Thundershowers. Lou Silberman is here, and gives talks on Psalms and Qumran.

I read Maritain's essay on Descartes today (in connection with Fénelon, but it is revealing in relation to Zen).

The task for Zen in the West is probably a healthy reaction on the part of people exasperated for four hundred years by the inane Cartesian spirit – the reification of concepts, the idolization of reflexive consciousness, the flight from being into verbalism, mathematics and rationalization. Descartes made a fetish of the mirror which Zen shatters.

March 21, 1963
> The earth is given into the hand of the wicked
> He covers the faces of its judges
> If it is not He, who then is it?
>
> *Job 9:24*

He takes away understanding from the chiefs of the people and the pieces of the earth and makes them wander in a pathless waste. They grope in the darkness without a light, and He makes them stagger like a drunken man.

Job 12:24–25

He leads counselors away stripped, and judges He makes fools.   *Job 12:17*

Because of the multitude of oppressions people cry out; they call for help because of the arm of the mighty: but none says "Where is God my maker, who gives songs in the night, who teaches us more than the beasts of the earth and makes us wiser than the birds of the air?"   *Job 35:9–11*

Heavy snowflakes fall, flying in all directions. But when there is no wind they descend so slowly that they seem to have no intention of staying on the ground. And in fact nothing remains when they have fallen. Then the pale sun comes out for a moment, shines uncertainly on the grass, the wheel, the pale logs, the rusty field, the fence, the valley. It is St. Benedict's, the first day of spring.

And I am ready to sing or do a doxology of justification for my injustices.

I am sick of the sight of my Herder book because, in my thoughtlessness and pique, I did not get it properly cleared by Farrar Straus, who had a right to first option. Same, though I simply told them of my intentions, in the case of the book being done by Macmillan. I make myself sick! Why didn't I think? Sick, sick. And God is right. There is nothing in me that can be justified.

Dan Walsh has been invited (through Ethel Kennedy) to give a series of lectures to a group of "official families" in the White House, and Robert Kennedy was asking Dan (in Louisville, Monday) if they could not get me also, later, sometime. Dan is for it, and says if R. Kennedy asks the abbot face to face etc. etc. For a moment I was for it (that's how sick I am), but I went to bed and lay awake thinking about it and saw soon enough that this was not for me to want.

What does the Attorney General want, giving a talk in Bardstown? And what do I want giving talks in the White House?

But everybody is asking everybody for favors. To please the judge in Bardstown, the abbot asks R. Kennedy to give a speech in Bardstown. And to please Sturm at Harpers I ask Ethel K. to meet Bruno James. And Robert Kennedy asks Dan to ask the abbot . . . etc. etc.

March 22, 1963. Friday after mid-Lent
The lovely 4th tone antiphon at the Benedictus _"qui biberit aquam_ [who drinks of the waters]." The Samaritan woman will be in the long Gospel. Stars in the cold spring sky. A zen line in Job: "Is it by your wisdom that the hawk soars?" (39:26).

March 27, 1963
"Ecoutez Dieu et point vous-même: là est la vraie liberté, paix et joie du Saint Es-prit." ["Listen to God and not yourself: in that lies true freedom, peace and the joy of the Holy Spirit."] _Fénelon_
The ms. of Fénelon's letters has arrived – of course only a selection. Well translated, very appealing.
"Les pécheurs veulent toujours ce qui leur manque, et les âmes pleines de l'amour de Dieu ne veulent rien que ce qu'elles ont." ["Sinners always want what they don't have, and souls full of the love of God don't want anything except what they already have."] _(Fénelon)_

A brilliant sunny day – perfect spring – joy all day after Communion and Mass in the sunny chapel. Said Mass for Christian Unity, not the long Mass of the Wednesday (the man born blind) which was sunny right after my own thanksgiving.

After dinner began a book on Nicholas of Cusa recently requested by the library – (Dolan, introduction and selections). He is someone to whom I am much attracted. I have only read the _De Visione Dei_ and that only in translation, and found it dry. Nevertheless something tells me to keep trying. His manly idealism fascinates me. And there are so many conflicting judgments about him that I want to arrive at one of my own!

Perhaps Cusanis is comfort to which I respond inordinately after reading the first two of Hannah Arendt's articles on the Eichmann case. It's incredible, and shattering. The trial is not just an indictment of one man or one system, but is in fact a sordid examination of conscience _of the entire west_ and one which has proved singularly inconclusive because no one seems to grasp anything definite about it (if they have even _tried_ to grasp anything). All that remains is a general sense of loss, of horror and of disorientation. And even the horror is diffuse and superficial. Where does one begin to respond to the multiple indictment of our world? The stereotypical answers all collapse, and there are no new ones, and there is no faith! . . .

Yet the total irrationality of the Eichmann affair must not make us distrust reason or humanity themselves. The temptation is to think that reason and conscience themselves have been exploded by the inane cruelties of our age! That opens the way to a more complete surrender to a more absolute irrationality, and a more total cruelty.

Saturday, in this same bright sun, sat and talked with Victor and Carolyn Hammer and drank brandy among the pine saplings near the old lake. It was wonderful! Nothing ever tasted so good, and it restored my faith in Europe. (It was Spanish brandy.) They brought books on Fénelon (most of which I need not read) and one small volume of fine selections. He, at least, had a conscience, and put it at the service of statesmen, if they would listen to him. I like his letters to the young prince, the Duke of Burgundy, and his warm, discreet, paternal kindness towards all whom he advised. And his *clarity*, his reasoned judgment, his insight. I like his *quality*. Contact with such minds is indispensable. Nor does it hurt to drink a little clear, heartwarming brandy in the spring sun. All this is not yet gone out of Europe, and perhaps there is also a little of it among us here in America. Let us not assume there is too much, however!

Diabolical elements in the extermination of the Jews: privileged classes were established. German Jews, ex-servicemen Jews etc. would receive "better treatment."

In *accepting* these distinctions and applying for them the Jews themselves became accomplices *approving of* the means for the destruction of their race and even in many cases collaborating with them. Yet in the long run the distinctions themselves were meaningless.

Machinery for human self-destruction. The loss of moral senses, the abdication of conscience are *signs of the proximate extinction of the human species itself*, unless there is a change, a moral recovery.

Eichmann appealed to the fact that he had practiced "blind obedience" and "corpse-like obedience." *Kadavergehorsam* [corpse-like obedience]. He declared that he had lived his whole life according to Kant's moral precepts and the Kantian conception of duty. But this, says H. A[rendt], contradicts the above bec[ause] Kantian judgment rules out blind obedience. Later he added that under the final solution he had "ceased to live according to Kantian principles." Rather he had distorted it to mean "Act as if the

Führer would approve of it if he saw you!" Importance of this German concept of obedience as going beyond duty to identify oneself completely with the legislator.

For Eichmann – what bothered him most was that *he had made two exceptions and allowed Jews to escape*, thus neglecting his "duty" to the Führer. Virtue = is act against his inclinations, even the most human.

All along, the terrible thing about the Eichmann case was the fact that his motives were always *motives of conscience* and duty, not of fanaticism! H. Arendt then raises the question whether this invalidates the concept of "a law that supposedly speaks in all men's hearts with an identical voice."(?) [Question mark circled in journal.]

March 29, 1963

Israelite conception of "existential connexion between act and consequence" (Von Rad) rather than punishment as a forensic retribution. The trouble with the Eichmann affair – a completely unrealistic morality – a forensic concept which has broken down. The existential evil is most evident, but cannot be grasped except existentially. No machinery can deal with such horror. The *acts themselves* are a retribution, and lead to worse acts and worse retribution. What judgement could *add anything* to the judgement implied in the very acts?

March 31, 1963

Warm spring Sunday, Passion Sunday, wrens singing and the nobility of the *Vexilla Regis* [Banners of the King]! Such substance in that hymn, solid words, solid melody, from the days when Europe had foundations! Thought of Poitiers and St. Radegund, and again of Fénelon, and his *Dordogue.*

Did I say I was bored with Fénelon? Perhaps the *least* interesting thing about him is his "spirituality" – the "*doctrine*" which is still perhaps in some way thought of as dangerous! Much more interesting than his relationship with poor Guyon is his relationship with the Dauphin, for whom he wrote *Télémaque*, and whom he would have advised had he come to the throne. But the Dauphin died before the old king, who hated *Télémaque*, in which his absolutism was attacked by a bishop he despised as "*chimérique*" – not belonging to the world of power. Now Bossuet, on the other hand: power was something he understood.

If they hated Fénelon's spirituality and wanted to find quietism in it, it was because they knew its apparent powerlessness was a protest and an indictment of the spirituality that went with absolutism.

———

That notorious illuminist, the Holy Ghost.

Now the mauve hills are stained with green.

As if I would write a novel about a southern place called Mauve Hill.

The fire on Friday: we went out after the thin dinner, and smoke boiled around the little hillocks at the end of St. Bernard's field. Arrived just when the flames were entering a small wood, leaping up fiercely on the brambles and into the cedars. We went down through the blackberry bushes to where a house was tucked in a hollow: an old man in it, in a pale jacket: not worried. We defended the house badly, nearly setting it on fire ourselves with a back fire that got away. Great flames roaring up in the brambles and sage grass. Twenty feet up in the air through some willows overgrown with honeysuckle – that was the original fire, and our backfire stopped it on that side. Then off into the next hill, but with so many monks it was soon out.

I remember the house as we left, tucked prettily into the fold of smoking hills, an unforgettable, old, unpainted Kentucky house with a rusty tin roof and a rickety porch, and an elm tree ready to be green, and a wasted, washed out, barren dry clay road leading up to it. The archetypal Kentucky house, almost a log-cabin yet.

Bro. Robert left, and left me a hammer handle which a man living in the woods over by Hanekamp's old place had made for him. He too was bewitched by the mystery of Kentucky houses and wants to go live and maybe teach school back in the hill country. He will do better there, if he gets there, than in this monastery where today the abbot, because of his leaving, was compelled to carry out this usual exercise on self-justification and one-upmanship.

The clear fact is that Bro. Robert was in a lot of ways a good monk and a contemplative, sensitive and aware in ways that Dom James never heard of and is not capable of conceiving. They are to him, no doubt, chimerical. For instance what would he ever want with that hammer handle? Anyway, scorn had to be poured on the "unfaithful" who, through their own fault, defect, abscond and leave. It is always entirely *their* fault, never the fault of the abbey, or of its abbot, or anyone in it. Yet these ceaseless tirades are effective in keeping the thought of leaving on everybody's mind.

A talk by Hans Küng in Chicago, on freedom in the Church!!

April 2, 1963

Adolf Eichmann, in his last words at the foot of the gallows –

Declared himself a *Gottes[un]gläubiger* – (one who did not believe in a personal god).

And then addressed those present

"After a short while, gentleman, we shall all meet again."

"Such is the fate of all men. Long live Germany, long live Argentina, long live Austria; I shall not forget them."

H. Arendt comments.

"In the face of death he had found the cliché used in funeral oratory, but his memory had played him one last trick, he had forgotten that he was no Christian and that it was his own funeral. It was as though in his last minutes he was summing up the lesson that his long course in human wickedness had taught him – the lesson of the fearsome, word- and thought-defying banality of evil."

This is incomparable.

And yet I am sure he had forgotten nothing and remembered nothing – he simply automatically recorded what was inappropriate, because to such a person there is nothing really appropriate but only something that vaguely seems so. And I am sure that a Catholic manual of apologetics could find a way to crown it all by "proving" from it man's uneradicable instinct for immortality.

All it proves is . . . nothing.

H. A.'s summation of the case is important. The whole question of justice raised by it is not "merely technical"; it has to do with the nature of the crime and the nature of our predicament. E. was condemned not just for a more massive and better organized anti-semitism, but for a crime against *humanity as such*. This is unintelligible without a valid concept of human nature.

And then (but this is not a legal question – or far worse, psychological and moral one) . . .

"This new type of criminal, the *hostis generis humani* [enemy of the human species], commits his crimes *under circumstances that make it well nigh impossible for him to know or feel that he is doing wrong*."

In conclusion: is a criminal anyone who decides what races will and will not inhabit the earth and decides to eliminate "undesirables"?

April 7, 1963. Palm Sunday

Quiet sunset. Cool, still day and another fire over toward Rohan's Knob. Peace and silence at sunset behind the woodshed, with a wren playing quietly on a heap of logs, and a detached fragment of gutter hanging from the end of the roof; bare branches of sycamores against the blue evening sky. Peace and solitude.

Fr. Matthew insists he has seen a deer again in our woods.

Daily I rot. That is, my health is good, but little pieces and parts of me begin to work less and less well, and I don't especially care. I am used, and wearing.

Fire last Wednesday in the knobs behind our own hills. We went out, and climbed through the forest, and I and the novices never made it to the right knob, saw smoke snaking along it, went around by the road to get nearer and missed it. We were overtaken by dark in strange woods but did not get lost. Later: the hill that had been burned stood like a city huge in the dark and the still burning stumps were like lighted buildings. Many of the monks were waiting in Calvin's store on 31E and the juke box was playing and of course nobody had any money. Two boys from the woods, with hair all over the place and sloppy hats, and one with a beard, were drinking cans of beer, and said roguishly we ought to come over Saturdays when it was real lively.

I like Guerric's Easter sermons.

The University of Kentucky has offered me an honorary L.L.D.

The Catalan translation of the *Seven Storey Mountain* arrived yesterday.

P[ierre] Bonnard, the post-impressionist painter, has died, after instructing someone where to put the last blob of yellow on a last great painting, already bought by the owner of Gimbel's.

But who has not died? Nils Bohr. Robert Frost. Robinson Jeffers (all last year). So many others.

I am so happy that the Pope has written an Encyclical on Peace announced for *Holy Thursday*.

April 11, 1963. Holy Thursday

A lovely spring morning. Things really getting to be green, just before they fully clothe themselves in foliage. I see a little stand of timid willows picked out thinly in the sun along the creek in the bottoms, against the shadow of the opposite hill.

The other day there was a beautiful whistling of titmice – and now today one of them lay dead on the grass under the house, which may well have been some fault of mine, as we dumped some calcium chloride on a couple of anthills – not as a poison but as something to move them elsewhere. What a miserable bundle of foolish idiots we are! We kill everything around us even when we think we love and respect nature and life. This sudden power to deal death all around us *simply by the way we live*, and in total "innocence" and ignorance, is by far the most disturbing symptom of our time. I hope I at least can learn, but in the light of Holy Week I see, again, all my own internal contradictions – not all! Hardly! But the fact that I am full of them. And that we all are.

A phenomenal number of species of animals and birds have *become extinct* in the last fifty years – due of course to man's irruption into ecology.

There was still a covey of quail around here in early fall. Now I don't hear a single whistle, or hear a wing beat.

April 13, 1963. Holy Saturday

Two superb days. When was there ever such a morning as yesterday? Cold at first, the hermitage dark in the moonlight (I had permission to go up right after Lauds), a fire in the grate (and how beautifully firelight shines through the lattice-blocks and all through the house at night!). Then the sunrise, enormous yolk of energy spreading and spreading as if to take over the sky. After that the ceremonies of the birds feeding in the dewy grass, and the meadowlark feeding and singing. Then the quiet, totally silent, day, warm mid morning under the climbing sun. It was hard to say psalms: one's attention was totally absorbed by the great arc of the sky and the trees and hills and grass and all things in them. How absolutely true, and how central a truth, that we are purely and simply *part of nature*, though we are the part which recognizes God. It is not Christianity, indeed, but post-Cartesian technologism that separates man from the world and makes him a kind of little god in his own right, with his clear ideas; all by himself.

We have to be humbly and realistically what we are, and the denial of it results only in the madness and cruelties of Nazism, or of the people who are sick with junk and drugs. And one can be "part of nature" surely, without being Lady Chatterley's lover.

So that was one good day.

Then, this morning: a charming visit of two Spanish families (or part of them as I suppose they are large families). First, Emilio Garrigues, brother of the Spanish Ambassador in Washington, with his wife and daughter, then Villalba, the Spanish consul at Boston, with his wife and daughter (the latter with a black mantilla and a round face and black eyes and a Goya complexion – I suppose about fifteen).

We talked for an hour and a half, very seriously and animatedly about all the questions they asked, and they were very direct, sensible, intelligent, lively. It was such a relief to meet *people* [underlined twice]. One thing that struck me is that Americans are not simple at all. We (I suppose I had better include myself) are by comparison with this Spanish frankness and aplomb, artificial, complex and trivial. How I enjoyed talking to them, and how good it was to have them here and to remember that all this exists still: the reality of Europe. It is not a dream after all, it *does* exist. There has been, and still is, such a civilization with good people in it, tormented no doubt with their ambiguities. Garrigues' daughter was a charming child, an overgrown fourteen or fifteen, tall, silent, not as obviously shy or forward as she would be if she were American – but just quietly growing into what she will one day be. And it is nice to think what she will be; I think both the girls are potentially quite spiritual, but it is hard to say as they were silent, and silence at that age might mean anything.

A kind of complement to yesterday morning. The bright world, and the people in it. How good God has made all things. And yet they are no happier than I, I am no happier than they, and for all of us there is a secret of acceptance we have not learned.

April 16, 1963

Hot, all the ground and woods dry, clouds overhead that give no rain.

It is Easter Tuesday. The less said about the Easter celebration the better. Pomposity, phoniness, display, ultra-serious, stupid. Interminable pontifical mummering, purple zucchetto, long train, Mexican novice as train bearer (he always manages to get a Mexican or a Philipino or a Negro to carry his tail), all of course for the "glory of God." The Church was morally, spiritually stifling with solemn, unbreathable unrealities.

It was the plush, the ornamentation, the mummery in Church that struck me as *secular*. The spring outside was sacred. At the lake, Easter afternoon, the purity of the green buds, the wind skimming the surface of the water, the utter silence, and a muskrat slowly swimming to the other side!

———

Two novices have left. That brings us down to 6 choir novices and 8 brothers (one in simple vows). But two postulants are coming this week. The main reason is the extraordinary unreadiness to admit postulants now – and I can see reasons for it. Most are turned away by Fr. Eudes, but those he does not reject, I eventually do! There is no point getting people in here who cannot in any way make sense out of this life, even when they are convinced they "like" it.

Reading [Étienne] Gilson's *The Unity of Philosophical Experience* [New York, 1948] – very lively and articulate. Also something about Karate and Aiki – a curious book for zombies maybe – casts a strange light on the American character and its infantile fascination with major ways of power. Always talking about 6 foot 6 marines who are black belt judo experts and people showing off *karate* tricks at parties ("Hand your drink to your girlfriend. Then . . ."). Of course the point of the book is that the little Jap weighing 95 lbs throws six marines out on their cans, but that is just another twist. What has become, in 20 years, of the "shifty little Jap" image!! Now he is magic. Still *Aiki* sounds like a very respectable discipline, basically spiritual, and something we could use.

There has been practically no rain for a month – only a brief, providential shower the night of that fire in the knobs two weeks ago.

April 19, 1963

Hot dry wind, still no rain. There are supposed to be tornadoes in Indiana. Cloudy sky, sinister fallout-like mist, humidity, wind, and no rain. You can hardly see across the valley.

In the U. of L. library yesterday I found a fine story of Jakob Boehme – the "Supersensual Life."

April 20, 1963

There was a light shower yesterday evening and today everything is brilliant. Around the hermitage all is neat and pleasant while Bro. Mark cleaned up with a power mower – there is something to be said for machines (though over there Bro. Benedict fills the orchard with poisons). Dom Columban [Bissey] arrived today for the visitation. I received a letter from Dom Aelred Graham in answer to a card about his book on *Zen Catholicism*, which I have reviewed (for *America*).

April 23, 1963

After a hot, stuffy weekend, last night there was a good thundershower and I was glad of the rain, though I lost some sleep. Today was beautiful as spring should be, and best of all a couple of quail started up under my feet behind the hermitage, and the cock with his trim black crest whirred off into the pines. I had thought they were all done for.

I wrote a note of commentary, perhaps for *Liberation*, about the race question, which builds up more and more to an explosion. A copy of a disturbing letter about the New Delhi-Peking peace-march and the state of affairs in India, where non-violence has become an abstraction and everyone's getting ready for war. The situation in Asia is extremely ugly.

Yet Pope John's encyclical *Pacem in Terris* [*Peace in the World*] was read in the refectory – it finished yesterday.

The document is in every way sane, lucid and admirable. Above all it contains a surprising passage that opens the way to more open cooperation with the Communists in trying to keep peace. This is most important, because the idea that Communists are incarnate devils has almost become a dogma of faith in the Catholic U.S. Yet the only way to peace is by cooperation.

The effect of hearing such things said is greatly heartening, and there are perhaps real hopes of [left uncompleted by Merton].

April 24, 1963

The riches of this day. First of all the day itself. Brilliant. Cloudless. The trees almost fully in leaf but not quite. (Except the oaks, which are usually later than the rest.)

The ikon of St. Elias, which Jack Ford brought me from St. Meinrad's, and which yesterday I put up on the east wall. Fabulously beautiful and delicate and strong. A great red transparent globe of light, with angelic horses rearing in unison, and angels lifting all of it up to the blackness of the divine mystery – from, below, the dark curve and shelves of the mountain from which Eliseus reaches into the globe to touch the mantle of the prophet, who stands in a little, finely drawn, very simple, Russian peasant's cart (in the globe of fire!).

Below Elias sleeps: that was before, when he had sorrow. The angel leans over him, and mentions the hearth-cake to the sleeping prophet.

What a thing to have by you! It changes everything! Transfigures everything!

———

And outside the door, a double bloom on one large violet iris, standing out of the green spears of the daylilies. And on the tongue of one bloom walks a great black-gold bee, the largest honeybee I ever saw. To be part of all this is to be infinitely rich.

Father Alphonse died this morning and I was kneeling by his bed, and we said the wonderful prayers, calling upon all the prophets, patriarchs, martyrs. Such prayers! And I discover that I was very fond of this crusty, simple, rude old man.

The relic of St. Bede over my heart, preparing me for May.
Work on Fénelon, which I keep as a meditation, not as work.

April 30, 1963
After more dry, stuffy days we finally got sufficient rain yesterday, and again last night and now it is cloudy, dark, cool, green. Read Gordon Zahn's talk to the Center in Santa Barbara – about the same question he raises in his book. Why religious groups are not potential centers of *dissent* when secular society challenges their basic ethical principles, or have they really abandoned these?

What is religion, for the most part, in this country? A "source of peace," a refuge from conflict? So – an Eichmann factory, maybe! Certainly we preach the Cross, but not the cross of resistance; only the cross of submission. And never mind to what. Submission to power – any power that adjusts itself to the Church.

Got a very friendly letter from Dom Aelred Graham about my article on his *Zen Catholicism*. He invited me up to Portsmouth – but the permission would never be given.

May 8, 1963
The other day, on the advice of Notker Balbulus, "If you love God's creatures, read Ambrose's *Hexaemeron*," I began the *Hexaemeron* of Ambrose. A book of great charm because it is a poem of love, primitive, childlike and erotic joy in creation, and yet with great intelligence and strength. We can well read such books if we do not take them as science, and the scientific view of the evidence will not make sense until it, also, becomes play.

Elements of play in space-flight. But the great death play of nuclear war: the awful, stupified, obsessed *seriousness* of technology, especially war technology.

Finished the preface to Fénelon's letters the other day. May has been beautiful, especially after my Mass, in the sunny chapel, looking at the willow and listening to the birds. And the bright afternoons, with the new ikon of St. Elias and the new shelves, the books. Yesterday came across D[ylan] Thomas' wonderful poem "The Holy Spring."

May 10, 1963

Much trouble in the South, Alabama. Negroes demonstrating, cops turning firehoses on them, getting after them with police dogs. The character of the Negro demonstrations is religious and non-violent, concerns mostly their right to vote, or rather the right to use their right to vote. Pictures of fat-arsed police, grin[ning], stupid and "efficient," arresting Negroes, dragging them off. Three of them after a Negro woman whom they have flat on her back, one with a knee in her neck. She was, it is alleged, "pushing" the police.

Les[lie] Dewart has sent the ms. of his important book on Cuba. The first thing I have seen that makes sense out of the whole business. But he points out the responsibility of Catholics in creating a situation which led Castro to Communism. And it was led to do this by its ordinariness and mediocrity.

Not that there was not great courage and generosity on the part of many who suffered torture under Batista for opposing him: but once Castro was in power, his Catholic supporters could not, says D., conceive of anything but an either/or choice between total repudiation of Communism or total acceptance of it. This, according to D., drove Castro to Communism.

Letter from the [Abbot] General came today categorically denying my request to publish *Peace in the Post-Christian Era* now that the Encyclical has said what I was saying myself! At the back of his mind obviously is an adamant connection that France should have the bomb and use it if necessary. He says the Encyclical has changed nothing in the right of a nation to arm itself with nuclear weapons for self-defense, and speaks only of "aggressive war." I suppose the letter was composed by his secretary, Père Clement: it reflects his obtuseness.

Such a complete lack of sensitivity to the real spiritual problem of nuclear war is certainly discouraging.

The question arises – have I sufficiently "done my duty"? The question is absurd. I must continue to be faithful in every way to the cause of peace and when one means is denied me, to use a dozen others.

The argument that I am supposed to be a "contemplative" and therefore to remain silent is transparently artificial. True, this is a principle. But there is also a culpable silence. Silence is not an absolute, nor an end in itself. And if I am a writer (this seems after all to be admitted)? . . .

Today I see the whole question of my place in the Order with a new clarity. There is such a thing as fulfilling my obligations to the Order and yet definitely not being "of" it in their sense. It would be to me a problem of conscience if I allowed myself simply to become the kind of monk they apparently want me to be – a conformist, not rocking the boat, not speaking out, passive, mute, indifferent.

Dom James wrote one of his letters from Mepkin, mostly about chickens, but with several typical stories of the childishness that strikes his fancy. What a picture of monasticism!

Hot, dry, stuffy. No rain for more than two weeks.

Dom Gabriel agrees it is not for me to write about war, that is for the bishops. Fr. Ford said over a year ago – how do you expect the bishops to say anything without the moral theologians?

And the moral theologians? Sitting on their cans and preserving their reputations.

This is one of the situations that keeps the Church half dead.

In spite of the fact that I thoroughly disagree with the ideas of Dom Gabriel and of Dom James, and with a great deal of the thinking that is accepted throughout the Order and the Church, I have never been less tempted against my vocation or my faith in the church. I have never before seen so clearly that "agreement" with Superiors has little or nothing to do with it. They have their right to my obedience, but there is no need to be interiorly servile. One can be obedient and free, and even in a certain sense independent, at least interiorly.

The fact is, they have their ideas, and there is no changing them. And this is the Order in which I am. But I do not have to be obsessed with its *unrealities*.

May 11, 1963

> *"La finalité historique doit devenir 'intérieurement' et librement intelligible, car elle concerne la personne qui dégage à elle seule le sens de l'épreuve commune (et non l'individu, élément différencié dépendant du groupe social qui en demeure la 'fin' naturelle."* ["Historical finality ought to become 'interiorly' and freely understandable because it deals with the person who brings out, all alone, the sense of the common trial (and not the individual, a fundamentally differentiated element, depending on the social group which remains the natural 'purpose.'"] *L. Massignon*, Parole Donnée, *135*

He goes on to say each can find in the religion of his own life "*interférences expérimentaires* [experimental interferences]" between his own inner spiritual time and his time of historical events.

> *"Prises de conscience poignantes, étapes décisives dans la formation de leur science expérimentale de la compassion, des participations réelles, lourdes et intelligibles de tout leur être . . .* aux douleurs de la parturition sociale *qui tardent dans l'inconscience et le désespoir de la masse des opprimés."* ["Sharp realizations, decisive steps in the formation of their experimental knowledge of compassion, real participations, heavy and understandable in all their being . . . *in the pains of social birthing* which slowly form in the unconscious mind and the despair of the mass of the oppressed."] *137*

> *"Le déchiffrement de l'histoire est réservé aux êtres de douleur. . . . Seuls ceux qui parviennent à l'imitation du Dieu souffrant peuvent l'approcher."* ["The understanding of history is reserved to those who suffer. . . . Only those who imitate the suffering God can succeed in approaching him."] *(A. Beguin)*

Helicopters (in Algeria) – grasshoppers of the apocalypse. Massignon.

I told Bro. Sebastian (O'Daniel) I thought he had no vocation and he seem[ed] delighted and relieved.

Dewart thinks that the issue of war and peace depends on the decision and policies to be taken in the years Kennedy is president, in regard to Cuba. These are the crucial years, and this is the crucial decision. Perhaps. I think the C. revolution should be recognized as a fact. But this is not likely. I think the coming revolutions in South America may well precipitate the issue. The U.S. will not be able to handle them. Only if Russia continues to back down can war be avoided.

May 20, 1963

Saturday Rev. Father with Dom Laurence [Bourget], the definitor,[3] returned from the meeting of American Abbots in Georgia. It turns out they are to meet *here* next year and also all the novice masters are to meet here. And I was told, by implicit and equivocal hints, that I would be expected to give them all spiritual conferences. This I found very irritating and upsetting, for various subtle reasons: but I feel as if I had been partly flayed and salted because I am so aware of the implications and of the secret injustice that is done me by my abbot's neurosis.

Here is the thing: I have been repeatedly invited to Georgia. Not that I want to go. No permission has ever been given.

I have been invited to give a retreat to our nuns in California. Permission refused.

Dom Aelred Graham invited me to Portsmouth Priory for a rest and I could use one. I felt like replying that I could more easily get permission to take a mistress than to go to Portsmouth or anywhere else for a rest. Though it is certainly true I have the hermitage, and that's much.

It is not that I want to go to these places especially, but I do want recognition that I have just as much right as any other monk to make such journeys if the need arises. But this right I do not have. It was evidently said by the abbot that if the meeting were at some other monastery I would not be allowed to go. No reasons for this have ever been discussed with me.

On the other hand, when the canary is asked to sing, well, he is expected to sing merrily and with spontaneity. It is true that I have a nicer cage than any other canary in the Order . . .

But this upsets me so that I cannot sleep. And the stray dogs that Bro. Wilfrid feeds bark in the night when I *do* manage to sleep, and wake me up again. Today I feel hateful, and miserable, exhausted, and I would gladly die.

Everyone can come and see me in my cage, and Dom James can modestly rejoice in the fact that he is in absolute control of a bird that everyone wants to hear sing. This is the way birds stop singing – at least those songs that everyone wants to hear because they are comforting and they declare that all things are good just as they are.

One's song is forced at times to become scandalous and even incomprehensible.

---

[3] A monk appointed to serve as liaison between the Abbot General and members of a group of Cistercians who share the same language. See p. 396 of volume 3 for Cunningham's definition.

And so my own neurosis runs like a sore, and I know it, and see it, and see that I am helpless to do anything about it! And am, of course, guilty.

So it is that the Christian and monastic mind is admirably fitted to be a seed ground of neurosis. This is at once a weakness and a strength. Unfortunately I can't imagine, for the moment, where to find any kind of strength in this futility.

May 21, 1963

After a good night's sleep I realize how sick were my thoughts yesterday. And also I see that I don't really see or know the depth of my sickness, but anyway I am thankful I can at least recognize it.

It is easy enough to find the weakness – and the *possible* failures and limitations in other people, and then look at them only, excluding everything else. Doubtless there is truth in my intuitions about the abbot. But in all his complexity there is also a good will that has to be recognized, and a sincerity – a quest for truth that is quite genuine, certainly as genuine as my own. (If my own *is* genuine.)

But it makes no sense to oscillate like this from the good points of another to his bad points. This seems to be a way of seeing and understanding others, but it is a futile activity for the most part. Pointless analysis. There is finally a simpler, more existential way of simply accepting facts. And it is this, not sterile moral analysis, that is demanded of a Christian.

The fact remains that if I have to give those conferences, I can give them and I don't have to be so frantic, so suspicious, so resentful, and so afraid of getting hurt. What if they don't agree with my ideas? They may be readier to agree than I think, and there is after all a common sincerity in a common quest for rational solutions. I should be able to join in this too, and accept what they may have to offer. Doubtless it is perhaps largely a silly game. But it has *some* meaning, surely.

Qui exaltas me de portis mortis ut annuntiam omnes laudationes tuas in portis filiae Sion. [You deliver me from the gates of death that I might announce your praises in the gates of the daughter of Sion (Psalm 9:13–14).]

Marvelous vision of the hills at 7:45 A.M. The same hills as always, as in the afternoon, but now catching the light in a totally new way, at once very earthly and very ethereal, with delicate cups of shadow and dark ripples and crinkles where I had never seen them, and the whole slightly veiled in mist so that it seemed to be a tropical shore, a new discovered continent.

And a voice in me seemed to be crying, "Look! Look!" For these are the discoveries, and it is for this that I am high on the mast of my ship (have always been) and I know that we are on the right course, for all around is the sea of paradise.

May 25, 1963

Busy week after the wonderful empty day of last Tuesday.

Naomi Burton was here Wednesday and Thursday. My publishing affairs are in confusion and I was disturbed at my own mistakes and imprudences.

Naomi very solicitous and friendly – but I do not see eye to eye with her on this war business. She is firmly stuck in a position that refuses me any good reason to protest, at least as I have done. She thinks of "what I represent to so many people etc." What does that have to do with it?

It is true that I perhaps ought not to be crudely polemical on a journalistic level – but have I been? Not so much.

She agrees that I can say the same things some other way.

A cop on the Red Squad of the Chicago police is shocked that I am writing about war, says I should rather be on a "spiritual Los Alamos project" and suggests what? What else but Theresa Higginson and devotion to the Sacred Heart. This is Catholicism!!

May 26, 1963

Reading [Werner] Heisenberg's *Physics and Philosophy* [New York, 1958], which is an exciting book. The uncertainty principle is oddly like St. John of the Cross. As God in the highest eludes the grasp of concepts, so in the ultimate constitution of matter there is *nothing really there* (except Aristotelian potency, perhaps – and H. is willing to admit this).

Heisenberg and quantum theory – at least the Copenhagen interpretation – is the end of conventional 19th century materialism – and the joke is that this materialism is now unmasked *as a faith*.

Soviet scientists now have to attack Heisenberg on purely dogmatic grounds, exactly as the Holy Office attacked Galileo. It is an article of Soviet faith that mechanical laws of motion, electronic activity etc. *must* be a confirmation of the religion of dialectical materialism. Ergo.

Heisenberg shows that the naive objectivity of conventional physics is on the same plane as the ancient conviction that the sun revolved around the earth. A pragmatic observation *Quoad nos* [as far as we are concerned, concerning us], but not objective fact. And the Soviets struggle to maintain this naive objectivity. *Eppur si muove.* [It still moves.][4] Yet with great sophistication quantum theory also includes the "factual" concepts of daily life, knowing they are not factual, and yet they are part of the observer's reality. This leads to a fabulous new concept of nature *with ourselves in the midst of it,* and destroys the simple illusion of ourselves as detached and infallible observers.

Today is the fourteenth anniversary of my ordination to the priesthood.

I wish I could say they had been fourteen years of ever-growing fulfillment and order and integration. That is unfortunately not so. They have been years of relative happiness and productivity on the surface, but now I realize more and more the depth of my frustration and the apparent finality of my defeat. I have certainly not fitted into the conventional – or even traditional – mould. Perhaps that is good. I am not a J. F. Powers character. Yet the frustration is the same. (I do not know if I am a [George] Bernanos character. I am not a [Graham] Greene character.) But this business of defeat is there, and I see it is perhaps in some way permanent. As if in a way my priestly life had been sad and fruitless – the defeat and failure of my monastic life. (Perhaps. For after all how do I know?)

I have a very real sense that it has all been some kind of a lie, a charade. With all my blundering attempts at sincerity I have actually done nothing to change this.

I have certainly not been a model of priestly virtue. It does not seem that I have willfully arrived, i.e. with my eyes wide open, in a serious matter. But there have been repeated failures, failures without number, like holes appearing everywhere in a worn-out garment. Nothing has been effectively patched. The moths have eaten me, while I was confusedly intent on what seemed to me to be good, or important – or necessary for survival.

There has been a kind of dazed desperation in my half-conscious attempts to preserve my identity, while being worn down by the ever renewed futility of a half-productive existence.

Lately I have been uncharitable and unjust, in matters that could have been objectively serious, but my attention was fogged, my mind was obsessed with some form of survival. I was saving myself in some futile

---

[4] This was Galileo's conclusion even while submitting to the Church's condemnation.

neurotic pattern. I saw afterwards where there could have been unconscious malice.

I have not always been temperate, and if I go to town and someone pours
me a drink, I don't resist another or even a third. And I have sometimes
gone beyond the *trivium perfectum* [the perfect third]. A monk?

Probably the chief weakness has been lack of real courage to bear up under the attention of monastic and priestly life. Anyway, I am worn down. I
am easily discouraged. The depressions are deeper, more frequent. I am
near fifty. People think I am happy.

My Mass every morning has certainly been a joy, and I have attended seriously to it; there has sometimes been great, and simple, meaning in it,
and always the realization that it was far greater than I could understand.
But there have also been moments of unspeakable anguish and tension.

I suppose that in the end what I have done is that I have resisted the su-
perimposition of a complete priestly form, a complete monastic pattern. I
have stubbornly saved myself from becoming *absorbed* in the priesthood,
and I do not know if this was cowardice or integrity. There seems to be no
real way for me to tell.

However, I do know there is a difference between the dead routine demand repeated meaninglessly (?) for the thousandth time, and the response
to the living need of a person, in a letter, or in direction, or in a class. I
know I have often missed this response too, but it seems to me that these
are the acts in which, by being a priest, I am also being myself and being
Christ.

I am not so sure about the others, the frustrating and seemingly pointless
acts of mechanical obedience demanded purely and simply by the organizational pattern.

May 29, 1963

Heisenberg – on the impact of technical and scientific knowledge upon
traditional cultures, etc.

This "process . . . *has gone far beyond any control through human forces.* One
may rather consider it as *a biological process on the largest scale* whereby the
structures active in the human organism encroach on larger parts of matter
and transform it into a state suited for the increasing human population."
[Merton's emphasis] Physics and Philosophy, *p. 189*

I think this is really a very practical way of looking at it, and far from re-
ducing morality to determinism, it gives morality the only dimension in

which it can really cope with our situation. One must first recognize reality, before he can deal with it. The traditional concept of nature is not opposed to this. It does not exclude grace.

Applying this to politics in the nuclear age.

"The continuation of the status quo may not always be the correct solution; it may, on the contrary, be most important to find a peaceful means of adjustments to new situations, and it may in many cases *be extremely difficult to find any just decision at all.*

"Therefore it is probably not too pessimistic to say that the great war can be avoided only if all the [different] political groups *are ready to renounce some of their apparently most obvious rights – in view of the fact that the question of right or wrong may look essentially different from the other side.* This is certainly not a new point of view; it is in fact only an application of that [human] attitude which has been taught [through] many centuries by some of the great religions." [Merton's emphasis] *p. 191*

June 1, 1963. Vigil of Pentecost

It is hot. The Pope, Pope John, is dying and perhaps dead. Already yesterday at this time he was in a coma, in an oxygen tent, with the Papal guards around his apartments. Last night he was conscious for a moment, they say, and smiled and blessed those around him. I have been thinking of him all day and praying for him, especially at the high Mass after None. The world owes him a great debt, in his simplicity, and it is hard to feel that we can do without someone like him. He has done so much in four years, four and a half, to remind people that Christian charity is not a pure fiction. Yet, in spite of it all, will people ever again have confidence in love? Will they not think that everyone who has spoken of love has finally betrayed them? This is what they want to believe. And it is the most threatening thing about the current climate.

The Black Moslems, with hard, shining heads, with frowns, with muscles, drilling for self-defence, have ceased to look upon anything at all in the world as funny. They are one of the few fanatical movements for which I am able to have the slightest respect.

But Martin Luther King – who is no fanatic at all – is perhaps one of the few really great Christians in America. His "Letter from the Birmingham Jail" is a terrific thing. It says "the churches" have failed the Negroes. In the end, that is what the Black Moslems are saying too. And there is truth in it. Not that there is not a fair amount of liberal and subjective sincerity. But the implication is that this kind of sincerity is so subjective and so ineffectual as to be worse than meaningless. It is a personal luxury, which enables the individual to feel concern – without doing anything.

Monday I began a private retreat and I need it – at least to get some order with my writing and my contacts, and my projects, and my concerns, of which there are too many.

June 2, 1963. Pentecost
Redite parvuli fili ad sinum matris vestrae aeternae sapientiae, sugite larga ubera pietatis Dei; transacta plangite, imminentia vitate. [Return, little children, to the bosom of your mother, eternal wisdom, suck from the abundant breasts of the love of God; beat your breast for what is past, and avoid what will weaken you.] *St. Gregory,* Hom. XXV. *no. 10*

June 3, 1963. Whit Monday
Retreat at hermitage. Mass at 4, came up shortly after 5, through the mist and the wet grass. "Open the ground of hearing . . ." (Eckhart)

Time here seems quite a different kind of measure, and in fact it is. For time is constituted by relationships and here all the relationships are different: I am convinced that the tensions of our community life are delusions and obsessional because of the *unreality* of our activities – the basic unreality of our relationships. Unreal because much too artificial and contrived.

In any case, here one has a sense of being both fully relaxed and fully alive, and having nothing to do, or rather still perhaps wanting to read and think, and not being able because of the sweetness and fullness of time that is too good to lose. The *immediacy* of the relationships is all too good to be lost. The sun, the summer tanager (I finally connected the song with the bird), the clear morning, the trees, the quiet, the barely born butterfly from the cocoon under the bench – etc.

Seriously, my projects and relationships, including correspondence and much of my work, are sheer waste. The only thing that can be said for them is that they seem at times to be more real than what goes on in the community and probably are.

Relationships with the novices, though, are meaningful and healthy, though I question the value of my conferences, maybe I am working in support of a delusion.

June 4, 1963

Pope John died yesterday. A holy and good man, and he was both because he was first of all a *man* – that is to say, human. This is the great meaning of his papacy, of the Council, of *Pacem in Terris*. Not humanism, "but the bare statement of the fundamental value of *humanity*." *Pacem in Terris* is not theological. It simply says war is inhuman, and therefore a sin – (not war is a sin and therefore you must not use the bomb). Certainly everyone loved him, and statements to this effect, though spoiled by the fact that language is too exhausted to convey it, are probably sincere. May he rest in peace, this great and good Father, whom I certainly loved, and who had been good to me, sending me the stole and many blessings. And I don't think he has stopped being a father to us, to me. He will one day be canonized, I think (if we last that long), and I do not hesitate to ask his intercession now.

Solitude – when you get saturated with silence and landscape, then you need an interior work, psalms, scripture, meditation. But first the saturation. How much of this is simply a restoration of one's normal human balance?

Like waking up, like convalescence after an illness. My life here is most real because most simple. In the monastery it is also real and simple, at least in the novitiate. The more I reach out into "the world," the less simplicity, the more sickness. Our society is gravely ill. This is said so often and I have said it so often, and saying it does not seem to help. Knowing it does not seem to help. My concern has been probably sincere, but in great part futile. I don't want to turn off into desperation and negativism, but there has to be a far greater reserve and caution and *silence* in my looking at the world and my attempts to help us all survive.

In England – the "Regional Sects of Government" – underground bunkers for military dictatorial cadres to run the ruins after a nuclear war. These places have been discovered and denounced by radical pacifists and everyone is up in arms at the betrayal of "official secrets." The governments of the world are utterly sick, mad, deluded. Society has to be reorganized from top to bottom, and who is there to do it? Those who seem, and claim to be most sane, are perhaps the least to be trusted.

Identity. I can see now where work is to be done. I have been coming here into solitude to find myself, and now I must also lose myself: not simply rest in the calm, the peace, the identity that is made up of my experienced relationship with nature in solitude. This is healthier than my "identity" as a writer or a monk, but it is still a false identity, though it has a temporary meaning and validity. It is the cocoon, which masks the transition stage between what crawls and what flies.

(*Contemplativus*) *res mundi mundo profecit, et seipsum Christo devota mente restituit, a quo sibi donari immortales divitias orat.* [(The Contemplative) leaves the things of the world to the world, and restores himself with a devoted mind abandoned to Christ, from whom he prays that He will give lasting riches.] Regula Solitariorum [Rule for Solitaries], *Grimlaicus, C[hap].* 10

June 5, 1963
Peculiariter autem ad professionem nostram pertinet nihil honoris in hac vita requirere sed honores fugere. . . . [It peculiarly belongs to our profession to seek no honor in this life, but to flee honors. . . .] Regula Solitariorum, c. 23

In spite of the above, today is the day I am supposed to receive, by proxy, an honorary L.L.D. at the University of Kentucky. Victor Hammer will be there to receive it for me. I don't suppose I am inordinately elated. Here I sit and listen to the sound of a wren echoing in the pines and the mist. It is an Ember Day and I am hungry and I would be very pleased if a crow would fly along with a cup of coffee. I could use one.

Receiving an honor:
A very small gold-winged moth came and settled on the back of my hand, and sat there, so light I could not feel it. I wondered at the beauty and delicacy of this being – so perfectly made, with mottled golden wings. So perfect. I wonder if there is even a name for it. I never saw such a thing before. It would not go away, until, needing my hand, I blew it lightly into the woods.

In the afternoon: I knew there was an intruder in the front room of the hermitage, where I could hear movement. I went to see, and it was a Carolina wren which had been thinking of coming in already the day before yesterday. It flew out again, as though it were not welcome!

June 6, 1963
This experience of solitude is important and most valuable. How badly I have been needing *whole days*, and days *in succession* out here. At last I am

getting a decent perspective again, and there is no question that my desire for solitude has been basically right, and not a delusion. I thank God that I have, by His grace, at least come this far and not made the fatal wrong steps that would have probably led to a failure without clarification (for instance trying to make a go of it as a Carthusian).

1. In the monastery the organized artificiality of the life, while not destroying the essence of the monastic spirit, does to a great extent obscure and falsify it. Not enough to be really harmful, no doubt – certainly the life is very beneficial to those who have merely arrived in it, and to the young monks, also to some of the old ones whose lives have remained simple.

2. For my part, I am under pressure and deeply "involved" in the silly business of keeping the place going – though I admit there is nothing silly about a novitiate as such, and I love the novices, want to help them to keep clear of foolishness and have their lives make sense. But I am mixed up in the work, the policies, the running of the organization: and though I am mixed up in it, there is little or nothing I can do to make it really meaningful or effective. Just help the abbot keep the thing going more or less smoothly, the way he believes it ought to go.

3. My "monastic life" in the community besides the organized prayer of the office which is good (but *artificial* – and sometimes overdone). I have a lot of reading and thinking, most of which goes into conferences and direction for the novices and juniors. The consequence of this is that I need to get away to the hermitage to try to recover some semblance of a personal life of meditation and prayer.

4. The consequence – I do get here, but long enough only to recover my senses. It is not so much a matter of real contemplation as a necessary recreation, a breathing spell. And it is a joy. But this is not deep enough.

5. I find now that with *more time* out here I go beyond that, as I should. It is no longer a "prayer" answered in the silence and peace of nature, but beyond that, more deeply interior, more a prayer of faith *without* the external medium of visible creation (which I did not think I was using as a medium, but I was). More Biblical – the psalms mean immensely more as days go by.

6. The greatest thing has been a recovery of the real dimensions of the mystery of Christ – and I think that really puts the seal on it all. A recovery, so to speak, of a deep and primitive faith – with the realization that it is a pure gift. What a renewal, and how thankful I am. My spirit is once again breathing after a long time of stuffiness and suffocation.

MONASTIC SPIRIT

1. Importance of the Biblical element, of real monastic tradition (not ritual "traditions").

2. Importance of restoring the distinction of action and contemplation *within* the monastery: that is to say, the distinctions between "little habit," the *stamphoroi*, and the "great habit" (*megaloschevoi*). In other words, some way in which a mature monk may find a way for further development, and not be held back all his life either to the basic level of the lowest common denominator, or to the pseudo-maturity of a monastic office which becomes an escape into activism (and not the real sharing of wisdom).

3. Importance of a tradition that opens out in *full continuity* into a wisdom capable of understanding the mystery of the contemporary world in the light of *theoria*. I.E. – Sensitivity on the issue of *peace*, racial justice, but also technology, and the great spiritual problem of the profound disturbances of ecology all over the world, the tragic waste and spoilage of natural resources etc.

In Europe, where the concern for "monastic tradition" has been most alive, there has at times been a marriage between monastic tradition and political reaction. For instance – German monasteries which were very well up on patrology and monastic theology and which at the same time supported Hitler, and therefore, whether they knew it or not, were involved in Auschwitz, the Blitz, etc. etc.

June 11, 1963

Another week, then.

Came back to the community three days ago, Saturday, because dentists were here from the U. of K[entucky] and I had a tooth that was thought to be a problem (and was not). They filled it.

Worked at the typewriter in the p.m. and saw Fr. Abbot etc.

Back at the hermitage for two good parts of today – in the morning, cool and light, I said Mass late.

Proofs of Dorothy Day's new book came from Harper (with a request for comment). It looks good.

In the refectory: interminable repetition of news stories about the Pope's death. Always the same details, rearranged this way and that, over and over, until the whole thing sounds like a story by Robbe-Grillet.

The cast iron bed, the thick red carpet, the four relatives from Sotto il Monte, the cast iron bed, the bed table with a black telephone and bottles of medicine, the thick red carpet to muffle the sound of feet. The relatives from Bergamo, Xaverio, Giuseppe (I forgot the other), and Assunta, who had been a nurse. The Pope calls his relations to the bedside. There is a rosary on the bed table. The Pope calls the relations. Assunta was a nurse. There's a thick red carpet. The Pope said, "Think of Papa and Mama" in Bergamesque dialect (who told the reporter?). Assunta, who had been a nurse, dipped a cloth in a silver bowl of water and mopped the Pope's brow. Four relatives from Sotto il Monte were there. Four red damask chairs. Assunta, with a silver bowl. A rosary on the table.

Poor Pope John! None of this idiotic reporting can change his greatness or his glory! And for all that he died a noble and Christian death, a holy death, that was not a cliché, however much they tried to make it one.

June 12, 1963

Came out of the house and looked at the pasture where the calves usually are. Empty of calves – there was in it only a small white colt, a thoroughbred, running beautifully up the hill and around and down again, with a great smooth stride and with the ease of flight, then breaking into rough and delightful cavorting, then back into the smooth canter. How beautiful is life!

But it was when he was dismembered that Halley could cry, "I am the truth."

June 18, 1963

The conclave begins tomorrow, for the election of a new Pope. I very much doubt if they will find anyone as good as Pope John. However, among those 82 cardinals there ought to be a good one. I wonder if there is not a possibility of Card. Agagianian being elected – some seem to think it possible. I doubt it.

I do not speculate much. I like the German cardinals but they do not have a chance. I like Card. Montini of course . . . and would not be surprised if he were the next Pope.

Anyway, this morning I said the Mass _Pro eligendo summos pontifice_ [for election of a Pope].

Other names – possible successors to John XXIII:

Agagianian – seems a good prospect – a respected diplomat.

Confalonieri – a better one still: secretary to Pius XI – Sec. of the Cong[regation] of Seminaries and Universities – has apparently some of Pope John's goodness.

Morella – succeeded John XXIII as Nuncio in Paris – but conservative.

Roberti – canonist – may get elected as a mediator between extreme parties.

Urbani – Patriarch of Venice and another pastoral type like Pope John.

I suppose I would like to see Urbani or Confalonieri get it – or *Montini*.

A new biography of St. Anselm has come in. It seems excellent (by R. W. Southern).

June 21, 1963. F. of the Sacred Heart

A joyful and exciting day, cool, with a great confabulation of crows in the east, and a woodthrush quietly singing in the west.

The conclave began yesterday, and this morning, while we were chanting the Night Office, Cardinal Montini was elected on the 6th ballot. It was announced in Chapter and I offered my Mass for him. I think he has the makings of a great Pope, but in his pictures he looks thin and tired.

In the refectory they played a tape of the broadcast from St. Peter's Square, the noise of the crowds, [Alfredo] Ottaviani's announcement, *Habemus Papam* [We have a Pope] and then the roar that went up after he got halfway through the name – John Baptist . . . He choked on "Montini."

The blessing of Pope Paul VI was clear and strong and very slow, and it was so moving that I did not feel like eating.

It is good to have seen this day.

June 26, 1963

Hot again. Hard to sleep at night with the forage blowers roaring all night in the alfalfa – teams of laymen driving them and dehydrating the stuff, all night. Is this the way to make our living as monks? Perhaps this is the price of contemplative leisure for some of us, but it does not really make sense.

Last night there was a fire at the dehydrator, which I did not see, but the fire engine going off sounded like six trucks. What a roar! Noise all night, and when it is nothing else, someone is out in the woods with dogs, hunting raccoons and filling the night with howls. So the sick world continues.

————

Last Sunday (23rd) Dom Vital was anointed (in Church), but he is still up and around, looking exhausted. He will not last long at this rate. But he is one of those who *cannot* stay in bed, or in an infirmary room.

Have read St. Anselm's *Proslogion* [*A Discourse*] and having for the first time considered the ontological argument, have come under its peculiar spell. It is certainly much more than a mere illogical confusion of orders, or an illicit transition from the level of words to the level of being. On the contrary, it begins and ends in being. It has extraordinary faults, impossible to define and describe because of the underlying spiritual experience which it suggests. I talked of this to the novices on the F. of St. John Baptist, which was a beautiful day, with great East Anglian clouds over St. Theresa's field.

Trouble with Farrar Straus drags on. Without fully realizing what I was doing, I violated the contract last year with those books given to Herder and to Macmillan. Now there is a threat of legal action (by FS against Macmillan) because they want to go ahead with the book anyway. I hope to persuade Macmillan to simply forego the publication and let me take the book back and hide it on some shelf forever, and we can all forget it. Wrote to Naomi today for advice about this.

This may at last be a way to change my way and stop publishing, at least stop publishing such books as that one on Prayer – which I have not had the courage to do so far. It would be so much better if I just wrote what was really in my heart to write. But I find the other things spilling out continually. Of course it is easy to see why. The novice conferences supply material that can quickly be put together as a book: but this is not the way good books are written. This is really a vice. And I suppose I am as attached as the alcoholic to his bottle. Breaking it will not be simple.

July 5, 1963

I have decided that the best way to solve the problem of the contract with Macmillan is to return the $5000 advance and ask for the ms. back with the understanding that I do not intend to publish the book *anywhere*. Sent a letter off to Warren Sullivan at M. today.

The Abbot is away on visitations. Fr. Anselm (Steinke) has not been around for some time. Many supposed he was in the hospital but it appears he is trying to get out of the Order and into a diocese. At one time I had thought of him as a good possibility for the next abbot, though since his return from Rome he was obviously too unsettled. The affair in California (where, as provisional superior of the foundation at Vina, he was not elected abbot) seems to have thrown him.

Swami Shivaprem, a yogi from Rishikesh (India), who is teaching yoga in Milwaukee, was here for three days. He is very much of a monk and I found we got along very well – had very much in common. For instance I felt I had much more in common with him, as far as the spiritual life is concerned, than with the average American secular priest.

I wonder if there are any educated yogis who are *not* deeply influenced by Christianity. This one certainly is.

He gave several good talks to the novices.

Fr. Pachomius, the thin, amiable and meek Cellarer of the struggling primitive Cistercian community at Erlach (Austria) was here too. Arrived first after Fr. Abbot left, otherwise I would not have been able to speak to him!! Monks of primitive observances are not *personae gratae* around here.

I finished my article on St. Anselm and the ontological argument but am still reading the R. W. Southern book, which is excellent, and very interesting with all its material on Canterbury.

July 7, 1963. Day of Rec[ollection]
I am disturbed at my combativeness. I still have so much of it. It comes out most when I think I have a just cause. And also I do not understand it. There is so much more in it than meets the eye. I come out for "justice" and "truth," but I come out swinging at everything. Of course the issues are enormous, and what makes it all worse is that I am not sure of my own position and my own approach. Often I am premature, my opinions are ill-considered and undocumented, and on the strength of a couple of fairly good intuitions I may end up by a useless and harmful blast that takes in the good with the bad in one general explosion. For instance in those letters which Leslie Dewart is using in his book on Cuba. This is perhaps stretching things too far, but I felt I should do it – if I come to regret my decision I will not be surprised.

———

The reasonableness of Knowles's essays in the new collection printed as a "homage" gives me good things to meditate on, on a day of recollection. It has been hot, clammy, rainy, stuffy, but a good day of prayer.

July 8, 1963
César Vallejo – the most truly "Catholic" in the sense of universal poet of our century. The voice of man, speaking with intelligence and compassion and absolute sincerity. His austere and chaste imagination – the art of the Inca. Can't read a poem of his without wanting to translate it, for love of the rude sorrows and nobility of his speech.
    Greater than Picasso in painting.

> *Il tiempo tiene un miedo cienpiés a los velajes.*
> [Time, for watchers, feels a centipede's fear.]

> *Sufriendo como sufre del linguaje directo del léon.*
> [Suffering as one suffers from the direct language of the lion.]

July 9, 1963
Cool morning. The corn is high – over my head already.
    A train comes slowly and busily down the valley, whistling first at Dant Station, then New Hope, now Gethsemani, soon New Haven.
    A helicopter came over, no better name for it than chopper with its insane racket, insect body, thin tail, half dragonfly half grasshopper (*Sauterelle de l' apocalypse!)* [Grasshopper of the Apocalypse!]. Flew over three times, in a circle around the monastery. What for? Just to make a noise.
    War on the ants in the hollow and behind the hermitage – millions of them in huge hills. Andy Boone got in to it with whiskey bottles full of kerosene which he sticks upside down into the anthills. But the ants just move and start again five feet away.

This book [bound journal in which Merton is writing] gets ragged and is ending. Need a new one.
    Letter from Marco Pallis and an essay by him on the question whether there really is such a thing as a "problem of evil." I ought to do a dialogue with him in *Continuum* – will have to think of it carefully, not get too involved in too many such things. But this, I think, would be highly worthwhile.

———

Ping Ferry sent a copy of an excellent hard-hitting talk on the failure of colleges which he gave in Detroit.

We have had more education for more people, for a longer period than any nation in history. The result is that we are not prepared for the new world which, ironically, is principally of our own making.

The system which seeks only to prepare people to make money – in individual careers, has not taught anybody to think about the momentous collective problems of the age.

It has interpreted individualism only as the promotion of self-interest, without bothering to teach people to think for themselves.

An infernal concerto of chain saws broke out in the woods on the hillside behind the new water works, just before Sext. A deep one and a tenor, a roar and a yell of hot metal, diabolical intervals of "harmony" in utter fury, while three or four oaks went down in quick succession. I did not get close, but I could see the naked *torsos of natives* hired by the cellarer, and a white panama hat, and the typhoon of stygian hymnody continued, with an awful unnatural shuddering of boughs. A frightful portent, but it did not last long. The trees crashed and were cut up, or partly so, by dinner time. And now I suppose they will lie on the ground and rot for ten years, and no one will ever know what it was all about in the first place. Somebody's brainstorm – it was set to the right music.

I am not physically in good shape. Asanas that were easy a year or two ago are becoming difficult, and some impossible. My breathing is more labored. I am knocked out by a little digging in the sun or a half hour with a brush hook.

July 10, 1963

An anthem from Canterbury. 11th Cent.

> *Gaude dei genitrix, virgo immaculata.*
> *Gaude quae gaudium ab angelo suscepisti.*
> *Gaude quae quaeruisti aeterni luminis claritatem.*
> *Gaude mater.*
> *Gaude sancta dei genitrix virgo.*
> *Tu sola mater incorrupta.*

Te laudat omnis factura domini.
Pro nobis supplica.
[Rejoice, mother of God, immaculate virgin.
Rejoice, who received the angel's greeting.
Rejoice, who sought the clarity of eternal light.
Rejoice, mother.
Rejoice, holy mother of God, virgin.
You alone are the incorrupted mother.
All creatures of God praise you.
Pray for us.]

Beginning to get acquainted with St. Anselm's marvelous Marian prayers.

A new machine, sailing through the distant horse-pasture, by the little bell-house, looking like an Ohio riverboat or a Saul Steinberg drawing, driven by a brother in a white sun helmet. What is it? An atomic-powered river gunboat? An agricultural pagoda? It seems to be made out of aluminum, and has a paddle wheel in front. A great deal must go on inside. It has ventilators protruding in every direction. Can be heard a mile away. Chews up the grass and leaves it shred[ded]. What for?

I keep remembering how old Fr. Amedeus said "My God!" in his retreat sermons. He had polyps or something in his nose and it came out as "My GOND, my GOND!"

The Vanderbilt faculty not coming for retreat in September, but rather in October – or next spring?

July 14, 1963
We have now the new photocopied edition of Erasmus, and I am reading the *Ratio Verae Theologiae.* I admit I am charmed by him. He reads so well, speaks with such clarity and sense, and is so full of the light of the Gospel. I am also reading K. Rahner's new little book on Mary [*Mary, Mother of the Lord* (New York, 1963)] and I am struck by the similarity – the same kind of clarity, simplicity and breadth of view. It is the same mutual climate without the subdued passion and the humor of Erasmus.

Two Negro students from Louisville were here on retreat and I arranged to have a talk with them, as I am supposed to be doing a piece on the race situation, for *Ramparts*. I talked with them about an hour with great pleasure. Two nicer people you could not want to find. They look at the events of the time with realism and humor, and are in no sense extreme one way or the other. Certainly not bitter. Accepting absurd things with tolerance and charity. The mad lady in Louisville who writes to the paper that she can no longer go into any of the parks because they now admit Negroes – a Southerner from the deep South, weeping on television in Georgia because she saw a black boy and a white girl walking together in Louisville. One of these students has a girl friend who is almost white, and if he goes out with her he is liable to be stopped and questioned by the police!

Another white southern youth, questioned on TV as to *his* bright thoughts on the situation, said his suggestion was to "kill 'em all off."

In addition to so many other things, and far worse things still, this is what they have to live with. Louisville is better than most places and there will be integration of public facilities in September.

But otherwise – fifty-seven varieties of the runaround.

I think the Kennedys are sincere with their civil rights bill, but the problem is to get it through Congress, with all the cornpone Neanderthals officiating there! (P. D. East's word. I keep hearing from him now, and have some copies of his fantastic "Petal Paper" and its withering satire of the South. I am surprised he can stay in Mississippi and keep alive.)

John Griffin wrote that Clyde Kennard had died last Saturday – a victim of fantastic injustice and cruelty, again from Mississippi.

Macmillan – i.e. W. Sullivan – returned the check I had tried to return to them, and said they wanted to go on with the book, that it ought to be published, etc. and that they would fight it out with Farrar Straus.

Fr. Peter coughing, spitting, sighing upstairs, while birds sing in the garden.

July 17, 1963
Caput tuum ut Carmelus, et cornu capitis tui sicut purpura reqis cincta canalibus.
[Your head is like Mt. Carmel, and the crown of your head is like the purple of a king girded with pleats (Song of Songs 7:5).]
This is the feast of Our Lady of Carmel.

Almost cloudless sky, bright sun, it will be hot.

The Ikon of Elias is burnished and beautiful.

With ardent hope and compunction I dedicate this day, and myself, to Our Lady.

If this day is to honor her I must spend it without any rancor in my heart. I know that I see my own falsity reflected in Bro. – and yet he is holy. I do not think of this much, but I do think of it, and am impatient with myself and with my lot, and my stupid mediocrity. It is so clear that I am in part a phony, and I suppose this comes from my fatal versatility in self-examination and self-expression. What good does it do to say I see this, and that I recognize its total futility?

The whole trouble is in my fatal tendency to see myself in relation to others, my life in contrast with some other life, everything. I do in at least an implied contrast with what someone else does. And who is better?

"Take no thought for or against it."

Perhaps it is true to a great extent that the untruth in my life *does* come from my doing so many things that are not strictly in accord with my vocation, writing on controversial topics, against the desire of higher superiors (I do not write on what they have forbidden, only on what they perhaps unwillingly tolerate). Yet there is no question of the seriousness of the need, and of the demand of my own conscience that I write at least a little on some of these things – that I at least express an opinion, as I did on peace – and it had its effect!

So too I think it is vitally necessary that I speak up for the Negroes. But after that?

I have undoubtedly written and said things that will definitely be regarded as "rash" – for instance the letters Dewart is using in his appendix to the book on Cuba.

All I can do now is await developments, with a sincere effort to be humble (if that be possible!) and to pay close attention to everything that is said and to obedience, even when some demands seem to be disconcerting. I must recognize the danger of first doing my own will, though I know at the same time that a certain abusive idea of obedience is taken to justify and promote inertia in the Church.

No question that I need much more faith in the Church, and much more delicacy of conscience in ref. to obedience, without nevertheless becoming passive and inert about my duty in the present world crisis.

It *is* a crisis and I *do* have duties, a certain initiative *is* demanded.

July 18, 1963

Diligebat autem anachoresios plurimos, frequenter expetens solitudinem. Et illic dies in oratione persistens dominum supplicabat ut a tantis se fraudibus clementer eriperet. [He loved to go far into the desert, often seeking solitude. And there he spent his days in prayer, asking the Lord that in his mercy he would be delivered from all deception.]   Vita S. Pachomii, *C. II.*

Charmed by the life of Pachomius – and have found much useful material in Ladenji's "Essai." Too many generalizations have falsified our view of Pachomian Cenobitism.

Ferial office long (i.e. *slow*) with office of the dead. Very hot and stuffy.

July 19, 1963

I am halfway through the *Ratio Verae Theologiae* of Erasmus, loving the clarity of his style, his taste, his good sense, his faith, his Evangelical teaching. If there had been no Luther, Erasmus would be one of the greatest doctors of the Church – officially I mean. He is perhaps anyway, though he is very simple. I like his directness and his courage. These qualities were all canonized in [Thomas] More. Humble Erasmus is content to be sainted in his friend.

But that's it: how can one be anything but a friend to such men?

Yesterday came a personal letter from Pope Paul, thanking me for my letter of congratulation on his election, signed by him and conveying or rather "lovingly imparting" upon me and the novices "our special fatherly Apostolic blessing."

I was very moved at the Holy Father's charity, and it helped me to be much more humble toward the Church, recognizing my debt and obligation to her. I am too prone to get angry when I think the Church slow and stolid and inert, that she does not respond to the human needs of the times, etc. I suppose it is natural for one to be impatient with plumes and

Sedia gestatoria and cappa magna [Papal chair and great cape of honor] etc. But the humanity of the Popes and their love does come through!

There is a little tremor in the first of the capital P's for *Papa*. I hope he does not have a weak heart – will pray that he be preserved for us! The "P" of Paulus is magnificent, though it looks more like a "G." The downstroke is sharp and firm, and the sweep of the circle is graceful and strong too. That first letter took all the ink.

Am going over the "letters to a white liberal" on the Race question. Had difficulty getting started last week, but finished all right on Wednesday.

July 20, 1963

A vile, stuffy hot night.

Yesterday was the most unpleasantly hot day of this summer so far, and just to make everything perfect, got a letter from Bob Giroux with all kinds of allegations that I was betraying him by turning over his *Letters* to Macmillan. Evidently the battle is in full swing and he had been talking to some character who told him some beautiful lies. He phoned and said, however, that he had misunderstood the situation and apologized, having found out that I had tried to return the advance and withdraw the book from publication.

I was glad he called, after sweating on the phone for 20 minutes. It cleared the air like a small cloudburst.

Much of the problem has come from his uncommunicative disposition – but the root of the trouble was my own impatience to get the *Reader* done, and that was nothing but self-love and ambition, unworthy of a monk.

I will try again to get the book away from Macmillan (Fr. Abbot can write the next letter) and withdraw it completely from publication.

Have finally put screens in the cottage – a great improvement. They make it seem smaller, cooler and more mysterious. Also make it harder to see in from outside, which is convenient if I want to change clothes!

Partial eclipse of the sun today, lasted about an hour.

In a sermon of Eckhart – God wants to give His greatest gifts. Love is the most noble and the most common of His gifts.

July 21, 1963. VII Sun. after Pentecost

A cool evening – or cooler than last evening and the one before. I am on night watch. It is still light, though everyone is in bed. A robin still sings in the garden and tall gold lilies shine in the dusk. While I was anticipating the night office of St. Mary Magdalen a female tanager captured a grasshopper on the path a few feet away, and after dinner, as I sat under the broad woodshed roof a woodchuck came out of the weeds and chewed at leaves five or six feet away from me, not out of tameness but rather for sheer stupidity. Woodchucks must be shortsighted and depend mostly on hearing, or so I think.

The mystery of my monastic community as my place of salvation and encounter with God. I was talking of this in the conference this afternoon and it is getting now, at last, into my bones. Though I *can* be solitary, I no longer have to make an issue out of it, and if I *am* solitary, it can be for love of God and a part of my community life, not an expression of a stronger psychological or spiritual need. A contribution to the community's life of worship.

July 22, 1963. F. of St. Mary Magdalen

I am reading Karl Rahner's essays on grace – at least those available in translation, as I do not have time to struggle with the German. They seem clear and obvious. I sometimes wonder why Rahner is considered so dangerous. Perhaps because he is too clear and not involved in the technical mumbo jumbo that makes others unreadable. In a word: a *readable* theologian is dangerous.

How true it is that the great obligation of the Christian, *especially now* is to prove himself a disciple of Christ by *hating no one*, that is to say by condemning no one, rejecting no one. And how true that the impatience that fumes at others and damns them (especially whole classes, races, nations) is a sign of the weakness that is still unliberated, still not tracked by the Blood of Christ, and still a stranger to the Cross.

[Gabriel] Marcel (in *Dieu Vivant* [*Living God*] IV) speaks of the "*dogmatisme des esprits posés* [dogmatic attitude of serious persons]" who refuse to recognize any *difference* in man's present situation. It is only another crisis, given time we will emerge from it as we always have in the past. This implies a rejection of the revealed *eschaton*, so clear in the N[ew] T[estament]. (Not that this is *necessarily* the end, but we cannot deny that it might be, purely on the assumption that the very idea of an end is not to be taken seriously.)

Marcel, contemplating the world in which he grew up and which now lies in ruins.

"Il ne suffit pas de dire que ce monde-là est en ruines. . . . Il n'a pas été pulvérisé par accident, mais il portait au fond en lui-même le principe de sa destruction. . . . Cette constation qui nie le fond des choses pose un coup mortel à la conscience que l'esprit posé croit avoir de lui-même." ["It is not enough to say that the world is in shambles. . . . It has not been ruined by accident, but it carried deep within itself the cause of its own destruction. . . . This statement which denies the heart of things strikes a mortal blow at the consciousness that the serious mind thinks it has of itself."]

Hence to go on *"comme si rien n'était* [as if nothing were the matter]" is scandal and absurdity.

For this is to neglect and ignore the *revelation* that has been made, of an abyss opening out before us.

Then he goes on to analyze superficial optimism based on a specious idea of unity based on rapid communications, congresses, etc. This false unity comprises usually 1) reduction of differences, 2) "accepted" resentments in which each one eyes the other in the same state of frustration and tries to keep him there so all will be "one," 3) ideology-propaganda directed ag[ain]st the scapegoat, maintains unity of the "elect" (i.e. the masses), 4) under influ[ence] of propaganda – masses "experience" the mass as transcending the individual – sharing sense of power in concentration on one object *"autorité collective"* [collective authority], 5) fascination of number bringing on spiritual blindness, demanding self-renunciation before the crowd.

Conscience eschatologique [Eschatological Conscience] – for Marcel

1. Refusal to accept mass-mind, technological "unity" etc.
2. Refusal to accept *"optimisme des esprits posés* [optimism of the affectatious persons]."
3. Awareness of conc[entration] camps as figures of the world to come (under technology).
4. Awareness of the *lie* involved in equating these horrors with those of other times.
5. Awareness of the imprudence with which the ideals of other times are invoked and revered by the very ones who, claiming to follow them and use them as used and generally understood, have actually destroyed them.

6. Recognition that much (all) that used to be taken for granted is now problematic and there are fewer and fewer answers.

7. Recognition of "statism" as impotence disguised as absolute power.

8. The Egocrat conscience = not "*le moi captif* [the captive self]" in the habits and prejudices of sensible world which thinks all is "business as usual," but "*le moi de l'amour et de la Prière* [the self of love and prayer]" which can face the event is joy of the person one with many in Xt.

Letter from Dom James read in refectory today. About his visitations at the Genesee, in Utah etc. These foundations certainly sound dull. One is left with a sense of desolation, after all the details of their business arrangements, retreats etc. and what they say to the Mormons. It is true that a lot of this is irrelevant, but still one knows that Dom James says what he sees and that is not much: of course, what he says about this monastery must sound equally desolate and futile. The clichés about the nobility of the contemplative life only reinforce the impression. One feels the emptiness and desperation with which so many of them escape into jobs. Yet there must be some real life there too, as there is here. But how? . . . Largely I suppose inarticulate and in anguish – or in simplicity. Anyway Dom James' letters always depress me. But now I don't care any more about the level of life in the monastery. It is enough for me to accept God's will, and by no means as a negative gesture of desperation – it is the only really positive thing I can do.

July 25, 1963

> *Nous ne cessons d' être harcelés par les mots: ils nous dévorent. . . . Nous passons la plus grande partie de notre temps à rédiger des circulaires, des manifestes, des rapports, à écrire des articles, des essais, des romans. Nous nous précipitons en foule aux conférences dont le nombre croit chaque jour en raison inverse de l'intérêt qu'elles présentent.* [We don't ever stop being plagued by words: they devour us. . . . We spend most of our lives editing pamphlets, manifestos, reports, writing articles, essays, novels. We rush in crowds to conferences whose numbers grow each day in inverse proportion to the interest they hold.] *M. Moré, in an old dimi [indecipherable] for* Dieu Vivant *(12)*

This morning at meditation I was disturbed and distracted again by the thought of the meeting of novice masters and abbots to be held here – but it is still ten months away. No matter, I really have such repugnance for the whole idea that I shudder at it. I can think of all the ways in which it will be useless, boring, absurd. For all the other novice masters it will be a vacation: for me only an extremely boring and difficult task added to my usual work. And I reflect how little I really have to say, how little interest I have in organizing talks and discussions, etc. Of course, I have a vow of obedience, and it is only out of obedience that I can face the thing at all!

Yet I have much less feeling of repugnance for writing that is perhaps almost equally useless – though there may in some way be more point to it.

Certainly I must refuse to draft a statement on the Race question for the Cath. Civil Liberties outfit. And I can't go helping on the FOR statement of purpose. This is outside my territory.

The new magazine put out by American Pax – more elaborate than I expected – yet less effective than the English Pax bulletins.

Ambivalence about certain poetry magazines. I really think I have no business at all in _El Corno Emplumado_, but still I doubt, like good stuff from Cuba there, and communication must remain open – is this a delusion? Many would be ready to tell me so, but can I believe them?

"_Le témoignage exigé de chacun de nous est beaucoup plus de transparence que de paroles—une parole, même juste, peut soulever des pris[?] de contradictions: rien ne résiste au rayonnement du silence rempli de charité._" ["The witness required of each of us is much more than transparence than words – a word, even an exact one, can raise a lot of contradictions: nothing can resist the radiation of a silence that is filled with love."]

"_Une végétation trop exubérante étouffe l'arbre de notre vie intérieure: ne suffisait-il pas d'y faire une bonne trouée, en renonçant franchement à toutes sortes de travaux et d'occupations à la petite semaine sur l'utilité desquelles nous nous faisons tant d' illusions?_" ["Too abundant a foliage can stifle the tree of our interior life: doesn't it suffice to make a good break in it, renouncing all kinds of insignificant (small-time) work and occupations, about the usefulness of which we have all sorts of illusions?"]

More translations of Vallejo?

Translate Susanna Sora – ? Though I am charmed by some of her poems and by her personality, so like that of Raïssa Maritain, very contemplative but with so much more poetic sophistication!

Perhaps I may someday do something of Susanna's, but after much reflection. I must after all honor her silence with some of my own.

"_Une théologie, pour être vivante, doit se greffer sur la substance même de l' histoire, non sur petits faits divins quotidiens!_" ["A theology, in order to be living, ought to be grafted onto the very substance of history, and not onto the small, daily divine acts!"]

I think I could talk to Dom J. today about giving up the idea of the Vanderbilt Divinity School faculty retreat here – their Dean seems to have trouble arranging it anyway – and maybe also the one which Paul Peachey is trying to arrange – of pacifists. I don't think I ought to be conducting *any* retreats.

July 26, 1963

How high the corn is this year, and what joy there is in seeing it! The tall crests nodding twelve to fifteen feet above the ground, and all the silk-bearded ears. You come down out of the novitiate, through the door in the wall, over the trestle and down into this green paradise of tall stalks and silence. I know the joy and the worship the Indians must have felt, and the Eucharistic rightness of it! How can one *not* feel such things – so that I love the Mayas and Incas as perhaps the most human of peoples, as the ones who did most honor to our continents.

The irreligious mind is simply the *unreal* mind, the zombie, abstracted mind, that does not see the things that grow in the earth and feel glad about them, but only knows prices and figures and statistics. In a world of numbers you can be irreligious, unless the numbers themselves are incarnate in astronomy and music. But for that, they must have something to do with seasons and with harvests, with the joy of the Neolithic peoples who for millennia were quiet and human.

Great cumulus clouds piled up over the valley, high as Mont Blanc, and probably as cool. Looked at them while thinking over my reading from Banya Ibn Peguda – Spanish 11th century Jew, who wrote in Arabic. Trans. into French by Chowaigui in *Dieu Vivant*. Splendid Preface to "*Les Devoirs des Coeurs*" ["The Duties of Hearts"]. B. I. Peguda is the most attractive, and most convincing, of all Jewish mystics to me. Strength, wisdom, truth, and such perfect solitude! I want very much to read more of him after this first taste.

An article in Portuguese (from Brazil) on Vallejo and how the Communists have tried to shanghai him for their cause. No one with such integrity could be a pure party poet. There is too much religion and honesty in Vallejo for the compromises of a Neruda. It is precisely because of his honesty that they *need* him – and have to get him after he is dead.

___

Fr. John of the Cross has sunk into the world like a hunter into a deep swamp. Rev. Fr. talked to him on the phone in San Francisco. What is said of him does not sound good. If he really goes wrong, he will go terribly wrong. And what is my part in this? Trusting his talent and his wisdom, I encouraged him.

July 29, 1963

Read a good article in *Revue Biblique* on Xtians in St. Luke, and skimmed through another on Amencinope (Egyptian: source for Proverbs).

Hot, damp, tropical. Heavy rain this morning.

I said a Requiem Mass for César Vallejo (inexplicably, chain saws howled all through it and stopped at the Communion). The rain came after that, heavy grey sheets of it veiling the knobs and flooding the new water works.

I sent the article on the race problem to *Ramparts*, for August 1 deadline.

There are some very stirring quotations on religious life, from Anglicans, in A. M. Allchin's *Silent Rebellion*, especially R. M. Benson. There is a special quality and excellence in the Anglican view of monasticism, with a very genuine touch of protest, of "witness *against*" the torpor of the Anglican establishment. Yet how much does it mean? Is it merely a precious indulgence of a very small minority? I am singularly moved and disturbed by this book, and am certainly glad to be a Roman, as emphatically as Newman was.

If it were not for the heat, I could think myself in England. Everything has the dark velvety green of Surrey or Warwickshire, and next door is a real meadow, since Bro. George has mowed it.

July 30, 1963

Reading again St. Thomas on the divine missions, in connection with grace, and am left a little uneasy with texts that used to seem so clear and final. For instance that the Holy Spirit is a gift given us to be "used and enjoyed." Of course there is the whole question of the Augustinian *fruitio* [enjoyment] etc. Still, this might lead to misunderstandings. It is not clear enough – or too speciously clear! It cannot simply be accepted at its full value.

On the other hand the Oriental Christian doctrine on "essence" and "energies" seems to bring much light into this question.

In fact it seems to me that *the whole question of grace* is something I must begin again to study in a light more germane to the contemplative and monastic life.

Magnificent article of Evdokimov on the Desert Fathers in the latest *Collectanea*.

Celibacy – collective *refusal* to procreate, to continue activity that has reached its term. (But a creative refusal. Opp[osed] to the destructive refusal, proliferation of missiles and condoms!)

Virile ascesis [manly ascesis] – not simple retirement. (My country gentleman meadow!!) Building a city "*non pas en marge mais à* la face *de ce monde* [not on the edges but in *front* of the world]." Yes! but temptation here. Athos? A fine city but with its own mouldy conformism and its own sins too!

In any case the monastery proclaims the abolition of history.

Nothing to do with fake optimism, millennia of beautiful activism!

Anti-conformism because the world of the living presents a *lying* vision of being. Hence ascesis distorts, deliberately, the measures of profane ethic.

"*Les 'fils du Christ' – créer l'atmosphère de mépris et d'abjection, de devenir les 'plus petits' de ce monde et de toucher à la limite de l'humilité.*" ["The 'sons of Christ' – to create a climate of being despised and rejected, of becoming the 'least important' in the world and to reach the very limits of humility."]

"*Dendrites,*" chained in trees, living as birds, no longer touching the earth in arks of air above the flood.[5]

"*Le refus de la cité humaine et de l'Histoire provoque un retour vers les conditions de vie* préhistorique." ["Rejecting the city of man and History brings about a return to the conditions of *prehistoric* life."]

Measure *within* the lack of measure.

The Desert Fathers. To be read iconographically?

Ikon – says nothing of autonomy, character, etc.

Elle nous fait voir le rayonnement d'un homme au delà de l'Histoire. Le Saint assume et porte en lui l'Histoire mais la montre autrement; par transparence il en révèle une nouvelle dimension, où son sens est éclairé par la Fin et constitue une synthèse méta-historique. [It (the icon of a saint) makes us see the radiance of a man outside of History. The holy man carries History within him but shows it otherwise; by transparence he reveals a new dimension of it,

---

[5] *Dendrites* were Christian solitary ascetics who lived in trees.

where its meaning is clarified by its End and thus creates a meta-historical synthesis.]

"La tradition de l'Église est justement ce silence orant [. . .] d'où sort la liturgie et l'icône." ["The Tradition of the Church is exactly this silence (in the attitude of a person praying) . . . out of which comes the liturgy and the icon."]

Yet he says that a return to the desert *now* would be a rupture in tradition.

Desert Fathers – ikon of the total gift – not opposite to "good sense" of moderation and ethical norms.

Renouncing also culture.

All curiosity ends after the Gospel (Tertullian). *"Or toute curiosité commence après l'Évangile, mais autrement qu'avant."* ["All curiosity *begins* after the Gospel, but it is *otherwise* than before."]

Icons – show man who have become immaterial – but not unreal – on the contrary, more real. "Dressed in space."

Their action on the world is not "on" the world, from without, but from *within* by cosmic charity without limits.

Vomiting up the interior phantoms, the doubter, the double.

"Les Pères du désert ont pratiqué cette opération grandiose à la place de tout et une fois pour toutes." ["The Fathers of the desert practiced this great endeavor in place of everything and once and for all."]

The ascesis of the desert has radically transformed the human consciousness – by deep therapy, which formed an ascetic archetype of man!

But the desert phase is over. *Their* ascesis has prepared our return to history – having in it a life of prayer – Christian morality surpassing ascetic exploits (St. Basil). The hermit can then move fully in a world which is for him no longer bewitched, in this world he is *"Le dépositaire de la philanthropie divine* [The treasury of divine love toward the human race]."

(St. Greg[ory of] Naz[ianzen])

The blood wagon was here again – first time since last July.

I went out about 11:30, wrong time – it was crowded. But got through in about an hour, drank a lot of strong coffee and felt light and refreshed, though I don't know if this was due to the blood-letting or to the coffee. Anyway, seemed to feel the heat less.

Weighed 185 lbs. Pulse and blood pressure better than last year – on the whole I am in better shape – but need to lose weight. Certainly am not much from the point of view of "iconography"!

But seriously: the problem of worldliness is a great one. I do feel called by God to witness in some sense to His truth in the world, but because I have so badly lacked community I have also lacked direction and spiritual judgement, and when I think I am speaking for God, perhaps I am only after all trying to hear a favorable echo from dissenting groups which are opposed perhaps not to the "world" but only to the "establishment." There is a difference!

There is no question that the basic monastic values are the ones to which I must give *all* my attention, and I have failed in this badly, trusting not so much in the vows and in silence, as in my own ideas and *my conviction that I know what to say*. This may be a very great self-deception, since such a conviction can be sustained easily by the mere fact that people listen to me readily and accept my statements. *And this is no reason whatever for speaking or for assuming that I know what I am saying!*

Fr. Callistus, the Prior, left to study in Rome yesterday.

Fr. Flavian was made Prior. Fr. Eudes took Fr. Flavian's job as Master of Students and Junior Brothers.

The cantor from O. L. Genesee has been here for about a week (Fr. Stephen).

"Je crois de plus que ce que nous appelons tristesse, angoisse, désespoir, comme pour nous persuader qu'il s'agit de certains mouvements de l'âme, est cette âme même, que depuis la chute, la condition de l'homme est telle qu'il ne saurait plus rien percevoir en lui et hors de lui que sous la forme de l'angoisse." ["I believe more and more that what we call sadness, anguish, despair, as if to persuade ourselves that it is a question of certain impulses of the soul, is really the soul itself, and that since the fall the condition of man is such that he is not capable of perceiving anything in himself and outside of himself except in the form of anguish."]

Bernanos

Light – no light – call it nothing. The illusion that could at any time damn me is pitiable; I know it and I do not know it, it is not given to me to see, I am prevented by "honesty" from seeing it or is it perhaps not discernable? Is it only a pitiable human sickness? But for it I have displeased God, and perhaps would again, and perhaps do without knowing it.

Whatever it is, it is now deep, hidden, in a way ineradicable, only God's mercy could do anything about it. Helpless with what I cannot let myself know. Helpless if I imagine I can know it as "known," and not experience it totally in myself as what – ? Anguish perhaps. Disgust is not enough. It is another illusion. *But one cannot have illusion unmasked without despairing* (except when the unmasking is done by mercy, and perhaps after all mercy hides our sins from us – *beati quorum tecta sunt peccata* [Blessed are those whose sins are washed away]!).

Temptation now perhaps only takes the form of a *poem about* the temptation that "would help me to understand it" – (or enjoy it?).

It is the "joy" of knowledge, the primeval curiosity for what is without wisdom, for the *false depth*, for the enchantment of the self, or better, for the false paradise which is the self, enchanted with its own illusion, its very pure and proper and unique illusion. Its very own illusion, which is so sweet because it is life (until it is experienced inside out as anguish).

My anger at the community is my anger at smelling out, half consciously, very craftily, the same kind of illusion in everyone, and some more especially, perhaps most especially the abbot, who have made a fine art out of it and is therefore a "success." And it begins more innocently and artlessly with the younger ones even with the beginning of their contemplation!

So that from the very first, love and the illusion that destroys love begin together, and sooner turn to frustration and anguish, in that we live on our own poison, and it is even sweet to us, though we may recognize that it is also bitter, bitter to ourselves and most of all to God.

Other dimension – the vast global drive toward destruction.

The great general temptation is to acquiesce in this gravitation toward death because it seems to be the only "solution" to the insoluable problem of the central illusion, the inescapable personal temptation. Only answer is acceptance of the Cross in the temptation itself (the personal one – the general one is in God's hands).

The priest at the funeral of Bernanos –

Cette exigence d'exister, cette angoisse à l'idée que peut-être il avait fait semblant de vivre, ce sont elles qui marquaient d'une insatisfaction dévorante, son aveu sur lui-même, son regard sur nous, son jugement sur le monde. [This need to exist, this anguish at the idea that perhaps he had pretended to live, these are the notions that marked with a devouring lack of satisfaction, his avowal about himself, his gaze at us, his judgment about the world.]

1962   (from a Korean friend)[6]
      This is the year of the tiger. It leads the dance.
1963   Next year will the Rabbit lead the dance
1964   Following which in 1964 the dragon
1965   The Snake
1966   The Horse
1967   The Sheep
1968   The Monkey

[6] These notes are *not* part of the journal proper, but rather were written on the rear endpaper of the bound journal volume and not dated.

Index